Pamela Couture

We Are Not All Victims

International Practical Theology

edited by

Prof. Dr. Chris Hermans (Nijmegen),
Prof. Dr. Maureen Junker-Kenny (Dublin),
Prof. Dr. Richard Osmer (Princeton),
Prof. Dr. Friedrich Schweitzer (Tübingen),
Prof. Dr. Hans-Georg Ziebertz (Würzburg)

in cooperation with the
International Academy of Practical Theology (IAPT),

represented by

Heather Walton (President) and Robert Mager (Vice-President)

Volume 18

LIT

Pamela Couture

We Are Not All Victims

Local Peacebuilding
in the Democratic Republic of Congo

LIT

Biblical citations are from the New Revised Standard Version Bible, copyright 1989, Division of Christian Education of the National Council of the Churches of Christ in the United States of America. Used by permission. All rights reserved.

Links to the headlines from *The New York Times* are provided on the citations page.

Research photos can be found at http://www.emmanuel.utoronto.ca/WeAreNotAllVictims

Funding for this project was provided by Dianne Schumaker of Kansas City, Missouri, the United Methodist Committee on Relief (UMCOR), the Association of Theological Schools' Lilly Endowment Summer Research grants and Henry Luce III Fellows in Theology, and by the Emmanuel College and Victoria University research funds. Housing in the Democratic Republic of Congo was provided by North Katanga Annual Conference, Bishop and Mama Ntambo Nkulu Ntanda, and Gaston and Jeanne Ntambo.

This book is printed on acid-free paper.

Bibliographic information published by the Deutsche Nationalbibliothek
The Deutsche Nationalbibliothek lists this publication in the Deutsche Nationalbibliografie; detailed bibliographic data are available on the Internet at http://dnb.d-nb.de.

ISBN 978-3-643-90796-7

A catalogue record for this book is available from the British Library

© LIT VERLAG GmbH & Co. KG Wien,
Zweigniederlassung Zürich 2016
Klosbachstr. 107
CH-8032 Zürich
Tel. +41 (0) 44-251 75 05
E-Mail: zuerich@lit-verlag.ch   http://www.lit-verlag.ch
Distribution:
In the UK: Global Book Marketing, e-mail: mo@centralbooks.com
In North America: International Specialized Book Services, e-mail: orders@isbs.com
In Germany: LIT Verlag Fresnostr. 2, D-48159 Münster
Tel. +49 (0) 2 51-620 32 22, Fax +49 (0) 2 51-922 60 99, e-mail: vertrieb@lit-verlag.de
In Austria: Medienlogistik Pichler-ÖBZ, e-mail: mlo@medien-logistik.at
e-books are available at www.litwebshop.de

"It is as if you are around a village campfire
and many people, coming in and out, are telling their stories.
You have penetrated the Luba mind."

Dr. Raymond Mande, March 2014

* * *

"Kujatalala ekwabana biya."

Luba Proverb meaning "you will eat peacefully,
when everybody received his portion of the share."

* * *

"Blessed are the peacemakers: For they shall be called the children of God."

Matthew 5:9

In Memory of:

Dr. Mireille Mikombe

Rev. Dr. Boniface Kabongo Ilunga

Rev. Tschimwang Muzangish

Mama Kahole wa Ngoy

Not primarily memorializing the lives of 5.4 million Congolese
who died in the wars in Congo from 1996-2003,
nor even celebrating the sixty-eight million Congolese who survived,
this book bears witness to the creativity of unknown numbers of Congolese
who resisted the violence
and are now inventing
DR Congo's first reign of peace.

.

Table of Contents

Regional Geography of Democratic Republic of Congo

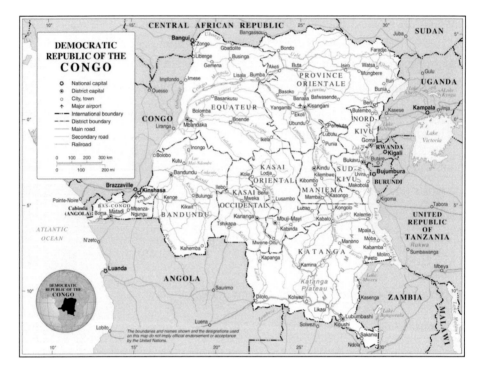

https://upload.wikimedia.org/wikipedia/commons/8/8e/Un-congo-kinshasa.png

Political and Ecclesial Timeline

7th-17th Centuries	Luba ancestors inhabit Katanga.
17th Century until present	Luba empire organizes traditional society.
1884-1960	Belgium colonizes Congo. European Powers recognize Congo Free State as King Leopold II's private colony, then, in 1908, as Belgium's national colony.
December 27, 1947	Ntambo Nkulu Ntanda is born in the village of Kahilo, near the town of Kabongo.
1960	Belgium grants independence to Congo.
January 17, 1961	Prime Minister Patrice Lumumba is assassinated.
November 25, 1965	President Joseph Kasavubu is deposed in a bloodless coup.
1965	Joseph Désiré Mobutu takes dictatorial power and renames Congo Zaire.
1994	Rwandan genocide creates refugee crisis in Zaire.
1996	Laurent Kabila seeks to overthrow Mobutu. Ntambo Nkulu Ntanda is elected United Methodist bishop.
1997	Laurent Kabila overthrows Mobutu and renames Zaire the Democratic Republic of Congo. Mama Mujing organizes orphans in Kamina.
1998-2003	Rwanda invades Congo; the war engages seven African nations and twenty nations beyond Africa. North Katanga Conference purchases Kamisamba Farm; Ilunga Mutombo organizes building and agricultural projects; Pastors Kahunda, Tschimwang and Nyengele supervise systems of care for internally displaced people.
July 1999	Warring countries ratify Lusaka Ceasefire Agreement but disregard the agreement until after 2000. Building and agricultural projects increase; internally displaced people continue to flow into Kamina.
May 2000	United Methodist General Conference discusses resolutions to press for an end to the war.
November 2000	United Nations Peacemaking Force (MONUC) is established and expanded the following February. United Nations Panel of Experts on Illegal Exploitation of Natural Resources and Other Forms of Wealth

	issues its first report (2 June, 2000). Building and agricultural projects increase; internally displaced people continue to arrive in Kamina.
2001	Laurent Kabila is assassinated; his son, Joseph Kabila, is appointed president. Building and agricultural projects in Kamina increase; internally displaced people continue to arrive.
May 4, 2001	Lusaka Peace Negotiations reconvene in Addis Ababa in October 2001 and fail.
2001	First American visitors arrive in Kamina. American and European visits continue regularly.
February 25-April 19, 2002	Peace negotiations resume in Sun City, South Africa without success. UN Special Envoy Mustapha Niasse continues the negotiations.
July 2002	Rwanda withdraws troops from the DRC.
2002	Building and agricultural projects increase; missing people, believed dead, continue to appear in Kamina.
December 2002	The Global and All-Inclusive Agreement on the Transition in the DRC is ratified. Joseph Kabila continues as president with four vice-presidents representing different political parties.
April 2003	Addendum to Global and All-Inclusive Agreement ratified. Internally displaced people begin to return to their villages in the former war zone.
2004	Government organizes North Katanga Mai-Mai peace conference; conference is held in Kamina under church auspices.
July 30, 2006	Congolese elect Joseph Kabila as President.
2006	Bishop Ntambo sends the first reconciliation missions to Moba and Kalemie.
March 23, 2012	M-23 rebels, backed by Rwanda, begin a new war at DR Congo's border with Rwanda.
September 2012	Interfaith leaders visit the United Nations, North America and Europe to build international pressure on Rwanda to withdraw from the DRC.

Acknowledgements

This story is based on testimonies recorded in English, French, Kiswahili, and Kiluba, translated by Pastor John Mutombo, Fabrice Ilunga Mujinga, Mbuyu Mwilumba and Pastor Ilgha Monga Ilunga, in Kamina and Lubumbashi in January 2008, and in Lubumbashi, Kamina, Kabongo and Kaboto in October 2009. Seventy-eight persons witnessed, in some cases for several hours or over a period of days and on multiple occasions. On the basis of this information I nominated Bishop Ntambo for the Tanenbaum Peacemakers-in-action award, which he won. Joyce Dubensky and members of the staff of the Tanenbaum Center for Interreligious Understanding graciously allowed me to include insights from further interviews with him that we conducted in preparation for his biographical chapter in *Peacemakers in Action: Profiles of Religion in Conflict Resolution Volume II*. Throughout the entire research project, I have consulted members of the community of Kamina when they have visited or resided in the United States or Canada, drawing especially heavily on the time and availability of my primary interpreter in Kamina, Pastor John Mutombo. Reverend Dr. Guy Mande Muyombo verified valuable historical background, Reverend Dr. Boniface Kabongo translated the minutes of the North Katanga Annual Conference, and Dr. Raymond Mande offered important literary advice. Without these people and opportunities, a book in the form that echoes Luba storytelling would not have been possible.

In Lubumbashi and Kamina in March 2014, Dr. Kimba Kyakutala Evariste and Dr. Boniface Kabongo translated as I read the storylines to the primary witnesses. They confirmed, corrected and expanded the chapters. Dr. Guy Kasanka, after hearing his chapters, said, "I am pleased. It is as if you were there." That was my goal.

In order to convert my academic prose to creative non-fiction I studied with Nancy Barry, Hope Edelman and Fritz McDonald in courses at the Iowa Summer Writing Festival. Shaughnessy Bishop-Stall at the University of Toronto School of Continuing Studies mentored me, editing the manuscript, chapter by chapter, for four years. The La Crosse, Wisconsin writers group responded to some of the stories. Western commentators on drafts of the manuscript included Roger Girouard, Samantha Cavanagh, Judge Maurice Cullity, and James Glass in Canada, Beverly Thompson and Stephen Simmons in the United States, and Rene Sephton in Australia. Hrach Gregorian suggested the title. My colleagues at the Society for Pastoral Theology and the International Academy of Practical Theology heard various portions of the work in progress. I am especially grateful to Stephen Graham and the Association of Theological Schools, who agreed to bring Dr. Raymond Mande from Lubumbashi to Pittsburgh, Pennsylvania, to read and respond to the entire manuscript when I presented it in November 2014 to the Henry Luce III Fellows in Theology. My utmost appreciation goes to Dr. Raymond Mande and Reverend Dr. Boniface Kabongo for their Luba critiques of the entire book. Karen Wishart of Emmanuel College library provided additional research support, and Vicky Fisher at the Black River Falls, Wisconsin public library filled numerous interlibrary loan requests.

I am grateful for the support in the Democratic Republic of Congo to many people and groups. All housing was provided as an in-kind contribution: Bishop Ntambo Nkulu Ntanda and Mama Bishop Nshimba Nkulu and Gaston and Jeanne Ntambo in Lubumbashi; Bishop Ntambo and the managers of United Methodist guesthouse, Pastor John Mutombo and Pastor Kahunda, in Kamina; the United Methodist guesthouse and Prophet Mechac in Kabongo and Kaboto. Mama Sila and her assistants at the Methodist Guesthouse in Kamina have made me comfortable during my visits, providing excellent food, clean and hot water, electricity by generator during the days of electric rationing, laundry services, and help with various errands for cell phone minutes, medicine, and other important comforts. Jeanne Ntambo lent me her clothes when my suitcase did not arrive in 2008. Faustin and John Nday provided safe transportation by car, and I am never more secure than when flying with Gaston Ntambo, the expert pilot of Wings of the Morning, who evacuates desperately ill persons from rural villages and delivers necessary medicines to hospitals and clinics of the interior. Several people, including the traditional chiefs of Kapukwe and Kapukwe-Kaniema and Prophet Mechac, Secretary Mutalala, and their assistants travelled long distances to Kamina to complete the story.

I, myself, twice experienced the relief of the sick who are evacuated from the interior by the pilot Gaston Ntambo and the longstanding United Methodist medical mission, Wings of the Morning. I am especially grateful to John Mutombo, Mama Sila, Bishop Ntambo, Dr. Kasanka, Dr. Kashindji, the nurses at the Lupandilo Nursing School, Dr. Y. Nanabhay of Milpark Hospital, Johannesburg, and MEDEX who cared for me during a mysterious illness in 2009, and Rachel Gabler, who travelled with me in 2014.

The project expenses were funded in 2008-2009 by Dianne Schumaker of Kansas City, Missouri; the United Methodist Committee on Relief (UMCOR); and the Lilly Endowment, through a research grant provided by the Association of Theological Schools. Grants from the Henry Luce III Fellows in Theology Program and Victoria University's research fund provided a sabbatical year and travel funding in 2013-2014, without which the completion of the work would have been impossible. I am grateful for the support of former President Myron McCoy and my colleagues at Saint Paul School of Theology, Kansas City, Missouri, who allowed me initial research leave in 2008 and 2009; and former President Paul Gooch, Principal Mark Toulouse and my colleagues at Emmanuel College of Victoria University in the University of Toronto, who cheered me on to the completion of this enormous task. I also thank Boram Lee, of Emmanuel College, Robert Mager of Université Laval, Quebec City, and Stephen

Simmons of Moravian Theological Seminary in Bethlehem, Pennsylvania, who provided technical support for manuscript preparation.

"Peace is not just the absence of war," says witness Betty Musau Kazadi, echoing a mantra of the church. This testimony of religiously-based local peacebuilding in North Katanga demonstrates the potential contribution of every person to activities, small and large, that are necessary to create and sustain a just society—so that, in times of social conflict—peacemaking, or bringing an end to hostilities, and peacekeeping, or building society, can be effective. We all have our part to play.

A Methodology and Epistemology of Right Relations

> "Congo Lurches Toward New Crisis as Leader
> Tries to Crush a Rival."
>
> *The New York Times*, May 12, 2016
>
> "Then you will know the truth,
> and the truth will set you free."
>
> John 8:32

The story of the methodology and epistemology of this project begins with a moment in which I recognized my own global "colonization"—or the ways that we in northern and western nations absorb and live by stereotypes about people in the poverty stricken countries of the global south. When I visited Kamina, Democratic Republic of Congo (DRC) for the first time in July 2003, I knew something of what to expect. I had met with Bishop Ntambo as part of the steering committee of the United Methodist Bishops Initiative on Children and Poverty four times a year for seven years, had heard him speak about his personal story and his vision for Kamina, had seen his hand-built model of a parsonage community center, and had watched videos of his community's construction work. I had experienced him as articulate about the war, compassionate about his people, and committed to the children we sought to assist. Still, on my first trip to Kamina, I was astonished by the breadth of Bishop Ntambo's projects and the energy of his people. But why should I be surprised? My reaction reminded me how deeply ingrained are the stereotypes of Congolese poverty and dependence. I experienced a town and a people who held up a mirror to a construct I carried that I thought I had discarded.

In Kamina I stood in Bishop Ntambo's office, thinking, "This man is a combination between Martin Luther King, Jr."—Bishop Ntambo's acknowledged hero— "and Franklin Delano Roosevelt, with a New Deal for Kamina. Someone has to document this." That impulse, I now realize, serves as an antidote for colonial relationships. As Mark Gopin writes in *Healing the Heart of Conflict,* "I have been astonished on numerous occasions to discover how easy it is for the use of basic positive emotions…above all, honor, to quickly transform a relationship between supposed sworn enemies." If honor can transform enemies, how much more might it recreate relationships of people desiring to overcome the legacy of colonialism? Could I take the best gift I had to offer, my research and writing skills, and use them to "honor" the work of Bishop Ntambo and his community?

Some months later, when I approached the Bishop about a book on Kamina, I foregrounded the delicate relationships between the North and the South. I wanted his story to be told in depth rather than in church news snippets, but I did not want to supplant a Congolese writer. I asked him, "Should a Congolese write the story about development in Kamina, or should I? I want to see it written, but I don't want to co-opt it." He was adamant. "You should." I heard the subtext: *because right now, if you don't, no one else will.* I had resources—time, money, advanced education—that his poverty-stricken, war-torn people were struggling to attain.

On May 17, 2007, exactly ten years after Laurent Kabila took the presidency and renamed Zaire the "Democratic Republic of Congo," Bishop Ntambo and I met in the Indianapolis airport to plan the book about Kamina. By that time, I knew about the Kamina peace conference with the Mai-Mai. I proposed that the book should focus on what Kamina had done to promote peace.

"Yes. It's what we are doing." We spent the day in a booth at TGIFriday's restaurant, recording the story of peace in Kamina from his perspective.

The entire methodology became framed by a series of decisions seeking a goal of "decolonization." But it was not primarily guided by decolonial theory. Rather, the practice-oriented term of "right relations," used by Canadians and indigenous people when they refer to their visions and hopes for a just relationship with one another, better expresses the methodological frame. The standards for "right relations" are not found in books written in abstractions that many North American and indigenous people alike cannot access—rather, the norms exist within face-to-face relationships. This person-to-person accountability, above all, guided the project and dared not be breached.

The Methodology I Brought: The Theory and Practice of Narrative Therapy

I have taught practical theology and pastoral care since 1988. Over the years I'd questioned the way certain theories set up pastoral psychotherapists and clergy as experts and clients or parishioners as dependents. The theory of narrative therapy had resolved this dilemma—and not surprisingly, it had been developed in relationship to indigenous people in New Zealand and Australia. Ever since Christie Neuger introduced me to it, I've taught every class the theoretical assumptions taken from Gerald Monk, John Winslade, Kathie Crocket and David Epstein's *Narrative Therapy in Theory and Practice:*

- o   People are experts of their own lives.
- o   "Discourse—how we tell our story, and how others tell stories about us—matters."
- o   Discourse "positions" us: position determines power relations.
- o   "Problem" stories prevent us from moving forward.
- o   Problems are externalized when our identities are not defined by our problems.
- o   "Alternative stories" help us write a new future based on our strengths.

o   Stories conflict. "Alternative stories" emerge when we discover differ-
    ences in stories.
o   When we are engaged in healing, we join together in the creating of
    stories, which recreates our knowledges of ourselves and of our world.

And to these I have added:

o   Stories of God and the supernatural may be problem or alternative sto-
    ries.

In other words, the way the world tells the story of war and peace in the
DRC matters. When journalists and historians write to a secular audience nar-
rating the country's history of violence, they erase the existence of the indigenous people who are working for peace and collude with a perception of a violent Congo. Similarly, when church reporters focus primarily on the safety of
white missionaries, they erase the suffering of the indigenous people.

Social witness and recognition, according to narrative therapy theory, is central to healing, as is the ability to contribute to a cause beyond oneself. I had
come to Kamina to write the "alternative story"—one that foregrounds the
peacebuilding that the Congolese people themselves are doing against the background of violence—to offer the world, the church, and the Congolese people
a more balanced image. I wanted the Congolese—specifically the Luba people—to find that their dramatic efforts to keep and build peace had been recognized by the outside word.

The Methodology I Brought: The "Problem Story" and the "Alternative Story"

Exotic stories of suffering and violence sell. It's relatively easy to find books
that fit within the dominant storyline about the DRC: the government officials
are corrupt; the government and the multinationals are in cahoots perpetuating
the war or, alternatively, the wars in Congo are really ethnic civil wars; villagers
are victims and perpetrators of violence; Christianity is impotent and indigenous religion fosters magical beliefs; the real stories come from towns near the
Great Lakes or along the Congo River and the rest of the DRC is still a mysterious and savage heart of darkness. Some truth resides in each of these images—but they are far from the whole story.

Competent and well-meaning journalists have a sense that something is
missing in their accounts. Brian Mealer's *All Things Must Fight to Live*, a memoir of a white journalist travelling through the DRC, foregrounds violence and
death. He says, "As a reporter in the Congo, I'd always bristled at the question,
'why do you concentrate on the negative and never report on the positive?' It
usually came from Africans themselves and struck me as naïve." Even though

in the second half of the book he changes his mind and, as a matter of conscience, wants to see "recovery," the violent lens he has established earlier in
the book dominates.

Histories of the Congo wars, such as Jason Stearns' *Dancing in the Glory of
the Monster,* are well researched through newspaper reports, non-governmental
organizations, and United Nations documents, many of the same of which provide the background verification for *We are Not all Victims.* In the Introduction
to the paperback edition of *Dancing in the Glory,* Stearns writes: "I was nagged
by two regrets. . . .I was afraid that I had undersold the Congo's many virtues,
highlighting the tragedy and bloodshed. . . ."

Other histories of the war, such as Gérard Prunier's *Africa's World War:
Congo, the Rwandan Genocide, and the Making of a Continental Catastrophe*
and Michael Diebert's *The Democratic Republic of Congo: Between Hope and
Despair,* focus on conflict in the Great Lakes region, along the Congo River
and in Lubumbashi, and do not reflect the experience of rural bush areas such
as North Katanga.

These books confirm a pattern that I identified in my analysis of newspaper
reports in 2007, presented to the Oxford Institute for Methodist Theological
Studies: that Congolese people are positioned as victims and perpetrators; that
both Christianity and indigenous religions are seen as impotent or even as a
source of violence; and that stories coming from towns along the Congo River,
especially eastern Congo, leave intact the stereotypes of the Congo inland as
ruled by exotic mystery and savagery. In contrast, the alternative story shows
the Luba as agents of their own peacebuilding, using both indigenous and
Christian religion as warrants for peace, and engaging in these activities inland,
where people live ordinary lives and rise to extraordinary courage when the
times call for it.

The Role of Peacebuilding Theory

In January 2008 I first interviewed Dr. Raymond Mande Muyombo using a set
of questions I'd formulated out of peacebuilding theory. My abstract questions
yielded abstract answers—and, I realized, not the deeply personal experience I
was seeking. We finished *my* questions, and then he said, "And this is what I
really want to tell you..." My first decision was to bracket peacebuilding theories so I could hear what the people considered important. I did not want to "fit"
people into pre-existing theoretical constructs.

So before arriving in Kamina, I had ditched my first interview schedule in
favor of three open-ended questions that allowed people to tell me their story:
"How did you contribute to peace in Kamina? How do your religious beliefs
undergird the work that you do? What do you think about a white American
woman writing this Congolese story?" These questions, with probes, allowed

me to hear the experience of people during the war. Instead of conducting pre-scribed interviews, I gathered testimonies from social witnesses. After finishing the research, I've returned to religious peacebuilding literature to determine how the people exemplify existing theories.

Briefly, the story reflects some key challenges to mainstream peacebuilding theory by experts in local religious peacebuilding. Marc Gopin posits that the key to understanding the theory of peacebuilding lies in the spirituality of those who are actually engaged in the act. They are highly self-reflective people, able to struggle with ambiguity and admit their faults—we see this quality particu-larly in Bishop Ntambo. Local religious peacebuilders understand the power of gesture and symbol—in this story ritual and the symbol of white lime repeat themselves in many contexts. John Paul Lederach has suggested that the com-plexity of peacebuilding does not progress in stages, often depicted in a bell curve, but builds in a more circuitous fashion. Even though this story follows a dramatic arc for literary purposes, it is important to see how activities of the different stages of peacebuilding continue throughout each "stage" of pre-con-flict, conflict, and post-conflict. The entire story is one of "moral imagina-tion"—moral imagination not of one individual but of an entire community, in conversation with each other, and each making his or her contribution.

Luba Epistemology: *Bwino bonso ke Bwino, Bwino kwikala ne Bantu*

My commitments to the assumptions behind narrative therapy made it easy to put myself in the hands of my local hosts. When I arrived in Kamina, John Mutombo, a trained interpreter, had been assigned by Bishop Ntambo to assist me. (Some qualitative researchers would call him my "trusted informant"; par-ticipant action researchers would call John my "co-searcher.") In his able hands, I fulfilled the local protocols. But he was formed within his culture, not by social scientists. Through *bwino,* described by Mutombo Nkulu N'Sengha as Luba epistemology, I can understand why John did what he did.

John's actions exemplified the Luba proverb *Bwino bonso ke Bwino, Bwino kwikala ne Bantu* that means "true knowledge consists in living in harmony with our fellow human beings." The research project should edify the commu-nity, not create conflict or suspicion.

On the night I arrived, he invited the local religious officials to come to the Methodist guesthouse to hear about the project. On my first afternoon, John sauntered me into town, walking at a quarter of my usual speed, introducing me to prominent citizens and government officials. A few days later, he arranged for me to visit the royal Luba ministers at the court at Kinkunki, although *Ka-songo Nyembo,* the Luba king, was absent. At Bishop Ntambo's bidding he organized a trip from Kamina to meet General Mbuza Mabe at Kamina Military Base. Bishop had noted a few people in Kamina who had to be interviewed immediately, as they were departing shortly; in addition, John and Bishop had identified residents and religious leaders in Kamina, including Muslims, who could offer testimony at the guesthouse.

When, whom, and how to visit—and when others should visit us—was carefully orchestrated consistent with Luba culture. We called on the officials at government offices, the king's court at Kinkunki, and Kamina Military Base, but with few other exceptions, all of the testimonies in Kamina were gathered at the guesthouse. John wanted to be careful not to demonstrate any favoritism toward members of the community by privileging them with a visit. He made one exception for Mwilumba's wife, Alphonsine, who was recovering from surgery.

I visited Alphonsine and the family at their hut in the section of town where many internally displaced people lived. John interpreted for the 2008 testimony, giving me the opportunity to hear the family as a whole and giving Mwilumba the chance to express himself in Kiswahili as a father and husband. When he originally told me his story of flight and accident in English at the guesthouse, he presented himself as a chipper, dramatic storyteller; in the presence of his family, who fled on their own after he was injured, his face settled dark and heavy, his eyes somber as he relived their suffering.[1]

In 2009 I was privileged to see the contrast between their temporary, two-room mud hut in 2008 and their new concrete Kamina home in 2009. They had been able to re-establish themselves in Kamina to pursue the older children's education, even though Mwilumba had returned to Tanganyika district to supervise a school. By 2014 the family had moved to Kabalo; I vetted chapters with Mbuyu and Cherita in Lubumbashi, who conferred with their parents by telephone.

The place of testimony also became significant in the second research trip, when we travelled to Kabongo with Dr. Kasanka and Kaboto to hear Prophet Mechac. Experiencing the road between Kamina and Kabongo and seeing the hospital and airstrip where the Zimbabwean army camped provided a sense of texture in Dr. Kasanka's medical story. The visit with Prophet Mechac had a dynamism all its own, described below.

Luba Epistemology: *Kuboko kumo Kubunga ke kololanga*

In 2008 John identified two other interpreters, Fabrice and Mwilumba, who assisted. Consistent with Luba culture, particularly with the proverb *Kuboko kumo Kubunga ke kololanga*, or "one single hand cannot comprehend things,"

---

[1] Cover Photo: John Mutombo, interpreter, and Pamela Couture, with Alphonsine, Mwilumba and their children, January 21, 2008. Photo property of Pamela Couture.

they spontaneously proposed people who could contribute to the story. (Qualitative researchers know this method as snowball sampling). Word about the project spread, and without being asked, the witnesses themselves sent others to tell their story. Even John was astonished when Kanda-Fwanyinwabo, Chef de Groupement Ngoy Mwana, a traditional chief from two hundred kilometers away, unexpectedly arrived at the behest of the Kinkunki ministers! Then, a few weeks later, a civil engineer who had heard about the project appeared with a version of the Luba genesis story that his father had written on the back of a blueprint for an electrical plant that the man had not looked at since the 1960s. John might have been somewhat apprehensive but did not resist when Fabrice suggested that I interview his uncle, Kebi Konkeka, who had been a Mai-Mai commander and had integrated into the Congolese army at Kamina Base. Finding different people with a perspective on the story of peace in Kamina had become a community project.

By the end of two weeks of testimony, I had identified a set of practices that contributed to the community's peace efforts: calling on Christian and Luba traditions; caring for widows and orphans; building infrastructure through agricultural and constructions projects; organizing relief for internally displaced people; building relationships with leaders in traditional and local government, the military, and other religious traditions; building relationships with American and European donors; engaging in conflict transformation with the Mai-Mai, and reconciling war-torn churches in Moba and Kalemie.

I also realized that men's experience dominated the emerging story—and I had been given three male interpreters, in front of whom women were hesitant to testify, except in generalities. So I asked to speak with four of the female leaders, alone, with two translating who spoke fluent English. I told the women that many other writers had focused on rape and violation of women during the war, and I was focused on peace. Could they help me frame the way women should be represented in a peace story? The very long conversation on that rainy evening clarified: an agenda for peace, for and by women, still needed to be created and fulfilled. They wanted my help with that.

Luba Epistemology: *kilemeka ne kulemeka bantu ne bintu bya Vidye*

Another central Luba proverb, *kilemeka ne kulemeka bantu ne bintu bya Vidye*, guides the Luba people "to respect sacred life in oneself and in other creatures." As a result, my interpreters were at ease probing and distinguishing different kinds of religious experience. Their attitudes melded well with my own pastoral counseling training that seeks to understand and respect the ultimate meaning behind people's actions. Once they learned I was open to varieties of religious experience, their cultural self-understanding overcame their tendency to want to guard themselves in front of visitors who might hearken to the attitude of early 20th century missionaries, from whom the community learned that Christians should consider all traditional religion as "magic" or "sorcery." If they had hid their own distinctive culture, my interpreters would have stunted the research.

Respect for the sacred as the witnesses understood it allowed me to record the story of a wide range of spiritualities with some common elements. One of the most powerful and original gleanings from the stories has to do with the ways that different people negotiate between Luba traditional religion and Christianity—from Bishop Ntambo and Kanda-Fwanyinwabo's "hands off the other" approach, to Alphonsine's iterative reasoning, to a wide spread belief in the authority and trust of mystical experience that finds itself in many different forms both in Luba culture and Christianity.

My own religious experience contains a mystical component, so I took their direct experience of God seriously. They clearly responded to my openness. As I began to absorb their experience, my own spirituality began to "Luba-ize." In fact, Luba spirituality fused with my own mystical horizon on two explicit occasions, both in association with gathering testimony from Prophet Mechac.

In January 2008 local witnesses in Kamina had urged me to hear Prophet Mechac; they considered him critical to the story. Then, I could only speak to him through a broken cell phone connection. In October 2009, during rainy season, I asked to visit Mechac at his village, Kaboto, a nine hours drive into the bush beyond Kamina.

Epistemological Wonder: The Creator revealing Godself?

In October 2009 we received word that the Prophet could receive us in Kaboto. John Mutombo and Dr. Kasanka conferred with the church's driver and mechanic; they patched together durable transportation by moving tires from one church vehicle to a more mechanically sound one. En route we stopped at a compound to negotiate for barrels of gasoline; I observed the process of purchasing and siphoning gasoline in bulk.

The professional driver, Faustin, a mechanic, our cook, John Mutombo, Dr. Kasanka and I rode in the cab. Two Kabongo Hospital physicians were waiting in Kamina for the next train, which was expected within the month; they hitchhiked in the truck's bed with the gas and our food. We planned to drive the two hundred kilometers from Kamina to Kabongo in one day. Although it was rainy season, the skies remained clear. The deep ruts in the road created treacherous cliffs; I learned that a professional, experienced driver is a necessity, not a luxury.

After driving eight hours, we arrived in Kabongo near dusk. As the weather was holding, we dropped the physicians at Kabongo's Methodist guesthouse and proceeded to Kaboto.

As we left Kabongo, we drove in the pitch dark through a market with small candles and fires lit, and behind the stalls I saw the first bolt of lightning. For the next hour, only our headlights and lightning on the horizon illumined the dirt road. This road lay flatter than the one between Kamina and Kabongo; it also seemed far less travelled. We were much deeper in the bush villages. We approached a bridge over a brook. John turned to me and said, "We are almost there."

As we veered left, a sudden wind pounded the truck as if from all directions, rocking it to and fro as we approached the village. A guard directed us to a particular hut, and using all our strength against the wind, we forced our way inside where our hosts waited. Once the door was shut, a monsoon-like rain pounded the hut. For the next hour or so, our delegation sat on benches, face-to-face with Prophet Mechac, Secretary Mutalala, and some of the other ministers, unable to speak above the driving wind and rain. I mouthed the words to the Prophet: "It's like we are on Mount Sinai and God has appeared." John could not hear to translate. The Prophet and I looked directly at each other throughout the storm: me drinking in his calm, patient face; he watching whatever he saw in me.

The African spirituality I had begun to recognize and absorb during stories I heard in the guesthouse had been writing its narrative on my soul. This experience punctuated it—the people's intimate contact with spiritual powers that far transcended their own; their absolute confidence in God's providence; their sense that contact with spiritual power provides safety against all that threatens harm. I also realized how easily this religious experience could be translated into rituals that sustain people's spiritual contact, and, when things go wrong, their need to assign blame to a combination of evil spirits and people.

Epistemological Wonder: The Presence of Evil?

In March 2014 it was critical to review Prophet Mechac's storyline with him and his ministers. Bishop Ntambo left a message on the Prophet's cell phone; Mechac's assistants had to climb a hill to the highest point to retrieve the messages and return the calls. I had heard nothing in return and given up hope when, on my last Friday, Minister Mutalala swung open the screen to the guesthouse door. I recognized him immediately. He had been sent to Kamina to prepare for the Prophet's arrival on Sunday. I was expecting to leave Kamina on Tuesday.

Pastor Kabongo, who served as interpreter on this trip, arranged with Mama Sila, who was now cooking for the guesthouse, to prepare a welcome feast of roasted goat, spinach, and bukari for the Mechac and the ministers who were expected to come with him. That Sunday the thunderstorms raged, and the Mechac and his entourage did not arrive. At nine p.m. Pastor Kabongo, Secretary Mutalala, and I ate from the feast. Mama Sila carefully reserved the leftovers.

The delegation appeared in the middle of the night. Four middle-aged ministers had shared the driving of two motorbikes with the eighty-year-old Prophet as a passenger. They had encountered thunderstorms, and their motorbikes had stalled several times. Pastor Kahunda, now the manager of the guesthouse, sent for Mama Sila to feed them. By ten a.m. the next morning Prophet Mechac was dressed in his sky blue business suit and tie, ready for the manuscript review.

We had begun translating and revising chapters under the cool shade of the mango tree in the side yard; I repeatedly looked down at the manuscript to read and then back to Mechac and his ministers to watch their body language for expressions of concern or agreement while Pastor Kabongo interpreted. I glanced down; I looked up; a bloody streak shot across my eye within my vision. Again I glanced down and looked up; it changed shape, spreading, deepening. The transcript of the digital recording notes me saying, calmly,

"Something is wrong with my eye."

My first thought: *Chinja-Chinja's* megwishi *is messing with the project.*

I immediately flashed to a question I'd asked Pastor Kabongo the night before, "Where does Chinja-Chinja get his power? Why can he command six thousand men and the next Mai-Mai commander only a couple thousand?"

"From the *megwishi*, the evil spirit who lives in the lake. The *megwishi* selects a person and lives through him." Does that explain, I thought, how Pastor Kabongo could describe his childhood friend Chinja-Chinja as a good and kind man, despite Chinja-Chinja's war crimes and Pastor Kabongo's terror at meeting him? In tLuba culture, is Chinja-Chinja like a man possessed?

My second thought: *You are sitting in the presence of the Prophet Mechac. Ask him to pray for you.* I did. We stood, and placing his hands on my head, Mechac and his ministers prayed in Kiluba, no translation needed. The bleeding seemed to abate.

We worked through the day and finished by four o'clock. Pastor Kabongo brought all of his children to be blessed by Mechac, who prayed over them as he had over me.

That night, I initiated the second medical evacuation of my research.

Embodied Epistemology the Context of Right Relations: Illness

Early in our initial interview in the Indianapolis airport, Bishop Ntambo spoke of health care as a peacebuilding activity. During the testimonies I heard stories of illness. In 2009, a few days after the trip to Kaboto, I was unable to get out of bed and became increasingly weaker until I was evacuated to a tropical medicine facility in Johannesburg.

Among the Luba, disease—its hold, its mystery, its threat, its lull, its community, its loneliness—is embraced by many people's compassion. When I became seriously ill in Kamina, the doctors, the nurses, the members of the community who visited, and the pilot taught me about their care for the sick. But I know most about the people's capacity for compassion kinesthetically—through the touch of Mama Sila, the internally displaced grandmother who cared for me at the guesthouse, as recorded in my research notes.

> By Monday I know four sensations: fog, nausea, intense and erratic heat, and exhaustion. The disease saps my energy; I am spent. Watching me, John masterfully proposes an intercultural interpretation. "Perhaps you will feel better if Mama Sila bathes and massages you the way that women are bathed and massaged after they have a baby."

> "Yes, I think I would like that."

> Mama Shela, or Sillah, or Sila—I have seen her name spelled three different ways but she pronounces it strikingly like the American name Sheila—has for years provided a constant presence at the guesthouse. She prepares food alongside the chef, now Papa Hubert, cleans the house, does the guests' laundry, and in many small ways acts like a dorm mother. She speaks only Kiluba or Kiswahili, not French or English, but she observes everything. She knows the personality and the needs of her guests, even without speaking their languages.

> A widow since the 1980s, Mama Sila frames her timeless face each day by wrapping her head in a headdress, hiding her hair. She may be in her sixties or seventies or eighties—John says I daren't ask and that probably, even she does not know how old she is. She fled to Kamina in 1998 when the war neared her home in Kikondja. When she testified, she vividly portrayed the psychological confusion of internally displaced people when they flee— "You think you have grabbed the baby and you've grabbed the chicken, and the baby is still back at the house." Walking through the bush and dodging the war for a week, she arrived at Kamina and sought the assistance of the bishop. She was selected as one of the first widows to staff the orphanage with Mama Mujinga, and then, after 2000 when the guesthouse opened, she became the guesthouse Mama.

Mama Sila knows I prefer to bathe in the morning. In 2003 and 2008 the guesthouse had running water because the bathroom faucet was able to drain water from a tank in the backyard. The tank was filled manually, so I took "African showers" using only a few cups of water, knowing that every drop had been carried on someone's back. This year the running water has been disconnected, so guests bathe the African way. Every morning Mama Sila heats a ten-gallon bucket of water and carries it, leaning only slightly from its weight, from the stove behind the house to the bathtub in the house's center. Each day I see her back as she enters the bathroom; I admire her strength. This generous and heavy water is intended as one person's hot water ration. I finally learn to luxuriate by splashing the entire bucket, cup full after cup full, on my body, leaving the bottom of the bucket only damp. I was cleaner on this trip than ever before. Until the fog set in.

When the water for my bath is ready, I gather clean underwear and socks and find a tube of body lotion. My purple bandana hangs in the bathroom where I have used it as a washcloth. Mama Sila hauls the hot water and waits patiently in the bathroom. As I undress, I am aware that Mama Sila has frequently wrapped my *kikwembe*, properly draping it and securing it, but I have never before stood naked in her presence.

In my wobbly state I must scale the walls of the large, white, claw-footed iron-cast bathtub. She holds my left hand tightly while I place my right hand on the top of the edge of the wall of the tub. I am able to lift my right leg, shifting my weight to my right so that I can position my left leg under my body. Now, I am standing unsteadily in the tub. I am slightly taller than Mama Sila. I must balance myself with a hand on her shoulder.

Normally we live in the world with a tacit knowledge of our bodies, an unacknowledged sense of our physical strength and an uninhabited space around us that protects our innermost vulnerabilities—our fears, our anxieties, our loves, our hopes, our sentiments—from immediate availability to interpersonal relationships. This emotional no-man's-land allows us to venture toward others, protecting that tender space which is dearest inside us. In this space we reform our innermost feelings for presentation to the outside world. People who care about us deeply walk up to the edge of that protected space and invite us, waiting for us to meet them. As I struggle to stand in the tub, watching Mama Sila, the psychological space protecting my innermost emotions from the people around me has narrowed from space to merely a line.

I watch Mama Sila put the bandana in the water. She quickly and confidently softens it by squeezing the water through it, holding the center of the cloth in one hand and sliding her other hand down the length and corners of the fabric, soaking it several times. She soaps the bandana and takes my left hand in hers. And then, she plays my body with the precise touch of a concert pianist. She scrubs my left arm, rhythmically, pulsating up and down the length of my arm from wrist to shoulder, as if establishing an underlying pace for her bathing. Keeping that time, she scales my shoulders, rubs grace notes across and under my breasts, and sounds deep, resonant chords over my torso. She turns me toward her to reach my right side, and, as if playing a refrain, she scrubs my shoulders and my back, firmly and confidently. I doubt that she will scrub a woman's hidden, pressed-together, sweatiest parts, but I am wrong: she keeps the rhythm when she reaches from my arms to my armpits, from my torso to my vulva, from my back to the crevasse between the cheeks of my buttocks. She rests momentarily to breathe, and then she bends to repeat the action from my arms on my legs, lifting my feet, encircling my toes. She twists her hand, motioning to me to bend over, and she pours the heated water over my head with a cup, wetting my long hair for sudsing. As I steady myself with my hands on either side of the tub, she massages my scalp and runs her fingers through my soapy hair. She has gently entered the intimate emotional space that is close to my raw, unprocessed feelings; as I lift my head tears cascade down my body in equal proportion from my hair and from my eyes. Her delicate, firm, precise touch communicates protection that I, for now, cannot find inside myself.

I stand in the tub while she pats my body dry. I remember a time when, as a young child, I stood on the toilet lid so that my short grandmother could dry my body after my bath without bending down. This moment of the tender touch of my grandmother has stayed with me for another fifty plus years. When Mama Sila dries the folds of my ears that she has carefully washed, I know she has bathed as many orphaned children as women giving birth. After she helps me from the tub, I sink, with a few sobs, into her embrace.

Then, wrapping me in a towel, she guides me from the bathroom across the hall to my bedroom. I hand her a tube of lotion, and as rhythmically and methodically as she has bathed me, she applies the lotion from neck to foot. She dresses me as she would a child, holding my underpants, helping me find the opening for a shirt that she pulls over my head. Finishing her work with me, she leaves to dump the water and clean the bathroom, and I walk to the living room. Shortly, I begin to shiver uncontrollably and I find a wool blanket in the bedroom and wrap it around myself. My quivering subsides after ten minutes. As my hips had begun to ache from lying in too still a position on the love seat, I had given her Ben-Gay rather than body lotion, a mistake I will not make after my future baths.

By Tuesday morning, when Mama Sila bathes me and massages me with lavender body lotion rather than Ben-Gay, I expect to be feeling nearly new, as Gaston has promised. Instead, the fog, the nausea, the erratic intense heat, and the weakness have reached a steady level, and I begin to suspect that more is wrong than malaria.

Bishop Ntambo had intended that I would finish my visit by teaching pastor's school; when I withdrew, he asked if I would simply greet the pastors. Gathering all my energy, I rode in the truck the seven kilometers to Kamisamba Farm, and looking out over the hundred men and a few women sitting in blue plastic chairs and on the ground, I spoke of the illnesses they had endured. "My illness is part of the research," I told them. "To know something of how you have felt." I remember the look of deep compassion that spread across room of eyes beholding me as they heard the translation.

Compassion meets vulnerability without violation, and when compassion communes iteratively within relationships, it becomes the heart of "right relations."

The next day I was flown to Lubumbashi on the same medical evacuation flight that removes the sick and dying from rural villages. My understanding of the community's experience of disease was limited by the fact that my insurance company, MEDEX, had arranged for me to connect immediately to a commercial flight to Johannesburg and then to travel by taxi to Milpark Hospital, which housed a South African tropical disease treatment center.

Embodied Epistemology Within the Context of Right Relations: Ritual

Luba honor people and occasions through ritual, and ritual becomes an opportunity for expressing the generosity and hospitality that is key to "right relations." My 2003 trip to Kamina ended with a party in the Bishop's backyard—the entire community, from orphans to government officials, gathered. Newly donated bicycles and garden implements were distributed; our delegation presented gifts we had brought; the Luba women wrapped each female visitor in a hand sewn *kikwembe* and each male visitor in a brightly patterned shirt; musicians played, traditional dancers performed, and everyone danced.

In 2007 I told John I wanted to host a party to thank the people who had participated in the research. He liked the idea, but it had to be culturally orchestrated. He thought through the guest list and the seating chart, negotiated with the chef for an appropriate menu, gathered tables and chairs from the church across the street so that we all sat at one long banquet, and thought through the appropriate honoraria and gifts for various people from the money I had remaining and the generic gifts I'd brought.

At meals in the guesthouse hands are washed in a traditional way: a plastic basin of warm water is placed on a chair, with an empty tub on the floor beside. People stand in line, and one by one, extending their hands. Mama Sila dips a cup into the warm water and wets the hands slightly; then the washer sudses with bar soap; finally, Mama Sila streams the water over the hands to rinse them and gives the person a towel. When the time came for handwashing, I took the cup and spontaneously began Mama Sila's ritual actions. The reverse symbolism was not lost on the community: John, who was busy orchestrating the seating, stepped in at the end of the line.

"I want my hands washed. It's like Jesus," he murmured.

The women had told me that they intended to confer on me a Luba name. That night, at the end of the meal, they named me *Inamiso*— "mother of the nations without discrimination." Bishop Ntambo later said that *Inamiso* can be a name or a title—for me, it is the latter. With this naming they both commented on the work I had been doing but and imposed on me an obligation to live up to its meaning.

Creative Writing and Practical Theology

When I returned home in 2008, the words downloaded into my computer and the testimonies written on my heart, I faced another decision of "right relations": I did not want to objectify the witnesses who told me their story by coding and analyzing their interviews. I wanted to present them in their subjectivity, to write so that they could testify directly to the reader, as they had spoken so eloquently to me.

Congolese peacemakers are not believed to exist because their stories aren't told, just as American women were not seen as contributing to American history until the 1970s, because their history hadn't been written. The Congolese people who risked their lives for peace needed what the women's historian Gerda Lerner called "compensatory history" — "in which the historian [scholar] wanders, like Diogenes with a lantern, seeking to identify women [peacemakers] and their activities." This, Lerner reminisced, provided the foundation upon which women's history redefined the structures of the academic discipline of history.

Lerner edited women's source documents; I collected an oral history, tape recording the stories and then weaving them into a narrative. I am convinced that the form of the story represents the best first portrayal of the work of this community.

As I began to experiment with the writing, I discovered I had to know the persons in much more depth to write a narrative than an analysis. The 2008 research trip, that I had imagined as a trip to vet the manuscript, became one in which I sought to fill out the story that was developing.

As I worked on this book, a turn toward creative writing occurred within my academic discipline, practical theology. Practical theology has many methodologies, usually involving a correlation between social sciences and theology. I have usually been identified with the liberation stream of practical theology. But I found that in this case, the liberation stream dovetailed with one identified with aesthetics, explored in the International Academy of Practical Theology conference in Quebec City in 1999. In my presentation at that conference, I had experimented with creative writing, prefacing my more theoretical talk with a vignette that artistically introduced the principles I sought to elucidate. In 2015, as I wrestled with various techniques and structures of creative non-fiction, Heather Walton, now president of the IAPT, published *Not Eden: Spiritual Life Waiting for This World,* which provides both a theory of spiritual writing and examples of her own spiritual memoir. Walton's work, and the IAPT working group on Poetics, created a niche within which my work could reside as practical theology.

My decision to write the narrative as creative non-fiction, made for "right relations," required me to learn a new writing craft. I attended courses at the Iowa Summer Writing Workshop and the University of Toronto Continuing Studies and meetings of the Canadian Creative Nonfiction Collective Society (CNFC), as well as doing my own reading. I wrestled with various definitions of creative non-fiction—from the very strict definitions of "true stories," as outlined by Lee Gutkind in *You Can't Make This Stuff Up,* in which every detail of every scene or dialogue must be verified, to the metaphoric understandings of truth described by indigenous essayists in *Crisp Blue Edges: Indigenous Creative Nonfiction,* to the middle way of my Canadian colleagues in CNFC who primarily locate truth in the clarity of "the contract with the reader."

The Contract with the Reader: The Truth in This Book

This book tells a true story of a community. Philosophers debate the meaning of truth: is truth perception, verifiable fact, or social construction? In this work of creative non-fiction, honesty demands an understanding between the author, the witnesses, and the reader about "what is true." I made my literary judgments according to one overarching standard: that the reader might experience, intimately, the spirit of a community of local Luba Congolese Methodists and their colleagues who, out of their religious motivations, sought to build the peace before, during and after the recent wars in the Democratic Republic of Congo.

In this story of a community, personal and communal truths interpret national and regional political, historical, and ecclesial events that I verified through public documents. Multiple testimonies identified key rural village events. I narrate meanings given to these events as closely as possible to the way they were experienced by the witnesses who found their lives changed.

No pseudonyms are used, except in the case of two people who requested anonymity. At the time of their original interview, all contributors consented in writing to having their stories included in the book. Each chapter is based on the testimony of the primary character. Most of these witnesses were interviewed multiple times over a period of seven years in the course of three research trips, telephone calls and Skype interviews. Witnesses with primary storylines, and secondary characters as far as possible, have shaped the narrative by reviewing their chapters, augmenting or correcting the information where necessary, and then giving additional consent for the way I have developed their story. In some cases, I have created symbols, metaphors and vignettes that support the meanings that the witnesses have tried to communicate to me. The witnesses confirmed these, too, as appropriate to the spirit of the occasion.

The interviews were conducted in English, French, Kiluba, and Kiswahili. Local interpreters John Mutombo, Fabrice Ilunga Mujinga, Mbuyu Mwilumba, Ilgha Monga Ilunga, Boniface Kabongo, Kimba Kyakutala Evariste, and Raymond Mande Muyombo added meaning to the story by rendering local language responses into English and by suggesting witnesses who offered additional perspectives. I have recreated the dialogue of those speaking native languages in standard English. Bishop Ntambo's "African English" contributes to his identity, and he values the African voice as it is communicated within the cadence and grammar of African English-speaking persons. Therefore, for English-speaking characters, African English has been somewhat retained so that the reader may encounter those witnesses more intimately. As the book documents *religious* peacebuilding, I have sought to interpret the witnesses' spirituality—their struggles, confidence, doubts, and negotiations between traditional indigenous and Christian religion—by closely following their interviews and then confirming with them the way I have recreated their story. A careful reader will notice that the spirituality of the witnesses differs significantly: they portray 'varieties of African religious experience,' especially as they relate their Christianity to their Luba tradition.

Even though I have sought information from the witnesses about scenes and dialogue, such details may not have been of utmost importance to them, or the limits of time and distance did not allow me to pursue specifics that the story's narrative coherence ultimately required. In such cases, I have created probable scenes and dialogue that were approved by the primary witnesses around whom the story was built. While I have not created composite characters, at times I have created one scene that allows me to communicate a witness's spiritual struggles that actually occurred over a long period of time.

I initially positioned myself as their ghostwriter. Over the next years, as I reflected on what I had learned from the witnesses, I came to understand myself as their spirit-writer: my spirit, *mutyima muyampe,* literally, my thinking heart, accompanies their *muya,* literally, their soul, in these words. Inevitably, my voice intersects with those of the people who lived this story first hand; my witness, in ongoing collaboration with theirs, has brought this story to the page.

Finally, these witnesses represent truths borne by many other Luba people who first hoped for a better future after the Mobutu era, then fled from war and cared for refugees, and now continue to make peace after the war. Many such Luba people remain unnamed in the text, even in the list of witnesses. To their efforts, also, this work is dedicated.

Congo is diverse. The Luba community in this book presents one among many communal perspectives on the recent history of events in the geography that Europeans constructed as *Congo.* In 2016, as in 1996, the people of the Democratic Republic of Congo face a turning point as they conduct a difficult election. Will the work of peace throughout the country provide an adequate foundation for the various linguistic groups who inhabit this land to find a way, together, toward their common flourishing?

Congolese names are notoriously difficult for the western reader; therefore, for clarity, a glossary of the primary characters and villages, in the order of their appearance in the story, can be found in an appendix at the end of the book. The full list of witnesses, as they identified themselves for the purpose of contributing to this story, include:

Bishop Ntambo Nkulu Ntanda
Willy Kaseki, DAF/Sendwe

Pasteur Kasongo Kazadi, Kamina District Superintendent
Pasteur John Mutombo
Dr. Rogers Galaxy
Dr. Mireille Mikombe
Pasteur Boniface Kabongo Ilunga, Kamina District Superintendent and pro-
    ject interpreter
Mutelwa Kabulungo Jean
Pasteur Kitenge Lumaliza Joseph
Thomas Kalonda
Prof Mwembo LM
Dr. Gustave B. Kyosha
Mr Hatari Salumu/Communauté islamique
Dr. Rashidi-Mussa
Oliver Monga
Darlene Cox
Cynthia Tozer
Les Maxwell
Pierre Mukolomone
Cond. Kebikonkeka
Pasteur Mukalay Kichibi
Me. Kakazi Ngoy
Pasteur Kayembe Besheta
Ilunga wa Mukumbi
Mwamba wa Ngoy Kyabula
Kanda-Fwanyinwabo, Chef de Groupement Ngoy Mwana
Greffier Kabwe-Kyamu
Mutonkole Kilungu Michel
Kamchape Kasase, Commissaire de District et du Haut-Lomami
Ilunga Kalonda, Commissaire de District Assistant
Mme. Suzy Mwema
Pasteur Monga Kamuyombo, Directeur de l'éducation chrétienne
Dr. Kisula Ngoy
King Kayamba
Mama Nkulu Sila
Mama Kahole wa Ngoy
Prof. Raymond Mande
Mujing Mwad Honorine
Sinbani Valery Chantal
Kay
Kalemie Local Pastor
Gaston Ntambo
Mbuyu Mwilumba Mathias, project interpreter, and

Moma Kabila Alphonsine and their family:
    Mwilambwe as Mbuyu Esquin
    Kongolo Kirongozi Patrice
    Mpungwe Baraka Cherita
    Mbuyu wa Katekamo Eschler
    Onda Kongolo Nizette (Dada)
    Djete Kalwashi Harris
    Mayombo Mwepu Kalume Nevadou (born in Kamina)
    Ntambo Nkulu Ntanda Bishop (born in Kamina)
Guy Mande Muyombo
Devis Mulunda
Mark Harrison
Phil Wogaman
Mujinga Mwamba Kora
Kabongo Hubert
Prophet Mwenze Ngoy Kasambula Mechac and his ministers:
    Ilunga Mutalala Godefriod, Secretary
    Ilunga Kiluja Moise
    Kamwanya Wangoy Adalbert
    Makadjamba Mbayo Seta
Lusanga Kitenge
Rev. Kazadi Kakabamba
Rev. Twite Kanonge
Banza Tina
Longo wa Kusamba
Kalonda Vautour
Félix
John Nday
Mr Kasokwe
Commissaire for Kamina Mr. Muzinga
Kasongo Ndalamba KK Hanspeter
Ngoy Nyengele Mbuyu Mianda

Their Story

In Chapter I: "Anticipating the End of Mobutu—Caring for Children, Protecting Missionaries, Engaging in Agriculture and Construction (August 1996-May 17, 1997)" a series of characters reveal the spirit of the times as they anticipate social and ecclesial transition: young people's excitement about the opportunities of a new social order, especially if a Luba takes over Zaire; older leaders' apprehension about violence in the transition; Kabila and the traditional chiefs' use of tradition to avoid bloodshed in Katanga; and the church's honeymoon with a new Bishop who has a vision for development in Katanga.

In Chapter II: "Joy and Peace—A Vision for Development (May 1997-July 1998)" the characters show the interlude of hope, joy and anticipation in the lull between the first and second wars in Congo.

In Chapter III: "War Engulfs Two-Thirds of the Democratic Republic of Congo—Development Continues, Relief Work Escalates (July 1998-July 1999)" the characters communicate their disbelief, apprehension, and sense of being overwhelmed, as they befriend their displaced colleagues from Tanganyika and then organize care for a steady stream of internally displaced people who seek assistance from the church. Government suspicion lands on anyone associated with Rwanda or Tutsis, including Bishop Ntambo's family; likewise, rebels seek to co-opt the resources of skilled elites, such as the Bishop's son, Gaston Ntambo, a pilot. The church leaders urge Bishop Ntambo and his family to go into exile, so secondary leaders must execute day-to-day decisions. Within a few months, word spreads on rural pathways that the Kamina church will help all refugees, and religious leaders seek international assistance to meet the demand. The end of the section documents Bishop Ntambo's emotional struggle as he and his wife decide to return to Kamina.

In Chapter IV: "The Lusaka Negotiations Fail—Development, Relief and Social Networks (July 1999-January 2001)" Bishop Ntambo leads a variety of development efforts and builds relationships throughout the local community and beyond, despite the repeated failure of the political peace process and the beginning of conflicts between villagers and Mai-Mai. Stories from villages deeper in the bush, including the villages of Kabongo, Kitenge, and Kamungu, towns on the border of areas marked as "inaccessible" on humanitarian maps, show the effect of the war and the growing conflict with the Mai-Mai on local, rural villagers.

In Chapter V: "The Mai-Mai Continue the War—Development, Relief, Social Networks, and Conflict Mediation (January 2001-September 2004)" the text braids storylines focused around the peaceful town of Kamina and its development initiatives and the conflict-ridden villages of Kaboto and Kitenge, some two hundred kilometers in Kamina's perimeter. In outlying villages religious leaders such as Prophet Mechac and Pastor Kora begin to intervene with the Mai-Mai. Officers from Kamina Military Base speak to the pastors at the Annual Conference, urging their participation in defusing the Mai-Mai threat.

Chapter VI: "Kamina Hosts the Mai-Mai Conference—Conflict Transformation (September 2004)" tells the story of the fragility and success of the conference, as experienced by the local villagers. It documents the initial call from the government and the arrangements and strategies developed by Bishop Ntambo and other local religious leaders. As the relationship between the government and the warlords has become toxic, the spiritual leaders are asked to persuade the warlords to attend. When the most powerful Mai-Mai commander, Chinja-Chinja, does not appear, the Kamina United Methodist District Superintendent, Boniface Kabongo, once Chinja-Chinja's childhood friend, is dispatched to convince the warlord to come to Kamina. Bishop Ntambo and Pastor Kabongo know that many others have died on such missions. Throughout, the section seeks to reveal the logics of the Mai-Mai, as well as the culture's respect for and authority conferred on spiritual leaders—the condition that allows such a conference to take place.

Chapter VII: "Peacebuilding After the Mai-Mai Conference (October, 2004 and following)" documents the notable efforts by Bishop Ntambo and his leaders as they reconcile congregations in the war zone in 2006. In 2012 they intervene internationally when the M-23 movement destabilizes the border between DRC and Rwanda; this effort leads to Bishop Ntambo's September 19, 2012 testimony in the United States House of Representative's Committee on Foreign Affairs, Subcommittee for Africa, Global Health and Human Rights. Afterwards, he negotiates disputes among Congolese politicians in order to help to stabilize the country.

In the Conclusion "The Peace to Build" I offer my interpretation of what this story contributes to DRC peacebuilding theory that is not acknowledged in secular histories: 1) that hunger fuels the local conflicts over resources, creating systems that are a microcosm of the well-documented illegal resource extraction that occurs on an international level; 2) that religion and tradition motivates people to seek the peace, and 3) that motivated by spirituality, the local people themselves have created a complex, organic model of peacebuilding, including capacity building, conflict transformation, and development.

In the Appendix I provide a list of characters to assist the western reader to distinguish the Kiluba names.

Prologue

"Where's the Peace to Keep in Congo?"

Headline, *Chicago Tribune*, February 14, 2000

"The wolf shall live with the lamb,
the leopard shall lie down with the kid,
The calf and the lion and the fatling together,
and a little child shall lead them."

Isaiah 11:6

Kamina, Katanga Province, Democratic Republic of Congo
September 24, 2004

Mama Mujing Mwad Honorine crept close to the wall of the orphanage leading to the door to the children's sleeping quarters, her face lowered, her spine hunched, her hands gripping a ten-gallon bucket of water. She felt his presence across the interior playground, and she dared not stare at terror. And yet . . . she lifted her head ever so slightly to the side and peeked, searing the remarkable image into her brain.

There ambled Chinja-Chinja, the famous Mai-Mai warlord, casually clad, surrounded by his followers who wore traditional garb—their loins wrapped in animal skins, their sides adorned with spears, their necks weighted with necklaces that bound together human genitalia. Chinja-Chinja, whose name translated 'slain-slain,' commander of six thousand warriors who carried out his vicious commands. Chinja-Chinja, who, by the persuasive powers of the Bishop and his clergy, agreed to attend the peace conference where the Governor of Katanga Province, Kisula Ngoy, hoped to bring the Mai-Mai threat to an end. Chinja-Chinja, who, for the next five days, would live, eat, and consult his ancestors for guidance through his deadly rituals, here in the dormitory of the orphanage in the front of Mama Mujing's compound. Meanwhile, Mama Mujing and the widows who staffed the orphanage, women displaced by the war, would feed, cuddle, and calm the fears of fifty-four war orphans who were now contained in the building close to the rear entrance. While Chinja-Chinja consulted his spirits, Mama, the widows and the children would pray to their God, hoping their God was stronger.

Mama's gospel tells the story of one man who lays down his own life for his followers. After his death, he is entombed with boulders sealing the entrance. Some women rise early in the morning to dress his body with herbs and ointments; they discover the tomb is empty and his body is gone. This tragic story has a miraculous ending: this man appears in visions around which his followers regather. They hear that they, too, may be asked to die in love for others.

Mama Mujing would have been one of the women who discovered Jesus' empty tomb; she would have been one prepared to die in martyrdom. But nowhere do Mama's scriptures—words that defend widows and orphans—say that church leaders may pledge the lives of fifty-four innocent children as collateral for peace. Nowhere do the scriptures say that religious authorities may hold hostage the women and children of an entire city. And yet, by agreeing to convene the Mai-Mai peace conference in Kamina and housing the most feared warlord and his delegation in the orphanage, Bishop had, in effect, done just that.

Chapter I

To Anticipate the End of Mobutu— "To Feed My People" (August 1996-May 17, 1997)

Historical Introduction

After many false starts—perhaps, just perhaps—the people were bringing the Mobutu era to an end. Young adults anticipated a time when they could rapidly establish their work and their families; older adults, their optimism tempered by promises and uneasy transitions, cautiously hoped for peace; children feared the change in their parents' fortunes. No two people experienced the political ferment alike.

Mobutu had taken the name Mobutu Sese Seko, which meant "the all-powerful warrior who, because of his endurance and inflexible will to win, will go from conquest to conquest leaving fire in his wake." His *Los Angeles Times* obituary stated:

> Mobutu once bragged in an interview on CBS-TV's "60 Minutes" that he was one of the world's richest men—this as Zaire's infrastructure crumbled. Many of the country's paved roads had been swallowed up by the encroaching jungle, hospital patients were forced to provide their own medicine, and almost every police officer, regular army soldier and civil servant had resorted to banditry as a means to survive.

While Mobutu played politics on the world stage as a Cold War ally of the United States and Europe, he pocketed international aid and extracted taxes throughout Zaire. The entire country suffered, but different regions of the country encountered specific dynamics of Mobutu's plundering. Mobutu was born of the Ngbwandi people in the city of Lisala in Equateur Province, and his base of support lay in the south-central capital city and province, Kinshasa. Shaba Province (renamed Katanga after May 17, 1997), in the south of Zaire (renamed Democratic Republic of Congo), housed the country's second largest city, Lubumbashi, and enriched the Kinshasa-based government through its extensive copper wealth. So, Mobutu, for the Luba people, became a foreign oppressor to be resisted. The liberator, Laurent-Désiré Kabila, was a Luba person, a native of Katanga Province.

In 1996 the United Methodists of rural Katanga elected a new spiritual leader, forty-nine-year-old Bishop Ntambo Nkulu Ntanda. The Mobutu era had reduced his villages to misery. He had one mission: "To feed my people." He believed that, with the wisdom of established lay colleagues and the energy of new young leaders, his goal could be achieved. And with a leap of Biblical faith nuanced by wonder at the opportunity and doubt before the task's difficulty, he laid the foundation for his work. Development of rural Katanga, the way to fight hunger, drove his initial vision.

For the elderly and middle-aged and youth and children, for those living in the big city and in towns and in rural villages, for civilians and military, for Christians and traditional chiefs—something new lay ahead, in both government and the church—but in what way would it come?

Pastor Ntambo Becomes Bishop of a Ghost Town

"In Zaire They Finally Ask, Who Follows Mobutu?"

New York Times, September 13, 1996

"How lonely sits the city that once was full of people!
How like a widow she has become,
she that was great among the nations!
She that was a princess among the provinces
has become a vassal."

Lamentations 1:1

Kamina, Haut Lomami District, Shaba Province, Zaire
August 1996

The train puffed, groaned, and halted before the one-room depot at Kamina. As it settled on the track, the newly elected Bishop Ntambo Nkulu Ntanda heard the singing, and, turning toward the window, saw a crowd of people, swaying, clapping, drumming, cheering. He smiled broadly. *His people!* Suddenly shy, he averted his eyes from the crowd to his hands that were folded on the brightly patterned shirt that covered his large stomach—but only for a moment. Recomposed, he reached for the hand of his wife, Thérèse Nshimba Nkulu, and beamed brightly at her full face. Her eyes soft and damp, she squeezed his fingers in return. He rose awkwardly, stiff from the three-day, halting train ride from Lubumbashi. Hands of his travelling companions reached for the luggage that was stored at their feet, and Ntambo and Nshimba crammed into the train's aisles behind the delegates to the Central Conference who had elected Ntambo Bishop.

Step by step, they wriggled toward the door, following the delegation that left the train first. At the top of the steps, Ntambo paused and looked directly at the mass of singers. The drummers beat hollowed logs, energetically accompanying a hymn of praise and triumph, stirring the music toward frenzy. He waved heartily, and then grasping the railing, swung to the ground. Turning to Nshimba, he held out his hand to steady her. When they were only a few steps beyond the door of the train, people crushed around the choirs toward him. Bishop's delegation pushed against the crowd, moving them back.

Women, their hands flapping at their mouths, punctuated the singing with ululations. "*Eyo-mwa, Eyo-mwa,*" Mama Nshimba responded, embracing the women who came closest.

The men, one after another, grasped their left fingers round their upper right forearms and extended their sweaty right hands toward Bishop. "*Eyo-vidje, Eyo-vidje,*" Bishop Ntambo greeted them, shaking each one.

Peering around the choirs, the dark eyes of children, toddlers straddling the hips of girls not yet pubescent, dolefully watched the stout man and smiling woman disembark the train and enter the crowd. Whoever this man was, he was well fed. He must be rich. He was one to be followed.

Even with the crush of activity immediately before him, Bishop's eyes rested upon the children. He recognized their look, felt the pain in their stomachs gnawing at his gut. As a toddler he had nearly died of malnutrition. His oldest son, Gaston Ntambo, had owned his first pair of shoes when he was nine, given to him by a missionary. Only now, as a bishop with a salary paid by the international church, had the fear of sporadic hunger been eased from Ntambo and his family. But the specter of an empty stomach regularly visited his parishioners in Kamina.

How will people think of me if I am fed and do not feed them?

* * *

A few days later, sleepless, Ntambo gazed at the night sky of the southern hemisphere, as if the hazy stars and expanses of mysterious, celestial universe might reveal the secret meaning of the last month. The election results had surprised even him, given the opposition by key leaders. He had been elected a bishop, but of what? The large swath of south central Zaire over which he was now the principal Protestant leader contained no provincial center of urban activity. He did not govern the network of Methodists among the ten million people of Kinshasa or even among the two million inhabitants of Lubumbashi. Bishop Onema and Bishop Katembo oversaw these major metropolitan areas.

He had become Bishop of a wasteland of dispersed, thin, hungry people in a country forgotten by the world. He aimed to feed his rural people, physically and spiritually, nothing more, nothing less.

Though the late Bishop Wakadilo had moved his office to Nyembo Umpungu after the soldiers of Kamina Military Base looted the town in 1991 and 1993, Bishop Ntambo intended to re-establish the episcopal headquarters in Kamina, in the middle of the Shaba province. Here he knew the tribal leaders and their ways. As a spiritual leader he could call upon King Kasongo Nyembo at Kinkunki, just a few kilometers from Kamina, even though Ntambo's home village lay two hundred kilometers away, within the jurisdiction of King Kabongo. He hoped that these relationships would help him feed his people.

But—it was a huge undertaking. Once a thriving rural metropolis, Kamina had become a ghost town.

The new bishop pondered the last seven years that had hastened Kamina's decline. In the 1980s Mobutu plundered the wealth of the country for his personal gain, and the economy in Kamina had struggled. But most people still had enough to eat. Then in 1991 and 1993 Mobutu's soldiers at Kamina Military Base had destroyed the city's business and agricultural base. Goats and chickens, the staple sources of protein, no longer roamed the townspeople's yards. Small businesses, the center of the barter economy, had closed. Transportation, by train to Lubumbashi or by bike around Kamina and the surrounding villages, had stilled. No hospitals had medicine. No schools had books. Only a few churches and a little food, mainly cassava and fish, remained.

Under the influence of Arab slave traders, under the power of Belgian King Leopold II's *Force publique,* and then under Mobutu—a Congolese life was a looted life.

And now, with Mobutu ailing from prostate cancer and with no plans for a successor, Bishop hoped that the death of the despot might offer a new era for Shaba—a time when the province could build its future, unencumbered by inordinate taxes from Kinshasa. A Congolese life as a stable and sated life, one that could be built strong, as if with fired bricks, and nourished by the fish of the river and the crops from green, lush fields—yes, that's what he sought for his people!

Equally possible, political tensions in the eastern refugee camps on the borders with Rwanda and Burundi could explode. Bishop shivered, remembering his narrow escape through Burundi after President Ndadaye's death. But those borders lay more than a thousand kilometers from Kamina.

The new bishop knew that the destitute people of Kamina, who believed deeply in supernatural powers, expected to be fed. They believed him to be a Moses who could call down manna from heaven, even if they were not practicing Christians. Before dawn that morning the hungry had crowded his door, asking for food and medical assistance.

And his mother had prayed for this! When it became clear that he might be elected, she had called her brother and his wife. The three stayed together in her house, fasting during the days of the election and calling upon God's will to be done. A devout Roman Catholic, Bishop's ninety-six-year-old mother, Kahole wa Ngoy, did not share her son's United Methodist commitments, but she had guided him to invoke the presence of the Holy Spirit in times when even he had vacillated.

Her faith had sustained them through the looting. In 1991 she was at home in Kamina with Nshimba, six children, and other members of the family when the shooting started. With bullets ricocheting around them, she had called her children and grandchildren to the center of the house. They knelt while she prayed over them. She remained calm. They survived and were comforted.

As a result of maternal and divine intervention, Ntambo now bore the responsibility for feeding the people physically as well as spiritually, and even *she* believed he had the power to do so.

All eyes in Kamina were upon him, most importantly, the eyes of the hungry children. Later that morning he walked silently to the church's office building down a side path that led to the main street through the center of Kamina. Even though people should have been hustling to work at this time, he was alone and allowed tears to rim his eyes, knowing what would come next. As he approached, their small forms came into view. A few lay on the concrete sidewalk, others leaned on each other by the wall of the dirty, white, two-story building with black painted lettering, "*l'Église méthodiste unie.*" As they saw him, they began to stir, one moving after the other, waking those who still slept. He anticipated their plaintive cry in Kiluba, "*Papa, wafwako, wafwako!*" He had come prepared. At the building he stepped over the open sewer that lined the street, counted the children, and cut the bunch of bananas into pieces. He gave each one a portion. Then, he willed himself to turn his back on them, walk through the doors, and enter his new office.

Pastor Kabongo and Raymond Mande Test the New Bishop

> "Zaire War Breeds a Human Catastrophe"
> *New York Times*, October 25, 1996

> "Restore us to yourself, O Lord,
> that we may be restored;
> renew our days as of old."
> Lamentations 5:21

Kamina, Haut Lomami District, Shaba Province, Zaire
October 1996

For Pastor Boniface Kabongo, in Kamina, the political earth barely trembled: who heard the troublemakers a thousand kilometers away in the eastern Zaire beating their war-drums? A few voices in North Katanga murmured, 'perhaps one more uprising of the *Banyamulenge*', the Tutsi Zairians who lived on the border with Rwanda. But Pastor Kabongo's ecclesial earth was shaking, like the rapid-fire arms of musicians calling everyone to the installation of a new Bishop, their sticks pounding hollow log drums under the canopy of branches and brightly colored cloth that protected the assembled from the baking sun in the side yard of Kamina's largest church, Centre Ville.

The newly elected bishop had concluded his speech. As Kabongo applauded happily, he leaned forward in his blue plastic chair and craned his neck, trying to look over the heads of the well-wishers who sat in front of him—rows and rows of pastors, district superintendents and leaders of women's groups from the towns and villages of Haut Lomami and Tanganyika Districts[1] of Shaba Province, most of whom had biked or walked for days to participate in a celebration that occurred only a few times in a lifetime. Even the national television and radio from Lubumbashi had broadcast the entire event. The women of Kamina had turned out in force, making ample preparations for the feast to come. Pastor Kabongo could smell the banquet that waited: stewed goat and beef and lamb with savory gravy, fire-grilled chicken, dried fish in oil, with steamy boiled bukari and rice, all provided at the expense of the church. The visiting bishops from Lubumbashi and Kinshasa, dressed in white preaching gowns, lounged on overstuffed chairs facing the podium from the left, clapping and chatting happily with one another. Local government officials in western business suits sat on the chairs facing the podium on the right, nodding their heads and applauding, affirming what they had heard.

The ceremony had followed tradition. When Bishop was properly introduced and stood before the congregation, men and women presented whatever gifts they could bring: small amounts of money, offerings of salt, traditional arrows, a leopard skin. They had sung the hymns and heard the prerequisite speech, outlining Bishop's vision. "We will renew our institutions—build parsonages, churches and schools from durable material, make sure our children are educated and healthy, invest in our hospitals."

In a ghost town, it was a great day. Pastor Kabongo's spirits soared with excitement—the momentum of the occasion carried him along with a great smile on his face.

But that night, lying in bed, he found himself being skeptical of his elders, including the new bishop. *Another speech, more promises from the older generation.* He had heard it all before.

* * *

Raymond Mande Mutombo Mulumiashimba busied himself in Bishop's new office in Kamina, arranging tables and chairs and backing the filing cabinets against the wall. He made do with what furniture could be scrounged locally, just to get organized. He and the new bishop had decided to open a study office here in Kamina, from which Bishop could conduct his pastoral relationships, and a transit office in Lubumbashi, where his projects could be administered. Kamina had no effective communications, no source of supplies, no operative

---

[1] A clear district map of the DRC can be found at http://siteresources.worldbank.org/EXTINSPECTIONPANEL/Resources/Annex29.pdf.

bank, except through Lubumbashi. Any progress Bishop could make quickening his vision depended on the link between these two offices.

After Bishop Ntambo was elected, Mande had visited him to offer both his congratulations and his services.

"Bishop, you are elected a bishop. Now to be a bishop means many things to me. A bishop is a leader, and leadership is incarnated in you. A bishop is a pastor; you are the pastor. So there is nothing I can teach you there. A bishop is a visionary; you have a vision. A bishop is an administrator. So he should know how to organize his paperwork. How are you going to do that?"

"I don't know. Maybe I can request a missionary in Kamina to help me."

Mande had waited for this moment. Yes, missionaries from the United States and Europe had started the church in Zaire, and over the last seventy-five years they contributed much. But as a young man Mande had run the Methodist chapel at the University of Lubumbashi. A missionary identified him as a talented administrator. He had been recruited to work with the missionary and the United Methodist Church on a USAID project developing hospitals. Since 1986 Mande had cleared many containers of construction and medical supplies through customs—he knew how to organize paperwork and negotiate with the government. And, he was working on his doctorate in English literature at the University of Lubumbashi. He could translate documents and write reports in many languages. He also had a keen interest in metaphor—exactly how the imagination communicated a vision with symbols.

Why should the new bishop turn to the missionaries when a Congolese layperson was capable, trained, and desiring to be used? But Mande felt his way through the conversation slowly, testing whether the new bishop could trust a Congolese colleague as his partner or whether he felt he needed to be surrounded by the status provided by the missionaries' presence.

"OK, you can recruit a missionary. But myself, I can help you do that."

Bishop straightened, his eyes brightening. "Really?"

Ah, we are thinking alike.

"Yes."

That day Bishop and Mande began to organize Bishop Ntambo's administration, laying the cornerstone of Bishop's vision. Then, they turned to writing his speech for his installation. That task satisfied Mande most of all—Bishop giving his ideas, Mande creating images and words, Bishop saying, "Yes, that's what I mean!" Now Mande felt sure—his organizational experience and his literary interests could serve Bishop well.

And, Mande thought, they could even be friends.

* * *

After the installation celebration Mande and Bishop had pondered the unan-swerable question. Laurent Kabila, a Luba, one of their own people, seemed to be behind an uprising in the east. Would Kabila try to take Katanga? To lead Katanga to become a free state?

Belgium had quelled Katanga Province's secession from Zaire in 1965, but some people still harbored the secret desire to separate Zaire into countries that respected ethnic, linguistic and kinship ties. Bishop wondered whether he could hear up-to-date news of Zaire in the United States. Mande would have to keep him informed.

That night Ntambo opened the suitcases next to the mound of clothes that he and Nshimba had piled on the bed; Nshimba began to neatly fold each item into a small square. It was the first week of November 1996, and soon they would board a plane for St. Simon's Island, Georgia, where they would meet their colleagues from around the world at the United Methodist Council of Bishops' meeting. They were expected to attend the Council twice a year for five days, with other meetings before and after. At best, the trip from Kamina to the United States took four days: a day from Kamina to Lubumbashi when travelling by plane was possible—if not, the train or truck ride might take sev-eral days or a week—overnight in Lubumbashi, a day from Lubumbashi to Jo-hannesburg, two days from Johannesburg to the destination which could be an-ywhere in the United States. For African bishops, an entire Council meeting took a minimum of three weeks, sometimes months.

"Put it in, very carefully. Don't bend it." Ntambo handed Nshimba a bifold poster board, the base for a homemade model of churches and parsonages he hoped to build in Kamina. He had been in charge of religious education for the conference, and he knew the value of a visual aid. But he had misgivings. Per-haps it was too soon to share his vision. He had to be confident of his friendship with colleagues around the world before he sought donations from churches that might contribute to the work of his people. But, he wanted to be prepared to show his model if anyone asked what he hoped to accomplish.

He wanted every church, every parsonage to demonstrate for the families of the community how they could feed themselves. But, his vision would require leaders, workers, laborers—people of his generation, but also, dedicated young people. Once, as a young man, he had been selected from a crowd and encour-aged by the political leader Sendwe Jason to pursue his dreams—what devel-oping talent could *he* recruit? And how would their lives change, if Kabila did take Zaire?

The Student John Mutombo Seeks Work with Kabila

> "Last Chance: 'Memory: Luba Art and the Making of History' Museum of African Arts, SoHo, closing this month"
>
> *The New York Times*, September 6, 1996

> "Sarah conceived and bore Abraham a son in his old age, at the time of which God had spoken to him."
>
> Genesis 21:2

Kitenge, Haut Lomami District, Shaba Province, Zaire
September 18, 1996

The rebel Kabila certainly would overthrow Mobutu, and John Mukana Mwembo Mutombo planned to be where he could take advantage of the new political opportunity.

The train shuddered and stopped, not at a depot but on the track in the bush, north beyond Kamina, almost in Kitenge. Stopped, again. John watched as a few men and women slowly arched from their seats, shuffled down the aisles, and crowded toward the exit of the train. Glancing out the window he saw that a few of the very uncomfortable ones had already disembarked and were making their way into the surrounding trees and shrubs. The men walked a short distance to the side, faced away from the train, and stopped. The women tread a little further—John glimpsed bright cloth through the bushes behind which the women squatted. He refocused his gaze on the aisle of the train, leaving the people outside their privacy. The engineer, John knew, was working to restore the train's engine. This stop might last a few minutes, or a few hours, or a few days. Such were the trains in Zaire—no sanitation, no food service, frequent stops—and waiting.

John, twenty-seven years old, was conditioned to be patient, even by his conception and birth. His mother, the first wife of his father, had been unable to conceive, so his father took a second and then a third wife, each of whom bore him children. Then, late in life, John's mother, like Sarah and Elizabeth of the scriptures, became pregnant. The community watched, wondering about the child. The live birth on December 25, 1968, from a womb believed to be barren, endowed the baby John with spiritual significance. The curse was broken.

As John grew, so did tension in the family. The children of the second and third wives became adults and established families of their own, competing with the younger special child of the first wife for their father's attention and resources. When John was fifteen, surrounded by friction, mystery, and hope, John's mother put him on the train to Lubumbashi where he could live among her relatives and get an education. Now, twelve years later, after perfecting his

knowledge of seven languages, graduating from teacher's college and beginning his pedagogical training, John was returning to visit his parents' rural
home in Kitenge.

John settled into his seat and relaxed his stomach, an automatic response
that allowed him to cope with one more breakdown of the train in what had
become a two-week journey. With the train halted, however, John could feel an
unusual sensation in his body, pushing forward, forward. The pulse of his heart
had matched the rhythm of the train's movement and now refused to rest. He
had new hope for his future: soon, he believed, the Mobutu regime would be
overthrown by Laurent-Désiré Kabila.

* * *

His hope had been born in danger. John had matriculated at the University of
Lubumbashi in October 1989, the year of the student massacre. Mobutu had
promised that the government would pay 60% of the tuition and then reneged.
Students organized and protested; some had gone missing. Finally, in May
1990, the leaders discovered a Kikongo-speaking Ngbwandi student, one of
Mobutu's kin, reporting the students' plans for protests on a "motorola." They
tortured the informer until he identified others who had aided Mobutu. The
campus grew tense.

In a dorm room students reported in hushed tones what they had seen that
day; John listened intently as they speculated on what might happen next. Police had appeared on the campus; what did it mean? Would the police protect
the students or did they have ulterior motives? Some students thought it best to
leave the university; many from rural areas had nowhere to go; those from Burundi, Rwanda, Uganda and other countries believed they would be protected.
While John focused on the debate, a friend whose father worked for Mobutu
approached him and whispered.

"John, the Ngbwandi student has died. Police have surrounded the campus.
Leave now. Come with us."

So John was in a different part of the city on the night of the massacre. The
next day, the rumors flooded the market, the streets.

"They cut the electric lines early in the night—the Guard went through the
campus killing any students who did not know the Kikongo password—the university is closed; go home."

The students believed that the United Nations and the Vatican had organized
transportation to remote parts of Zaire where the students lived; John had taken
a train first to Kamina and then to Kitenge. Even there the word spread: "The
bodies of most of the students presumed dead have not been found—the airport
was near—perhaps the students' bodies were taken by plane over the jungle
and dumped in a distant area."

A year later, in 1991, John had returned and entered Lubumbashi's *Institut supérieur pédagogique* (ISP-Lubumbashi). In the next five years, students resisted Mobutu but avoided open protest. Charges had never been filed against those responsible for the 1990 massacre. Most Katangans believed Mobutu had retaliated against the protesters. His people, still in power, denied it.

Then in 1996 came more rumors: a liberator named Laurent-Désiré Kabila seemed to be gaining the power to overthrow Mobutu.

* * *

In Lubumbashi, people in the campus, the market, the restaurants—everywhere—chattered about what they heard on the international radio stations: Kabila, a man from the diaspora, a man whose ancestral home was Katanga, a Luba, was making war against Mobutu in the northeast. Mobutu's popularity with the western nations had diminished. Would international pressure now restrain Mobutu or derail his opposition? Or, was it civil war? This time, would not only the campus but also Lubumbashi's population of two million people be crippled? Where would the people in Lubumbashi get water, food, or electricity? How could they find transportation to take refuge with relatives in the rural areas, away from the fighting?

The official Zairian news stations proclaimed Mobutu's power as if nothing had changed.

And then, the British Broadcasting Corporation, Radio France International, and Canal Afrique, the international news agencies, reported that Kabila and his Alliance for the Democratic Forces for the Liberation of Congo (AFDL) had taken Kisangani, the interior port city on the Congo River. Kabila was advancing on the capital, Kinshasa.

In the café Lipamu, under normal circumstances, waitresses flowed between white, square, plastic tables where eight people sat in civilized comfort, eating omelettes, toast and coffee. But now, waitresses squeezed between the tables that were jostled into a topsy-turvy pattern as extra people drew up a chair, seeking word of what was happening in the east. The television bolted to the ceiling of the café broadcast news of Mobutu's power. At the tables beneath, people shared the word from the international radio stations, little by little ignoring the television.

John sat with a group of students, munching on a piece of toast but not tasting it.

"Kabila took Kisangani. He was able to break through Mobutu's resistance."

"Kabila is recruiting students."

"Yes, whenever he takes control of an area, he does *chembe-chembe*. He teaches his philosophy of self-determination, he trains leadership. That's why he wants students—to work in his government."

"Philippe is already gone. He had enough money and flew to Goma."

"So what do you think?" John asked. "Will Kabila really take control?"

"Oh, he'll win. Mobutu is crumbling. Even his own soldiers are fed up."

"We are young. They sent word. If you are educated and in your twenties and thirties, you can have a place in the new government, in the new army, no more waiting, waiting, waiting like under Mobutu. We will have a job. We will have a future."

"There is a train going to the eastern part. We can join him."

The students at the University of Lubumbashi were ready for such an opportunity. Their futures had dangled; some had been lost.

John became convinced and boarded the train. First, he would visit his parents in Kitenge. Then, he planned to meet Kabila's people in Kabalo. To imagine a Luba leading Zaire: it changed everything.

The Child Chantelle Flees Mobutu's Army

> "U.N. Presses for Truce to Help Refugees Trapped in Eastern Zaire"
>
> *The New York Times*, January 25, 1997

> "You shall not abuse any widow or orphan."
>
> Exodus 22:22

Moba, Tanganyika District, Shaba Province, Zaire
January 1997

This man, Kabila, overthrowing Mobutu—it was as if some force had shaken all the furniture and crashed the china and the knick knacks, everything by which eight-year-old Chantelle identified her life.

Chantelle cowered in the corner of the living room, her arms locked with her brother's, as she watched her mother pushing their clothes into the blue and red checked vinyl sack. Mama laid Chantelle's baby brother in the brightly colored wrap of her *kikwembe*, hoisted him to her back, and tied a knot tight across her bosom. They were moving, again. Kabongo, Kabondo, Kitenge, Kalemie, Moba—and now?

"Go." Her mother nodded toward the door.

Chantelle looked at her mother nervously. "Where's Papa?"

"Papa'll stay here. Mobutu's army put down their guns. Papa and his men are going to join Kabila's army, but Papa will not be a commander. We have to go."

Chantelle's eyes swept longingly around the living room, where, for the last year, she had offered food or drink when Papa received his officers. The sheer curtains fluttered in the breeze, billowing over the brown, overstuffed furniture that ringed the room. A lace doily rested over each pillow of the sofa where a visitor placed his head. Guests had rested their bottles of Fanta on the glass coffee table adorned with plastic flowers; sometimes, Papa had allowed Chantelle to taste the fizzy orange drink. The television in the blond wood bookcase had always chattered in the background, reminding the visitors of Mobutu's power and wealth. So many men in uniforms had sat with Papa at the long, wooden table over which the dictator's picture hung. And now. . . Chantelle could not finish the thought.

Her mother faced her older children. "Hold tight to your charms!"

Chantelle followed Mama onto the veranda and into the garden, squeezing her fingers tightly around her small bundle, wrapped in cloth, until her fingernails bit into the palm of her hand.

* * *

In the military camp Chantelle had ventured from the compound only in the company of her mother. By her mother's side she felt safe to walk down the road from the commander's mansion, beneath the banana and mango trees, past the officers' concrete houses with tin roofs and private gardens. Next came the administration buildings, and between two of them, an open area with a concrete slab and a thatched roof, the space for community meetings. Here, Mama had met with the other officers' wives. Many of the children had run together in the grass between the buildings even when the adults were not meeting, but not Chantelle.

She knew that this military camp, like the others, was divided into two parts—the near side for the officers, the far side for the enlisted men and their families. When Chantelle accompanied Papa as he drove through the reaches of the camp, she saw familiar sights. There, the families lived in one-room mud huts with thatched roofs like the ones Chantelle and her parents had occupied when Papa was on the police force. She knew the drip of rain that inevitably dampened the hut during the rainy season. The families shared a common garden, and often, they argued over the harvest that never yielded enough.

Chantelle knew how soldiers found food when gardens did not produce. In Kabongo she had heard them boast about the way they threatened the village people.

"A good goat the old Mama had!"

"The radio, and ooh, the young girl!" The soldiers' laughter had made Chantelle shiver.

She also knew the pain in her stomach when food was scarce.

When Papa was enlisted, he often told Mama, "They did not pay again today." Soldiers got money from the army every now and then. Some days, Chantelle knew her father had been paid because the family ate, but her friend's family still had no food.

When Chantelle had asked why her friend did not eat on the payday, she explained, "He said he had other problems." Sitting in the yard, they had watched as a man followed her friend's mother into her hut. "Soon we will have food," her friend smiled. Many children knew that when their fathers spent their money elsewhere, another man visited their mothers, and shortly thereafter, the mothers fed their children.

When living people could not or did not provide and protect, women and children sought the help of the ancestors. Charms hung openly in trees. But the blessing of the spiritual protection for some always held the threat of curse for others. Chantelle hated what the children did.

When they played, they imitated the soldiers they saw in the camp. The young ones had their sticks and stones. They imitated all the ways that rituals could keep the bullets from hurting them. Sometimes the older boys and girls killed an animal and used its blood. They made its bones, ears, and noses into necklaces like the ones worn by the combatants. Eventually, the children were invited to participate in real traditions and got real guns. In not too much time the adolescents became part of the army; then they taunted the younger ones.

Once the family moved to the commander's compound, Chantelle knew that children who resented her privileges could accuse her of using witchcraft to hurt them. She protected herself by staying inside. Even at eight years old she had come to hate everything about the military camp, but for a while, she had felt safe in the mansion.

* * *

Now, Chantelle sensed that Mama was worried. Mama had hastily prayed in front of her family idols and then had scooped the ash of human nails, animal bones, and herbs into small pieces of cloth, tying the little bundles. She gave one charm to each of the children, tucked one into her bosom and one into the baby's shirt. The ancestors would now guide them on their way.

"Keep it with you," she urged her children, "so no harm comes to you."

They walked through the metal gate and hurried down the road away from the commander's compound.

Doctor Kasanka and the Student Suzy Celebrate *Kifunga Mulango*

"As Rebels Gain in Zaire Army Morale is Declining"
The New York Times, February 8, 1997

"I am black, but comely, O daughters of Jerusalem."
Song of Solomon 1:5

Kolwezi, Shaba Province, Zaire
September 1996 through early 1997

Kabila, Mobutu, whomever. Dr. Guy Kasanka had his political leanings, to be sure. But right now, he wanted to be an adult—to find work and a wife—regardless of who was in charge of the country.

Beginning adult life in urban Congo—it was a series of starts and stalls. In the last years of the 1980s Guy Kasanka had attended the political meetings at the University of Lubumbashi. He had survived the student massacre. His education was delayed while the university closed. Finally, the university reopened, and his education progressed as he concentrated on learning medicine. He graduated. But securing a good position—now *that* was difficult. And finding a suitable wife had entirely eluded him.

* * *

Suzy reached toward the center of the gleaming, teak dining table, a china bowl in each hand, and lowered the steaming plates of chicken and tilapia. Scarcely aware of the three men who joined her uncle at his table, but feeling good in the smart, fitted green skirt and tee-shirt that perfectly suited the occasion, she murmured "*Bon appétit*," smiled, turned, and rejoined her aunt and her female cousins in the kitchen.

She was glad that, for the first time, her father had allowed her to travel alone to visit his uncle's family in Kolwezi for a few weeks of the school vacation. He normally worried over his daughter and kept her close to home. But it was her last year before graduating from secondary school, and her wealthy uncle's invitation to visit and become acquainted with her extended cousins suited all of them.

Her parents, modest villagers in Kombove, earned enough to pay her school fees without fail. But they did not have the means of her uncle, who managed the Kamoto mine. When Suzy arrived at her uncle's family's home, she knocked on the metal door to the compound, was given entry by the security guard, stepped over the threshold, and stopped short. Before her stood a rambling concrete villa with a wrap-around porch and a separate guesthouse. Awed, she raised her head to absorb its grandeur. It was the perfect place to spend her last secondary school vacation. The joy of her first trip away from home in this lovely abode loosened the bounce in her step, brightened her smile, and allowed her to enjoy the sway of the fabric that hugged her hips.

* * *

"And what do you think, Dr. Kasanka?"

"*Pardon.* I don't know much about mining," Kasanka fibbed, pretending that he'd been silent out of ignorance, chiding himself for his lapse of attention. He was dining in the home of Monsieur Kabemba, the director of the important Kamoto sulfite ore mine; he'd been brought here by his friend, Nyembo, who worked for Gecamines, the national mining company. He and Nyembo had discussed the industry often enough that, yes, certainly, Kasanka had opinions, especially about the health risks of mining operations. Newly graduated from medical school, he was now a man: it was time to prepare for his future, to express opinions among people with power. But it was also time to find a wife. He had not found a girl who interested him—until this one walked into the room.

Staring at his plate, he glanced sideways and caught Nyembo stifling a smile in his direction. He dared not speak. The girl had taken away his concentration—it was as if she had captured his emotions and carried them back into the kitchen, out to the garden, onto the paths through the compound, to the external porch where she might now be. The conversation continued, while he nudged the food from one side of the plate to another, struggling to bring himself back to the dining room. In a few minutes he regained his composure.

He gulped, then leapt into the conversation. "Monsieur Kabemba, who is the girl in the green skirt? Does she live with you?"

Now, Nyembo smiled and nodded slightly.

"She is my niece from Kombove, visiting for the school vacation," Kabemba said. "She is in her last year of secondary school and very intent on her studies."

"I like her. I am looking for a wife. May I meet her?"

He was prepared for the interview that would follow this opening. It helped that Nyembo could vouch for his seriousness, his commitment to one wife, his character, his promising future. Finally, Monsieur Kabemba agreed to contact the girl's father for permission for Kasanka to visit the next day.

* * *

"Suzy, today you need to stay nearby," her uncle's wife told her in the morning. "You will have a visitor. One of the men who ate with your uncle."

"Which one? And what does he want with me? I don't know him."

"He is just a young man, he wants to talk to you."

Soon, Suzy was called to the living room, where she sat opposite one of the men from yesterday's dinner party.

"Let us introduce ourselves," the man said. "My name is Guy Kasanka. I have just graduated from the medical school in Lubumbashi. I studied general medicine, but I am interested in further studies in surgery and in public health."

"I am Suzy Mwema. I am in the fourth grade in secondary school. I intend to go on to college and study law."

"I am a doctor."

And so, they continued in this way, introducing their interests, their families and their future dreams. Finally, Kasanka told Suzy why he had come. "Mademoiselle Mwema, I am here to ask you to marry me. Would you be willing to become my fiancée?"

"No," Suzy replied. "I am only eighteen years and five months old. I want to finish my studies."

"I, too, need more time to find a job so I can properly support you. But we can spend the time getting to know one another. All I am proposing is an engagement."

"No," Suzy replied.

Patience and determination had served Kasanka well in secondary and medical school; now they aided him again. "All right, I will give you time to think about it. I will call again."

Taking his leave of Suzy, he reported to Monsieur Kabemba that she had not agreed to an engagement, but that he, Guy Kasanka, was an educated man who was willing to wait for an educated wife. He would visit again. And he did, every day for the next week.

The day before Kasanka was due to leave Kolwezi, Suzy contacted her father in Kombove. "A man, a friend of a friend of Uncle, has visited me every day."

"Yes, I know."

"At first I wasn't interested, but over the week, I have found him appealing. He is a doctor and willing to wait to marry until I finish my education. What do you think?"

Throughout the week Suzy's father had been conferring with Monsieur Kabemba. His enthusiasm for the man had grown. "If he values your education, if he will provide well for you, and if you find him attractive, you may go ahead."

That day Suzy agreed to become engaged to the young doctor.

* * *

Kasanka had travelled to Kombove to meet Suzy's family, and they agreed to accept his proposal. So they invited him to return for *kifunga mulango,* the ceremony in which the couple would formalize the engagement before Suzy's extended family. So Kasanka prepared to travel with his friend, Nyembo, his uncle and his cousin to meet with Suzy's family.

It would have been easier to buy the necessary soft drinks in Kombove but the supply could be low, leaving Kasanka empty handed. Taking no chances, the betrothed-to-be bought cases of Coke and Fanta in Lubumbashi, loaded them into a car belonging to his uncle, and arrived with ample beverages at Suzy's home.

When Kasanka and his supporters stood before Suzy's compound, Suzy greeted them at the gate. She led them to the living room where the entire family was already seated. She offered them the chairs that had been saved for them.

Suzy's father waited for a moment of silence. Opening his arms wide, he began. "Welcome to my house! So. Why are you here?"

Nyembo responded. "We are here as Kasanka's family, to accompany Kasanka who is here to marry Suzy."

Suzy's father turned to Suzy. "Suzy, tell us the story."

Suzy said, "Papa, family, I want to introduce my fiancée, Dr. Kasanka."

"Oh, that's Kasanka? Do you really mean what you say? Is Kasanka the only man you want in your life?"

"Yes, Papa."

Turning to Kasanka, Papa spoke. "Sir, have you ever married before?"

"No."

"Are you engaged to any other woman?"

"No."

"Sir, do you really love my daughter?"

"Yes, Papa, I love your daughter with all my heart."

"Look, Sir, we are a Christian family. Our daughter is still a student. Will you commit to wait until she has finished her studies?"

"Yes, Papa."

"We don't support polygamy. Will you promise that you will not take another wife?"

"Yes, Papa. I am also a Christian and devoted to Suzy, only."

"Sir, Nyembo, have you something to say?"

"We have heard what the couple has said. We are the members of Kasanka's family. We are here today to give the pre-dowry."

Suzy's father turned again to Suzy. "Suzy, are you really sure that you want us to take this pre-dowry from Kasanka?"

"Please take it with your heart."

Standing in the center of the living room, Kasanka drew an envelope from his pocket. As Suzy took it from him, the women began to ululate. The men clapped and cheered. Kasanka and his friends reached for the cases of Fanta and Coke and began to distribute the drinks among the guests. The women of Suzy's family hustled to the kitchen and reemerged with plates of rice, potatoes, tilapia, chicken, and *sombe,* vegetables, they had prepared for the feast.

The welcome was heartening, but Kasanka did not yet know what kind of dowry payment Suzy's family expected—money, clothing, a goat? What kind of contribution would they want from Kasanka before the wedding festivities?

While eating together, Kasanka and Suzy's father agreed that Kasanka would provide Suzy's family with a sewing machine, two goats, a *kikwembe* for Suzy's mother, a large basin, and fifty US dollars in cash. Kasanka offered to make payments in instalments over the next several visits to Suzy in Kombove.

They were well matched—a young, educated, forward-looking couple, waiting for the future to unfold before them.

The Pilot Gaston Rescues the Missionaries

> "U.N. Chief Says Abandoning Aid Force for Zaire Was a Mistake"
>
> *The New York Times*, February 13, 1997

> "'Do not lay a hand on the boy,' he said. 'Do not do anything to him. Now I know that you fear God, because you have not withheld from me your son, your only son.'"
>
> Genesis 22: 12

Kafakumba, Shaba Province, Zaire
February 1997

The rebellion in Zaire had created a very dangerous situation for Congolese with assets—especially for one who had an airplane and could fly it.

Gaston Ntambo, a tall, mahogany man in his early thirties with broad shoulders and a solid face, had dressed himself in a smartly ironed white pilot's shirt with gold epaulettes, black trousers, and shiny shoes. He circled the Cessna 172 that rested on the concrete floor of the garage-like hangar at the edge of Lubumbashi's main airport, its entrance wide open to the runway and the airliners preparing to take-off into the towering, black clouds. He had just completed the first pre-flight external examination, but thunder still cracked overhead. So he began again, as if the vibrations threatened to dislodge a necessary wire. Outwardly, he appeared composed, authoritative; inwardly, he fretted. Concentrating on the plane and his pre-flight routines calmed his jitters.

He had received a satellite phone call that morning from the eldest of the American missionaries. Two weeks earlier, when Gaston had evacuated the others, he had urged the man and his wife to leave.

But no, this couple had refused. "I've weathered a lot of violence in Zaire," the seventy-year-old missionary had said. "I'll finish the pastor's school and then drive out." But now something had changed—his car wouldn't start. Would Gaston pick him up this afternoon in Kafakumba?

* * *

An African kid becoming a pilot: it's unthinkable. Had a miracle made it possible?

Gaston's route to the heavens began when a missionary pilot gave him a pair of shoes. At nine, he was, oh, so proud. So dignified. So confident. He felt the soles under his feet, protecting him from stones. For the first time he ran without worry, he jumped without expecting to wince when he landed. All the other kids admired him: "Gaston, let us try your shoes!" Such a privilege, such a wonder. They strutted in his shoes, but eventually, the shiny black leather enveloped only *his* feet. He felt destined for something special, even though his father only made ten dollars a month as a pastor. Someday, he would fly an airplane like the missionary who gave him the shoes.

As a young adult he got a job working in the Lubumbashi treasurer's office of the church's mission agency, the General Board of Global Ministries (GBGM), and the missionary said, *he gets it, send him to school for accounting.*

At Davis Business College in Toledo, Ohio he saw a table of guys with flight jackets and sunglasses.

"Who are they?"

"Student pilots in the flight school."

"Really?"

Every day Gaston went to the airport to watch planes. His host family found a banner pilot in the church—*you can pick up the banners and then fly the plane back.* Again, he got it. The family found flight instructors with whom he could log miles. They made it possible for him to enter flight school. He accumulated hours to become a pilot. He attended another meeting of GBGM to discuss joining the flight ministry in Congo. Judas Jefferson, an African-American staff member, pulled him aside.

"Some people in that meeting are saying Africans can't fly."

"I will disappoint them." The fire of challenge burned within him. He returned to flight school and passed his instrument test a year ahead of time with a grade of 96%. In 1995 he returned to Congo to fly medical missions.

* * *

He had launched his life in record time for a young man in Zaire. By the time he was twenty-four, he had earned his pilot's license and married; shortly thereafter, he and Jeanne had had twins, named for the couple who hosted him in Ohio. They had settled in Luena, his hometown, and he flew medical missions—taking supplies to rural clinics and bringing villagers to Lubumbashi for treatment they could receive nowhere else.

He had watched people die, and he especially mourned the pregnant women.

Once, he had been called to transport a woman who had had a dead fetus in her womb for three days. When he landed on the dirt runway and emerged from the plane, she was being comforted by her relatives. She asked him for water.

Should he give a sick woman water? He didn't know. It seemed the compassionate thing to do.

He lifted a cup of water to her lips. She sipped, and then, she died. Right there.

He had also watched people live.

A villager's raw skin weeped; the man writhed in pain. He had been burned over sixty percent of his body. No trains, no trucks, only bicycles travelled over the mountains from his village, Gombe, to Lubumbashi. But a small airstrip allowed Gaston to land. The villagers laid blankets on the seat of the plane, making the man as comfortable as possible. Gaston delivered him to Lubumbashi to the hospital.

Several months later a stranger appeared at his door in Luena—the villager, his body healed, had walked for several days to thank his pilot for saving his life. *And,* Gaston thought with satisfaction, *the miracle of being flown to Lubumbashi had brought the man to faith.*

Most of the time he didn't know what had become of his passengers. But he knew that these poor people in remote villages had already tried herbs, natural healing, and rudimentary local clinics. To be flown deathly ill to Lubumbashi, well, it was their miracle like becoming a pilot had been his.

And then, in 1996, Kabila's rebellion against Mobutu began. As the war approached Katanga, the white American missionaries, who had long been associated with the Mobutu regime, had good reason to fear Kabila's rebels. The ham radios buzzed—where was the fighting? When did they need to leave? Who had the church's planes, and where was the fuel located? Before each flight, Gaston and Jeanne evaluated whether Gaston could fly into remote villages before the rebels arrived. A missionary pilot fell acutely ill as the war neared his village, Matoba, and Gaston retrieved the sick pilot and flew his family to safety in Zambia. The war threatened another missionary family in Mulongo; again, Gaston evacuated them to Ndola. He picked up the Swiss doctors at the Kabongo Hospital and brought them to Lubumbashi.

As one of the few Congolese pilots in the country, Gaston knew he was dangerously valuable to the army, to Kabila's rebels, and to the various political parties who were emerging in Zaire, each with its own armed force. If Gaston were detained, the army or the rebels could commandeer the church's planes. If he or his family were kidnapped, they could force him to fly for them. But he had resisted calls to fly for Mobutu's army or for the rebels. As a medical evacuation missionary, he flew for Jesus, no one else. He was clear about God's will for his life. He transported medicine into rural clinics and poor, sick people from remote villages to the medical center in Lubumbashi. He assisted God through the church, and that was the only way he used his gifts.

In Luena he and Jeanne stood out as one of the few families with resources—food, a car, gasoline—and in the way that rural Congolese expected others to share what they had, people came to his house even in the middle of the night, asking him for fuel and transportation. He and Jeanne decided to move to Lubumbashi where, if trouble came, they could blend in with the crowd. And there, he tried to protect the church's plane, unless the trouble came to Lubumbashi.

* * *

OK, one last trip to evacuate a missionary and his wife. To Kafakumba, one more rural village with little entertainment where the people always crowded around to gawk at the plane's landing. It was a tricky in the best circumstances—dodging the people, the goats, and the lake that bordered the runway.

The thunderstorms passed and Gaston flew, scanning the terrain below him that he knew so well. The Kafakumba *aerodrome* appeared in the distance and grew larger. Here, goats wandered on the airstrip; he always swept close to the ground to frighten them into the trees. As he approached, his eyes scanned wide-angled across dirt lanes leading to the airport. All empty, except the missionary who was waving his arms in front of the hanger. Strange. No villagers had come out to enjoy the entertainment.

Gaston circled the airport and positioned the craft for his second approach. As he neared the ground, he saw newly dug holes in the earth by the sides of the landing strip, the ends of machine guns pointed toward the air. Jeanne, in Lubumbashi, was monitoring the radio. During the usual landing description Gaston added, "I see machine guns, hidden by the landing strip, pointing toward the plane. I may have flown into the hands of the rebels."

His wheels touched down. *Stop before the lake, keep them from shooting and damaging the plane*, he muttered, instructing himself. Then he prayed. *Jesus, be with me.*

The plane rumbled to a stop, and he u-turned back toward the hanger. Now, he faced the sixty or so raggedy-clad, armed young men running toward the plane, surrounding it. But whose soldiers were they? And why had the missionary led him into this ambush?

He rolled to a stop near the hanger where the yellow jerry cans of fuel were stored. He checked his instruments, turned off the propeller, removed his headset, and opened the pilot's door. The men pressing toward him reeked of dirt and sweat; they had not bathed in many days. As he stepped to the ground, he felt the pressure of their fingers digging into each of his forearms. He stood eye-to-eye with a uniformed officer. His stare hardened; he did not flinch.

The officer jabbed him in the chest. "You're the hero, coming for this white man, this traitor with the satellite phone. You're aiding the rebels. You're under arrest. Tomorrow we will take you to Kinshasa and figure out what to do with you."

"I'm a medical pilot. A church pilot. Let us go."

The officer motioned, and then men jabbed at Gaston with their guns. Mobutu provided no protection now. Mobutu's soldiers were already marching the missionary, his wife and the one Congolese pastor who had remained with them down the lane that led into the village. Behind, surrounded by other soldiers, walked Gaston, outwardly dignified in his pilot's uniform. They soon entered the missionary's walled compound, which was now surrounded by armed child soldiers.

* * *

Once inside the house and left alone, the missionary told Gaston that the army had forced him to lure the plane and its pilot to Kafakumba. But the missionary still had the satellite phone, the cause of much suspicion. "What do you think I should do with it?" he asked.

"Get rid of it. Dump it in the lake over there," Gaston replied.

"But it's a very expensive piece of equipment."

"It's the reason we're in trouble. So what's it really worth?"

The missionary glanced at the ground and changed the subject. "I have about four thousand dollars I can offer as a bribe." It was an amount no soldier could resist.

In the bedroom, Gaston hung his shirt carefully on the back of a blue plastic chair, letting the wrinkles release so it looked ironed and new. Then he stretched out on the bed, hands behind his head, tracing the pattern of the mosquito net with his eyes. He contemplated their next move. He prayed.

Sometimes as a Christian you have to act so the Lord can help you.

He developed a plan. He doubted that the child soldiers guarding the house could distinguish his uniform from a general's. At the first streak of light, he told the missionary, his wife, and the Congolese pastor, "These soldiers guarding us are kids. I'll head for the airport, distract them. You walk to the landing strip in about five minutes, offer the money. We'll try to take off. It's better than staying here."

Gaston smoothed his shirt and tucked it into his pants. He strode out the front door, down the concrete steps, through the yard, and opened the front gate. The child-guards stood and pointed their guns.

"Put those down! Your general wants to talk with me."

As he expected, they lowered their guns and followed. Others joined as they trod the dusty lane, straight toward the landing strip.

The tall pilot, surrounded by armed boys, turned onto the grass around the hanger.

There, older soldiers lounged, smoking cigarettes. The officer who had met the plane loitered with them. Seeing Gaston, he jumped to full height and strode to block their movement. The loiterers jumped to attention and followed.

"I told you to stay in the house!"

Gaston set his feet solidly in the dirt. "I know you have your orders. But so do I. My Bishop directed me to pick up this missionary and his wife. If I don't go back today, they'll wonder what happened to me. They'll send a search-and-rescue plane."

The officer matched Gaston's conviction. "We're waiting for a Land Cruiser that'll pick you up and take you to Lubumbashi. Then you'll fly to Kinshasa. Go back to the house."

The missionary, his wife and the Congolese pastor had arrived on the edge of the crowd. The old man pushed through the soldiers, sidling up to the officer. He pressed the black sock full of money into his hand. "Let us go and you can take this," he whispered, forcing him to feel the width of the wad of bills inside the sock.

"I can't take that money! I would be dead in a few hours—what good would it be to me then?"

They had made their best offer—and they had lost.

Gaston heard the sound of a car engine and looked up. The Land Rover was pulling into the grass beside the hanger. The crowd of ragtag soldiers, children and adults, were backing away from the car, blending together.

The car stopped just short of the wing of the aircraft. Three soldiers jumped out, ran toward the missionary, and grabbed him. Soldiers from the landing strip joined them. In the confusion they turned their backs on Gaston and the missionary's wife.

Instinctively, Gaston pushed the elderly woman under the wing and toward the cockpit. Opened the door. Pushed her over the pilot's seat. Leapt in one step onto the plane's running board. Swivelled, backed onto his seat.

He closed the door partially in front of them, like a shield. He relaxed briefly: with him between her and the crowd, it would be more difficult for the soldiers to capture her, also. But the pilot's door provided them with slim protection against the guns.

He peered through the opening. The soldiers holding the missionary had progressed to the far side of the car, but the Congolese pastor had flattened himself against the door. The soldiers were shouting at him to move.

"He knows all about Congo, he's been here long enough!"

"…a traitor!"

"…the reason we aren't progressing!"

"…take him to Kinshasa."

As Gaston heard the heated words, he saw a figure who remained in the car with the windows rolled up. A man sitting in air-conditioned comfort, a man pampered, protected. *The real boss, the one I have to see. The only one who can call off the crowd.*

Then, slowly, he instructed himself. *Remain calm, don't do anything stupid, don't get shot, you mean nothing to them.* Then he pled. *Jesus, be with me.*

He opened the door to the plane and slowly climbed down the steps. He walked toward the window of the car, his eyes fixed on the face. Slowly, the boss-man turned toward Gaston, and seeing him, startled. He rolled the window down.

"Do I know you?" the boss-man asked.

"I don't think so."

"You look very familiar. Tell me about your parents."

"My mother is Nshimba and my father is Bishop Ntambo Nkulu Ntanda."

The boss-man shook his head. "You don't know who I am? I am your mother's cousin." And in the way the Luba people use the words of more intimate family relations to claim respect and authority: "I am your uncle."

Gaston smiled. His inner voice shouted, *whoever this man is, of course, he is my uncle!* The ties of extended kin were strong among the Luba. No relative wanted family blood on his hands, the wrath of the ancestors plaguing his life.

The commotion on the far side of the car had quieted; the soldiers now watched Gaston and the boss. Then he opened his car door, stepped out, and faced the soldiers. "Let the people go," he ordered.

He turned back to Gaston and spoke in a hushed voice. "Get to Lubumbashi now. Leave the country. It's too dangerous for you. I will try to clean this up, but it will not be easy for me. Greet your parents."

* * *

The Cessna lifted Gaston, the missionary, his wife and the Congolese pastor into the clouds. Gaston thanked Jesus for the miracle, for he knew of no one in his family who was in either Mobutu's government or the military. A few hours later, Gaston, Jeanne and their children slipped into Zambia. From there he could seek refuge in the United States. He had already earned his pilot's license in Ohio, and now was a perfect time to return to complete the course in airplane mechanics.

Mama Mujing Gathers the Children

> "A Three-Cornered Struggle to Redraw Zaire's Political Map"
> *The New York Times*, April 12, 1997
>
> "Let the children come to me, for to such belongs the kingdom of heaven."
> Luke 18:15-17

Kamina, Shaba Province, Zaire
April 1997

Under Mobutu, Kamina, sitting at the juncture of three railroads, always had its street children; now, with Kabila's rebellion sweeping across Zaire, more children appeared each day. The government authorized care, but only the church was in a position to organize it.

By February Bishop and Mama Nshimba had returned from the United States, and Mama Nshimba had visited Mama Mujing in her yard. They talked under the shade of the tree, enjoying the breeze.

"Bishop is wondering if you would organize the children sleeping around the church center so we can open an orphanage," Mama Nshimba had said. "You will need to get to know them all, find out where they came from, whether their parents are alive, why they are sleeping there. And then you will need to negotiate with the government. I will help you, but we are away so often that Bishop wants someone else to be in charge."

After their conversation, Mama Mujing sat for a long time, a voice in her mind singing like the birds that herald the sunrise: *My whole life has trained me for this.* All of the hardships, all the disappointments of her life, suddenly made sense in light of her mission.

A kaleidoscope of memories flashed through her mind. She saw her father as a young man, prosperous and educated. She imagined his face, and pride leapt gleefully in her heart. Papa had been a business partner with Gecamines in Kolwezi. He had provided a home and possessions; the family always had enough food.

Then, she remembered the quick fear and hard determination in Papa's eyes when, in 1980, the army pillaged Kolwezi, looting and even killing. Under Mobutu, such was their payment, their right, to take whatever the villagers had. And, of all the things the soldiers could loot, the virginity of a daughter was the most precious. Mujing was eleven years old and pubescent; her vulnerability beckoned. She saw herself holding her hands over her ears to block the soldiers' shrieks and popping gunfire, then releasing her hands slightly to listen to her parents' hushed, anxious voices, and, tense with fear, shrivelling small as she tied the outer wrap of her *kikwembe* tight around her hips.

As if trying to circle his arms around all his family at once, Papa had marched Mama, Mujing, and her eight siblings on foot to Zambia where they could catch a bus to Lubumbashi, the headquarters of Gecamines. As they feared, the army arrested them at the border and took them to Kasapa prison. But Mujing watched wide-eyed as Papa pulled out a stack of grimy currency, *Nouveaux Zaire*, and bought their freedom and safety. All was not yet lost; Gecamines hired Papa. The family had a small home and money for food. Then, like a recurring nightmare, the looting came to Lubumbashi. Protective and wise, Papa had guided them to Kamina. There, Papa's business struggled and the family hungered.

Papa had always said, "Go to the church, it will encourage you." Mama Mujing had followed his advice. When her parents had not had enough money for Mama Mujing to study past the grades offered at Lwanga High School, she had used the church as a place to develop her natural leadership abilities. She had organized the youth and, even as a teenager, began creating programs. Once she married, she was elected the new, young president of the adult women's group. She had proven herself.

* * *

And now, in April 1997, the children swarmed around her. At first they were an indistinguishable, amoeba-like mass. Soon, they had faces, names, and stories—then they became Bishop's children, well known to Mama Mujing and to the church.

Word quickly spread among the children: "Talk to the mama in the red dress. She has some food." So now the children crowded around Mama Mujing, eager to tell her where they had come from, who their parents were, and what had happened to them. She had her copybook and pencil in hand, ready to document those with whom she had not yet talked.

"Little one, where you from?" Mama Mujing knelt so that she engaged the girl eye-to-eye. The girl smiled at Mama, her face bright and clear.

"From Luena. My mother was very sick. She died. Papa got a new wife. When she had her own child, she told Papa that we were doing witchcraft on her children. Every time they hurt themselves, she blamed us. We became afraid and we ran away."

And the next, "My mother died after she had a baby. My father died when he had malaria. So I stay with others, trying to find something to eat."

And another, "My auntie told me to leave the train. They were going to Kalemie. She could not feed me anymore."

Mama Mujing carefully noted each child's name, home village, closest living adult relative, and place where the child slept at night. As she did, their personalities emerged.

The little girl might have been seven or eight—it was hard to tell. She had worked with her friends to fashion her hair, gathering it into small clusters across her head, creating a cross-stitch pattern on her scalp and short, stubbly braids that stuck straight out from her head. She had had enough pride of self for that, at least. Her chocolate skin smoothed across her face, proclaiming her innocence. Despite the ragged dirty green-checked dress, her brown eyes reflected a sense of self-possession.

Around her most of the children looked like they might be eleven or twelve years old. One boy smiled, happily licking his lips. His eyes twinkled with good-hearted mischief. Another girl was giggling, the corners of her mouth turned up brightly, enticing Mama Mujing to smile in return. Behind her, a sober young boy caught Mama's attention with a curious, questioning look, attentive, waiting. His friend, a boy with a wide forehead, plump cheeks, and a penetrating gaze stared at her with a sense of friendly demand.

They seemed so—energetic, laughing, eager, curious—so childlike!

Those without families belonged to the government. She took each orphan to city hall to record the child's vulnerability. As she waited, she shook her head in disbelief.

"How will I take care of twenty-five children? What if others come?"

The Traditional Chiefs Seek Peace for Katanga

"U.S. Decides Time is Ripe to Elbow Mobutu Aside"

The New York Times, April 29, 1996

"For I am about to create a new heavens and a new earth; the former things shall not be remembered or come to mind."

Isaiah 65:17

Lubumbashi, Shaba Province, Zaire
April 1997

The King of Kayamba territory smiled with satisfaction. A new sun was rising. If the rebel leader Laurent Kabila took Zaire, as it seemed he soon would, *this* government would actually respect the authority of the network of traditional leaders, just as the authors of the recently enacted law had hoped.

Kabila had asked the Governor of Shaba, Kyungu wa Kumwanza, to convene the traditional kings, the *mulopwe,* and chiefs. Kabila and Kyungu originated from the same village, Ankoro, and adhered to the same traditions, including the white lime, the symbol of the chief's power over war and peace in his lands. So Kabila requested the chiefs' permission to enter Shaba peacefully. But Kabila's supplication meant more than compliance with custom. His initiative signalled his intention to formalize a working relationship between traditional and national government. Through such a move Kabila could secure the cooperation of the Luba leaders.

The Luba kings and chiefs, from the most powerful territorial king to the lowly head of a small village, exercised their responsibility for white lime in conflicts large and small—in wars and in fights in clans and even between families. Their ministers knew how the chief should use white lime to bring honesty, fidelity, and forgiveness to his people. They told slightly different versions the same story.

> There was a time, maybe the wartime, maybe a fight between two families or clans. To reconcile them, first the chiefs call for the white lime. They mix it in a calabash. They will ask the people involved in the conflict to share it, to put it in their mouths as a sign that they are willing to be reconciled. Then they spit saliva and they vomit. This way, they throw the conflict, the problems, out.
>
> The people bring food for a feast. They offer only very white animals: white chicken, white goats, white lambs, everything white with no spot. These animals signify that the conflict resolution will be successful. The animals invite the blessing of the ancestors and *vidje mukulu, shaka panga,* God the Supreme Being, the Creator.
>
> The elder guides the ceremony and asks them to eat and drink. The bowls and the dishes used for that ceremony will be buried, and the parties declare, "We will never again come to the same kind of behavior."
>
> The elder announces that anyone who returns to the conflict will be cursed.
>
> Everyone goes to a special tree. The elder takes the axe and cuts the tree as his signature. It remains on that tree as it grows, and people see it and remember, *this day* we ended the conflict. If you break that tradition, now that's where you see cuts in the family. Some will be born blind, mute, crippled and you will see different kinds of limbs.

The white lime in the possession of the chief symbolized his wisdom, his connection with his spirits, his ability to discern justice, his peacekeeping role. Any invader seeking to rectify a problem in the territory of the chief had to request entry. The invader would be welcomed only if the chief were persuaded that the cause was just. The chief could seek the advice of the diviner, who coated his face with lime and entered a state of ecstasy to listen to the spirits of the ancestors. Ultimately, though, the chief decided.

* * *

The kings and chiefs of territories such as Kayamba had already met with their leaders of groups of villages. They had agreed enthusiastically—give him the lime! Welcome him, without bloodshed! It was a precious gift. By receiving their permission, Kabila also had the right to call on the chiefs to share their traditional power—their fetishes, their deities, their rituals—all that kept them safe in times of war.

King Kayamba turned his head slowly, observing the assembly. Old rural chiefs, renowned for their practical wisdom, sat side-by-side with middle-aged chiefs who had been formally educated, like Kayamba himself. What political change they had witnessed in less than a decade! They had participated in the democracy conferences in Kinshasa in 1991 and 1993. They had sought a place for traditional government. But in those conferences, as one said, "When Mobutu offered a goat, he held onto the rope around its neck."

They stood, one by one, and expressed their opinions; then they sat, respectfully relinquishing the floor, letting the next speaker complete what the former had said, fulfilling the Luba proverb: *kuboko kumo kubunga ke kololanga*—"one single hand cannot apprehend many things."

They agreed that Kabila brought the right message. *We need to depend on ourselves, to lead our people to determine their own lives, to work for our livelihood rather than beg from others.* But the power of strong nations had thwarted Luba self-determination before. In the 1960s, when Sendwe Jason and Tschombe Moise led Katanga's rebellion, the Belgians might have helped Katanga become its own country. But as the western nations negotiated their will for the future of Congo, those powers sponsored the Ngbwandi man, Mobutu, to rule all of the former Belgian Congo. The kings and chiefs mourned—the last fifty years could have been quite different for the Luba people! But the Canadian and Australian mining companies, and a large network of businesses that connected them to the United States, China, Libya, and the Middle East, profited handsomely from their land. *They do not want Zairians building their own lives and making their own decisions.*

Still, Mobutu had dominated them long enough.

The kings and chiefs knew that any government would still have outside controllers. Kabila could not take Zaire without Rwanda's help. What would Rwanda want in return? The Rwandese already had their tentacles in the mining industry. Belgium had always encouraged Gecamines—a Zairian company!—to put Rwandese in positions of power. *Rwanda will have their eyes on our minerals.*

But first, they concluded, Mobutu must go. Kabila and Rwanda offered their best hope.

They also believed that Kabila's message endangered him. Could they, as kings and chiefs, provide him some security? They agreed to send a message welcoming Kabila.

"And who will speak for us?"

"King Kaponda's territory includes Lubumbashi and a large rural area."

"But most of Lubumbashi is in King Shindaika's territory. He is older. He is wise. He must do the ceremonies."

King Kayamba drew a deep breath, knowing the significance of the moment. The issue of designating a spokesperson for the Luba people was as historic as the fact that Kabila had asked for the meeting. Mobutu had played with royal succession. In 1971 when Mobutu renamed the country Zaire, he had implemented "Zairianization" or "indigenisation." Mobutu had appointed Ngbwandi men to governmental and police positions in Luba territory. He sought to place people friendly to his regime within the Luba court, setting aside those born to be kings and chiefs. Succession disagreements had made the Luba people vulnerable. In the recent political turmoil, the Luba leaders had worked hard to clarify royal lines and authorities. Now, the assembly would decide on their spokesperson, giving him the power to negotiate for them. They called a name.

"Shindaika. Shindaika!"

Mobutu, his regime, his old political alliances had to be replaced. Mobutu had brought nothing but despair to the Luba people, all the time enriching himself and favoring his kinsmen and political partners. The Luba kings had a divine responsibility to uphold tradition, to do their part, to right past wrongs, and to welcome a new age.

They had worked together, and the council had passed the white lime to King Shindaika to welcome Laurent-Désiré Kabila.

Pastor Nyengele Muses: The End Has Come, What Next?

> "The Congo Victors Meet the Zairian Vanquished"
>
> *The New York Times*, May 20, 1997

> "My soul magnifies the Lord, and my Spirit rejoices in God my Saviour… He has brought down the powerful from their thrones, and has lifted the hungry with good things, and sent the rich away empty."
>
> Luke 1:46-47, 51b-53

Manono, Tanganyika District, Shaba Province, Zaire
May 1997

The older generation of Luba people had lived through many rounds of political upheaval. They wanted Mobutu gone and cautiously hoped for stability from the emerging leader, Kabila. But would such a massive political transition bring a time of violence and chaos to Zaire? And was that time now?

Pastor Nyengele stood in the doorway of the church, watching the image of the man on the bicycle fade until he disappeared in the darkness. A few minutes earlier the rider had stopped briefly to inform the pastor of the happenings in Goma, Kisangani, and other cities to the north and east. Without such couriers, Manono would have had no news, as the small city had deteriorated under Mobutu's rule. The town no longer had electricity, phones, or other communications. But, fortunately, messengers kept the town leaders informed. Even after his visitor vanished from view, Pastor Nyengele gazed into the night and pondered the words of hope: Mobutu had fled. Laurent Kabila would soon take possession of the capital, Kinshasa.

Bishop Ntambo had sent Pastor Nyengele to Manono only a year earlier. In 1996, when Bishop was elected, Nyengele completed his term supervising a large number of churches in Kabalo, a town in Tanganyika District. Bishop had asked the pastor to take charge of the Manono Center Church, a large rural congregation of five hundred people. From his pulpit Pastor Nyengele had watched the changes in the relationships between the soldiers and civilians as political events unfolded.

The villagers feared the soldiers from Manono's military base, not knowing whether they offered a threat or protection. But here in Manono Center Church the civilians sat in pews next to Mobutu's soldiers. They intermingled. They got acquainted.

Pastor Nyengele had preached brave sermons, challenging the soldiers to stop the looting and raping of civilians that the military had been taught was its due. He believed they could change. He saw in every person a divine light that was dimmed but could not be extinguished. In some cases, he had been able to reach the goodness that still dwelt inside. A few joined the choir, others supported the church financially.

Pastor Nyengele stared after the courier, thinking of his civilian and military parishioners. If Kabila took Kinshasa, if Mobutu's rule ended, it would certainly change the congregation. So much of the future depended upon events far away, over which the people of Manono had no control.

* * *

Kamina, Haut Lomami District, Shaba Province, Zaire

John Mutombo had boarded Kabila's train in Kabalo, and for two days now, he had watched the people who lined the tracks in the towns along the way—Katutu, Ngwena, Kitanda, Kasumpa, Makena, Sohe, and finally, John's hometown, Kitenge. Villagers waved palm branches and sang, "*Mukombozi, mukombozi,* liberator, liberator." John waved back.

John's diligence had earned him the respect of the new government, so he had been rewarded with a window seat on the train. He had landed a position as secretary to Émile, one of the administrators in Kabalo. His seven languages proved useful—he sorted documents, sent communications. When not in his office, he participated in *chembe-chembe,* Kabila's leadership classes, required of all people in his administration. John spent at least six hours a day studying philosophy, sociology, political science, public administration and physical education. The responsibilities of his position consumed him—except, of course, for the one hour a week during which he trod across the town to the public ham radio to call his new fiancée, Aimerance. He was faithful to her—he never missed the call.

When the train reached Kitenge, while the leadership team addressed the crowd, John found Aimerance. He took her hand and led her to his seat where she unpacked plantain, roasted peanuts, pineapple and avocado to supplement the meat that the administration provided.

"I love my job. We can marry now," John proposed. He showered her with gifts from Kabalo. Aimerance was pleased. But in less than an hour, the train whistled, announcing its departure, and she disembarked.

The train chugged through towns and villages, to Kamunza, Lenge, Kamungu, Kabongo, and Fukuyi, where leaders made speeches and well-wishers waved palm branches.

Finally, they approached Lukoka, the last stop before Kamina. John's eyes widened. Here the crowds here swelled larger than any they had seen. He sat on the train, watching out the window, waving at the villagers while Kabila's foremost administrators greeted King *Kasongo Nyembo* and the military general of Kamina Base.

In Kamina the administration planned to install a district commissioner, Sadiki; a leader of the party, Ramazani; and a head of security, Banza. The traditional chiefs made it seem easy—they had sent word that they and the military would welcome Kabila's people without bloodshed.

But as the train neared Kamina, the message was passed: be cautious. All this excitement could foretell a trap.

* * *

Mama Mujing had donned her bright red shift—her best, the one in which she shimmered. She had examined the dress of each of her children—her biological offspring and her charges at the orphanage. She added a belt for one and straightened the collar of another, until they looked their finest. She strapped a calabash of cassava flour to her back, ready to distribute it when the little party arrived at the train. *Vidye mukulu* had smiled, and all of the pilgrims would greet Kabila's administrators and military throwing white flour, the symbol of joy! The children, too, could partake of the ritual. Even the youngest would remember the celebration the rest of their lives.

* * *

When the train stopped in Kamina, John saw the Luba King *Kasongo Nyembo*. John had heard that the king had met with the general at Kamina Military Base and that he had been reassured that the officers were ready to pledge their support to Kabila without resistance. Now, the king and his ministers stood to witness the historic transfer of power.

John imagined the Luba royal preparing for a day like this one.

First, *Kasongo Nyembo* would have dressed in his trousers and shirt. Around his belly he had wound a white cloth, a sign of happiness, and tucked it into his belt. But for the king, joy intermingled with power, so over the white, but not entirely covering it, he wrapped a leopard skin. On his head he placed the tidy hat with the red band from which white feathers protruded. To this, he added symbols of Luba success and achievement: his assistant would have placed the calabash of limestone powder in the crook of the king's right arm and then offered the animal whip, which the king grasped in his right hand. But only the king, not his assistant, dared lift the mahogany carved staff that signalled his royalty.

John knew that when *Kasongo Nyembo* touched the staff, determination surged through him—for a moment the king was connected directly with the spiritual energy that sustained the Luba people through Mobutu's thirty-seven-year reign. Most likely, the king had consulted his diviner: his ancestors had promised to accompany the Luba into the future.

For the first time in over a century, the king's court at Kinkunki would welcome a Luba as their political and military leader. Mobutu's grip on the people had loosened: the Ngbwandi could no longer intrude into the Luba affairs. It was a glorious day.

* * *

Lubumbashi, Shaba Province, Zaire
May 14, 1997

Of late, Dr. Kasanka smiled a lot: he was preparing to leave. He had successfully courted Suzy. He had procured his medical license. The Methodist Bishop had appointed him to a post at the hospital in Kabongo. When Suzy finished her education, they could marry. While preparing to relocate, he often used the ham radio at the Methodist headquarters to talk to the nurses at the hospital. They described the conditions he would find when he arrived, and he double-checked their supplies. Since he was making the long trip, he was assembling medical equipment to bring. He did not want to leave without something he would badly need.

But today, he did nothing. He, his brother, and his good friend, Nyembo, sat fixated on the television, fascinated by the political events on Kilimasimba, the "mountain of the lion," near Lubumbashi. If the day went well, his new position in Kabongo, on which he banked his entire future, might truly be the great step forward he imagined. But if the ceremonies on Kilimasimba were a ruse, he might never reach Kabongo at all.

There, on the television, was Shaba's Governor Kyungu wa Kumwanza, a Mobutu appointee for two decades. The governor was suspected to be capable of treachery—he was believed to have organized the murder of the Kasai people in 1992 on Mobutu's behalf. But he was gaining credibility. He had called the meeting of the Luba traditional chiefs, giving them the opportunity to formally extend their welcome to Kabila and avoid unnecessary bloodshed in their lands.

Kyungu wa Kumwanza now seemed to favor Kabila. But was it a trick? Had he truly become loyal to the new regime, or was the entire drama an ambush—one that anticipated the doom on Kilimasimba of the chiefs and the enthusiastic townspeople?

* * *

Tanzania, May 14, 1997

Bishop Ntambo sat motionless, listening to the radio.

"The key question," Bishop wondered aloud to Mama Nshimba, "how much does military still support Mobutu?" The reception of Kabila's administration by the traditional chiefs and the military in Kamina had been promising. Kamina Base, the largest military camp in the nation, twenty kilometers from Kamina, reported directly to Kinshasa. Technically, it was still under Mobutu's control. But, as the military had promised, a delegation from Kamina Base met the train of Kabila's people in Kamina wearing white hatbands. They read a declaration, transferring their loyalties to Kabila. It had happened in Kamina: would history repeat itself in Zaire's second largest city, Lubumbashi?

Mobutu's greatest support lay between Kisingani, a city on the Congo River in eastern Congo, and Kinshasa, the capital near the mouth of the river in the western Congo. After taking Kisangani, Kabila's troops inched toward the capital. They were nearly stopped by Mobutu's soldiers in Kenge, on the Congo River outside Kinshasa. Finally, Kabila's troops, led by the Rwandan General James Kaberebe, broke through. No one knew what lay ahead in Kinshasa—or whether events there would spark a fire in Lubumbashi, as they had when the students were massacred.

Bishop Ntambo and Mama Nshimba hoped for the best and prepared themselves for the worst as they listened to the events on Kilimasimba.

Kabila and his troops climbed one side of the mountain: the Mobutu governor, Kyungu wa Kumwanza, his staff and the Lubumbashi military, the other.

At the top they met. Quietly. No ambush.

The Kabila era had begun.

* * *

Manono, Tanganyika District, the Democratic Republic of Congo
May 20, 1997

The eerie shout of a woman drew Pastor Nyengele to the front door of his parsonage. He hurried down the lane toward the town center. Villagers had come to the doors of their huts; now, men, women with babies on their backs or hips, and young children joined him. Once they rounded the corner to the main street, he saw that a small contingent of Kabila's soldiers had arrived. They were speaking loudly to those who were assembling. "His Excellency President Laurent-Désiré Kabila is now in Kinshasa and has decreed that the country will be called— Democratic Republic of Congo!"

"Have you heard?" the man beside Nyengele exclaimed. "The camp of Mobutu's soldiers is already empty. Not one shot fired!" He made a fist and pounded the air. Nyengele smiled and made a fist in return, but his heart twinged with sadness. He knew that the soldiers, his parishioners, were caught between the old regime and the new. Even though they, too, had had enough of Mobutu, they also feared retaliation from the soldiers of the new President. For now, it was best that they had deserted.

The liberator Kabila had arrived. Did these astounding events also reveal the reign of God? Had the millennium of joy and peace, promised in the book of Revelation, begun? Or was the announcement a brutal illusion, a false hope, with treacherous days ahead?

Be cautious. Nyengele returned to his hut.

Chapter II

The Year of Joy and Peace—Bishop Ntambo's Vision for Development (May 1997-July 1998)

Historical Introduction

The people of Kamina did indeed experience May 1997 through July 1998 as "the year of joy and peace," but ominous national events foretold Congo's "gathering storm."

Kabila's liberation movement had been backed by Rwanda. After the Rwandan genocide in 1994, the refugee camps in eastern Congo had been filled with millions of Hutus who had fled from the new Tutsi regime led by Paul Kagame. The camps mostly housed innocent civilians, but militant Hutus opposed to the Tutsis also found refuge there. Mobutu reached out to the Hutus. The Kagame regime supported Kabila, it declared publicly, as a way of reducing the Hutu threat against the Tutsis.

For the first few months after Kabila declared himself president, he and his Rwandan allies worked together. Shortly, Kabila proved to have a mind and agenda of his own, and the relationship between the Kabila and Kagame governments became strained. The conflict came to a crisis when Kabila ousted all of the Rwandans who had been given positions in the Congolese government.

Bishop and his leaders in Kamina had launched projects—largely in agriculture and construction—nourished by the hope that development could "feed my people." But the time that followed, it turned out, was less the promised millennium of God's reign than a Congolese Camelot, which, whether in England, the United States, or the Democratic Republic of Congo, provides only a moment of fragile happiness.

Bishop Announces his Vision for Development

> "On Visit to Congo, Albright Praises the New Leader"
>
> *The New York Times*, Dec. 12, 1997

> "Then Jesus asked, 'Were not ten made clean? But the other nine, where are they? Was none of them found to return and give praise to God except this foreigner?' Then he said to him, 'Get up and go on your way; your faith has made you well.'"
>
> Luke 17:17-19

Kamina, Haut Lomami District, Katanga Province, Democratic Republic of Congo

December 1997

The political transition had occurred with little violence in North Katanga. Development seemed within reach. Bishop stood and leaned forward, his eyes gleaming, his excitement overflowing. "*Jambo yenu*, Committee Executive!"

"*Jambo sana*, Bishop!"

"Hallelujah!" he cheered, waving his fist.

"Amen," the committee shouted in unison. And they settled in their chairs, their eyes riveted on Bishop. He began to read his formal address.

"North Katanga needs builders, people with servant hearts who can recreate all that is decaying here. North Katanga needs everything—water, food, electricity, schools, hospitals, huts made from durable materials. We will begin with churches and parsonages made of fired brick, not mud. Buildings that will last and will be beautiful."

Bishop's speech had resonated with the message that was being proclaimed by Kabila's people, the new philosophy being talked about all over town. "Take your future into your own hands. Don't steal: work! Be self-determined. Make your life what you want it to be!"

Everyone knew that North Katanga should have birthed a vibrant economy. Instead, its wealth had been looted by one occupier after another, leaving the people poor. In the 19th century, even this deep in central Congo, King Leopold's *Force publique* had whipped villagers into harvesting rubber and ivory, cut off their hands if they resisted, and taken the profits back to Belgium. In more recent years the famous copper mines filled the pockets of Americans, Canadians and Australians with cash. During Mobutu's reign eighty per cent of the taxes collected were sent to Kinshasa. Zairian soldiers, stationed at Kamina Base, unhappy that they did not benefit from the political reforms of 1991 and 1993, had pillaged the local population. After the 1993 looting, the economy had slowed so much that even the local brewery had closed.

"First I will show you my vision." He unrolled a green cloth on the table in the center of the room. "Each parish will have a church made of fired brick, a durable church, one made with tin roofing and cement." He placed a model of a small church on the cloth. "And each church shall have a parsonage made of the same materials—one that does not have to be rebuilt every five years." Again, he placed a replica of a smaller building on the cloth. "And every pastor will have two bicycles, one for himself, one for his wife"—and he placed people with bikes on the cloth— "and a Bible. And each parsonage will demonstrate food production"—and he placed hoes on the cloth— "so that it is a community center. And each parsonage will have a fishpond."

He looked up, his eyes sparkling. He had their attention. Everyone's gaze was riveted on his model of the parsonage compound. "Now you say, how we get the bricks? The cement? The tin roofing? We make the bricks, ourselves. We need a farm."

The church owned farms in areas of the conference far from Kamina: Kanene, Kamungu, Lunge, Nyembo, Mwanza, Samba, Kabongo. But none were accessible to the residents of Kamina.

Bishop continued speaking. "Monga wa Nzaji is selling. His old Belgian farm has best soil in Kamina. It's good property by the river—termite hills for bricks, an oven to fire them. We have money from Millenium Fund."

All around the room heads nodded and murmured approval.

"A training center to teach cultivation, care of livestock. Crops from the farm to provide source of income. All of the work of the farm provides jobs—clearing, hoeing, tilling, harvesting, rebuilding, teaching."

Bishop smiled broadly, his eyes dancing. "If you agree, we meet Monga wa Nzaji tomorrow."

The next day members of the committee went to the farm, seven kilometers from Kamina, and negotiated a purchase. Seeing Kamisamba, they imagined the future.

"And where we get money for tin roofing, for cement? I have already shown my vision to my good friends in the Council of Bishops. I raise money in America."

Where the church people had felt malaise, they now were teeming with energy. The years of neglect and decay, the Mobutu years, surely were coming to an end.

Mama Mujing Embraces Chantelle

"A New Model for Africa: Good Leaders Above All"

The New York Times, March 24, 1998

"Rejoice before the Lord your God—you and your sons and your
daughters, your male and female slaves, the Levites resident in
your towns, as well as the strangers, the orphans, and the widows
who are among you—at the place that the Lord your God will
choose as a dwelling for his name."

Deuteronomy 16:11

*Kamina, Haut Lomami District, Katanga Province, Democratic Republic of
Congo*

April 1997

Now that the political transition had occurred, perhaps the children, even the
orphans, could experience something of a stable childhood.

The boys and girls, different heights and sizes but all small for their ages,
skipped across the grass and sand of the orphanage yard—squealing, tagging,
laughing. But the new girl and her brother huddled to the side, away from the
others, digging a stick in the dirt. Every now and then they glanced toward the
children, but then they immediately looked away.

It always took time.

Mama Mujing sat in a blue plastic chair in the shade of the roof that lined
the porch of the U-shaped Center for Abandoned Children, watching the children play. She kept her eye on the pots on the fire. The beef cubes had stewed
all day; she had set those aside. The balls of bukari, too, waited in a pan, covered
to protect them from the flies. Now, the rice had nearly boiled, the beans had
softened. Three of the children had stopped their playing and dawdled at her
side, sweating from the heat but sniffing the joy to come. Mama Mujing wiped
her brow where large beads of sweat formed from the humidity, the heat and
the fire.

When she called the children for dinner, the three by her side were the first
in the queue.

The children received their plates, and Mama Mujing served two cubes of
beef with gravy, a large helping of rice and beans, and *bukari* to each one. They
crouched or sat to eat, dotting the porch and the grass. When all the children
had been served, the two new ones, Chantelle and her younger brother, sat by
the wall. But now they looked in Mama Mujing's direction and stared.

"*Karibu!* Welcome!" She smiled softly but with energy. She beckoned
them, with an encouraging lift of her head. "Come!"

Slowly, the new ones rose, stumbled in her direction, and received their portions. "Wafako," they murmured. They slowly turned toward the side of yard.

"No!" she called, her voice lyrical, as if she were singing a very happy children's song. "You sit here with me. We eat together."

Mama Mujing sensed a special light in the children. So young, so many traumatic experiences, and so damaged. But Mama Mujing's love, the twinkle in her eye, the cheerfulness in her heart, had worked miracles on other children. She prayed that for these, one more might occur.

* * *

The city administration had called Mama Mujing.

"We have some new orphans in town. Their flight separated them from their mother. But they followed some people to Kabongo and found their father in a military camp. He was a commander for Mobutu; they knew where to look. They lived with him. Then he got sick. He asked the Kabongo administrator to care for the children. When the father died, the government had nothing to offer, so the administrator put them on the train for Kamina where children can be served. He asked me contact you, to see what you can do."

So many orphans. But it was clear—these little ones could not be reunited with extended family or friends. The children's center, already filled to capacity, provided their only security. As they had nowhere to sleep, Mama Mujing had invited them to overnight at her own home.

* * *

In the next days and weeks, the new girl began to sit by Mama Mujing as she cooked. Then they prepared the food side by side, Mama Mujing reassuring her by her presence. Mama did not ask anything about Chantelle's parents, but she invited Chantelle to stir the beans and rice. Chantelle remained shy with the other children, but soon, it seemed she was trying to reflect Mama Mujing's happiness, to be like this Mama who was being good to her.

One day, Chantelle spoke with unaccustomed boldness. "The children here, I watch them. They seem different than the children in the military camp. They do not seem jealous. They do not play nasty games. And they do not do witchcraft."

"No, we are a Christian orphanage. They are expected to get along. They have their small differences, and if they quarrel, I intervene. But they do not hurt one another. If they fight, they are set apart, and they learn. Here, let me introduce you to one of the girls your own age."

That day, Chantelle made her first friend.

John Becomes a Bishop's Aide for Public Relations

"One Year Later, Congo Seems to Languish"

The New York Times, May 18, 1998

"Come, follow me, and I will make you fishers of men."

Matthew 4:19

Kitenge, Haut Lomami District

April 1998

The political transition had occurred—peacefully—and it was a great time to be a young adult!

In Kabila's government John Mutombo had found the opportunities he had been seeking. He had proven his worth in Kabalo, and, a few months after Kabila took the presidency, had been appointed chief administrator of Kitenge. He and Aimerance had married. Life was good!

One day, John got a call on the ham radio. "A big leader is coming. A Methodist Bishop. You need to welcome him with proper honor."

John knew the man, but still, he was suspicious. Assemblies were forbidden. This bishop might be a political opponent of Kabila. John planned the welcome but took precautions. The police led the way on motorbikes to the center of town where they met Bishop's entourage.

The church choirs drummed and sang their welcome; the women's brightly colored *bikwembe* swayed around their hips. The whole city of Kitenge attended the ceremony.

The traditional chief of Kabongo greeted Bishop, taking his hand and holding it. "*Wafwako*, you are the first Bishop from the Kabongo district, we are glad you have come, feel free."

John spoke next: "Bishop, on behalf of the people of Kitenge, I welcome you."

Three dancers approached, dressed in grass skirts, necklaces and ankle bracelets of bones and shells, their faces painted. They swung their arms and stomped the traditional Luba welcome.

"*Wafwako*," Bishop exclaimed, clapping his hands and bowing in the direction of the dancers. He turned to the crowd. "I greet the traditional chief of Kabongo, the government official, the religious leaders, all the people. Peace to you!

"To have peace we have to develop ourselves. When the lame man begged Jesus, Jesus said, 'take up your pallet and walk.' And the man did, by faith. I say to you: we have nothing, no silver, no money, but in the name of Jesus, we stand up. As a church, as a people, we want to walk.

"A man named Martin Luther King, Jr. spoke to American people of peace. He was black like me. He led them up the mountain—we too can climb the mountain!"

The sky was clear, as were John's thoughts: *He is truly a man of God. And one who is educated.*

The music, the drumming, the speeches continued, as if Bishop were a new chief.

The day went well, and John began to relax.

The morning after Bishop arrived, a man approached the sentry guarding the front door to John's office. After a few words, the guard entered the building and stopped in front of John's desk. "Bishop's superintendent in Kitenge, Pastor Kabongo, is here to see you."

Kabongo had been a friend of John's older brother, but why would he be calling now, on behalf of Bishop? John started, frowned, and glanced toward the gun on his desk. He had learned to be wary. Bishop seemed to support Laurent Kabila's presidency, but he could still be part of the ever-present opposition.

Reading John's thoughts, the guard shook his head. "You can trust Pastor Kabongo. He was my pastor in Bukama. Last year he moved here. Bishop promoted him to district superintendent."

A few moments later, John received Kabongo. He was a solid man with a self-confident expression, the kind that commands respect. "Bishop wants to talk to you without your bodyguard. He knows a little about you."

John's skin felt prickly. So, his earlier suspicions were well founded. "I can't go into the city without protection."

"You are safe. He wants to talk with you as your father, to hear about your future plans."

Kabongo paused, but John said nothing. So Kabongo explained further. "He does this when he finds a young person whom he believes will become a leader. You see, when he was young during the revolution, he was in a crowd. He raised his hand and asked the speaker, 'How will independence serve the people of Congo? And will young people be able to get an education?' The speaker was Sendwe Jason. *Sendwe Jason!* Sendwe was impressed and called for Ntambo, to inspire him. So now he does the same for others. He wants to get to know you, to encourage you. That's all. It's an honor to be identified by him in this way."

Still, John was unsure. "I will consult my family and let you know. *Wafwako.*"

"*Eyo-vidye.*"

When John told his mother, her eyes danced. She bent at the waist and ululated. "John, talk to the man of God!"

"Ask him to pray for you," Aimerance urged.

Like a Luba leader who seeks his mother's advice and trusts his wife's food, he acted on their wisdom. He sent word to Bishop that he would visit the next day at four p.m.

At the appointed time John and his guard approached the home of the businessman where Bishop was staying, the nicest in all of Kitenge. John told his guard to return in an hour and knocked.

As the door to the compound opened, the singing and dancing began. Bishop's people were expecting Monsieur Mutombo, the head administrator of Kitenge. Caught with the joyous spirit, John played a little game.

"It is good to meet you again, Sir, my Bishop," in English.

"Oh, so you speak English, man. So where do you come from?"

"*Niko mwana inchi*, I am the home boy," John answered in Swahili.

Bishop smiled, asking in Kiluba, "*Sapulanga*, how are you?"

"*Biyampe*," John answered.

"*Où avez-vous fait les études?*" Bishop asked, playfully, changing to French.

"*À l'Université de Lubumbashi.*"

Back to English. "Let's talk over here." They walked a few yards to the side of the property to the *payotte* where the businessman received his guests—a one-room screened-in porch with a thatched roof, ringed with comfortable overstuffed furniture, a coffee table, and a television. Bishop opened the door and motioned to John to sit.

"What language are you most comfortable in?"

"Any one, but as we are here, we can use Kiluba, our language."

Then Bishop became serious, his eyes intense. "Great job. The roads are clean, and sanitation is organized so the city is pleasant. In Mobutu's reign people were beaten during a welcome, women were pushed around. But you have achieved harmony between the civilians and the police. Yesterday, we could only tell the police by the uniforms."

"Thank you, my Bishop."

"You don't draw attention to yourself. In Mobutu's reign there was such a distinction between the leader and the population. You have built a reputation, but you don't lord it over others. The church is happy with your administration." Bishop paused, drew a breath, and continued.

"So how did you come to this position?"

John told him the story, how he had narrowly escaped the student massacre, how he had become engaged to Aimerance in Kitenge, how he had built his reputation in Kabalo with Kabila's administration.

"You are a good man, a moral man. You want to build your country. You are also ambitious; you want to make opportunities for yourself. So let us speak honestly. As you get more power you will be offered advantages by the government and the military, with strings attached. Will you maintain your current ideals? Or will your ethics be compromised? In order to keep favor, will you do the bidding of others who are more concerned with increasing their own power and wealth?"

It was as if Bishop were holding up a mirror in which John could see his future. He pondered Bishop's wisdom.

Bishop continued. "But for Congo to change, we need people, in all kinds of positions, who take risks. What your dream doing this? To be minister in government? Politician? People who supported Kabila get rewarded. How can I support you?"

John swallowed hard. "I want to continue my studies. If I could learn more, I would leave the government."

"There are ways to get funds. You can apply outside the country."

John jumped on the possibility. "You have a scholarship to offer?"

"No, not now, and besides, I don't want you to move from this key position. I can't offer you an income as good as this."

"The potential with the government is good, but I am just a volunteer, paid occasionally, by commissions." The system of commissions allowed some of Mobutu's middle managers to be paid by gratuities for services done for the population, saving the government salaries. This system had not changed in the Kabila government. "I haven't committed myself to a paid job."

Bishop replied, "I don't have a scholarship to offer. But I can make intro-ductions. In the Methodist Church you will work in the environment where *wuzungu*"—white people— "from America come and go. You can talk to peo-ple, make friends. That can lead you somewhere. You can work with me, since you are just a volunteer."

"I will consult my family. *Wafwako*." They stood, shook hands, and joined the crowd outside. As he greeted the people who were gathered, John felt their respect, their confidence in him, the authority he enjoyed as the administrator of Kitenge.

* * *

John's mother responded exactly as he thought she would. "This is my prayer. The church is your right place."

John talked with his father separately. He thought his father would comply with his mother's wishes; it was easier that way with multiple wives. So John was surprised when his father said, "John, no. The church will demand too much of you."

If his father disagreed with his mother, his father had to be right.

But Aimerance was the most persuasive. "I remember the time I saw you beating the man lying on the ground. I didn't like it. I saw in you a bad man. If you continue that way, we won't get along."

A man had been brought to John's office. He had raped a woman, and it wasn't the first time. Kitenge had no court, only John's judgment. John wanted to set an example. So outside his office, John beat the man where a crowd was watching. Then he called the police to take the man to jail. Aimerance had been in the crowd, watching.

"The man had to be corrected!" John protested. "You should think of the victim. It was the third time he had repeated the same act—a rape! I tried to talk to him. He didn't understand rape is wrong. He thought it was his right. You talk to me as a church member. You say, 'Jesus wouldn't beat him, Jesus would offer grace and love.' There is mercy, but there is justice. He could only change if he was beaten."

Aimerance objected. "Mercy, justice, all the fancy language—you sound like a university student. Yes, he was a bad man. But you acted like Mobutu's soldier, the way you made him bleed. He hurts the woman, you hurt him. Does it change him in the long run? Or do you just feel self-righteous, that you are different than he is? But are you? You both think you have the right to hurt others. The power of government will corrupt you. You need to work for the church."

Aimerance prevailed. That evening John dined with Bishop and agreed to join him in Kamina.

* * *

Bishop had appointed John as his assistant for public relations. He translated for a missionary couple who worked in Kamina when people came to their door with requests. His time with the government turned out to be useful, as Bishop built relationships with everyone, including politicians. He was beginning to know the church people and to make friends with the *wuzungu*. His future in the church looked different, but bright, and most importantly, Aimerance was happy.

Pastor Kahunda, District Superintendent, Organizes Relief

"New Congo Ruler Facing Rebellion from Former Allies"

The New York Times, August 04, 1998

"As it is, there are many members, yet one body. The eye cannot say to the hand, 'I have no need of you,' nor again the head to the feet, 'I have no need of you.' . . . If one member suffers, all suffer together with it; if one member is honored, all rejoice together with it."

1 Corinthians 12:20-26

Mulungwishi, Katanga Province, Democratic Republic of Congo
End of July 1998

Pastor Kahunda sat quietly on the train, his face turned toward the window through which he watched the mountains rise high into the mist. By focusing on the scenery he could ignore the twenty-five colleagues with whom he travelled, without appearing to do so. He needed some moments without the people's requests, without organizational responsibility, without conversation. Even so, Bishop's magnetic voice interrupted his reverie, catching his attention. Kahunda glanced at his spiritual leader, a few seats ahead of him. *His vision, his energy!* Kahunda thought. *But I am his detail person in Kamina. Details make the vision happen.*

The Annual Conference had ended. The people had celebrated, prayed, sung hymns and danced, and were returning to their homes. Kahunda had attended to the minutiae. He had made his contribution. He felt tired but satisfied.

Bishop had gathered his district superintendents—the pastors who supervise a group of congregations in an area and report directly to him—from the governmental districts of Tanganyika, near Lake Tanganyika on the border with Rwanda, and from Haut Lomami. Now they rode the train together, headed south for two weeks of leadership training at the seminary in Mulungwuishi. Ahead of them lay a rigorous curriculum of organizational theory, public speaking, community development, preaching and Bible—the kinds of topics Bishop thought were important for the leadership of the church in North Katanga. Kahunda would again care for many details, so on the train he was grateful for a moment's rest.

* * *

For several months the word had spread that President Laurent Kabila and his Rwandese backers had been at odds. The pastors had heard a series of ominous announcements, making the pastors from Tanganika nervous. Kabila had dismissed all of the Rwandese in his government and asked them to leave the country. In the refugee camps near the border of Rwanda and Congo, fighting had broken out.

Bishop's voice barked, unusually demanding. "Kahunda, bring your radio to the seminar room so all of us can listen!"

Kahunda scrambled to comply.

As Kahunda tuned, the superintendents pulled their chairs close. All day the ham radio operators of the churches in Kalemie, Moba, Nyunzu, Kongolo and Manono had reported the rumors. Some superintendents had slipped away to listen, abandoning their study sessions. Now, the entire body succumbed to its desire to hear the news first hand.

A few minutes before eight p.m. the voice on the short wave radio announced, "President Kabila is going to speak."

And then the pastors heard the dreaded words: "The Rwandese aggressors have entered Congo at the northern edge of Lake Tanganyika."

Even though Kahunda had expected it, he sat stunned by the news. Their fears had been confirmed as reality.

* * *

Pastor Nday, the superintendent from Lubudi, a village far from the fighting, broke the silence. Nday sighed with discouragement. "I pastored the Rwandese when I lived in Vyura. I know them. This will be a long war."

"My family!" Pastor Kichibi's eyes flickered with fear. His city, Kalemie, lay just south of the border between Congo and Rwanda on the western edge of Lake Tanganyika across from Tanzania—a strategic target for Rwanda's invasion of Congo. After the Annual Conference had concluded, Kichibi's family had returned to Kalemie without him.

The superintendents from the rural areas of Tanganyika District—from the villages of Kabimba, Moba, Nyunzu, Kabalo, Kongolo, Manono, Kiyambi, Ankoro, Kitanda, and Kitenge—differed in their sense of the danger.

"We will be all right," Pastor Kabongo from Kitenge declared. "It's a very long way inland to most of our villages. There are no river routes. Kalemie is south of Rwanda. If the fighting spreads from the refugee camps, it will follow the Congo River north toward Kisangani and Kinshasa. I believe even Tanganyika will be safe."

But his words did not reassure Kichibi and some of the others. "If Nday speaks the truth, we need to return home to our families and our churches."

Kahunda sympathized with his brothers from Tanganyika. "We will pray for you and your families every day."

Bishop sat quietly, berating himself, swimming in fear. *I am guilty. We heard the rumors. Why did we have this meeting, ask them to leave their families behind? I have asked too much of them.*

They continued to study and listen to Kahunda's radio. The next day they were stunned by more news: Kindu had fallen.

Then Bishop stood, walked around his chair and rested his hands on its back, assuming his authority. The pastors looked in his direction. "We end the seminar. We take the next train to Kamina that continues to Kalemie. I worry till I know that all of you are with your families and that you are safe."

* * *

Bishop and Kahunda stood together at the depot in Kamina. The train whistle blew. They watched as the locomotive lumbered out of sight, taking many of their pastors into the feared unknown.

Kahunda sighed. "Perhaps Pastor Kabongo is right, they'll be okay."

"That's what I thought when I took my family to Burundi," Bishop murmured.

The images of their escape from Burundi in 1993 flashed through his mind. He had been invited to be a missionary for Bishop Ndorichimpa, so he had relocated Mama Nshimba and the children to a house in Bujumbura. The country had recently elected the first Hutu President, Ndadaye. He sought to reconcile the Tutsis to a Hutu government; Ndorichimpa wanted an evangelist to do the same through the churches. Ntambo had a history of teaching church members to "love their enemies," so he was chosen. A week after they arrived Ndorichimpa introduced Ntambo to President Ndadaye, and Ntambo preached to the president's family. A week later Ndadaye was assassinated in a Tutsi revolt against the new government.

Word of the killing spread. Ntambo and his family huddled in their home on the main street of town as Tutsi soldiers paraded up and down. The Tutsi were brown skinned, lean and tall, and had facial features more like Europeans. Ntambo believed that in colonial times they had been taught that they were superior to the Hutu, who had Bantu features: black skin, with large noses, full lips, and a short, squat stature. The Hutu and the Luba were both Bantu people, similar in appearance. In such an atmosphere, soldiers would not bother to distinguish Ntambo's Luba family from the Hutu they sought to kill.

They knew if they stayed in the house, they would all die. In the night Ntambo and Nshimba hatched a bold plan to reach the Congolese embassy— one that might allow at least some of the family to survive.

They drew the children together; the youngest was then eleven years old. "We will walk one by one, with Papa first, and then each of you following about thirty or forty feet later till we reach the Congolese embassy. Mama will be last. If one of us is killed, ignore it and walk on. Follow whomever is ahead." They hugged one another and prayed. "God watch over us and keep us safe."

Then Ntambo stepped out into the Tutsi-dominated street. The children followed at intervals, and then Mama Nshimba.

Miraculously, they all survived.

Now, the fear he knew then gripped his heart. Many of his district superintendents might be asked to make similar, hard decisions about the lives and possible deaths of their families and congregations.

Bishop turned to Kahunda. "We hope for the best. But we must prepare for them to return to Kamina if they can't reach their homes."

* * *

A week later Kahunda called Bishop to report that the office had just heard from the church at Nyunzu on the ham radio. Kalemie had fallen to the rebels; Nyunzu was fleeing. Four of the district superintendents and their families would be returning to Kamina on the next train.

That night Kahunda gathered the pastors of his district at the Kamina Centre Church. They sat solemnly, waiting for him to speak. "Some of our colleagues from Tanganyika have fled from the fighting. They and their families will be our guests. We will house two of them in the orphanage; two others will stay in parsonages. Could we divide, so that three parishes could host one colleague and his family? Who will volunteer to collect food and cooking utensils for each?"

In the first week of September 1998, twenty-eight internally displaced persons—District Superintendents LuNkombe, Watate, and Maloba and their families—arrived by train in Kamina. Others, including Kichibi, had gone to their homes to discover that their families had fled to Tanzania, and the superintendents continued on, searching for them. They had not been heard from.

* * *

Two weeks later, about the third week in September, Kahunda was surprised when two hundred people swarmed around his door, hungry, thirsty, dirty. They had arrived on foot.

Kahunda and his family hurriedly brought buckets of water. Their guests cupped their hands and drank gratefully. Kahunda ran to his neighbors to collect bananas, peanuts, or whatever food they could spare. Word spread, and people brought *bukari*, beans and fish to the grateful refugees.

Kahunda again gathered his pastors, this time with the displaced district superintendents, to work out the details of relief. "Now we have many more guests. Bishop will assign housing to them. We will develop a central depot at the Centre Ville church where congregations can bring clothing and utensils. We will divide into seven groups of congregations. Each will bring food to the depot on a different day. Superintendents from Tanganyika, we ask you to divide the supplies among the different families. Take it to your family and your parishioners where they are staying. Each person receiving food will register, so that we know who is in Kamina, who has become separated from their families, and who is searching. Who will be the secretary, to take the names of all who come and family members who are missing?"

From that day on, every day for almost two years, new guests arrived in Kamina, until they numbered twelve thousand.

Chapter III

War Engulfs Two-Thirds of the Democratic Republic of Congo—North Katanga Divides into a Relief Zone and a War Zone (July 1998 – July 1999)

Historical Introduction

During the second half of 1998, "Rwanda's war of aggression," aided by Uganda and Burundi, overwhelmed Katanga Province's Tanganyika District and sections of Haut Lomami District. Early attempts by Zambian President Chiluba and other African leaders failed to resolve the conflict, and by September, Zimbabwe, Angola and Namibia came to DRC's aid. For the next year Rwanda and its allies advanced, and it seemed, no peace effort could hold. Bishop Ntambo's area became divided between a relief zone, centered in Kamina, and a war zone, beginning at the town of Kabongo and stretching north and west.

Under these circumstances, "to feed my people" became far more complicated than creating development projects. Kamina became a destination for internally displaced people. Meanwhile, the people of Kamina did not know whether their city would be overtaken by the war or whether the Zimbabweans at Kamina Military Base, twenty kilometers away, could secure it. "To feed my people" meant caring for widows, orphans and sojourners; employing local and displaced people in church, parsonage and school construction and agricultural projects that supplemented the local food supply; organizing medical care; and building relationships with other religious, government, and military leaders and traditional chiefs. Mundane tasks, such as transportation of people and goods, required monumental efforts.

People grieved, loved, struggled, worked, died and lived.

The people faced more serious challenges "than even our parents faced," noted Pastor Ndalamba from Kabongo district. Of those who survived, many internally displaced, direct victims of the war transformed their agony into leadership, working with colleagues who hailed from more secure areas. Others who could have remained safe risked their lives. Faith called for improvisation, creativity and commitment, as the leaders of the relief zone penetrated the war zone and more and more displaced people from the war zone established their lives as guests in Kamina.

Bishop Ntambo Protects the Missionaries and the Tutsis

"Congo Presents Evidence of Foreign Invaders"

The New York Times, September 2, 1998

"As he came near and saw the city, he wept over it, saying, 'If you, even you, had only recognized the things that make for peace! But now they are hidden from your eyes.'"

Luke 19:41-42

Kamina, Haut Lomami District
Mid-August 1998

Bishop Ntambo frowned as he searched for options. Fortunately, Gaston had evacuated the missionaries safely to Zambia. But the *Banyamulenge*, the Tutsi Congolese pastor and houseboy—how to help them? He could not find a clear path.

The war at the Rwandan border, a thousand kilometers away and only a month old, had already put lives at risk in Kamina. Government officials had begun to arrest anyone who might have reason to join the rebellion against the Kabila government—those with ties to Mobutu's party, to Rwanda, or to Tutsis. Though the war raged far from Kamina, Kamina Military Base lay only twenty kilometers away. Potential traitors might convince the soldiers to aid Rwanda, giving the enemy an advantage at the center of the country. If Kamina Base fell, Rwanda might take Congo. Kabila's government officials were watching closely, routing out anyone who might be a spy.

First in the church to be scrutinized were the American missionaries. One night the government had pounded on their door, demanding their sophisticated satellite phones. John Mutombo had delayed the officials while the Americans hid the stuff. Before another incident could occur, Gaston had evacuated the foreigners. Bishop was relieved that they were now safe in Zambia, but the missionaries wanted some of their possessions. John, a chauffeur, and a female passenger were already underway, driving a car packed with their belongings through the mountain roads.

Next under suspicion, the *Mwenyamulenge* pastor[1] whom Ntambo had appointed to a parish in Kamina. A Congolese Tutsi, the pastor was feared by both sides, trusted by neither. He had originated from Uvira on the border of Congo and Rwanda. As one with features more like the Rwandese than the dominant Bantu, he was immediately associated with the rebels. Yet his loyalties lay with his country, Congo. A Congolese soldier might choose sides at will, depending upon where he thought the advantage lay, but the pastor's future, and therefore

---

[1] Banyamulenge is the plural form of the noun referring to Tutsi Congolese; Menyamulenge is the singular.

his sentiments, lay firmly with the Congolese church. Still, the government had arrested him.

Even as Bishop thought fondly of his pastor, hatred of the Tutsi clutched at his belly. Tutsis had killed in Burundi, had threatened his own family! *Nonsense*, Bishop chided himself, pushing away the xenophobic disdain. *Love your enemy*. His viscera had reacted to a stereotype, not to the reality of the human being he knew. He loved and respected his *Mwenyamulenge* pastor. But he did not know how to save him.

He had no options, in part, because he had sheltered a *Mwenyamulenge* houseboy from Burundi. When Ntambo's family fled for their lives, leaving all of their possessions behind, the boy, on his own volition, had watched over their house. When they returned, they had lost little. In gratitude, they offered the boy a position in their home and cared for him as if he were a son. He had returned with them from Burundi to Kamina. But the government had detained the boy, also, for no other reason than his ethnic and national identity. He, too, was in danger.

Bishop and his family were guilty by association with all of these persons. They had to tread lightly.

* * *

The chauffeur braked the missionaries' car as he, John Mutombo, and their female passenger approached the military barrier at Kibondo, a hundred and fifty kilometers south of Kamina. At the checkpoints near Kamina, the vehicle had been recognized, so it was easy to pass. Here, it blended in, one in a long line of nondescript autos and trucks, any of which might be hiding aid to the enemy. The driver pulled into the line of travellers who hoped to satisfy the Congolese army that they had legitimate business further south.

Finally, the guards approached.

"You are from the church," the soldier observed, noting the cross-and-flame logo on the side of the car. "What are your positions?"

"I'm the driver for some missionaries."

The guard nodded, dipped his head slightly, and peered at John in the center of the front seat.

"I'm the assistant to the United Methodist bishop. This girl is a passenger, a student who wishes to visit her family in Lubumbashi."

The guard turned back to the driver. "What do you have in the truck?"

"The missionaries' belongings. They have already gone to Zambia."

"What kind?"

"Personal effects and furniture."

"Let us see. Please get out."

The driver swung open the car door and stepped down from the front seat. John and the girl got out and stood with the driver. The soldiers began their search; they found nothing.

Then the commander strode to the car. John saw he wielded a staff with a face carved in the end. *His charm.* He banged on the car, then on its interior, finally on its seats. He stopped. He hit the seat once again with his staff. Then, he lifted the seat. The driver and John's eyes widened when they saw a stash of binoculars.

"What are these? To aid the rebels?" The commander cracked the staff over the chauffeur's shoulder and he fell to the ground. The commander struck the driver again, four solid blows. "Where were you when they packed the car?"

"Away."

The commander turned to John. "You, priest, we can't strike you, a man of God, but we'll question you. You sit over there." He pointed to a bench to the side of the checkpoint.

A soldier put his arm around the girl. "Come with us."

John had taken a step toward the bench, but he turned and put his arm across the soldier's path. "No, she needs to stay here. She is a student. *Under the care of Bishop Ntambo,*" he emphasized so that the commander could hear.

"Let her be," the commander demanded. The soldier dropped his arm from the girl. "Girl, wait in the car. Priest, wait on the bench. There."

Then they tied the hands of the chauffeur, pulled him to his feet, pushed him toward the guardhouse.

John sat. As he watched, he prayed. *Find the right words before they kill us. God, tell me what to say.*

And then, he imagined the missionaries looking for fish in the river.

The soldiers returned without the chauffeur. As John watched them approach, he saw in them the signs of hunger: they hung their heads, they dragged their feet. They straightened when their boss followed them out the door.

"So, priest, what do you know?" the commander demanded.

"You know, the missionaries liked fish. They had their own fishpond, and they went to the river. I've seen them use the binoculars to find fish to eat. Or to peer into the bush to find other small animals to hunt."

The commander looked interested, remained quiet. John paused, then continued.

"Are your men hungry?"

The commander nodded slightly.

"I was Kabila's administrator in Kitenge. Shipments can be late." John smiled, confident. "Keep the binoculars to find food. And we have flour, oil, and salt. Take it all, and you will have enough till you get your shipment. But let us be on our way quickly."

The commander relaxed. "We'll take it. Go." He turned to the soldiers. "Release the driver."

John unloaded the binoculars and foodstuffs from the car, leaving it all on the side of the road. Then he slid into the center seat and turned to the girl. She let go a sob.

"I wanted to be with my family with the war coming. But I should have stayed in Kamina."

John patted her. "We'll be all right now."

Shortly the chauffeur limped toward the car, moving painfully. He tucked himself slowly behind the wheel, his face drawn and tight.

They inched through the checkpoint and then, despite the driver's bruised legs and hips, sped down the dirt road to Lubumbashi.

* * *

"Police to see you." Bishop's guard had come into the house, a stricken look on his face.

"Coming." Bishop gave Mama Nshimba a long look, then stood, straightened himself, and walked out of the house to the door of the compound.

The policeman was chatting with Ntambo's guards. He grew silent when Bishop approached.

"Could we talk privately for a moment?"

"In my *payotte*."

When they were seated, the man said, "The police need your help. The government plans to execute your Tutsi pastor and your houseboy tonight. But we do not want to hurt you, Bishop. We do not want to be against God. There is a train this afternoon. Could you buy them tickets, make them disappear? If so, we will get them to the depot."

Bishop had been handed the option he needed for his *Banyamulenge*. And John, the driver and the girl had called to say they had had a difficult encounter with soldiers but they were now safe in Lubumbashi.

For Bishop's people in Kamina, the danger had retreated, for now.

Headmaster Mwilumba Hosts the Displaced

"Congo Peace Talks Open in Zimbabwe"

The New York Times, September 6, 1998

"Thus says the Lord: Act with justice and righteousness, and deliver from the hand of the oppressor anyone who has been robbed. And do no wrong or violence to the alien, the orphan and the widow, or shed innocent blood in this place."

Jeremiah 22:3

Kabalo, Tanganyika District

August 1998

The sun lay low in the sky as Papa Mwilumba hustled home from his duties as headmaster at the Methodist school in Kabalo. A diminutive man of five feet, he walked as fast as men with longer legs by quickening his stride. Today his smile further lightened his step. It had been a long, satisfying day. He had observed at the side of the class as the pupils stood at attention, ready to recite their lessons. The teacher posed the questions; the students replied quickly and lowered themselves on their mud benches. Mwilumba praised them both. The teacher bowed; the students looked at him with shy, smiling eyes. The headmaster warmed with pride at all they had accomplished. The day had ended well.

He turned into the lane that led to his house and contemplated his fields. He ran the farm like the school, engaging and encouraging his workers, and the farm prospered. Now in early August, the end of the dry season, the harvest of cassava, spinach and sweet potatoes remained plentiful. Goats and chickens roamed. The laborers ate all they wanted, as did his own family: his wife, his four children, and various other relatives. No one hungered.

Mama Alphonsine, his wife, sold produce and animals at market for cash. She brokered tilapia from the fishermen on the river, adding to the crops and meat. She profited well. With the cash, first she paid the school fees for Mbuyu, in Kamina, and then in Kabalo, for Patrice, Cherita, and nieces and nephews in need. Then she bought clothes and toys.

Between Mwilumba's salary and her sales, they had enough to care for their own family and to help others.

In another month, the daily thunderstorms of the rainy season would quickly turn the fields to a lush green, making the vegetables even more abundant. It was a good thing, too, as they had so many new guests to feed.

In the last two days five new mud and grass huts had been hastily erected behind Mwilumba's main house, symbols of the latest, fast-moving drama in Congo. Ten days earlier on July 28th President Kabila had expelled the Rwandese from his government and army. The next day Kabila's bodyguards had disarmed an assassin who tried to enter Kabila's office. On July 30th the Rwandese army, with help from Uganda and Burundi, had invaded Goma, the northern city on Lake Tanganyika, the great, long lake that stretched between the borders of Congo to the west and Uganda, Rwanda, Burundi, and Tanzania on the eastern shore. During the first days of August, the foreign army entered Congolese towns along the edge of the lake as far south as Kalemie. As the soldiers approached, civilians scattered, leaving everything behind.

The families of five Methodist church leaders from Kalemie had bushwhacked directly west for three days, finally arriving in Kabalo and seeking refuge on Mwilumba's farm. Here, they thought they were beyond the reach of the Rwandese. The roads from Kalemie to Kabalo were poor, and the train operated sporadically. They knew that Mwilumba, the church's school headmaster and director of youth activities, had enough land and food to welcome them until the fighting ended.

Perhaps the guests could return to their homes even before the rainy season began, Mwilumba thought. The Rwandese were spread thin—it would be hard for them to occupy the west shore of Lake Tanganyika and also control the 4700 kilometer Congo River. Some Rwandese troops had marched northwest from Goma to take the major eastern port, Kisangani, key to entering and conquering the waterway. But the radio reported that the Congolese army had stopped the aggressors. Kinshasa, twelve hundred miles to the west, was well protected.

Even now, South African leaders were meeting in Zimbabwe with Kabila and the Rwandese president, Paul Kagame, to resolve their differences. South Africa supported the Kabila presidency.

Surely, Mwilumba mused, *South Africa will make a deal and the Rwandese will go back to their country. It will soon be over.*

* * *

It was dark as Mwilumba, his wife, Alphonsine, and their children sat around the coffee table, breaking off pieces of a cassava ball and dipping the sticky white dough into the oily orange fish gravy. Mwilumba's son, Patrice, paused as he balanced some *linga-linga* leaves atop his cassava and fish. He focused his inquiring eyes on his father. "I miss Mbuyu. At the end of this year, may I join him in school in Kamina?"

Mbuyu and Patrice, just eighteen months apart in age, had always been close. They had constantly played together, and they had never fought. But at the beginning of the last school year Mwilumba had put Mbuyu on the train to Kamina with school fees and food money in his pocket. He now lived with Pastor Bondo and attended the best school in Kamina.

"Next year, yes."

Cherita, Mwilumba's oldest daughter, a year younger than Patrice, licked her fingers. "Papa, I need a new school uniform." Then she frowned. "I would rather wear a new *kikembwe.*"

Cherita was growing womanly, and the native dress, with a fitted bodice, long wrapped skirt and additional material draped around the hip, created a festive, happy, feminine aura. In addition to accenting a young woman's hips and bust, the outer wrap was functional—everything from sweet potatoes to babies could be collected and tied to a woman's back. She turned to her mother.

"Can we sew a *kikwembe* with material from Tanzania? The new bright green and yellow fabrics are pretty. I get *so* tired of the white blouse and a blue skirt. Two dresses, a uniform and a new *kikwembe?*"

"Yes," Mama nodded. "You sew enough doll clothes! Time for you to learn to sew your own clothes and clothes for others. We'll measure you. You've grown. We'll buy fabric in town tomorrow."

Cherita smiled. She examined her fingers and then, like a meticulous cat, cleaned the last oily spots.

Mwilumba looked at Alphonsine, his eyes dark, and lowered his voice. "I saw Congolese soldiers from Kamina Base in Kabalo today. They will stop the war from reaching us. But you and Cherita, be careful, stay with a group. We don't know whether their behavior has changed under Kabila."

Mwilumba did not need to state the obvious in front of the family: Congolese soldiers, under Mobutu, had always been allowed to violate women at will. But now that they were Kabila's soldiers, at least they could be counted on to defend the population.

The Depot Manager Ilunga Mutombo Supplies the Building Projects

"Genocide with Spin Control: Kurtz Wasn't Fiction"

review of "King Leopold's Ghost", by Adam Hochshild,
The New York Times, September 1, 1998

"They shall build houses and inhabit them;
they shall plant vineyards and eat their fruit.
They shall not build and another inhabit;
they shall not plant and another eat;
for like the days of a tree shall the days of my people be,
and my chosen shall long enjoy the work of their hands."

Isaiah 65:21-22

Kamina, Haut Lomami District
September 1998

Ilunga Mutombo stood upright, threw down the stick with which he had been digging stones from the ground, and stretched his arms high to relieve the cramp in his back. He inhaled the heavy scent of damp, freshly turned earth. After a few moments, he rubbed the muscles of the side of his back as he gazed with satisfaction at the small river in the far distance. The land sloped gently from the moldy Belgian mansion on the hill, past the crumbling brick animal pens, over the fields to the river. Scrubby bushes had sunk their shallow roots into the fertile but rocky soil. Once the rubble was removed, crops would once again rise from these fields.

Kamisamba Farm had been purchased by the church. A hundred men and women dotted the land, each one bending and swaying, cutting bush plants with machetes or digging out roots with hoes, unearthing stones with heavy sticks, standing for a moment to relieve the ache of the unaccustomed activity. For the last week, the men had worked the fields from dawn till dusk, the women joining them at noon after they hauled water and prepared the day's *bukari*.

Hopefully, Ilunga Mutombo thought, by next week they would have a field cleared, irrigation troughs dug, and beans planted that they could harvest yet this season. The weather was cooperating. The thunderstorms had been consistent, beginning about two o'clock in the afternoon. The natural slope of the field to the river drained away excessive water overnight. By dawn, the soil was loosened for the next day's work. Bishop and Ilunga Mutombo had agreed that the first yield would stock the kitchen at Mama Mujing's orphanage. After that, the crops would be sold for a small price unless people were hungry and entirely unable to pay.

He laid his stick carefully by the rock pile so that it would be ready when he returned—time to check on the bricks. He turned back toward the house where his motorbike waited. He had fuelled that morning; it revved at his first try. After riding half a kilometer, he spotted the eight-foot high termite hill. It rose out of the bush like a tall orange sandcastle, a cone well formed at the bottom, narrowing to a point at the top, the first of many such piles waiting to be cultivated.

Nearing the hill, he saw a large concave cut-out in its side that revealed the progress of the morning. The tower of termite excrement, exactly the right consistency for packing into bricks, had yielded several dozen that waited to be fired. The men had constructed a kiln not too far away; the brush and wood that had been cleared from the fields provided the fuel. Coming closer, he saw that the oven was already hot.

"Hey, Baba, how long?" Ilunga Mutombo asked the foreman, Baba Majita.

Baba Majita hesitated. "It depends. Maybe… another two days. If you bring food and coffee, the men can work through the night."

"Sure. I'll bring you something tonight, but I want the work to be finished. Do you promise?"

"*Wafwako.*" Majito turned to the team. "Ilunga Mutombo will bring us food to continue the work. Are you ready?"

The workers clapped and cheered. "*Ndiyo.* Yes, sir!"

Turning, Ilunga Mutombo swung onto his motorbike, rode back to the house, and parked. Now to check the progress in the field. Quickly scanning the horizon, he saw patches of earth, hills of stones, and piles of vegetation. Soon it would be time to hitch the oxen to the cart to collect the refuse and bring it to the area by the kiln. The men would sort sandstones into two piles: those of usable shapes and those that would be pounded into gravel. As soon as the cement arrived on the train from Lubumbashi, the builders would commence the new church and parsonage at Kinkunki Village. He walked toward the nearest worker to speak a word of encouragement. In this way, he visited each and every one so that they knew that they were important to Kamisamba Farm.

* * *

The oxcart moved materials around Kamisamba, but Ilunga Mutombo needed to truck stones and cement to Kinkunki. Ilunga Mutombo could not drive, but he contacted the church chauffeur, Félix.

Together, they rented a *gari* from an entrepreneur whose business had slowed. Ilunga Mutombo and six other men, some in the cab, some riding the flatbed, nudged it across Kamina to the fuel depot, learning its quirks. The men jumped off to push every time it stalled.

"Every truck needs encouragement, just like people!" Ilunga Mutombo murmured out loud. Félix patted the steering wheel, as if to start the engine with kind thoughts. The men pushed, the truck rolled, and the men jumped aboard, one more time.

In front of the green metal gate of the fuel depot Félix pressed the horn hard to be let into the compound. No response. He waited, he honked again, longer and louder this time, with an air of importance. The door opened and the guard inquired about his business. Young boys swung wide the metal doors, and once Félix had driven a few yards inside, they clanked the gate shut behind him. Ilunga Mutombo opened the truck door, swung his feet to the ground, walked into the kiosk and deepened his voice.

"You have heard about the church's project at Kamisamba."

Te-te, the owner, nodded slightly.

"Is it possible to buy a barrel of gas?"

"Not really. We only have a few litres." Te-te frowned, then his face softened. "But I know the project is important. I can try to make it happen. But, of course, there is a fee."

"I know it is difficult. But we can't wait for a shipment from Lubumbashi that will take three weeks. I hope you will help us."

"The church's work is important to whole community. I've heard the church is feeding many people." Te-te picked up a pencil and made notes in his book.

Ilunga Mutombo knew he was calculating the possible sources of gas in Kamina. Ilunga Mutombo's heart quickened, and he waited, watching the man's face. Finally, Te-te drew a line and wrote down a figure.

Te-te looked directly at Ilunga Mutombo. "I think my suppliers will want to help you. All right, I will try to collect a barrel of gas for you."

"How much will it cost?"

"Two hundred and seventy US dollars for a barrel, plus twenty for the cost of collecting." Te-te needed to pay his runners who would bring the gas, liter by liter, by bicycle.

Ilunga Mutombo knew that Te-te was his only hope, but he also was certain the owner would offer high. "How about two hundred fifty?"

"Make it two hundred sixty for everything."

"Yes, that works. Do collect the gas for us."

"I need to visit my suppliers. Come back in two days."

Two days later Te-te and Ilunga Mutombo rolled the barrel of gas to the truck. Te-te offered a siphon hose. Reversing the pressure by sucking quickly on it, Ilunga Mutombo inserted it into the gas tank. The whole procedure of fuelling the truck had taken two days—not so long, considering the obstacles. Then, the guards opened the compound doors. Félix put the truck in reverse and backed onto the dirt street.

It was seven long kilometers of rutted mud track from Kamina to Kamisamba Farm. Slowing to the speed of a bicycle, Félix carefully calculated the placement of each revolution of the tire as he picked his way through the hills and valleys of rain-drenched path. Occasionally, he stopped for the men to jump from the flatbed and wave him through the most passable route. It was a great achievement: he had laid the first tire trace through the kilometers leading to the rise created by the railway track. He reduced the gear and jostled the truck over the rails and down the hill on the other side.

"We need to smooth the road," Ilunga Mutombo thought.

The tumbling barns of Kamisamba came into view. As they pulled up, the men working the farm hurried to the truck.

Félix backed as close and carefully as he could to the tall pile of stones. The men passed them hand over hand to each other, loading the truck from front to back, gesticulating, arguing over how much weight the truck could support. Finally, Ilunga Mutombo called a halt to the loading, and all eight of the men piled on top of the stones to ride to Kinkunki.

* * *

The site for the new church lay just outside the land surrounding King *Kasongo Nyembo*'s headquarters on the primary road between Kamina and Kinkunki. A driveway led from the road through the trees to a cleared patch of land. Several huts were tucked back under the trees. The land had already been marked as a church site—the telltale upright posts, attached to a crossbeam, were sunk deep into the earth. Between each post a reclaimed piece of train track hung by a strap drawn through a hole drilled into the metal. When beaten in a regular cadence with a piece of rebar, the rail rang like a church bell. The clang called people to pray before dawn, to attend special events in the afternoon, and to worship on Sunday. But now the rail stood as a silent witness to the unloading of the first stones from Kamisamba.

The men jumped from the truck and began to hand off the stones, one by one. Children came running at the sound of a vehicle, stopped short at the strange sight, and drew near to watch. Slowly, mothers with babies on their hips or tied on their backs sauntered toward the children; they too gawked at the men on the trucks unloading the stones. A few older boys came round.

"You there, join in!" Ilunga Mutombo beckoned the boys.

And so, under the watchful eyes of the villagers, the first church was delivered from Kamisamba's womb.

Headmaster Mwilumba's Household Flees

> "BOOKS OF THE TIMES: No Ice Cream Cones in the Heart of Darkness"
>
> review of Barbara Kingsolver's *The Poisonwood Bible*
> *The New York Times*, October 16, 1998

> "And God spoke in these terms, that his descendants would become resident aliens in a country belonging to others, that would enslave them and mistreat them during four hundred years."
>
> Acts 7:6

Kabalo, Tanganyika District
September 18, 1998

Cherita stood in the corner of the hut, holding Dada on her hip, while Eschler clung to the skirt of her blue and white school uniform. She felt like she was dizzy with malaria—that sensation of schools of fish rushing round in her head, pushing her down, to lie flat. But she stood motionless, her dark eyes wide open and barely blinking. She tried to absorb the scene. In front of her, her parents and Patrice were digging a big hole in the earthen living room floor, while her grandparents piled the family's valuables nearby.

Cherita had arisen at dawn, as normal. She dressed for school and sat down with her brothers and sisters to eat cassava, peanuts and sweet potatoes while Mama drank coffee. Then they heard the strange commotion—outside—voices talking, crying out. Feet scuffling in various directions—not along the trail toward the river to fetch the morning water but toward the bush.

Mama hurried out the door of the house toward the activity, and Cherita, Patrice, Dada, and Eschler followed, stopping in the yard, watching. Mama spoke a few sentences to one passerby, who answered and continued on. She called to Papa, and together they talked with the next hurried travellers. Heads bobbed; fingers pointed; voices became louder. The guests emerged from their huts. Mama's elderly parents hobbled toward them. Soon, all of the adults who lived on the farm and some of the wayfarers were engaged in an animated conversation, talking loudly and gesturing to one another.

During the last few weeks the political rumors had been promising: Robert Mugabe, the president of Zimbabwe, had called together the African leaders, and this time—in the fourth attempt to end the war in Congo—the essential representatives had shown up. The guests on Mwilumba's farm believed the talks had succeeded and the war in Congo was ending.

Cherita had heard Papa tell Mama, "Soon the guests will be going home."

But in the last few days, confusing things had happened. Congolese soldiers from Kamina appeared in Kabalo, as well as soldiers from Zimbabwe. And now…

"There are soldiers coming. People are leaving for the bush," Mwilumba told Cherita and Patrice when he and Alphonsine returned to the house. "We will hide our belongings, go the bush with the others. Just a few hours—don't be afraid."

Cherita followed her parents back into the house, and she stood in the corner minding the youngest children, out of the way. She tried to steady herself. *No fear, no fear*, she repeated. But her eyes welled with tears when her prized possessions—her bicycle and Mama's sewing machine—were buried in the hole and covered with dirt.

* * *

By noon Mwilumba, Alphonsine, their four children, Alphonsine's elderly parents and their household guests had picked their way into the bush and found a bit of shelter from the sun in a clump of trees beyond the back of the farm. All afternoon they sat in the shade, watching groups of people weave their way through the scrub. They prayed. Occasionally, when a wanderer came close, Mwilumba intercepted him, hoping for good news. But it was not. Soldiers were still coming.

Black clouds rose on the horizon. The thunder cracked, and the sudden rain drenched everyone. By now they were thirsty, and they welcomed the downpour. They stood with their hands outstretched and cupped, trying to catch the rain. They drank what they could and licked their hands and arms to quench their thirst. The men took off their shirts and wrung them out, letting the water drip into their mouths.

The storms passed. As Alphonsine fed her baby, her toddler cried, "Dinner, Mama, hungry." She shared the milk of her second breast with her older child, till her breasts were empty.

As night neared, the entire household, family and guests, sang hymns and folk songs. Patrice and Cherita harmonized; the pure sounds of young voices singing in perfect pitch calmed the wanderers' souls.

Mwilumba decided. From everything they heard that day, it was better to stay the night in the bush and wait till tomorrow to go home.

For the last hour of daylight Alphonsine hung the wrap of her *kikwembe* over the branches of a tree, drying it as best she could. The sun reflected a bright red on the clouds, and shortly the sky went dark. Then she spread the damp cloth over some leaves as a place for her children to sleep, and they spent their first night in the bush.

* * *

The sun rose, waking those in the group who still slept. Patrice opened his eyes, hoping it was time to go home—he was now quite hungry. Here there was nothing to eat. If they walked back to the farm, they could dig sweet potatoes. But the ground would have been too damp for a fire, even if they had a match.

Shortly after dawn a small family walked near the place where the household had slept. The man wore the cap of a Congolese soldier and carried a gun, but he was accompanied by two women and children. Mwilumba, Patrice, and a few of the men walked out to greet them. This time the small party stopped and talked for many minutes. When Mwilumba and the men returned, Mwilumba's usual smile was replaced by lips drawn in a tight line. His voice dropped low, as he talked to the entire group.

"The Rwandese are outside Kabalo. The Congolese army is falling apart. The local soldiers, even the soldiers from Kamina Base, believe that the Rwandese will beat Kabila. Many of them have changed sides, integrated with the Rwandese, to fight for the winners. Rwandese have offered them food, water, and salaries. A few have left, like this one, if they have families in the area. But most have decided to help the Rwandese."

No one spoke.

Alphonsine's mother began to pray aloud, and the rest joined in. And then, they sang.

* * *

That afternoon Patrice's stomach hurt. Alphonsine and her mother had gone into the forest and returned with some strange fruit. It was sweet and juicy with a slimy, stringy texture. It tasted good on an empty stomach. After a short time,

Patrice felt queasy. Then his stomach cramped. No more of *that* fruit, especially without anything to drink. He would rather eat raw sweet potatoes.

People continued to trail through the bush, past Mwilumba's encampment, avoiding the well-worn paths. In the late afternoon Mwilumba's party heard something in the distance— like thunder, but not quite. Those who were talking stopped, those who were playing games in the dirt looked up, those who were snoozing opened their eyes. Pop-pop-pop-crash-pop-pop. The adults stared at each other, for a moment, wide-eyed. Then their mouths grew taut, lines appeared in their faces, and their chins sagged as they looked at the ground. The children watched the adults.

Again, Mwiluba decided.

"To Kadima." It was the next village with a Methodist church, a place of refuge. Slowly, at the speed that Alphonsine's parents could walk, the household turned their backs on the farm and joined the stream of people heading through the bush, away from Kabalo.

Doctor Kasanka Directs Kabongo Hospital

> BEST SELLERS (Editor's Choices): *The Poisonwood Bible* by Barbara Kingsolver
>
> *The New York Times*, October 25, 1998

> "Then the man of God wept. Hazael asked, 'Why does my lord weep?' He answered, 'Because I know the evil that you will do to the people of Israel; you will set their fortresses on fire, you will kill their young men with the sword, dash in pieces their little ones, and rip up their pregnant women.'"
>
> 2 Kings 8:12

Lubumbashi to Kabongo, Haut Lomami District

April 1997 through October 1998

Dr. Kasanka's feet hurt when he boarded the bus in Lubumbashi to go home for the night. He fell gratefully into his seat and closed his eyes. Each day was like the next—he rose early to attend to patients at the Jason Sendwe government hospital and then took the bus to the private clinic. The days he was scheduled to teach rising medical students at the university he had to travel to a third location. He could not imagine longer days with less reward—he worked like a grunt, received meager pay, saw no opportunity for advancement, no way to build his curriculum vitae. His disillusionment had become palpable, aching like the bottom of his feet after each long day.

Then, the miraculous happened. At a church meeting he was approached by a Swiss missionary doctor who badly needed a physician to assist her on the staff of a government-supported church hospital. He would live and work in one place, spend more time seeing patients than riding the bus, and learn the skills of hospital administration. As one of two physicians, the position provided him an opportunity to emerge from anonymity, to show his superiors his dedication and his skill. She had arranged for Bishop Ntambo to appoint him. He had placed his foot on the first rung of an important ladder. . .

But in Kabongo, a remote town in North Katanga. When he told his family, the conversation began, continued, and ended badly. All but one uncle disapproved; they had no respect for a doctor in a rural outpost.

He dreaded telling Suzy. Between his work in Lubumbashi and her home in Kombove they could visit regularly. Moving to Kabongo took him away indefinitely, too far to travel. The train from Lubumbashi to Kamina took several days through the mountains, then Kamina to Kabongo required another two hundred kilometers through the bush. It might take a month to reach Kabongo with train breakdowns and the irregular schedule. Suzy still had one year of secondary school to complete, so they could not marry, even though he had finished his payments to her family.

Suzy cried when he told her the news. "You will forget me. You will find another woman in Kabongo who is closer."

Now that they had visited often, she had fallen joyfully in love with the young doctor, his dancing eyes, his passionate dreams, his ideals. She did not want to be disappointed.

He took her hand in his. Looking down, he brushed the skin of her arm so gently that the hair stood upright to his touch. Then he gazed at her, confidently, softly.

"I want only you."

* * *

The train puffed one urgent, final chug and rested on the tracks in Kabongo. From his seat Kasanka scanned the waiting crowd and found the missionary doctor in her white lab coat. She was shifting from foot to foot, waiting for him. He stood, lifted his luggage, jostled though the crowd down the aisle. When he emerged from the train, she brightened.

"*Wafwako, wafwako!*"

"*Eyo-vidye!*" The suitcase he carried clunked on the ground. He beamed in excitement: his first position of real responsibility! He believed himself to be more than ready to share the challenge of rural health care with the missionary doctor. He climbed into her white pick-up truck, and she drove directly to Kabongo Hospital.

As they approached, Kasanka's eyes swept across the medical campus for the first time: several large, concrete buildings fronted by a grassy lawn, divided by a dirt lane. A white sign with black and red painted letters announced:

Hôpital général de référence de Kabongo: Église méthodiste unie au Nord-Katanga.

His professional home. His future.

The missionary doctor parked in front of a long, one-story, white and yellow building. A shaded porch stretched its length, covered by a red roof supported by square white pillars.

She and Kasanka mounted the chipped brick steps. The hospital staff in white coats waited in the foyer, anticipating their arrival. "Dr. Kasanka, our new doctor. Our staff: Elizabeth, Muluka, Sabin, Eric."

"*Jambo.*" They greeted one another, but before they could say more, the missionary doctor led through the rear door, walking down the hall, making more introductions. Kasanka and the staff followed.

Beyond the first building, another loomed, this one yellow, blue and white. A little bit of *wuzungu* Switzerland in the middle of Congo.

But despite the décor, the campus felt familiar: its layout was much like the general hospital in Lubumbashi, only smaller. Covered stone walkways led from one building to another and around each building, protecting staff and patients from rain and sun. As they strode past open doors to semi-private rooms, telltale hospital sounds—a newborn whimpering, a family talking in soft tones—welcomed Kasanka like the cozy smell of firewood in his mother's kitchen.

Then, a bleat. Kasanka turned, surprised. Three goats grazed in the yard, munching on the grass. "Yes, we need a fence to keep out the goats. And the chickens. But we have other priorities."

She led into the interior of the building. A small office, an examination room, a spartan but clean surgery. They were crossing an exterior hall that led to the maternity ward when pounding footsteps and shrill voices reverberated from the lawn. Kasanka stared at a dozen teenagers who raced and whooped between the buildings, arriving and vanishing quickly, before anyone could scold. Their energy vibrated the walls of the hospital.

The missionary doctor stood at Kasanka's elbow. She shrugged. "The cemetery is behind the hospital. We lost one of their friends this week. Just finished the funeral. Teenagers letting off steam."

Kasanka shook his head: he was not in the big city of Lubumbashi anymore.

After showing him the wards, the missionary doctor returned to the truck, drove down the lane, across the street, through a gate, and parked in front of a white concrete house in a cluster of homes surrounded by a wall. "Here's your place." She motioned to a cottage with green shutters next door. "I live over there, with the nurse."

* * *

Medicine consumed his time. Each physician had their own examining room, though they shared the surgery. As soon as he awoke, he walked down the lane to the hospital and immersed himself in patient care, observing the doctor's techniques and improving his own as they repaired a hernia, performed a Caesarian section, or removed an enlarged prostate gland.

Each night Kasanka went home to his lovely house of many rooms. He unpacked his clothes, but otherwise, settled little. Sometimes he watched television with the doctor, the nurse, and other staff members at her cottage. Even there they discussed their cases.

Otherwise, no one visited. The hospital was located in Lubyai village in Kabongo terrority, an overgrown rural area of nearly thirteen thousand people. Kabongo had no reliable electricity, no clean water, no cars, no infrastructure, and lots of grass to breed mosquitoes. Children went barefoot, and people and animals circulated through the town together.

At six p.m. the entire town slept. It offered no social life, no circle of friends like he had experienced as a medical student in Lubumbashi. He lay in bed at night, imagining what Suzy might do to make the house into a home: filling the kitchen shelves with bananas, peanuts, rice and spinach, preparing chicken or fish with aromatic spices, finding small trinkets to decorate the living room. But she was far away. He wrote letters, and they spoke weekly on the ham radio. It was not enough.

Then in late August came the news: the war in the eastern Congo was threatening the interior. Foreign missionaries were being evacuated. The missionary doctor, nurse and finance director should prepare to leave for Nyembo Mpungu the next day. The doctor hurried her goodbyes to the nurses and administrators. She assured them she would not be gone long. It was only a precaution—the war would surely end soon and they could return.

The missionary doctor hugged Kasanka. "You have adapted to Kabongo well. I will remember you in my prayers."

It was to be a temporary assignment of acting responsibility. But three weeks later, the missionary boards withdrew their personnel from Kabongo. After only six months of preparation, Kasanka took the helm as medical director of the Kabongo Hospital.

* * *

Kasanka and the nurses were performing a Caesarean section when they heard an airplane overhead, not the purr of the single-engine medical evacuation flight but the commanding retort of a jet engine. Then, an explosion. They looked up, searched each other's eyes, and bowed their heads to bring a baby to life.

A few hours later, army trucks rumbled into Kabongo and turned down the hospital lane. Uniformed officers approached the receptionist.

"We need to see the doctor in charge of the hospital," one said in Swahili.

"I will find him." She hurried across the yard, and the officers followed. She opened the door to the surgery. "Dr. Kasanka, there are soldiers here to see you."

Kasanka did not look up from the incision he was stitching.

"When I finish."

She closed the door and stood with her back against it, blocking their entry. "He must conclude his surgery first."

"We will look around." The officers crossed the hall and opened the doors to the office and examination rooms. They were scrutinizing the contents of the pharmacy when Kasanka caught up with them.

"You wanted to see me?"

"We're Zimbabweans, here to support the Congolese army. We'll defend the airport—from here we can retake Tanganyika District, Kalemie and Kabalo. We have medical supplies but need a field hospital, a place to bring casualties. We want to see your facilities, make them ready to receive wounded soldiers. In fact, we have some injured civilians we we'll be bringing to you later today. We're also looking for quarters for our officers."

"I'll show you. But let's disturb the patients as little as possible."

Just as the missionary doctor had introduced him to the hospital six months earlier, Kasanka now escorted the Zimbabwean officers, showing what the hospital had as well as all it needed.

By the end of the day, the army had camped at the airport and stationed sentries around the hospital. The officers moved into the available bedrooms in the missionaries' cottage and Dr. Kasanka's house. The quiet, too-lonely compound now bustled with activity, but not the homey kind for which Kasanka wished.

The bombing of Kabongo that day, Kasanka learned, was a case of "friendly fire." The Zimbabweans had been told that the Rwandese were advancing from Kabalo to Kabongo. They were flying overhead when they saw a van headed toward Kabongo. Believing it to be the Rwandese, the Zimbabwean plane bombed the van.

But they had been mistaken. The Catholic priest and some assistants had loaded their car with important items they wanted to protect, but as they left Kabongo the van broke down, so they turned around. The van faced Kabongo, and the passengers were sitting on the side of the road, waiting for assistance. They were injured from flying debris but only required first aid when they were brought to Kasanka.

The Kabongo airstrip and its hospital a kilometer away—the Zimbabweans had found a prime place from which to stage the war.

Pastor Kahunda Hosts Many Guests

"Long War Saps Spirit and Money in Congo"

The New York Times, December 30, 1998

"For the Lord your God is God of gods and Lord of lords, the great God, mighty and awesome, who is not partial and takes no bribe, who executes justice for the orphan and the widow, and who loves the strangers, providing them with food and clothing."

Deuteronomy 10: 17-18

Kamina, Haut Lomami District

November 1998

Pastor Ngoie Kahunda wa Kazadi looked across the now-empty church sanctuary, smiled, and then sighed. His success was bittersweet. Large problems loomed ahead.

When the first displaced families had arrived in Kamina, Kahunda was relieved to see the colleagues with whom he had spent time in Mulungwishi. He found it easy to ask the parishes— as protocol required, in the name of Bishop—to assist these early guests. Kahunda found lodging for his colleagues in the orphanage and in pastors' homes.

Two weeks later another two hundred displaced people came out of the bush, Methodist pastors with members of other religious groups, seeking the help of Bishop. These people were also known to the church leaders. They had walked from towns and villages, Kabalo, Nyunzu, outside Kalemie, far away. Kahunda had known them as lean, physically fit Methodists who, until their displacement, had eaten well enough, worked hard, and paid their children's school fees—poor people, but not destitute. But when they shuffled into town, Kahunda saw them in a strange, decrepit state: their eyes drawn, their clothes torn, their bodies caked with sand and mud. Some of their children and elderly relatives had died en route. Finding safety in Kahunda's office, many of them wept, first from relief and then from grief over the loss of their relatives and property.

"How to care for them?" Kahunda asked Bishop.

"I will encourage, you organize," Bishop had told Kahunda.

Bishop had gathered the displaced pastors and their families and spoken to them warmly, sympathetically. "'Come, all you who are weary and heavy-laden, and I will give you rest.' This is Jesus' promise in the book of Matthew. Kamina will be the place where Jesus' promise is fulfilled—a city of peace and hope for those who seek refuge."

The pastors murmured, "Amen!"

Kahunda and Bishop assigned the second set of families to different parishes that worked together to feed and clothe the guests. The faithful rose to the occasion: it was the gospel in action.

Now, every day, a few more people walked into town, hungry, dirty, bedraggled. Word had spread in the bush: the Methodist church in Kamina would help. So Methodists arrived with strangers who had joined them as they walked. They found their way to the conference office where Kahunda heard their pleas.

"Do you have water or food? We have not found clean water or real food in a week. Do you know a place we can sleep?"

He knew the weight—water, food, utensils, clothes—that now fell on the church members, so he gathered some of the recently arrived guests. "Go to the district commissioner. See if he can help you." But they returned empty handed, and Kahunda was summoned to the government offices.

"We are not organized to help these people. But you are the church—you will need to do it."

Day after day, Kahunda welcomed them with traditional greetings, *Wafwako, Praise God.* But he could find no words of his own to express the compassion he felt or responsibility that rested on his shoulders. So each night, when his anguish overflowed, he turned away from the people, sought a quiet corner, and prayed. Sometimes he reminded himself of the spirit of hospitality in the Old Testament:

"Once, you were a stranger in Egypt, and God led you out."

Or he read Matthew 25: 44-45. "Then they also will answer, 'Lord, when was it that we saw you hungry or thirsty or a stranger or naked or sick or in prison, and did not take care of you?' Then he will answer them, 'Truly I tell you, just as you did not do it to one of the least of these, you did not do it to me."

Or he prayed the 23rd Psalm:

> The Lord is my shepherd, I shall not want.
>> He makes me lie down in green pastures;
> he leads me beside still waters;
>> he restores my soul.
> He leads me in right paths
>> for his name's sake.
>
> Even though I walk through the darkest valley,
>> I fear no evil;
> for you are with me;
>> your rod and staff—
>> they comfort me.
>
> You prepare a table before me

in the presence of my enemies;
you anoint my head with oil;
   my cup overflows.

Surely goodness and mercy shall follow me
   all the days of my life,
and I shall dwell in the house of the Lord
   my whole life long."

Then he could go on.

* * *

On Saturdays, Kahunda met with Bishop and his team. New refugees often sat outside the conference office, waiting for assistance. The team had to pick their path around them, step by step, being reminded of the suffering that gathered in Kamina. So the team began their meeting with churning stomachs.

"You see them waiting there. They need so much, and we have so little to give them," Kahunda began on a Saturday in early November. "Every day more come. I hurt for them. When I can't help, I can't face them."

Even then—a knock on the door. It opened slowly, a grubby face appeared. "Please, just a little food, some water…"

The families of Kamina could not absorb their guests into the existing housing any further. The newcomers slept in churches, in government buildings, in makeshift shelters. Finally, they built mud huts at the edge of town. Within a few weeks, a suburb of tiny homes had expanded the usual boundaries of Kamina.

* * *

One Saturday in late November, after two months of receiving new guests every day, Kahunda made a proposal to the team. "Let's create one central place for a large distribution—have one large gathering of supplies—hopefully it will sustain our guests for a while."

Bishop seconded the idea. "I will ask the people of the surrounding towns as far as Malemba to give what they can; Ilunga Mutombo and the driver Faustin will pick up their donations in the truck."

On the next Sunday morning the pastors asked their congregations to bring all the donations they could to Kamina Centre, Katuba, Six-Four, and Centre Ville Church. After church Kahunda assembled the displaced superintendents. He directed them to rearrange the lines of wood benches into square stalls so that they could separate each category of goods. The air smelled of sweat and grit as the men worked, making the sanctuaries of the churches into a market.

Kahunda's family had already offered all the food, utensils, and clothing they could. But Kahunda remembered the words of Exodus 22:21: "once you were a slave in Egypt and the Lord delivered you, so do for your brothers and sisters, also." Surely, he could add to the items for the distribution—but what? Then he remembered the expensive, dark blue suit he had worn for his graduation from the seminary at Mulungwishi. He hustled to his hut, retrieved the suit, and piled it on the bin of clothing.

When they were prepared, Kahunda called the musicians. They beat the drums and sang rousing songs. Women of Kamina brought calabashes filled with salt, oil, and flour, balanced on their heads, and bundles of clothing and cooking utensils tied to their backs. Men carried couches, *air kabongo* chairs and mattresses. They deposited their donations in the appropriate stalls, and then stood outside the church, singing, clapping, and swaying to the music. When the collection was complete, Kahunda prayed for the hosts, the guests, and an end to the war. Again, the music resounded as the group sang in response. But the displaced families quieted quickly. They gathered around the superintendents from their district, who led each family in turn into the market to take what they needed from the stalls. All were served. They left quickly, eager to cook the food they had received.

Kahunda was satisfied with the way the distribution had gone. But a few men and women from Kamina hovered in the corner of the church, and when all of the displaced left, approached Kahunda. One man spoke for the group.

"Pastor, you have preached about our Christian responsibilities. Please understand—we suffer with our guests from Tanganyika. But our families can't donate much more."

Kahunda nodded, without speaking, the ache of hunger gnawing at his gut. The local population had reached the limit of its ability to give. His own family strained to feed the family now living with them. Kahunda, a lean, wiry man of medium build, carried no extra fat on his belly, but he ate less so that the cassava his wife prepared each day could feed more mouths. *How will the town continue to care for so many guests?* Kamina had become like a savannah that had been picked bare—no fruits, no animals, no termite hills, no wood. Just red clay dirt and a few scrawny plants to feed the people.

* * *

Bishop's team sat in the conference room in the Methodist building, well aware of the importance of today's agenda. No one spoke.

Bishop bowed his head. "I pray to God for the health of our community, for our displaced families, and for peace throughout Congo. Amen."

Then he looked at his leaders. "You are about to become like oxen, with a yoke around your shoulders. We cannot carry the burden alone any longer.

UMCOR is sending a team. They will see the need, and the international church will provide the funds. But you, the church leaders, the oxen, must organize everything. You must do all of the work. And no one, no one, may take what does not belong to him."

Kahunda, John Mutombo, Ilunga Mutombo, and others looked directly at Bishop and nodded. "We are ready!"

Then the room became so quiet that even the distant thunder dared not interrupt.

Bishop searched their eyes. Then he turned to Kahunda. "What is it?"

"We're worried about *you*. People with an education are a target for the rebels. We've discussed it among ourselves, and we agree. Leave. Go to America. We can carry on."

Bishop felt a jabbing pain, as if someone had thrown a spear into his heart. *To leave my people when they are suffering more than ever?* His mind raced. His presence endangered them. To the local Congolese army, he was suspect because of his connections with the Americans, the *Banyamulenge*, the Burundian. He felt stained, contaminated. *Even with them gone, I am tainted. If Rwanda takes Kamina, they will kill the leaders.*

Nshimba. She too was in danger. *How to leave?* Gaston and his family now lived in the United States. It was time to acquiesce to the one remaining missionary pilot who was also urging him to leave.

"Yes, you are right. I am no good to you dead and perhaps a danger to you alive."

The relief in the room was louder than the rain pelting the windows. Kahunda began to sing in Kiswahili, and they all joined in a hymn taught by the missionaries:

> When we walk with the Lord, in the light of his Word,
> what a glory he sheds on our way!
> While we do his good will, He abides with us still,
> and with all who will trust and obey.
> Trust and obey, for there's no other way,
> to be happy with Jesus, but to trust and obey.

Headmaster Mwilumba Assists the Soldiers

> "Talks on a Cease-Fire in Congo End: Peace Gets Only Lip Service"
>
> *The New York Times*, September 9, 1998

> "When you gather the grapes of your vineyard, do not glean what is left; it shall be left for the alien, the orphan, and the widow."
>
> Deuteronomy 24:21-22

Kadima, Tanganyika District

September 1998 through January 1999

Mwilumba's party, about thirty people in all, edged their way west to the shore of the Lualaba River. Once there, they picked a path that led directly south through the brush along its banks. The undergrowth scratched their ankles. The mosquitoes bit their legs and arms. They ate little. Their hunger had been quelled by anxiety and fear.

Over the next week other refugees joined them, until the crowd resembled a colony of ants fleeing their hill, some crawling fast and some slow, some skittering back into the bush before returning to the river. Alphonsine's parents rested often, giving Mwilumba time to talk with new travellers who had overtaken them.

Each refugee family brought more reports of Congolese and Rwandese soldiers gathering near Kabalo. Together, they speculated.

"Will the Congolese army defend the population?"

"The army is angry."

"The soldiers have not benefitted from President Kabila's government. They have not been paid. The Rwandese offer food and salaries, so the Congolese soldiers tell them about the terrain, the villages, the leadership and their loyalties."

To hear the newcomers talk, Mwilumba thought the entire army had defected to the aggressors.

When Mwilumba's group reached the river crossing, they traded some of their clothing for passage on a *pirogue*. They crowded with others into the large canoe on a moonlit night, submerging the sides almost to its gunwales. But the captain knew exactly how many people he could carry to the other side. He poled the boat into the current, ferried across at the narrow point, and landed them in the crook of the river's arm. The far shore wrapped itself protectively around them, shielding them from danger.

They walked two kilometers west, inland to the village of Kadima where they found the hut of a Methodist pastor. And there they learned that they had passed into territory currently controlled by a friendlier force.

On the western side of the Lualaba many Congolese soldiers had remained loyal to President Kabila. They had been reinforced by troops sent from Zimbabwe, Angola and Namibia. These allies were gathering at Katutu, fifty kilometers to the southwest. Some soldiers were already travelling northeast, preparing to resist the Rwandese invasion at the river.

The refugees had sought sanctuary near the front between the two opposing forces.

* * *

They lived in the church, all thirty of them, and made what they could of a normal life. The church gave them a few supplies: a yellow jerry can for water, seeds, and cassava to get by. They fished at the river and planted a garden. In the early rainy season, the spinach and cabbage quickly sprouted and grew.

Mwilumba gathered the young village children and began to teach. He instructed them in their letters, some simple words, addition and subtraction.

Every night they sang—folk songs, hymns they knew from church, Bible verses set to music, old melodies with new words that described their adventure. Patrice clicked his fingers to set the beat, and everyone joined the chorus, raising spirits, hoping again.

Mwilumba and Alphonsine hugged, kissed, and snuggled together as a couple. In quiet moments they found life in each other's bodies. Alphonsine's body changed in a familiar way, and she realized she was pregnant with their fifth child.

They sought news from Kabalo. Every day they heard of more aggressors. Finally, a traveller reported that the Rwandese army had captured Kabalo.

The family stood together in the church, leaning against one another, as Mwilumba questioned the traveller. He shook his head as he answered. "The Rwandese occupy your farm. They eat your food. They have sold all your belongings, even what you hid. Nothing is left."

Cherita lowered her head and stared at the ground in the middle of the church. Her bicycle, her mother's sewing machine. . . but her tears remained hidden, soaking her heart.

Mwilumba, Alphonsine, her parents, their children and the guests they had welcomed to their farm now slept together on leaves and branches in the church in Kadima. No way home, and nowhere else to go, except through military barriers.

* * *

Most days the refugees walked two kilometers from Kadima to Kyalo, the village by the river, to catch fish and haul water. There, they watched as well-armed soldiers arrived by foot and in trucks. The boss man, Major Mataruka, dressed in his crisp Zimbabwean uniform, strode through the village with confidence. He commanded all the soldiers—the ones dressed like himself and those wearing the colors of Angola and Namibia.

Mataruka distrusted the Congolese army. They were undisciplined and changed sides at will, today fighting for Rwanda, tomorrow, for Kabila. The next day, who knew where their loyalties would lie? The Congolese soldiers who helped the Rwandese gave them an advantage. The major had to even the odds, to find Congolese loyal to Kabila who knew the villages and the terrain. But first, he needed a translator. The Zimbabweans and Namibians spoke English, the Angolans Portuguese, and each a different native African language. The Congolese in this area spoke French, Kiswahili, Kiluba, and Lingala. The Zimbabwean commander could not communicate with the local people.

One of Mataruka's soldiers knew a few words of Kiswahili. So the major sent him to make friends with the ones believed to be least dangerous and most impressionable—the village children. The soldier drove his truck slowly down a lane between a group of huts, and a crowd of ragamuffins collected behind him, entertaining themselves by trying to outrun the truck. He halted.

"*Rafiki, rafiki*, my friends, my friends! You want chicken? sugar?"

Hearing the soldier speak Kiswahili, the children crowded round, pushing at each other, "*Jambo*, we greet you!" They grinned widely and stretched out their hands. The ones in the back of the crowd jumped high, trying to be seen.

The soldier threw bagged rations toward the children. They caught the packages, ripped them open and plucked out the contents. They chewed and sucked, looking up at their benefactor with doleful eyes.

"Now, tell me, who speaks English and your native language?" the soldier asked, holding high more ration bags.

"Mwilumba, the schoolmaster," a young boy replied, holding out his hand.

"Where can we find this Mwilumba?"

Several children answered in chorus, reaching. "Kadima!"

"*Jambo!*" The soldier threw the rest of the ration bags over their heads, away from the truck. They landed on the ground, and the children turned and scrambled toward them. The soldier sped away, eager to report his success to the major, leaving the little ones to collect their treats.

* * *

Mataruka and his soldier drove their truck down the dirt road into Kadima. Villagers working the gardens in front of their huts stopped and stared. *The army has never come to this village. What does it mean?* The major halted at a hut. He was met by a wizened old man.

"Mwilumba?"

"*Pale*. Over there."

The man grunted a command to a little boy playing nearby. The youngster jumped up and sprinted toward the church. When he found Mwilumba, he was breathing hard. "The army man wants you!"

What could they want with me? It is the last day for us! But before Mwilumba could gather his family, he heard a deep voice call from outside the church.

"Mwilumba! Please come here."

English? Mwilumba pulled himself up as tall as possible, almost five feet, squared his shoulders, assumed the authority of a headmaster, and walked out the door to face the major. "What do you want with me?"

"Are you Mwilumba?" The Zimbabwean waited till Mwilumba nodded.

Then the major continued in English, speaking slowly, allowing Mwilumba time to absorb his meaning.

"We are Zimbabweans. We support the local soldiers and President Kabila. We need someone who can translate English, Kiluba, Kiswahili, and Lingala. We have come from Namibia, Angola and Zimbabwe to help you. You can serve your country with us. You, Mwilumba, a schoolmaster, can be a patriot."

As the major was speaking, Alphonsine, the children, her parents and some of their guests edged their way behind Mwilumba. He felt their presence.

Mwilumba thought. Then waited. Finally, he spoke firmly, matching the tone and tempo of the Zimbabwean. "We are Christians. Teachers and musicians. Not soldiers. Before I go with you, I must consult my family."

"I will wait for your answer." The major turned toward his truck, leaving them some privacy.

Mwilumba faced his family, somber. "We have never been soldiers. Not in my family, not in Mama's family. It's not our character. No killing, no raping, no corruption. But we have fled into the bush. I have left my school, my pupils behind." He paused and looked deep into their eyes, one by one, reading their thoughts.

Then Mwilumba decided. "I will protect our country and those who came to help."

They nodded. Fifteen minutes later Mwilumba rode in an army truck to Kyalo for the first time.

* * *

From the end of September until the middle of January, Mwilumba spent each day with the army. He always arrived before the sun rose. Sometimes he walked briskly from Kadima to Kyalo; other times, he rode on the rear fender of the pastor's bicycle with Patrice peddling. The faithful little man beamed a smile when he reported at Mataruka's door each morning.

The major demonstrated a moment of warmth, flickered a smile. Then he became matter-of-fact and assumed an authoritative distance, briefing Mwilumba on his day's duties.

Over the next months Mataruka seemed to become fond of his new recruit. He shared his binoculars, and together they reviewed the land and the approaches over the river. Mwilumba explained the various routes from Kyalo to Kabalo. They analyzed the possible movements of Rwandese. They engaged others in conversation. Mwilumba identified Congolese persons the major could trust and brought them to advise him. Occasionally, the major's soldiers caught a Rwandese scout, and the major interrogated him with Mwilumba translating.

* * *

On the morning of January 18, 1999 Mwilumba appeared at the major's house. The engineer who was installing guns along the riverbank had just called on the ham radio. A Congolese woman, her child on her back, was trying to tell the engineer something. But they were getting nowhere. Would Mwilumba please go to the river and translate for the engineer? The major would finish the briefing after Mwilumba returned.

As he was standing at the river, engrossed in translation, Mwilumba heard a sudden whirr. His head jerked up in the direction of the sound. Beyond the engineer and the woman, he saw what looked like a two-foot bullet that had landed on the sandy bank. But nothing happened. He stepped back a few yards to see where the thing came from, looking across the river. He saw Rwandese on the opposite bank.

Suddenly, he heard a crash and felt tremendous heat. His body rose into the air. Then all was dark.

* * *

Patrice had returned almost to Kadima when he heard the explosions by the river. He peddled fast, entered the village, leaned the bike onto the wall of the church, and yelled, "They are shooting!" He hugged his mother tightly.

But there was nothing to do, except till the garden and wait for word.

Villagers had gone into Kyalo to market that morning. They scurried back to the village, bringing disconcerting news.

"A bomb landed. Papa Mwilumba is dead!"

Alphonsine shrieked and put her hands to her face. Cherita gasped, locked her mother in an ironclad embrace, and wept loudly. Eschler and Dada grabbed at her legs. Patrice stood silently, tears streaming down his face.

A few minutes later a second villager brought a different report. "They hit the guns on the bank. A woman and her child were blown apart. A soldier died. But Mwilumba lives. He was burned. He cannot see or hear."

Patrice grabbed the pastor's bike and steadied it, and Alphonsine hopped side-saddle onto the fender. Cherita picked up Dada and held Eschler close to her legs. "God be with you!" she pled. Patrice pushed the bike to a glide and then pumped as fast as he could. Soon, his chest and back were coated in his sweat and his mother's tears.

* * *

The soldiers confirmed the gruesome report. The first artillery shell had hit the Zimbabwean guns but not exploded. The second killed the engineer and blew the woman and her child to bits. Mwilumba, who stood a few feet away, was knocked onto the sandy bank of the river. The army had already moved him to their field hospital at Ngwena, the place of the first military barrier around Kyalo and Kadima.

Major Mataruka was sympathetic. "He has worked with us. We will fly him by helicopter to the military hospital at Kamina Base. But you can't go. We can't care for civilians."

"May we see him?" Alphonsine asked.

"Hurry."

At the field hospital Alphonsine saw what had become of her husband. His eyes and ears were badly burned; he could not see or hear. His skin had lost its pigment; he was as white as a *muzungu*. Mwilumba could not touch his wife and son to impart his blessing. When Alphonsine and Patrice said goodbye, they knew it was likely forever.

Doctor Kasanka Treats Patients in the War Zone

"WORLD; A War Turned Free-For-All Tears at Africa's Center"
The New York Times, December 6, 1998

"For we cannot pray as we ought. . .but that very Spirit intercedes for us with sighs too deep for words."
Romans 8:26

Kabongo, Haut Lomami District
January 1999

As he neared the military barrier beyond the village of Kamungu at 6:30 in the evening, half an hour after curfew, Dr. Kasanka expected trouble. He slowed his motorbike and lowered his feet to the ground, balancing the bike. The Congolese soldiers, in fatigues and maroon berets, met him with their guns pointed.

"Curfew is six o'clock! No passing!"

Kasanka had anticipated this moment and had tucked his passport visibly into his front shirt pocket. "May I show you my identity card? I am a doctor."

The soldier stared at him, unmoved, unimpressed.

Kasanka withdrew his passport and held it out to the nearest soldier. "Been treating villagers with cholera in Nyembo." His voice raised a note, pleading. "Patients are waiting at Kabongo Hospital."

He paused. The soldier remained silent.

"Please, I *must* travel another thirty kilometers tonight."

As he spoke, he looked the soldier in the eye, gently, firmly, not moving his head. But he worried that his voice had betrayed his anxiety. He mentally chided himself—perhaps he had yielded too much authority in the tat-a-tat.

The soldier ignored his outstretched hand and did not move the gun from Kasanka's chest. "We have our orders. No one passes after six o'clock!"

"I treat soldiers. If your wounded are brought to the hospital, they will not have a doctor to take care of them."

"No exceptions. Go back to Nyembo. Come again tomorrow."

Further entreaties would only endanger his life. Reluctantly, Kasanka turned his motorbike in the direction from which he had come, back down the road through the village of Kamungu. Then his face stiffened with resolve. Entering the village center, he asked to see the commanding officer.

* * *

In his new role Kasanka needed the patience and self-assuredness of old bull elephants greeting one another on a plain. The bulls, who in advanced age live away from the herd, plod toward one another with unhurried dignity until they face each other, touch their foreheads gently in greeting, back away, and turn to walk back across the plain to their solitary existence. They communicate an aura of knowledge and self-possession, an image of manly maturity.

Kasanka was the only doctor serving Kabongo Hospital, the whole of Kabongo, and the surrounding villages. Though he was always with people, the responsibility left him lonelier than ever. But instead of feeling like a wise bull elephant, he identified with the lizards that skittered along the wall of a compound, quickly changing color to adapt to a new environment, resting only occasionally.

As a medical student, he had enjoyed urban Lubumbashi. The city vibrated with energy: from the third-floor windows of the Methodist Center he looked out at the peach-colored Park Hotel, which boasted provincial lattice balconies and was surrounded by palm trees. Below him the cars and bicycles wove through one another on the street, and pedestrians spilled into to the public square at will. They promenaded into the central market and along the store-fronts and lolled about in bars and restaurants.

In the last year he had adjusted to the quiet of Kabongo, the rural medical hospital, the low bush trees and scrub brush, grasses and weeds, the quiet dirt streets, the thatched mud huts, the erratic electricity, the hauled water. The most difficult part had been the lack of social life. But he had gotten to know the people and established a doctor-patient relationship with many.

Now, as 1999 arrived, the village of Kabongo had transformed entirely, and Kasanka had changed with it. Most of his patients from the native population had fled. He treated strangers who arrived at a teeming rural war hospital. The soldiers and displaced people brought daily medical emergencies, but supplies arrived only occasionally through the fighting.

Kasanka would not have ventured to Nyembo had he not received special visitors a month earlier. The administrative assistant had opened the door to the surgery and announced, "Dr. Kasanka, MSF, *Médecins sans frontières* to see you."

Kasanka concentrated on the hernia he was repairing and murmured, "I am not finished."

When Kasanka was satisfied with the surgery, he joined his guests. They were already deep in conversation with the head hospital administrator. The doctors summarized quickly: they had an office at Kitenge and were visiting Kabongo to survey the medical needs of internally displaced people.

"You the only doctor here?"

Kasanka nodded. The visitor's eyes flickered for a moment with compassion, then resumed their direct professionalism. "We've brought some supplies and can provide medicines as you need them."

"*Wafwako*. We're waiting for medicines from the church, got some help from the Zimbabwean army and the International Red Cross. We'd appreciate anything."

"Who're your patients?"

"Everyone. The people of Kabongo, the people from the bush villages. Soldiers—Zimbabwean, Congolese, Rwandese. Displaced. Most of them have walked from Uvira, Kabalo, Nyunzu."

Many of the displaced from the towns in Tanganyika thought they were safe near the Zimbabwean army. They hoped that they would not have to walk another two hundred kilometers to Kamina.

"Be in touch on the radio."

"*Wafwako*."

* * *

The breathless man on the bicycle had swung his legs to the ground and had jabbered at the first nurse he saw at Kabongo Hospital. "Diarrhea, vomiting, fever, many people," he had panted. The nurse brought him immediately to Kasanka.

Cholera. A whole village can die in a few days, Kasanka diagnosed.

Kasanka checked his pharmaceutical cabinet. His supply of rehydration medications was very low. *Not enough for a village.* He stood for a moment, his head in his hands, agonizing. *I can treat cholera, if only I have the correct medicine and equipment.* But he lifted his head, remembering his visitors. If he could confirm the diagnosis, MSF might bring the proper pharmaceuticals and supplies.

In the hospital yard he checked his motorbike. It seemed capable of the forty-one kilometers from Kabongo to Nyembo. He made his decision.

"I must go to Nyembo. You're in charge here," he told the head nurse.

He packed his paltry supply of medicines in his saddlebag and added a jar of drinking water, some food and his exam kit. He tucked his identity card into his pocket where it was close at hand should he need it. Then, strapping an extra can of fuel to the back of his bike, he headed over the rutted, sandy roads to the village. Once, a thunderstorm roared overhead, and he rode into the bush, taking refuge under the canopy of trees. After that, he wove the bike between the red clay mud puddles that filled the ruts in the road.

The trip took two hours. He easily passed the military barrier at Kime, twelve kilometers from Kabongo, where all of the soldiers knew him. The barrier at Kamungu was more difficult. There, he had to explain and show his identity card. He reached Nyembo in the late morning.

In the village Kasanka was greeted by the chief. Four people had already died; many others were ill. He asked to see the children, examined them, noted their symptoms, and gave them what medicines he had. He counted the sick villagers. In the early afternoon he began his journey back to Kabongo where he could call for assistance on the radio.

* * *

Kasanka had followed the protocol precisely; everything was arranged. He would meet MSF at the village, introduce them, and help them organize the makeshift hospital ward. The doctors would begin the rehydration treatment early in the afternoon, and Kasanka could return to Kabongo.

He had left Kabongo at dawn and had motorbiked a few kilometers toward Nyembo when a bicycle came into view—an ambulance, outfitted with a seat for a sick person on the rear fender, travelling in the direction of Kabongo. He slowed.

"I am Dr. Kasanka from Kabongo Hospital."

"She has been in labor for two days. She's originally from Kabalo. Her family is walking behind. I am taking her to your hospital."

The woman's face was contorted, and suddenly she cried out. Then, as the pain subsided, her cry became a whimper. *Two days*, thought Kasanka. *She has certainly seen the village herbalist. She likely needs surgery.*

"I have an emergency in Nyembo," he told the woman. "But I'll only be gone a few hours. If your baby hasn't arrived when I return, we can do a Caesarean-section."

She nodded, without speaking.

As he motorbiked, his lizard-like mind raced back and forth between his patients in Kabongo and Nyembo. *This woman, and who else will arrive at the hospital while I am gone?*

He hoped her baby would be delivered while he was in Kabongo. But he knew it was unlikely.

* * *

In the cholera-stricken village just outside Nyembo, Kasanka arrived before MSF. When the villagers heard Kasanka's motorbike, the healthy ones ran from their huts to welcome him. One of them spoke. "More villagers are ill."

Kasanka took charge. "Healthy men, follow me." They walked around the outskirts of the village, and Kasanka chose the spot. "We will build our ward here. Get your machetes, clear a path and then an area in the bush beyond the village. Set aside any solid branches. When MSF arrive, they will have a tarp for a roof. It will cover the beds." He spent the morning with the men, preparing. Finally, they heard the slow chug of a truck engine picking its way over the rutted trails. The healthy villagers ran toward the truck, the men cheering, the women ululating.

Kasanka greeted the doctors, quickly leading them to the clearing. They worked swiftly, erecting the tent and unloading six of the special beds outfitted with holes so that the ill could defecate into disposable containers. Here, the patients would be less likely to infect others.

When MSF saw the extent of the illness in the village, they consulted with Kasanka. If he would begin the IV's on the first six people, they would return to Kitenge for additional beds. Kasanka had not expected to remain away from Kabongo Hospital for so long. But now he had patients in Nyembo.

"Of course," he replied.

"We'll be back in a few hours."

Within moments, the doctors left, and Kasanka turned toward the village. At first, the responsibility overwhelmed him. Then he straightened his shoulders. He knew what decisions faced him. As he walked toward the first hut, he prayed.

God, I cannot be the one who decides who lives. Only you must do that. I will treat the first six I meet who will likely survive. Let it be your will.

He entered the first hut. The family surrounded a young woman, lifting a jar of water to her lips. In the corner, an old man lay unconscious on a mat, a young man by his side. Kasanka spoke gently. "Carry your daughter to the ward, and pray for the soul of your grandfather." And so his journey continued until six patients lay in the beds. He poked their arms with IV needles and sent their family members away.

When MSF returned, Kasanka said his good-byes.

It was already six-thirty p.m., after the military curfew, when he turned his motorbike toward the village of Kamungu. He was tired. But having left his cholera patients in the hands of the doctors who could do more for them than he could, the image of the woman in labor on the bicycle formed in his mind and held fast. *God, let her live,* he prayed. He experienced a new rush of adrenalin, energizing him to ride the forty-one kilometers to Kabongo.

* * *

Kasanka fumed as he rode back into Kamungu to find the commanding officer. *The soldiers are stubborn. They like their power. Who do they think they are, gods over life and death?*

His bike nearly spilled in a rut in the road, so he focused on the path, which calmed him. The sun was setting. Entering the village center, he drove directly to the military headquarters. He sought to assert the strength of the bull elephant.

"I want to see the commanding officer," he said in a calm, firm voice.

"In a moment."

The officer arrived. Kasanka spoke swiftly. "I am the only doctor at Kabongo Hospital. I have been treating villagers with cholera in Nyembo. I have other patients I need to see in Kabongo."

"I remember you," the officer said. "I'll send someone with you to the barrier to verify your identity. Please wait."

Kasanka sat, worrying about the woman in labor, wondering whether her baby had arrived.

Finally, the commanding officer returned. "I can't find anyone. I'll go with you myself."

* * *

At eight o'clock in the morning Kasanka finally neared Kabongo. The confusion in Kamungu had wasted valuable hours. Once he had passed the barrier, he picked his way through the moonlight over rutted, damp roads. The barrier at Kime had not presented a problem; all of the soldiers knew him. In the dawn light he increased his pace, gunning the bike up to the hospital. He parked near the maternity ward.

A family sat outside on the concrete sidewalk. The women were crying. Kasanka felt his throat tighten as the nurse approached with tears in her eyes.

"The woman said she met you on the road. She could not hang on; she lost too much blood. The baby did not survive, either."

Kasanka could not speak. But his soul cried out like the wheezing, nasal, mournful trumpeting of an aged elephant, one who had seen much death in its long life. Its call rose and sharpened as realization yielded to anger and then to anguish. Aloud, Kasanka moaned lowly, a lament too deep for words.

Bishop Ntambo Dreams in Tanzania

"In Congo Carnage, How Many Died?"

New York Times, January 10, 1999

"I loathe my life; I will give free utterance to my complaint; I will speak in the bitterness of my soul. I will say to God, 'Do not condemn me; let me know why you contend against me. Does it seem good to you to oppress, to despise the work of your hands and favor the schemes of the wicked?'"

Job 10:1-3

Tanzania

January 1999

Now settled in temporary lodgings in Tanzania, Bishop Ntambo slept restlessly. Not wanting to wake Nshimba, he left their bedroom and laid down on the living room couch. Half asleep, half awake, he sprawled across the couch with his head lying cocked, his eyes closed, his legs outstretched, a light blanket across his chest and lap. Memory fragments circling his mind. Capturing him.

Kamina. Ghosts from ham radio.

Static, crackle. Voice.

"Hundred villagers, church members, killed today."

"People running, all directions. Old ones left behind. Children losing parents. Chaos."

"Rwandese forced brother rape sister family watched."

"Woman staggering on road. Crying, bleeding. Home alone, family fled. Gave birth, hut bloody. Baby lived. Tutsi enter, poking, chortling."

"Soldiers demand answer. How church got concrete, tin roofing, who sends? Who got money, connections? Bishop Ntambo. Army knows your name."

"District superintendent ran, hid radio. Soldiers arrested, found radio. Accused him to send messages. Shot him dead."

Ghosts laugh.

Kamina. My old Mama, one hundred and seventy relatives. How can honorable son, leader, abandon brothers, cousins, even his own mother?

Mama appears. "Go. Fly with missionary to Lubumbashi. We care for ourselves." Mama leaves for bush. Ntambo, Nshimba, children board Cessna.

Plane floats on clouds. Engine drones. Silence. Don't speak. Stare to pilot. Can't start engine. Hear each other think. Emergency landing.

Missionary calls commercial plane. Junk airline. *Trust mechanics have done right this time. Pray without ceasing.*

Land in Lubumbashi. Safe.

* * *

Lubumbashi. Main street. Soldiers, Congolese, Rwandese, Angolans. Each one pointing. "Bishop Ntambo? We kill his people. His family. Him. Every one."

Silence from Kamina. *Who to trust? Go to Tanzania.*

Tanzania. Pastors and members from Kalemie, Moba, sheltered in churches. More stories. Families separated, encounters with soldiers.

Congolese refugees, Tanzanian churches. Nshimba and children, safe. Me, dishonored. Humiliated. Crying for my people, dead, violated. Dreams, looted, again. No peace.

You, God, why you contend against me?

As if to break free from the cell of dreams and memories in which he was imprisoned, Bishop Ntambo roused, threw the blanket to the ground, and rose. The action offered momentary respite from his thoughts. Three a.m. What to do now?

Mama Alphonsine Protects the Children

"The African Question, Who is To Blame? The Finger Points to the West, and Congo is a Harsh Example"

The New York Times, January 16, 1999

"My eyes are spent with weeping; my stomach churns; my bile is poured out on the ground because of the destruction of my people, because infants and babes faint in the streets of the city. They cry to their mothers, 'Where is bread and wine?' as they faint like the wounded in the streets of the city, as their life is poured out on their mothers' bosom."

Lamentations 2:11-12

In the bush from Kadima to Kamina

January through April 1999

Mama Alphonsine rested with her elderly parents and her children, Patrice, Cherita, Dada and Eschler under the canopy of branches and leaves that covered the deep bush. That day, when the rains came, the family had taken refuge under a strong tree, keeping some ground dry for their camp. But the heavy rain had penetrated the forest more than usual. Now, they slept sitting upright, leaning against its trunk to avoid the moist ground. Alphonsine's father rested across her abdomen, the slight bulge of her pregnancy providing him a bit of cushion. Her embrace warmed him. He was so frail. He had lost any protective fat and most of his muscle. She worried that he would not survive the trek to Kamina, even at the slow pace they set for themselves.

After Mwilumba was burned by the bomb, the family feared that the Rwandese could make their way to the villages beyond the river. They had left Kadima and bushwhacked toward Kamina, where they could ask Bishop for assistance.

* * *

They hoped that the deep bush would provide safety from soldiers. One day they discovered that they were not beyond the possibility of military harm. On the trail they came across a woman, lying on her side, the wrap of her *kikwembe* still tied around her, bulging on her back.

"Wait," Alphonsine commanded softly, holding out her hands to the stop the others.

She walked ahead alone, stopping a respectful distance from the body. The woman had been shot and the blood from the wounds had dried. Insects were beginning to circle, land and pick, but no animals had yet disturbed her. The wrap held her child snug against her body. The baby whimpered indiscriminately but did not look at Alphonsine. *How long did they run? Where from? What now?* Alphonsine was tempted to untie the mother's wrap and lift the child from her back, but she hesitated. If the mother's spirit was nearby and restless, she did not want to provoke it carelessly.

Alphonsine returned to her family. She pointed a short way into the bush, off the trail. "Let's rest." They circled around and sat, no one directly facing the body that lay ahead of them.

"What to do?"

"If we leave the baby here," Cherita said, tears in her eyes, "it will die."

"Perhaps the family is in a nearby village. They will search for the mother. If we take the baby with us, the mother's ghost could make trouble for us for separating it from its family," her father said.

"We will wait to see if the family comes," Alphonsine decided. "We will pray and see if there is a sign."

Patrice and Cherita harmonized a mournful song, one that could soothe the mother's spirit. The family prayed, and then they sat silently. More insects swarmed around the mother's wounds, and the baby cried loudly. Alphonsine spoke. "It is time for us to move on."

"Perhaps it's better that the mother and baby die together. Spirits find each other. The mother will be comforted," said Alphonsine's mama.

"But our Christian faith tells us to protect the orphan," Patrice offered.

"Our tradition is strong, but Christ is the way," Cherita pled.

Alphonsine decided. "We'll take the baby. We'll make peace with the ancestors of the family, pray to them that we're doing a good thing for the baby and its mother, who is lost. She'll want her baby to live. Dada is old enough to share my milk."

They walked to the mother, stood around her and prayed. Then Alphonsine adopted the first of her orphans.

* * *

They crept along their way, travelling slowly. No tragedy escaped their view.

A mother with a very small baby overtook them. "My milk is gone. Can you milk my baby?" the mother asked. Alphonsine nodded. The baby suckled weakly at her breast, and Alphonsine's milk dribbled a few drops from the baby's mouth.

"That's all it wants."

"Wafwako."

"Eyo-mwah." Alphonsine handed the mother her baby, and the mother and her infant headed down the trail.

The next day, as they crept along slowly, they heard a whimper from the side of the path. It was the same baby, left to die by the mother who could no longer provide milk.

She must hurry on, to save her own life, Alphonsine thought.

Cherita picked up the child and handed it to Alphonsine, who looked at its tiny limbs, its swollen, malnourished belly. *This child will die. Better to let the others live.* Her limited supply of mother's milk now had to be shared between Dada and the child they decided to call Jesu. So far, the children were strong. She looked at Cherita and shook her head slowly. Cherita pled with her eyes, and Alphonsine acquiesced.

Cherita carried the child in her arms until it died. A few hours later they dug a shallow grave under a bush, laid the child within, prayed for its soul, and continued on.

All too often they came across babies, dead and alive, abandoned in the bush by their desperate mothers. At one point Alphonsine looked deep into the woods and imagined the forest floor littered with baby skeletons.

The family understood how people in flight made tragic decisions. They never judged, but they never grew accustomed, and they grieved each one.

* * *

Rape—the weapon to be feared, even more than the gun and the machete.

Alphonsine and her family met men, women, and orphaned children on the road and heard the stories. Some survived to tell of the horrific evil they themselves had survived; others mourned the death of their loved ones at the hands of evildoers. They spoke in different ways—some were numb and spoke hesitantly, some hysterical and weeping, some without any emotion.

Soldiers had come to their villages, separated the men and the women, and restrained the men at gunpoint so they were helpless. A group of them held the women, especially the young girls like Cherita but sometimes the old women like Alphonsine's mother, to the ground. First they raped them, one after another, emptying themselves, and when they were through, they took branches from the trees and raped them more. They heard of so many women who bled and died.

Alphonsine welcomed the orphaned children to join them on their road. Her family of adopted orphans grew to nine, so that sixteen travelled together. Cherita and the girls scoured the bush for food and Patrice and the boys held out their shirts to collect the rain to drink.

Every day Patrice and Cherita led the group in songs, hymns and lyrics they composed about their journey. Alphonsine and the family, original and adopted, prayed to Jesus Christ to keep them safe and to comfort the ones who had lost their families. And they asked their ancestors to make them invisible, to blend them in with the trees and the bushes so they could not be seen by the soldiers.

So far, for Alphonsine and her family, their prayers had worked.

* * *

Then they heard the worst story. A woman had recently delivered her baby, and her husband had fled. When the soldiers with guns and machetes entered her hut, they found the mother with her newborn, bloody signs of the birth around them.

She hugged the baby to her breast.

"What's this?" The leader nudged his gun at her hands and the baby's head.

"My baby."

Soldiers chortled.

"Have you ever cooked a chicken?"

"Yes. I can cook a chicken for you," she said, full of fear, hoping.

"Get a chair." She did as she was told, blood dripping as she walked, and the leader sat, laying his gun across his lap. The others stood by, grinning. One handed her a machete.

"We want you to cook this baby like a chicken. And if you hesitate we will shoot you. Get your oil and salt. Cut the chicken in pieces and fry it." And they roared with laughter.

She was too afraid to cry as she reached for her oil, her salt.

"Build a fire."

She gathered a few twigs and lit the fire. Then, in front of the soldiers, with their fingers handling the triggers to their guns, she bowed her head and wept.

"Do it. Prepare the chicken!" She did as she was obliged.

"Test the chicken—does it have enough salt?" She tested.

"We need some chili, we like *pili-pili*," the solders demanded.

"We don't have *pili-pili* here. But I can get you some."

"Just go. Be quick."

She left, taking the opportunity to flee down the road. Once she was out of the village, she wept, screeching, unable to be comforted by the people she met along her way.

That night, Alphonsine and her family prayed, weeping, for the poor woman and her baby.

* * *

For two days, they did not move forward on the trail. Papa had developed diarrhea. Alphonsine made a camp for the children nearby, while she tended her father. By now, Alphonsine bent with difficulty; her belly bulged with new life. But she cleaned him with leaves as best she could. Mama held his hand and prayed for his recovery.

Soon they knew. He would be not live to arrive with them in Kamina.

When he died, they dug a grave and lowered his body into it to protect him from the wild animals. They sang, soothed his spirit, commended him to Jesus and to their ancestors, and wept.

Raymond Mande Oversees Relief Shipments

"PUBLIC LIVES; In Congo or Kosovo, A Compulsion to Help"

The New York Times, April 20, 1999

"I give thanks to my God always for you because of the grace of God that has been given you in Christ Jesus, for in every way you have been enriched in him, in speech and knowledge of every kind."

1 Corinthians 1:4-5.

Lubumbashi, Katanga Province

April 1999

Raymond Mande pushed his way between crates, cartons and boxes stacked high above his head, till he came to the section in the Lubumbashi customs warehouse where officials stored the incoming shipments for the North Katanga church. There, his eyes roamed the stacks of twenty-five and fifty kilogram bags of cement and layers of tin roofing. He scanned from floor to ceiling, counting, checking off the goods on the transit manifest. Ten, twenty, thirty, forty, fifty kilogram bags of cement. Ten, twenty, thirty, forty sheets of tin roofing. Last time, from Tanzania. This time, from Zambia.

Mande had cleared items through customs for missionaries for many years now; he knew the routine. But Bishop's building projects had significantly excalated his workload. As Bishop raised money in the United States, the purchases of building supplies increased. All of the cement and tin roofing had to be imported, though the community scrounged locally for stones, sand, and termite dung. Then, the nine-month old war had changed Mande's work even more. North Katanga needed food—rice, beans, corn flour, oil, salt—and medicine. When the church sent money, he purchased what he could in Lubumbashi. But sometimes, even in the big city, supplies ran low. Increasingly, the demand required international shipments, and they had to be processed through customs.

He had his routine. Check the shipment. Go to the clearing agent. Fill out all the necessary paperwork, a process that might take two, three, four days. From the clearing agent to the customs office. Check the documents on file, the value of the items, how it should be charged according to the customs court. Determine the import tax, 5% of the value of the items. Go to the bank. Deposit the money, get a receipt to show to customs as proof of payment. Walk through the shipment with the customs inspector so he can see for himself the items that have been declared in the document, what is what. Inspector authorizes the release of those items.

Only now could Mande, with his team, truck the items to the church depot.

Every shipment, the same process. But Mande had gotten so experienced, so good at it, that all the churches—Roman Catholic, Pentecostal, Baptist—now used him as their go-to guy to process international shipments.

* * *

The routine held its surprise dangers, especially after the United States declared the "war on drugs." All medicines had to be tested to be sure that any white powder did not contain cocaine or heroin. And sometimes, a test showed a false positive, as it had in 1994 when he had gone to Ndola, Zambia to process a medical shipment for Kabongo Hospital with the Swiss missionary doctor in Kabongo and her nurse.

Mande and the missionaries had identified the shipment of medicines from Switzerland when two policemen accosted them.

"We need to test, to make sure you are not trafficking drugs."

"But we're medical missionaries! Here's our identification. It's medicine for the hospital!"

"Then it should be ok. But we need to make a test."

One of the policemen placed a tiny amount of white powder in a bag with some chemicals. Within a minute he had his result.

"I found what I am looking for! My test has revealed that it is cocaine."

"But no, this is medicine!"

"We need your passports." One policeman kept his eyes darting among the three; the other policeman took the little books, opened the cover of each one, glanced at the picture, quickly scanned the three detainees, and matched each passport to its owner. "Good. Now, you are under arrest."

The jail had three rooms, separated by chain link fences. "Heaven, Purgatory, and Hell," Mande joked to the women. Mande and the missionaries were the only ones held in the center cell, Mande's Purgatory, but they could see everything that was happening in the adjacent rooms.

In Heaven, the guards sat, smoking cigarettes and watching the two rooms of prisoners. In Hell the real troublemakers hung around, with nothing to do but to goad one another. The guards received a new prisoner, and the three detainees flattened themselves against the wall while the guards removed all but the new prisoner's most basic clothing and then strong-armed him through Purgatory and threw him into Hell. From Purgatory the women tried to turn their faces away from the men in Hell when they urinated or defecated, sometimes in the corners of their room, other times, wherever they happened to be. Eventually, they became used to the scene and could look without seeing. Mande just watched it all, thinking of the literature he loved, especially Dante.

In Purgatory Mande and the missionaries were segregated from the others. The women requested bathroom privileges. When they pled, "May we go?" the guards escorted them to the toilet.

And so it went for three days, until a policeman arrived and whispered to the guards, who swung open the door and beckoned to them. "You're free. The tests in Lusaka showed that it's medicine. Take your passports."

Mande demanded an apology. "I won't, I remain here, till the Congolese officials come to find me!"

The missionary doctor bit her lip. "Just forget it."

The nurse's urgent tone persuaded Mande. "Let's go!"

Mande and the missionaries hurried as they left the jail behind them. The three picked up their medicines and made their way to the border between Zambia and Zaire.

* * *

Words flew across the ocean and land and through the air, almost as if the speakers were in the same office. Bishop called Pastor Kahunda daily, eager to learn the exact progress of construction projects: how many bricks completed? Then Bishop heard other news: What? Kasanka, or one of the other doctors, had reported a cholera epidemic? Bishop then instructed Mande to request funds from UMCOR for medicine. Mande pounded on the manual typewriter, made a carbon copy, and faxed it to New York for approval. When GBGM wired money to Trust Merchant Bank, the treasurer withdrew the funds. Mande then purchased medicines in Lubumbashi and arranged for transportation, if possible by air, if not, by train.

All of this administration required Mande's capacity to work with detail, but he most liked his work as Bishop's amanuensis: *that* piqued his literary imagination. In 1996 he had begun his course work for his Ph.D. in English literature, and now, the ideas of literary communication—the process between writer and audience—swirled in his head. Mande's pen sought the perfect translation of Bishop's ideas—his vision, even his mind! —to his various audiences: other bishops, members of churches who became interested in North Katanga's projects, executive secretaries of church agencies. *I know Bishop. I translate his mind, but now, the people I address, I've never seen them. An executive of an agency, like GBGM, or finance. Another bishop, even the president of the council of bishops. Imagine! In which language do I speak to them?* The names had no persona, no culture, no sense of world associated with them.

Mande had not yet travelled in North America or Europe.

Mama Alphonsine Enters the Land of Hospitality

"The Downside of Doing Good: Disaster Relief Can Harm"

The New York Times, February 27, 1999

"Every third year. . .the resident aliens, the orphans, and the widows in your towns, may come and eat their fill so that the Lord your God may bless you in all the work that you undertake."

Deuteronomy 14: 28-29

Kabongo, Haut Lomami District

April 1999

Alphonsine paused at the entry to Kabongo, holding out her arm like a gate in front of the children. "Rest a moment."

Was it true…had they really arrived in Kabongo, out of the bush and beyond the reach of enemy soldiers? What kind of strange feeling sparked in her chest? Joy? For so long she had felt numb—no happiness since Mwilumba's accident, no grief since her father's death.

Depleted of emotion, she had drawn energy from a biological force deep in her womb that ignited her fierce instinct to protect her children. Her tummy bulged with Mwilumba's child, the one he might never meet. Cherita still carried the infant they had rescued from its dead mother; Patrice led Eschler and Dada by the hand. She hugged her aged mother, holding her upright, murmuring to her as one mother to another. "Surely, here, others will share our burden."

Then, Cherita and Patrice began to sing, pure, sweet sounds in perfect pitch, one of the many songs they had composed that praised God that so many members of the family yet lived.

* * *

The Kabongo district superintendent held out the tickets. "Bishop authorized the church to purchase tickets for all of you to travel by cargo train to Kamina. We expect a train soon. Be ready."

Alphonsine pressed her hands together as if she were praying, and her eyes flickered an appreciative smile. "Praise God."

As soon as Alphonsine heard the train whistle, she gathered all of the children and led them and her mother through the village to the station. After all they had endured, it was an easy walk. Here, they did not have to bushwhack through the underbrush or hide from enemy soldiers. They had food in hand, though the children didn't know it. The district superintendent had given Alphonsine dried fish for their journey, and she had kept it bundled in cloth, out of the children's sight, so they could make a quick entrance when the train arrived.

As Alphonsine and her family entered the depot yard, a member of the train crew yelled at the gathering crowd, waving them back from the tracks. Alphonsine stopped the children and stood still. She watched as the crew beckoned to a man who backed a truck to a cargo car. The crew and the man unloaded some barrels of palm oil and dried fish. *Businessmen still making money. A good sign.*

Passenger trains, crowded as they were, provided seats; cargo trains allowed passengers to travel among the transported goods. But Alphonsine's concern for comfort was shallow and her determination deep. She needed to load the children and her mother quickly into the boxcars, as not to risk being left behind. Another train might not come for a month or more.

Alphonsine pressed the children toward the smell of sweat, dirt, and urine that was intensified by heat that reeked from the boxcars at the end of the train. She chose one and mounted a wooden box that served as a step. *Putrid, but it would have to do.* She pulled the children one by one into the car. Then she created a seat for her mother on a barrel of palm oil close to the door, where she had ventilation and little need to move further.

* * *

They huddled together in the boxcar through the stops and starts of the train for several days, gasping for fresh air, holding one another to prevent each other from falling out of the car. Finally, they felt the last of the relentless, bone-rattling vibrations. The engine puffed and settled on the track. Patrice jumped from the boxcar to the wooden train platform, and Alphonsine and Cherita lowered the children and Alphonsine's mother to him. Finally, Alphonsine and Cherita sat on the ledge of the door and Patrice swung them one by one to the depot floor. Then the family hurried away from the bondage of the smell. They had endured the train and arrived in Kamina—free of the war and closer to the protection of Bishop.

It was mid-morning and Kamina's air was still cool. Alphonsine led her family down the familiar dirt road that served as the main city street and was astonished to find the stores without life of any kind. The Central Bank of Congo had posted a sign, *fermé*; no men touted their wares in small kiosks; no women sold vegetables on little tables. Kamina had declined since the looting in 1993, but the silence this morning was frightening. Had the war reached Kamina? Or had the threat of war simply stilled the market?

They walked slowly down the lane, into the residential area, and toward the center of town. The sweet smoke of charcoal fires rose from the rear of the houses, slightly thickening the air. *Women cooking!* Alphonsine knew how to char wood and bake bread over such a fire. With some help from the church, she might be able to feed her family regularly again.

Her family needed everything—food, water, shelter, clothing. But at the moment, as she neared the conference office, all of their suffering faded to the background. Instead, hope and fear, now unrestrained, overwhelmed her. Here, at the conference office, she might be reunited with her eldest son, Mbuyu, who was attending secondary school in Kamina. But most importantly, she might learn whether her husband, Mwilumba, had survived his accident and where he might be living. Or, she might learn that he was dead.

* * *

A month earlier Mbuyu had perched on the edge of the hard wooden chair in the one-room library in the first floor of the Methodist building in Kamina, flipping the pages of the biology book that lay open before him. He felt honored to study in the presence of the old volumes that surrounded him on the freestanding wooden shelves. They stood on their spine ends, but, with many empty spaces between the books, most fell to the side, one against the other, like weary travellers resting against one another. Still, the books befriended him, and Mbuyu felt a special kinship as he studied among them. He knew that his father, Mwilumba, the Methodist schoolmaster in Kabalo, would be proud to see him studying in this room.

His parents had arranged for him to attend secondary school in Kamina, boarding with Pastor Bondo. Mbuyu was the eldest son and took seriously the responsibility of getting a good education, setting an example for his younger siblings, and eventually, helping the family financially. But he had decisions facing him.

He wanted to be a pilot. He liked watching Gaston land the Cessna on the dirt airstrip in Kabalo. Gaston always communicated a sense of power and authority as he emerged from the plane in his bright white shirt with black shoulder epaulettes. Gaston, like Mbuyu, was his father's eldest son. And his father, Bishop Ntambo, must be very proud.

But, thinking of his dream, Mbuyu frowned. Mbuyu's father, Mwilumba, had opposed the idea. "If there is a war, maybe you will land in the hands of the rebels. Maybe you will crash in a lake. A pilot—there are so many risks."

If not a pilot, then what?

Mbuyu shook his head to interrupt his thoughts. He had been daydreaming, gazing into the bookshelves. But they did not hold the answer to his dilemma. He turned his attention back to his biology book and began to memorize the names of the muscles that the artist had drawn to show what lay beneath the human skin.

* * *

Mbuyu liked to spend Sundays at Pastor Bondo's church. He missed singing with his family, and at church he joined other musicians like himself. One Sunday afternoon he was waiting for the music to begin when Pastor Bondo's oldest son came running. "Mbuyu, come quickly! Your father is coming to the house!"

"It can't be! My whole family is in Kabalo!"

What could this mean?

When Mbuyu entered Pastor Bondo's house, he saw a human figure with the likeness of his father. The same facial features, the same expression on his face, but pink skin, like a *muzungu*—what?

At the sight of Mbuyu, tears flowed down Mwilumba's face. "I thought I would never see you again!" He opened his arms wide.

Mbuyu felt the familiar embrace that had encircled him since he was a small child. He hugged his father tightly but could not speak. Gratitude and then questions flooded him, head to toe. Finally, his father released him. He looked at his son, carefully.

"You do not know."

"I don't know anything."

His father told him the story—the war, the flight, the Zimbabweans, the accident, the family's separation. "I was treated at Kamina Military Base, and now Bishop is sending me to the hospital in Lubumbashi."

As Mbuyu listened, first, tears glistened on his cheeks, then, his head bent and his entire body shook with sobs. He tried to absorb the family's months of suffering, all at once.

"So Mama, Patrice, Cherita, the others—you don't know where they are? Even if they are alive?"

"No."

"I heard about a war in Kabalo and vague rumors about an accident. But I didn't know my family was involved!"

The following Monday, when Mbuyu tried to study, no words, no pictures, no ideas could touch his fear and loneliness. The library might as well have collapsed, his beloved books lying feebly beneath the rubble.

* * *

Pastor Kahunda opened the conference door.

"I am Alphonsine, Mwilumba's wife."

"So good to see you! We are ready for you. Mwilumba is eager to talk with you. He is in Lubumbashi where he is receiving treatments for his burns. We will bring him to the ham radio in a few days."

"Then he lives!" Alphonsine covered her face with her hands and sobbed with relief. Cherita and Patrice hugged one another and then swung Eschler and

Dada in circles. "Papa lives!" Pastor Kahunda smiled and waited, till the family composed themselves. *Lazarus, come out!* he murmured. Every day he relayed information to new arrivals about the fate of their relatives, and often, it wasn't so happy.

"We have sent for Mbuyu. You and your children can stay at Pastor Bondo's house for a few nights."

"May I meet him?" Patrice asked.

Alphonsine nodded. Patrice fled out the door, eager to find the brother he thought he might not see again.

"Mama Mujing will be here shortly to register the children who came with you. You remember Mama Mujing?"

Alphonsine nodded. "We met at women's meetings."

"She finds the children food, clothing and shelter, if possible. She is supervising the orphanage. She will be here shortly."

At the bottom of the steps, Patrice nearly collided with Mbuyu, who was rushing toward the conference room.

"Mbuyu!"

"Little brother!"

They laughed, hugged, slapped each other on their backs, looked again.

"Little brother, you have grown up! You have muscles and you are growing a beard! You are like me!"

"Of course! You have been gone a long time!"

Alphonsine could hear the raucous laughter of her oldest boys through the window. She had not yet seen Mwilumba, but her entire body filled with relief and happiness. Her most important prayers had been answered.

Suzy and Kasanka Marry

> "Congo: Rebel Gains Claimed"
>
> *The New York Times*, April 9, 1999

> "Look, O daughters of Zion, at King Solomon,
> at the crown with which his mother crowned him
> on the day of his wedding,
> on the day of the gladness of his heart."
>
> Song of Songs 3:11

Likasi, Haut-Katanga District
The month surrounding Easter, April 10, 1999

Kasanka laughed when he heard the whistle of the passenger train. His bag had been packed for a week. He had bought a seat. The train that would take him to his wedding in Likasi had finally come!

One night in January he had lain awake in his bed, listening to the occasional retort of gunfire at the airport, wondering what the next day would bring. He lived immersed in tragedy—every day he countered the effects of disease and violence with an undependable trickle of medicine and supplies. He comforted himself with images of Suzy. He relived the first day he had seen her, the beautiful girl in the swishing green skirt, and how he had courted her until she, and then her family, had agreed to their engagement. He thought how, as he made trips to her family's home to develop their friendship, their physical attraction grew into appreciation for each others' aspirations. Their dream for a future together took shape. Such a love, so powerful a swirl of thoughts and emotions. His bond to Suzy sustained him while he treated disease, cleaned and bandaged bullet wounds, and delivered weak, premature babies. Yet the question nagged him—she was so beautiful, he was so far away. Would she meet someone else?

And then he decided he could wait no longer. He had already paid Suzy's father the entire dowry. Yes, he had agreed to postpone the wedding until she finished secondary school, but that was before he became director of a hospital at the edge of a war. She had only a few months of school left—he wanted to marry her now, to be sure she was his, to bring her to Kabongo as soon as she graduated.

He rose from his bed and composed a letter to her father.

* * *

As usual, Suzy was studying, but she had more trouble than usual concentrating. Kasanka was due from Lubumbashi, the trains being what they were, sometime near the end of March. As the probable time of the train's arrival approached, Suzy listened for its whistle like a mother alert to her baby's cry.

"It's here!" She fled from the compound to the station, leaving her books opened on the table. And there he was, her love, the one she missed so terribly. As he leapt from the stairs of the train, she brimmed with pride at her well-educated, well-employed, deeply religious betrothed. He embraced her and she clung to him, as if she would never let go. Heads in the station turned and stared; weary faces softened to smiles at their effervescent love. The chatter in the train station energized; their joy was contagious.

* * *

The wedding, like the war, provided reasons for grumbling, even grounds for fighting.

Initially, her mother had objected. "He agreed to wait till she graduated."

Suzy's father defended the doctor's wishes. "Times have changed. He could be killed. We can see her love, and he has proven his faithfulness. If Suzy wants it, they should go ahead."

And so, with Suzy's father's blessing and despite her mother's misgivings, the couple announced their plans.

They discussed two possible dates: April 10 and April 17. Kasanka's cousin, Celine, had also planned to marry. "You take the 17th. We chose the 10th so long ago!"

"But Kasanka has travelled a long way. He'll only be here the first two weeks of April, and we want to spend them together, not waiting."

Celine grudgingly agreed to a double ceremony and reception on April 10th. Easter Sunday.

The two couples and their families got to work, nominating members of each family to the planning committee that would organize the reception and the food.

* * *

Likasi lay in the south, far from the fighting. Even so, the war created a sense of foreboding, like the dread that was written into the scriptures leading into Holy Week. The invitation list had to be carefully constructed, as the couple had agreed to one hundred guests—fifty for the bride and fifty for the groom.

Could some people be invited to the church and humbly accept that they could not attend the party after? Who should receive the formal invitations, so that they knew that they were indeed expected? And where would each of those persons be seated, in relation to the wedding couples? Who would be offended if they were not sitting near the bride and groom, and whom did the couples *want* seated near them? These details, even when carefully managed, often led to wedding wars that Suzy and Kasanka now sought to avoid.

When the day came, many of Kasanka's friends from Lubumbashi could not travel from Likasi to Lubumbashi. The war had depressed the price of transportation, and bus drivers went on strike. Even in this peaceful section of Congo, the war had snarled its ugly talons around the wedding plans.

* * *

Kasanka fulfilled his responsibility and visited the town clerk at city hall to arrange for the legal ceremony. The clerk bade him to return with his friend Nyembo and with Suzy and her father—and then the official questioned all of them, satisfying himself that Kasanka and Suzy genuinely wanted to be married and that the families approved.

"We have to be a bit careful. The legal ceremony will be short, just the necessities."

"Please, we have waited so long, say your word of blessing to the marriage. It will mean so much to us. You know our families. No problems." Suzy's winsome coaxing relaxed the clerk, and he felt the need to explain, not just command.

"It's not your family—the rebels can use any gathering as a camouflage for trouble. Be alert." Though Likasi had not been a site of fighting, its deposits of copper, cobalt and gold made it potentially valuable to combatants trying to attack Lubumbashi.

Kasanka smiled inwardly. After working in Kabongo, he simply assumed that fighting would provide the backdrop for all that he did. He had more experience than the Likasi town clerk with the threat of violence. But he did not intend to allow war concerns to constrict the overflowing joy he felt as the time to marry Suzy neared.

* * *

Easter, at the height of the war in Congo. Suzy and Kasanka: the beautiful young girl in the womanly green *kikwembe* and the up-and-coming doctor in his finest suit. Their festivities created a rare sense that peace and happiness could triumph despite the horror of war.

As Kasanka stood before Suzy and promised himself to her, his excitement overflowed—but out of habit he listened for any irregularity that could mar this moment. It was a skill he had honed in the surgical theater in Kabongo, where he had his full attention on his patient, all the while keeping track of any change in the environment around him.

"The basics" at the city hall took a full twenty-five minutes. Not fifty, as usual, but longer than necessary for the promises, the signatures, and the marriage certificate. The town clerk could not resist adding a few words to the legal ceremony. "May all of your ancestors keep you safe—and bless you with many children!" Forty family members cheered them on.

* * *

At the church everyone looked their finest. When Kasanka and Suzy stood at the front of the church and beamed their appreciation to their families and friends, they faced a sunrise of dazzling color—red, indigo, green, ochre—the most brilliant dyes of fabric that the *kikwembe*-clad women could find. Suzy had plaited her hair with intricate lines of tiny knots, woven together with long, brown and sand-colored hair extensions. Many of the women in the congregation had spent hours, similarly fashioning each others' hair. Their perfumes added a flowery fragrance to the air. The men looked their handsomest with dark western suits and strong colored neckties, yellow, purple, or pink, in bright tones that complemented the women's *bikwembe*.

Kasanka had arranged for two of the finest church choirs in Likasi to perform. The choir pulsed, vibrated and drummed, and then the preacher exhorted the couple; more singing, and the families and friends added their blessings. The drummers intensified the beat, and people rose to dance in the aisles. The drums and voices led the swaying crowd into ecstasy, as if the energy of the choirs and congregation could billow the couple's dreams to heaven. The spirit of the risen Christ filled the church.

The reception was a cosmopolitan affair and showed the far-reaching affection and influence enjoyed by the couple. The halls filled with a variety of languages—French, Tschiluba, Kiluba, Lingala, Kiswahili. Kasanka's family, and what friends could attend, mingled with Suzy's family and high school friends, renewing old friendships and making new acquaintances over a long buffet of goat, chicken, fish, *bukari*, *linga-linga*, *sombe*, *muchele*, rice, peanuts, pineapple, and bananas. More music, more dancing.

At midnight, Kasanka and Suzy had had enough.

"I'm ready for some time alone with you."

"Our family and friends have blessed us well, but it is time to leave." Their eyes met and twinkled with anticipation. Nyembo had arranged for them to spend two days alone at a guesthouse owned by a Gecamines mining commissioner.

* * *

On the third day after the wedding, Suzy and Kasanka sat with Suzy's auntie and Nyembo for the final, customary wedding ritual. Auntie and Nyembo came prepared to hear the details of their intimate relations. If sex had not gone well, either member of the couple could back out of the marriage. If it had, the family expected Suzy to be pregnant in the first year. If she weren't, Kasanka's family would customarily encourage him to find another wife who could provide children. Even though the Christian church taught that a man should marry only one wife, these traditions and the link between marriage and procreation remained strong.

Nyembo waited to hear Kasanka's report. "I am devoted to the one woman I want to marry, and with her, all of my happiness exists."

Suzy turned to Auntie. "I feel the same about Kasanka."

"We have agreed—we are a modern couple and the rest is our own private story."

* * *

A few days later they laid in bed in one another's arms, murmuring. They had lived in their own world for a week and needed to help each other face the approaching reality. The next day Kasanka would board a train for Kabongo and Suzy a bus bound for Kombove. She could only join him after she graduated in August.

He stroked her cheek with the back of his fingers. "It's as if life is so normal. So peaceful. I've not even thought about the war for days, not till I had to pick up the medical supplies this afternoon."

Her eyes searched his. "But I have. I have counted the days until you would have to leave me. Can't you ask Bishop to move you to a hospital closer to Kombove?"

He kissed her softly, gently, caressing her cheek. "I can't. Then the people have no one. The war makes the hospital extremely busy. It was hard to leave, even for a month."

She snuggled her body nearer to him and rested her face in his shoulder. "But you are now my husband. I'm worried about your safety."

"Just like when I wasn't your husband! I am the same man, devoted to you, but a doctor. And a Christian. Would Jesus turn his back on people who needed his care? No. Then how can I? The Zimbabwean army will keep us safe from the rebels."

She resisted the tears that formed. "You are right, and that's why I love you. But I'll miss you terribly between now and August."

He hugged her close to him. "Concentrate on your studies. I want a devoted woman, but an educated woman. You make me very happy. God has given you to me. It's been a very happy Easter."

"Every day I will pray for you, my love." She kissed him, gently at first.

Pastor Nyengele Flees Manono

"Have We Forgotten the Path to Peace?"

Jimmy Carter, in *The New York Times*, May 27, 1999

"Judah has gone into exile with suffering and hard servitude; she now lives among the nations, and finds no resting-place; her pursuers have all overtaken her in the midst of her distress."

Lamentations 1:3

Manono, Tanganyika District
May 8, 1999, 6:00 am

Pastor Nyengele sat with his wife and six children around their breakfast circle, eating their cassava. Pop, pop-pop-popo-pop, pop. Gunfire? Lots of gunfire, nearby, outside. Nyengele sprang to his feet, shocked by the crackling invasion of his morning's peace. He opened the door of his parsonage a few inches and peered at the street. Five soldiers had already passed his hut and were marching toward the end of the lane, their backs toward him, rifles drawn. Three people lay bleeding. Near the corner a toddler stood crying. One of the soldiers aimed and shot and the child fell. Nyengele quickly retreated and closed his door; his family, paralyzed with fright, sat stock still.

"Soldiers just leaving the street. Stay here; once they pass, we go."

Then, the back door opened. Two of the children of his parish appeared, breathless. "Baba Nyengele, our parents have already gone to the fields—we don't know what to do!"

"Come in. Shut the door. Stay with us."

The gunfire paused. The door of the hut opened again, and now the living room began filling with children who sought the pastor's protection. In a few minutes Nyengele's house overflowed with little bodies, some crying, some watching silently, intently.

Outside, the quiet continued.

"We are too many. To the church next door. Run!"

The church with its mud brick walls offered limited protection against bullets, but the larger space allowed Nyengele to pray and organize the growing crowd. Scenes flashed through his mind: here, Nyengele had preached a message of repentance to the soldiers at Mobutu's military camp and reconciliation to the civilians who sat in the same pew; here, he had mourned the flight of Mobutu's soldiers when Kabila arrived, even though he thought their departure was for the best. But he never imagined the scene that was now developing. The children of his parishioners lit around him like a small flock of birds.

"Baba, help us, we can't find our parents!" More and more children were coming to the church, seeking the pastor's protection, trusting his spiritual power.

Adults joined the group, some from other churches. "Our pastor has already gone, Baba. Pray that we will be invisible to our enemies. Pray that the bullets can't find us!"

How to pray? Nyengele stretched his arms toward the gathering crowd, lowering his eyes. "God, protect us from soldiers while we flee." He looked up. "Slip behind the church, toward the bush. We will meet at the next village."

* * *

Nyengele had been warned that the war might be coming to Manono. The night before two Congolese soldiers who attended his congregation appeared at the door of his hut. They had money, as the military are paid when the war starts.

"*Wafwako,* Pastor. We wanted to give this money to our parents, but we don't know where they are now. You are actually our parent. Please, take this money."

They held out a wad of dirty bills, honoring Nyengele as a wise elder, one whose care and concern the younger people could depend upon.

"No. Give it to the treasurer of the church."

"The treasurer is not here. The person who is here is *you*. We cannot find our father. We don't know what will happen—maybe we will die with this money. It will be lost. We want to give *you* this money."

Folding his hands in appreciation, Nyengele accepted the dirty wad of *Nouveaux Zaire,* equivalent of 230 US dollars.

* * *

Nyengele and his family arrived at the designated meeting place, a crossroads with a thatched roof compound on each corner. The crowd had swelled to nearly 500, mostly children. The owners of the village farms and their workers had already fled, leaving the houses empty, the fields unattended.

"We are too many to sleep in one village, even if it is deserted. We will spread out to three or four, with older children running between with information."

In the course of the day, messengers brought word: all of the nearby villages had been deserted.

* * *

God fed the Israelites in the wilderness, Jesus fed the five thousand on the banks of Galilee. *Please, one more miracle*, Nyengele prayed. The children gleaned cassava, sweet potatoes, *linga-linga*, banana and pineapple from the deserted fields. In a few days the food was gone, and the crowd swarmed deeper into the bush, toward the next villages and their remaining crops. Nyengele paid the farmers a few *Nouveaux Zaire,* silently thanking the soldiers whose money had become their salvation.

* * *

Water. Soldiers lurked by the river. So children dug holes, uncovering a quarter cup of dirty rain, lying on the ground, sucking it. The miniature wells seemed safer than the enemies roaming the banks of the river.

* * *

News. *Was Manono still in the hands of the rebels?* Oh, yes. Brave men wandered to the river, posed as fishers, talked with soldiers.

"Rwandese surrounded the Congolese and Zimbabwean armies. Zimbabweans broke through and retreated to Ankoro. Rwandese now occupy Manono. Kabila will lose this war."

No going back. Nyengele and his group trudged even deeper in the bush.

* * *

Nyengele's prayers had worked; no one in his protection died from the bullets of soldiers. But a more powerful enemy camped in their midst, and Nyengele had failed to pray for its demise before they were overtaken. Dehydration, starvation, diarrhea, fever, malaria. Children died, three or four a day, in one day, twenty.

Nyengele prayed for each little one. He commended them to the arms of the waiting God and to their loving ancestors. *But to bury them? Too many, too dangerous.* The small corpses lay where they fell and the living moved on, leaving the animals of the bush to feed on the flesh of the children.

Bishop Ntambo Returns to Kamina

> "Q and A/Dr. Craig Etcheson; Keeping A Record of Atrocities of War"
>
> *The New York Times*, June 13, 1999

> "Oh, Lord, do not rebuke me with your anger
>   or discipline me in your wrath,
> Be gracious to me for I am languishing,
> Oh Lord, heal me, for my bones are shaking with terror."
>
> Psalm 6: 1-2

Crossing the Atlantic Ocean
June 1999

Bishop Ntambo had followed the will of his executive committee, and, after leaving Congo for the Council of Bishops meeting in the United States, stayed safely abroad until the next Council met, six months later. But he was not idle. He visited many American churches, raising money for his vision: every pastor in Katanga should live in a permanent, fired brick parsonage equipped with a fishpond, a bicycle, and a Bible. American Christians eagerly provided support, and Bishop had raised tens of thousands of dollars for his development projects. Furthermore, the international church had initiated "Hope for the Children of Africa," a six-million-dollar campaign to build schools and orphanages, so Bishop anticipated even more funding for development. Bishop's dream of building the Christian kingdom in Congo had the financial backing to become reality.

But death and displacement jeopardized the dream. Bishop had talked with Pastor Kahunda daily, and he had heard every report that came through the ham radio system: most of the church leaders in Tanganyika had fled for their lives; many were known to be dead and even more were missing, their churches demolished and their property looted. Pastors, lay leaders, women's leaders. Children orphaned, wandering hungry in the bush. Wives widowed, now considered useless by Congolese society. His pastors, their congregants.

His people were suffering greatly. They needed their spiritual leader. He felt compelled to return to Kamina.

* * *

Terror. It gripped his belly, weakened his moan to a squeak, dizzied his head. He woke, dazed, but the plane's darkened interior provided no relief from his nightmare. Halfway across the ocean en route from Atlanta to Johannesburg, the pitchblack night surrounded him. Turbulence choreographed a dance of reading lights rising and falling like ghosts of his dead pastors and lay leaders, begging for mercy, warning of violence to come.

His eyelids drifted shut, and images formed in his brain. He stood before the divine whirlwind, finding words for his anger. *Why, God, why this violence now? Why have you destroyed our dreams? We can feed, clothe, employ your people. But they die in war, they disappear in flight. We are ready, eager. But you toss our hopes into hell. You kill even innocent children. You torment us, your believers. What have we done to deserve this suffering? Where is our savior, the once-and-for-all, the one who took the sin of the world onto himself so that no more needed to die?*

God remained silent. Ntambo shook once, and then he opened his eyes.

To comfort himself he switched on his reading light and took his Bible from his pocket. He flipped the pages to Job 40:3-5:

> Job answered the Lord:
> "See, I am of small account: what shall I answer you?
> I lay my hand on my mouth. I have spoken once,
> and will not answer;
> twice, but will proceed no further."

* * *

Ntambo understood his people's agony. Their families separated, relatives dead, children's education interrupted.

Now Nshimba sat by his side, returning with him to Kamina, risking her safety, ready to care for the orphaned children. *Why should my family and I survive when so many of my people have not?* He felt a flash of gratitude, then guilt and doubt settled in. *Does God have a purpose? Or am I just lucky?*

In his mind's eye he saw his family in Burundi in 1993—each one following the other with pretended nonchalance, twenty feet after the other, as they made their way to the Congolese embassy after President Ndadaye's assassination. They had escaped, unhurt, while others around them died.

When the political events made it impossible for him to return to Burundi, Ntambo had been assigned pastoral duties in eastern Congo. Nshimba had selected a house in Bukavu, a Congolese city on the Rwandan border. In 1994 Ntambo was in the United States, raising money for the church in Burundi, when a colleague came to him.

"Ntambo, did you hear from home?"

"No…what?"

"A plane crashed in Rwanda. Habyarimana and Ntaryamira were killed. We've tried to reach Nshimba—but she doesn't answer."

The presidents of Rwanda and Burundi—dead. More violence where Rwanda borders Congo—inevitable. When they had talked by satellite phone the previous night, Nshimba said she planned to go to Rwanda to the bank. Nshimba might now be caught on the Rwandan side of the border. He struggled to compose himself.

"It will be chaos. I need to find my family."

He secured a flight to Johannesburg; once in Jo'burg, to Lubumbashi, on the next available, a day later. From Lubumbashi, a flight to eastern Congo became more difficult. "Lots of people searching for relatives; flights aren't reliable," he was told. He managed to book a flight to Goma, a Congolese city he had never visited.

As the plane circled to land, he could see the crowds hurrying like a panicked herd of zebra on the plain, trying to escape the Rwandese lion that was pacing on a hill, choosing its next victim. Bantu people and their luggage crowded the streets, the lanes, the paths—heading out of Rwanda and into Congo.

Ntambo disembarked the plane and entered the terminal of sweaty, smelly, screeching people, the ones with money who were trying to fly anywhere, as long as it was away from the gunfire just outside the airport. It was six p.m., dark, no hotel rooms available. What to do? He bumped and jostled his way toward the door and the shooting.

A soldier stood alone, idly by the door, smoking a cigarette. Ntambo approached.

"If you can save my life, I will pay you. I don't know anyone here. I am Congolese, a Methodist pastor, from Katanga."

"My wife is also from Katanga! She will be happy to greet you. Come with me." Either God had provided, or Ntambo had gotten lucky. For the night, speaking Swahili in the soldier's home, he was safe. When morning came, he paid the soldier and worked his way through the crowds, avoiding the sporadic gunfire that intensified as he approached the airport.

In the terminal he recognized four ministers from the cabinet of President Habyarimana, the slain Rwandan. "I am Ntambo, appointed by Bishop Ndorachimpa, pastor to Ndadaye. How are you travelling?"

"Renting a plane to Bukavu."

"I can contribute."

"With you on board God may bless us."

The gunfire continued just outside the airport. As he sat in the rented Cessna, taxiing on the runway for take-off, his hands shook. Planes in the air were assumed to be enemies of Rwanda. If attacked, Ntambo could be incinerated in a mid-air ball of fire. No one would tell Nshimba that he died, where or how—*if she is still alive.* Still, this opportunity offered the only way to Bukavu.

The plane rumbled to the end of the runway, and Ntambo sucked in his breath and held it. Perhaps his last. The Cessna purred and lifted. Floated into the clouds, beyond the reach of bullets. He released his breath. *Praise God.*

When Ntambo walked through the door of their compound in Bukavu, Nshimba and the children were packed, waiting. The entire family clung to one another and cried. "The church got a message to us. We knew you were on your way, so we didn't leave."

"What about you?"

"God saved us. I went to the bank in the morning and had crossed back to Congo before the chaos started." She told Ntambo the story in detail, a long story.

The reunion with his family banished his sense of helplessness and gave him momentary calm. But in Bukavu, soldiers, both Rwandese and Congolese, roamed the streets, shooting at will. Refugees filled any crevice of shelter; food and water were increasingly scarce. Ntambo felt bold, but not reckless. Now that they were together, he could lead them as a father should, making decisions with Nshimba, hugging his children and praying for them.

Nshimba put her hand on his arm. "Refugees are fleeing into Bukavu. It is not safe."

Ntambo nodded. "We could rent a car, drive to Uvira, take a boat to Tanzania."

"But the road over Goto mountain—soldiers, bandits at every curve. And the boats, overflowing with people. We could drown. But I agree—here, our food will be stolen. We may all die. We should not test God."

Once more, Ntambo and Nshimba talked with the children about the dangerous journey ahead.

The long road up and down the mountain, winding through the bush and past unknown villages, terrified them more than the walk from the house in Bujumbura to the Congolese embassy. The crowded boat leaked, and the crew bailed water all the way down Lake Tanganyika. But this time, the family sat close together, praying silently and in whispers, until peace accompanied them.

Again, unlike so many of his pastors and their families, they arrived at their destination, alive.

"God has blessed us for a good purpose," Nshimba had cried when they were finally safe in Kigoma.

Or, we just were very lucky, Ntambo had thought. *My wife, your belief in providence is so strong.*

Now, safe in the plane to Johannesburg, Ntambo glanced sideways at Nshimba as she slept, took her hand, and held it tight. The torment shriveled. Her warmth radiated to him, and as it did, he felt her faith fill his heart, crowding out his disbelief. In that moment, the purpose was made clear to him. God had tempered them in the fire so that in this time of dire need, they could comfort and aid their people in Kamina.

* * *

Offering compassion, so complicated—like trying to hold an egg in your hand when the egg white is oozing through your fingers.

Take, "Blessed are the peacemakers." His favorite beatitude. At times, a word of comfort. Other times, when people wanted retribution—when they had experienced horrible violence and were not ready for peace—a condemnation.

Ntambo had been converted to Christianity by its message of non-violence. In this idea he had found comfort, and a black man he had never met had led him to discover it. Reading Martin Luther King, Jr. in 1964, he tumbled into a new life: he, a black teenager, could respond with love to the violence he had experienced from the white Belgian colonialists. The idea rooted itself in the core of his being.

Even in extreme personal suffering, it guided his life. When his three-year-old daughter died of a fever, a traditional healer announced that Ntambo was being punished. She claimed that ever since he had become a district superintendent, he acted as if he were better than the others. Her criticism in his time of sorrow slashed his heart like a machete. He wanted condolences, not harsh words. But he resisted the guilt she tried to inflict, her beliefs in divine retribution.

"If I am being punished because I have done good work for the Lord, then I will work a hundred fold until the Lord kills me, too." His words, his ability to turn her condemnation toward good, stayed the woman's tongue. He did not need to criticize her in return.

He knew his real comfort lay not in the words of the village but in his faith. *My daughter lives; she is resurrected with our Lord.*

But messages of non-violence and resurrection had missed the mark in the refugee camps. After he had left his family safely in Tanzania, he had returned to Bukavu to minister among the displaced. The church called him an evange-list, but he acted as a chaplain. He did not seek to change the people's beliefs but to offer the right kind of comfort.

The young girl he remembered most had lost her entire family, twenty peo-ple. She told him how she had seen her father's fingers cut off, one by one, till he bled to death.

"I hate the Tutsis. What do I have left? Why should I not kill myself?" *She cannot hear the word of non-violence,* Ntambo realized. *And for a young girl considering suicide, resurrection is not the answer either. Comforting her lies in helping her form a vision of her future.*

"Your opportunities will come, perhaps to be educated in America. Prepare yourself for them."

What to preach? When, and to whom? The challenges of pastoring thou-sands of similarly traumatized people lay ahead.

* * *

Their plane landed in Johannesburg, and the news made him cautiously opti-mistic. The South African president Nelson Mandela, the African Martin Lu-ther King, Jr., had convened the countries involved in Congo's strife. A new peace process was underway. Congo, Rwanda, Uganda, Burundi, Namibia, An-gola and Zimbabwe were meeting in Lusaka.

Surely, the war was coming to an end.

Chapter IV

The Lusaka Negotiations Fail and Mai-Mai Emerge—Peacebuilding Increases: Development, Relief, Social Networking and Building Capacities (July 1999- January 2001)

Historical Introduction

Beginning in October 1998, various representatives of African nations and Congolese political parties had met in Lusaka, Zambia, with the ostensible goal of agreeing to the terms of a ceasefire, during which a political settlement in the Congo war could be negotiated. A ceasefire agreement was finally signed by some parties on July 10, 1999 and others in the succeeding six weeks.

Since the beginning of the war, the fragility of the Congolese state had been exploited by foreign forces, whether allies or enemies of the Kabila government. For the first time, with the Lusaka agreement, the Congolese domestic agenda was brought back to center stage. If the cease-fire agreement was not implemented, the continuation of violence could postpone the National Dialogue, which was key to the deployment of a peacekeeping force, the withdrawal of foreign troops, the formation of a new Congolese army and the re-establishment of government administration on DRC territory. As long as the military situation remained unresolved, it was unlikely that the Congolese nation would be in charge of its own destiny.

The ceasefire was undermined by almost all parties involved, leaving civilian villagers to their local fates. On November 30, 1999 the UN Security Council Resolution 1279 created *Mission de l'Organization des Nations Unies en République démocratique du Congo* (MONUC). The first United Nations Expert Panel Report, commissioned in 2000, officially determined that arms trade, illegal mining and theft of minerals perpetuated the war.

During this time Kamina's agricultural and building projects increased, as more and more displaced people sought relief and jobs in Kamina. "Feeding my people" meant distributing food, clothes and medicine and becoming the largest employer in town.

The faith of the church reached into the local community, establishing new public relations with religious leaders and the military. Meanwhile, the ongoing threat of violence challenged the faith of ordinary people, leaving them to negotiate between Christian faith and traditional practice and belief.

Mama Sila's Family Flees from Mai-Mai

"Congo Refugees Flee to Tanzania"

The New York Times, July 2, 1999

"Deliver me, please, from the hand of my brother, from the hand of Esau, for I am afraid of him; he may come and kill us all, the mothers with the children"

Genesis 32:11

Kinkondja, Haut Lomami District

July 1999

Keep your presence of mind, Mama Sila told herself. *Count the children. Know who is with you.* Mama Sila forgot how old she was, but she remembered what she'd learned in the war in Kolwezi in 1973: when the gunfire starts, it's easy to get confused. *You grab the dog and you think it's the baby. Later, you discover you have left the baby behind and rescued the dog. You see a person shot, and you run to save your life. Then, you realize you have left the person you love helpless, bleeding to death.* War makes people panic, do things they otherwise would not.

After Kolwezi, she and her husband had built a hut in Kamina. When he died in 1982, she moved her family to Kinkondja, a village by Lake Kisale some two hundred kilometers away, where she dealt in fish. For sixteen years, she'd been a successful entrepreneur, working with her daughter, Chantelle Kalenga.

This morning Chantelle Kalenga had returned early from the lake, sobbing, with horrible news. The Mai-Mai militias demanded their fish. Her son, Mama Sila's grandson, Pateient, resisted, so they shot him dead.

"Go to Kamina!" Mama Sila did not take time to cry; rather, she grabbed her grandchildren's arms and turned them toward the path that led them away from Kinkondja, making mental note: 1-2-3-4-5-6-7-8. "Run! With your mother!"

But before she followed, Mama Sila withdrew a clean sheet from her shelf and strode down the path to the river where her daughter reported Pateient had fallen. She found him lying on the road, partially dried blood pooled around his body. She knelt to spread the cloth over him. As she did, passersby, members of her church, drew near. She looked up, her eyes determined.

"The Mai-Mai want our fish—we must flee to Kamina."

"Go. We'll bury our brother. We'll honor him."

Trusting the people of God, Mama Sila rose and hurried after her daughter and young grandchildren.

* * *

Over her lifetime Mama Sila had witnessed the rise and decline of the Mai-Mai. Back in the '70s, the underground rebels, like Laurent Kabila, had created the militias for the villagers' protection against Mobutu's soldiers: "Fight the dictator and his western backers. Call on your powerful, local traditions, your rituals. Be Congolese. Water-water, wash-wash, Mai-Mai. Become invisible and fight your enemy." But as Mobutu became more powerful, the militias nearly died out, even though a few die-hards from the old days remained.

Lately, she'd watched the Mai-Mai re-emerge among a new generation. In '96 and '97, when Kabila overthrew Mobutu, villagers recalled the Mai-Mai movement—some even said that Laurent Kabila reintroduced the idea, distributed arms, and trained new Mai-Mai militias among the Luba people. Mama Sila saw their power grow in Kinkondja, and she'd heard it was happening elsewhere.

Most Congolese men called the Mai-Mai "a good idea gone wrong." But Mama Sila, old and wise, never found them good. Because so-called "protectors," soldiers and Mai-Mai, always wanted fish from her meagre stores. And for what? Feed the Congolese soldiers, feed the Mai-Mai. It was not possible to catch enough fish, and the fighters would never be satisfied.

* * *

Mama Sila, Chantelle Kalenga, and seven children leapfrogged from village to village in the direction of Kamina. They concentrated on ways to get far from the Mai-Mai as fast as possible. They broke their own trail up a mountain, pushing away trees and vines, emerging three hours later, scratched and bleeding, on paths connecting the villages. Then the children asked for food.

"*Bukari*, Mama?"

"Not tonight."

Sunset. They dared not strike a fire that might attract the Mai-Mai. They slept beneath the blanket of the dim light of the southern stars, but by three o'clock, Mama Sila woke Chantelle Kalenga and the children.

"Let's move on." By now, the warriors should be sleeping off their drugs and their ceremonies.

Near dawn, they reached a village where they approached one of their customers. "The Mai-Mai are fighting in Kinkondja. A bit of fish, water for the children?"

"For you, Mama, we will share what we have." That morning they breakfasted well.

After eating and resting, they found their path. They hurried the children along, and when the little ones tired, let them ride piggy-back ride in the outer wraps of their *bikwembe*.

* * *

Mama Sila, a Methodist, distinguished her beliefs from traditional religion, and she led the children in Christian prayers. But as an old Congolese woman, she knew how the Mai-Mai thought, how the logic of tradition provided the rationale for their practices. They carried the charms of their families within their clothing. They dressed in the symbols of Congolese warriors—animal skins and feathers—and inducted new members, including children, through ritual washing that, they believed, made them invisible to their enemies. They conducted their traditional ceremonies in private, using marijuana and other drugs to create the ecstasy through which they contacted their ancestors. When they divined spirits, they determined who in the villages might be their enemies. They empowered themselves in the traditional way—by killing and eating the flesh of those who threatened them and making fetishes of their body parts, especially breasts and genitalia.

Mama Sila and Chantelle Kalenga answered the children's questions. "Why do they need our fish? They have food. They offered food to our friend Ngoy, so he joined them. Perhaps we should…"

"No! They'll tell you that they'll treat you well, give you more than your family. They'll tell you they only want good for Congo."

"But they showed Ngoy their power. They have charms. Maybe they'll protect us."

But Mama Sila had become a devout Christian and had rejected traditional ways. "Your protection comes from the church and your family, not Mai-Mai. We don't seek the power of our enemies, and we don't dress like them. We're Christians—we sing hymns, we dance, we live in our ways. We must hurry before they find us."

The Mai-Mai dress intimidated many villagers, but not Mama Sila. She didn't believe in their power. But the idea that militias could attract her children into their false beliefs, or that they could decide that *she* was a witch who wished them harm and should be killed, now *those* were problems to avoid. Better not to have any contact with the Mai-Mai.

* * *

After walking three days, Mama Sila's old feet swelled. She had walked too fast, carried too many children. Still, she wanted to reach Kamina as quickly as possible.

She and Chantelle Kalenga devised a new plan. They had travelled well beyond the outskirts of Kinkondja and immediate danger from the Mai-Mai. Perhaps some of the local villagers could help with transportation, as well as food.

She heard twigs snap in the path, bicycle wheels crunch on the sand, and a rider overtook them. His rear fender was laden with branches. She waved and the man stopped.

"*Jambo.* We have come from war in Kinkondja, want to reach Kamina. Could you take this little child on your handlebars, just to your village? We'll meet her there."

Each time a rider came across their path, she asked for help. Mama Sila no longer carried the children on her back. She hobbled to the next village, found the children, and continued walking until new cyclers took the little ones on their handlebars or fenders.

Making good time, they arrived in Kamina in a week. Now they were safe from the Mai-Mai.

* * *

Mama Sila and Chantelle Kalenga registered at the conference office, and Pastor Kahunda sent them directly to the orphanage. The orphanage offered a noon meal for children; it was about to begin.

In front of the small, horseshoe-shaped concrete building, a long line of children, their clothes torn and falling from bony frames, queued at the door, waiting patiently.

"Stand at the back of the line," Mama Sila directed her grandchildren. Then she entered the building and found a familiar face, a smiling, stout woman in a cheery red dress.

"Mama Mujing, you, in charge of the orphanage! You've done well for yourself in church!" Mama Sila had known Mujing as a mere child in their Methodist church in Kolwezi.

Mama Mujing looked up from the large kettle of beans she was stirring. "Mama Sila, *wafwako,* good to see you!" Then she nodded in the direction of another woman fluffing rice in a large pot. "Mama Alphonsine. Mama Sila."

"Chantelle Kalenga."

"We feed the children shortly. Please help. There are so many, more every day."

"*Wafwako!*" The dusky smoke of charcoal, the warm flickers of fire, and fragrance of the rice set Mama Sila's stomach to growling. She tasted a spoonful of warm, silky beans—just one—as a long line of children waited.

Mama Sila stood by the two pots, scooping rice on a plate, and handing it to each child. No telling their ages, they were so small, so undernourished.

A very short boy took his plate of rice and held it nearly above his head toward Mama Mujing. She spooned his beans beside his rice, and steam rose from his plate. He lowered the plate and put his nose close to it, inhaling deeply. Mama Sila handed rice to a taller child, who nudged the short one in the back with his plate. The young boy walked a step forward, stopped again, and breathed deep, inhaling rising steam. Finally, he lifted his head and took the spoon offered by Chantelle Kalenga. Mama Alphonsine helped him balance the plate as he walked to the other side of the room and lowered himself to the concrete floor.

As she spooned the rice for the remaining children, Mama Sila glanced his way. He was eating one bean and one kernel of rice at a time, making his food last. The taller boy sat down by his friend and devoured his meal. The tall one had finished, and the small one had half his plate yet to eat. The tall one opened his mouth toward the little one, who placed a bean on his tongue. The tall one opened his mouth again, and the little one shook his head. Then he lifted his plate to his mouth, sucked the rest of his food into his mouth, and licked the plate clean.

She walked over to the boys. "Good?"

"*Wafwako*, Mama."

"Your names?"

"Pierre."

"Jean."

Every day Mama Sila returned to the orphanage to mother the children. She comforted the lucky ones who had found a bed and a new family within its walls, and she prepared and served meals to the community children who came to eat three times a week. Within a few days she knew most of the names of the seventy-five children who depended upon the orphanage to survive.

Bishop Ntambo Rebuilds Kamina

> "Congo Rebels Take Big Step to Reviving Peace Plan"
> *The New York Times*, August 25, 1999

> "Let the nations be glad and sing for joy,
> For you judge the peoples with equity
> And guide the nations upon the earth"
> Psalm 67:4

Kamina, Haut Lomami District

Late August 1999

"Peace is coming to Congo, and we are ready!" Bishop beamed at his executive committee. He was on fire. His energy, his enthusiasm radiated, electrifying the whole room. His prayers had been answered. He was with his people again, seated around the table in his office in Kamina, reviewing their business and plotting future directions. God had tested them through the war, and, at this moment, was showering them with grace.

"Mama Mujing, tell us first about the children."

Mama Mujing, wearing her bright red dress, stood. "*Wafwako*, Bishop. We have thirty-nine children housed in the orphanage, and we are feeding another hundred. Some displaced women have volunteered to cook and care for the children; otherwise, the work would be too hard for me. We are grateful for your support."

"Of course, they are all my children. Now, we must build schools, not of mud but of fired brick, even a university, to educate them. Schools that say: you, too, can read, write, learn a profession. If you work hard, you can be a pastor, a doctor, an engineer. *Wafwako*, Mama Mujing. Pastor Kahunda, your hospitality report."

Kahunda glanced shyly out the window. Then he rose and stood behind his chair, tall, his arms at his sides. His smile sparkled. "*Wafwako*, Bishop, for the floor. We have registered about nine thousand guests in Kamina—many Methodist pastors and lay people from Tanganyika, but others on their path. Word is beating in the bush, 'you are treated well in Kamina.' We receive the money from UMCOR for salt, oil, seeds, clothing and medicine. Every morning we distribute food and clothes to people in need, in a rotation through the parishes. New arrivals build their huts outside town. We are doing God's work. Matthew 25." His smile drooped to a thin line. "The lines are long, and at times, the people are so desperate that they can be unruly."

"We will think more about security. *Wafwako,* Kahunda. Ilunga Mutombo?"

Ilunga Mutombo stood behind his chair, rubbed his calloused hands together, and spoke with excitement. "At Kamisamba Farm we are tilling the fields and removing the stones. The land slopes to the river—the soil is fertile, the crops lush, green. Beautiful. Wait till you see! We have employed local and displaced people to work the fields. We harvest enough beans each week to supply the orphanage, feed the community children, sell to the townspeople, and distribute to the displaced. Whenever we are able to hire more laborers, we open a new field."

Bishop smiled his approval. "It is my wish that Kamisamba Farm will be a training center, a place where the townspeople learn to cultivate new crops and raise cattle and pigs. We will find laborers to rebuild the barns so that we can raise livestock. *Wafwako,* Ilunga Mutombo. Dr. Kasanka?"

Kasanka rose to his feet. "The Kabongo Hospital treats all of the people we can. But we are always short of medicines, supplies. We work with *Médecins Sans Frontières* and the International Red Cross, but much is lacking in Kabongo. Here in Kamina, the Lupandillo Nursing School delivers babies for the displaced, who can't afford to pay at the government hospital in Kamina. We especially need hydration and medicines for *kwashiorkor* and malaria."

"I will communicate with UMCOR about more medicines. *Wafwako,* Kasanka. John, is Annual Conference prepared?"

John Mutombo stood. "The program is organized; the choirs are ready. People in Kamina will open their homes to guests, but we do not know what to expect. Many of the representatives from other areas now live here as displaced people. Many of our pastors and district superintendents are still missing. People continue to arrive every day. It's hard to know how many will attend."

"We will welcome our brothers and sisters and find shelter for them. Food will come from Kamisamba Farm. Something else?"

"Yes, some Seventh Day Adventists, friends of the former missionaries, have suggested that we make the former missionaries' home into a guesthouse where visitors could stay."

"Interesting. Let's talk about it. Now, let's visit Kamisamba Farm. But first, let's pray."

* * *

Bishop climbed into the front passenger's seat of the truck, Ilunga Mutombo, John Mutombo, Kahunda and Mama Mujing into the back seat, and twenty workers into the truck's bed. Faustin slipped into the driver's seat. He had fueled the truck for Bishop's first trip to Kamisamba Farm and left the truck guarded. He had a moment of anxiety: hopefully, the guard had not gotten distracted and no one had stolen the gas from the truck while it waited. He turned the key, the engine chugged, and the radio blared. He quickly switched it off. *Not the atmosphere for Bishop's ride. An overlooked detail.* As the truck settled into a steady purr, he relaxed.

Bishop turned to Ilunga Mutombo. "Fuel?"

"We purchase from the local broker whenever he receives a shipment, keep it locked in your yard, under guard."

Buying and protecting the fuel, one of Ilunga Mutombo's most important jobs. He guarded it against looters and tried to keep enough on hand that the truck could travel whenever supplies needed to be distributed.

"When we run out of gas, we have problems. We can't distribute food from the depot in town. If people are hungry, they'll walk the ten kilometers to Kamisamba Farm. Sometimes they harvest the beans before they are ready." Lack of fuel always contributed to disorder among the displaced.

Ilunga Mutombo and Faustin's truck were now good partners, as most days, they traversed the road back and forth, to and from Kamisamba. They knew every rut, every rise in the rugged dirt path, every place where the truck might sputter and cough. The truck jostled, limbering the joints in Ilunga Mutombo's back—to Ilunga Mutombo, a pleasant feeling, a reminder of progress being made. As long as the truck bumped its way over this road, the harvested food could be taken to the depot in Kamina for distribution, and the stones could be unloaded at the building site of the next church.

The truck shimmied up the rise to the railroad, crossed the track and descended to the other side.

* * *

"Stop." Kamisamba's first field came into Bishop's view, and Faustin halted.

Bishop swung open the truck door and perched on the running board, craning his neck. He felt the sun's hot rays and the breeze that reminded him that soon, the rains would begin. A field lay before him. The dry season irrigation had worked well. Long rows of shiny, green soybeans spread out before him like a giant fan, as far as he could see. Color dotted the field, a sign of the first shift of workers, hard at work. "Ahhh. Beautiful, just beautiful. And we pay the workers?"

"$30 a month, plus a portion of food for their families. People are eager to work here. They do not go hungry."

"How many?"

"Last year at Annual Conference time, 260. This year, 400."

"Praise God. Let's proceed."

Bishop banged the truck door shut, Faustin slowly roused the engine, and they rolled forward. The road flattened and sloped gently, and more of the farm came into view. Hills and furrows sprouting healthy crops, one field after another.

Bishop sighed deeply. Kamisamba Farm, the great mother, nourishing the people. Surely, this was a vision of the kingdom of heaven, the womb of the church as Jesus meant it to be.

* * *

The five-day Annual Conference beat as the church's heart, rhythm within rhythm. To open the conference, the choirs sang, the people danced. When new displaced people arrived every day and registered on the rolls, Bishop celebrated each person newly identified as having lived through the war. More singing and dancing. When the displaced reported the deaths of children and spouses, Bishop announced the names of people now known to have died.

Bishop made important announcements. "We will begin building three elementary schools of fired bricks. We will hire more laborers for these schools. We will pay the widows who volunteer at the orphanage. We will employ more people to help with both the children and the construction." The crowd cheered, and some cried tears of gratitude.

To close the conference, they sang the missionaries' song:

"Blest be the tie that binds, our hearts in Christian love,
the fellowship of kindred minds is like to that above.
Before our Father's throne we pour our ardent prayers,
our fears, our hopes, our aims are one, our comforts and our cares."

* * *

On the evening of August 24 Bishop gathered his leadership committee, his mouth set in a grim line. "It seems that the peace agreement has been broken."

Most parties had signed the Lusaka Agreement, and all had observed a truce for three days while the World Health Organization vaccinated children against polio. But that day, in Kisangani, a major town on the Congo River a thousand kilometers to the north, the war took a strange turn: Rwandan and Ugandan forces, allies who had invaded Congo, fought each other. Seven hundred people were killed, and even more Congolese were displaced. Rwanda had always claimed that it invaded Congo to protect itself against Hutu militants in the eastern refugee camps; Congolese had always suspected that Rwanda had offensive, rather than defensive, goals. This fierce, destructive battle between the aggressors might now reveal the true motives for the war to the world. While Bishop's committee speculated about Rwanda's aims, of this they were certain: only durable peace offered hope for Congolese stability. Most discouraging to them, the different factions did not seem ready to observe the peace to which they had agreed.

"We continue to build in Kamina. We do not flee." The hard lines of determination in Bishop's face showed everyone, it would be so.

Doctor Kasanka Treats Patients During the War

"Rebels Can't Conquer Hearts of Congolese"

The New York Times, August 13, 1999

"They had come to hear him and to be healed of their diseases; and those who were troubled with unclean spirits were cured. And all in the crowd were trying to touch him, for power came out from him and healed all of them."

Luke 6:17-18.

Kabongo

May through November 1999

To deliver a premature baby, to dislodge a deep bullet. Improvising, always improvising. The mother, her newborn—they can both survive. How to focus their energy on healing? Dr. Kasanka stood at the bedside of the displaced, malnourished mother. He held two, two-liter plastic bottles of hot water and a length of tattered sheet in his hands. She had borne her tiny infant an hour before. So many babies died from the cold, and Kabongo Hospital lacked baby isoletes. He was taking all precautions, giving them every chance to recover.

He had moved the mother from the surgery table to an iron cot outfitted with sturdy, full length wooden planks, avoiding the makeshift beds with broken slats. *Someday, perhaps Kabongo will have mattresses, linens, and pillows. I hope her husband finds a blanket to soften her bed.* The wrap of the mother's *kikwembe* draped the planks as a sheet; tomorrow, she would need to launder the bloodstains from her only dress. Her husband's bright coloured shirt, folded, cradled her head.

Fortunately, the new parents had been able to obtain a knitted layette, so the nurse had washed and bundled the baby well. The tiny girl had lain on her mother's chest for the first hour of her life, warming between her mother's breasts. *Now, to move the baby so they both can sleep.*

As Kasanka had requested, on the lawn outside the door to the maternity ward, the new father had stoked a small fire; he had warmed the plastic bottles filled with water. Now, the doctor laid the bottles on the mother's bed and wrapped the ends of the length of cloth around each one, leaving a loose sling between them. He placed the makeshift incubator at the mother's feet. Then he gently lifted the baby and laid her between the bottles, snuggling her close.

"The nurse will keep your baby warm. She will be right here. Make yourself comfortable and get some sleep."

"*Wafwako.*" The exhausted mother closed her eyes.

Satisfied, he returned to the surgical theater. The nurse had prepped a soldier who had a bullet embedded in his leg. Now, Kasanka stood before the soldier and prayed. *Guide my hands to make this extraction as simple as possible. Strengthen the soldier during my prodding.* Kasanka could not afford to use valuable anaesthetic on this fairly straightforward wound. Prayer had to suffice.

* * *

After leaving Suzy in Lubumbashi the previous April and returning to Kabongo, Kasanka had single-mindedly sought to chip away at the boulders that prevented him from practicing medicine. He had obtained medical supplies from UMCOR in Lubumbashi and, when he returned to Kamina in August for Annual Conference, had received a second small shipment. To sterilize, he needed soap; to operate, anaesthetic; to hydrate, salt, sugar, and clean water; to reduce fever, aspirin. The medicines that might last a week in Lubumbashi had to stretch a month or longer here in the bush.

He knew that many people he saw had first been treated by local herbalists, who had a ready supply of natural remedies that sometimes helped and sometimes hindered healing. When traditional treatments failed, the rural people came to the man of western medicine. He had become popular with the displaced people and soldiers. He could diagnose and cure when he had the necessary pharmaceuticals. When the medicine ran out, he offered his compassion, knowing that hope, also, provided a natural healing. He was guided by the Hippocratic oath and his religious beliefs: *Do no harm, do all the good you can.*

The sleepy, boring village of Kabongo had changed since Kasanka had first arrived. Now, he lived with the constant fear that violence could overtake the hospital. The soldiers who came to be treated could create a fight, or the hospital itself could be directly attacked. He kept an overnight bag packed, should he need to flee. But he resisted the impulse—he knew that here in Kabongo, he was saving lives. Most of the native villagers had fled to Kamina, and hungry, tired people from villages far away now slept in their huts. He treated dehydration, malaria and diarrhea among the displaced whenever he had the medicine. But he lost many children. He watched them die from *kwashiorkor*, a disease he had no means to reverse.

Zimbabweans and Rwandese came with bullet wounds and torn limbs to be cleaned and sewn; Congolese soldiers sought help for diseases of the bush, especially malaria. He mused on the trends, but could not account for the difference in their complaints. *Perhaps the Congolese soldiers fight less. They certainly eat poorly. Perhaps their traditions do prevent the bullets from entering their bodies.* He appealed to the Zimbabwean army, still camped at the airport, for needles, sutures, and plastic gloves. Sometimes, the Zimbabweans provided quinine for malaria, and then the Congolese soldiers were lucky, indeed.

And now, in late 1999, he was beginning to receive a new kind of patient: Mai-Mai. They would not give up their charms, their adornments, many of which, Kasanka suspected, could contaminate his hospital. But he also understood the strength of their traditional beliefs. He could not in good conscience refuse them treatment.

He took precautions. He established a ward for each kind of soldier: the Zimbabwean and the Congolese, the Rwandese, and the Mai-Mai, as a way to prevent not only contamination but fighting among his patients.

In Kamina, Kasanka had heard all about the Lusaka peace process; back in Kabongo, nothing had changed. Here in the bush, the combatants jockeyed for power over various swaths of territory. The displaced continued to flee; they had nowhere to call home. The Zimbabwean army, the International Red Cross, MSF and UMCOR—each provided a sparse and treasured measure of the medicines he needed in order to save lives.

* * *

Word came by ham radio from the Red Cross: a shipment of medicines had been flown into Budi, one hundred and twenty-seven kilometers to the north of Kabongo. A portion of the shipment could be made available for Kabongo Hospital, if Kasanka could pick it up. *Of course, he would find a way.*

As soon as he returned the headset to the receiver, an image of Suzy formed in his mind. Every time he prepared to venture onto the roads beyond Kabongo, he could hear her pleas. *Don't take chances. We have our future, our children ahead of us.*

The man you love saves the lives of his patients.

Yes, I know. Her image became distorted, as if she were sinking under her tears.

I love you. Her image rose again, distinct. She smiled. He had made an uneasy peace with his beloved wife.

* * *

Now, to find the best way to Budi. As a university student he had developed street smarts to keep himself safe during anti-Mobutu demonstrations in Lubumbashi; as a doctor, he had become experienced at talking his way through barriers guarded by soldiers in the bush. He had learned not to provoke, but also, not to succumb. He had become a determined bull elephant, aware of his predators, no longer controlled by the fear of them.

But leaving the patients behind—now, that raised his anxiety. He had isolated the combatants in separate wards to keep them quiet. The Zimbabweans fought on the side of the Congolese, but as a more professional army, sometimes openly disdained them. When shamed, the Congolese soldiers fought back. The Rwandese hated both the Zimbabweans and Congolese. And now, the Mai-Mai "protected" the villagers against all three. *Would they take advantage of the vulnerability of their opponents while they are in the hospital?*

Pastor Masengo wa Katondo had newly taken on the role of chaplain, visiting all of the soldiers, offering comfort, hearing their stories, calming them. When Kasanka found Masengo, he was standing by the side of a displaced woman, holding her hand, praying with her.

"Masengo, I need to go to Budi for medicines. I leave the peace of the hospital in your hands."

"God be with you. The hospital will be safe."

Need a car. Kasanka revved his motorbike and kicked up a trail of dust as he rode under the palm trees through the dirt streets of Kabongo to the office of the mayor. "I can obtain medicines from the Red Cross in Budi."

"We will drive my car. But Budi is near the fighting, and there are many barriers. We will take Congolese soldiers with us for security."

The driver dodged dirt, ruts and barriers, manned by Congolese soldiers, who required a small payment, every ten kilometers. They passed without problems until, nearing the outskirts of Budi, they halted before a makeshift gate of logs and leaves. Zimbabwean soldiers sat on either side of the road. At the sight of the car, they jumped to their feet.

Kasanka handed the soldiers his identity papers. "Dr. Kasanka, Kabongo Hospital, entering Budi to pick up medicines from the Red Cross. And it is late in the day. We will likely return to this checkpoint after the six o'clock curfew."

"Pass, doctor."

As Kasanka had predicted, the sun had set as they returned to the checkpoint. The trees stood like silhouettes against the fading light; charms hung from the trees. They saw no soldiers on guard. The driver straightened behind the steering wheel, alert.

"Something is wrong," the mayor said.

The driver slowed the car and stopped it in front of the barrier. As he began to open the door, Kasanka heard a shout outside the car, and the soldiers in the back seats raised their rifles to the car window. The muzzles of their guns faced those of a brigade of Zimbabweans surrounding them completely. The guards had changed their shift; the new soldiers did not recognize the car.

The guards shouted. "Ha! Rebels in disguise, are you? Have you shot Congolese soldiers and stolen their uniforms and guns?"

Kasanka turned his head toward the soldiers in the back seat. "Please, put away your guns." The Congolese soldiers lowered the barrels of their rifles, but only a few inches, to just below the window.

He turned to the Zimbabweans. "I am a doctor. We have received medicines from the Red Cross and are returning to Kabongo Hospital."

"People from Kabongo do not pass this way at this time of night."

"Doctors pass late at night when they are trying to return to their patients. We told the guards this afternoon that we would be returning after the curfew. Please, let me show you my identity papers."

"You will have to show the commander. We have our rules. Out of the car, this way."

"I know you have your job to do. Please, be calm," Kasanka said, as much to the Congolese soldiers as to the Zimbabweans. He knew that a frightened soldier, one who could not keep his head, even one friendly to Congo, endangered them most. "We are not rebels. Now, let's walk. Slowly." He spoke in his doctor's voice, as if they were patients in his hospital.

As he walked, keeping his eyes straight ahead, the face of Suzy formed before him. *Walk quietly with me, my love. That is how you can help us.*

They reached the commander's hut. He recognized them from earlier in the day, and the crisis passed. "You can release them," he said to the soldiers, but to the mayor: "It is too dangerous to drive through the night."

"We will stay at Kaloko, a village up the road. We do not want to be shot by our friends and allies."

* * *

Word passed through Kabongo that the hospital had a ready supply of medicines. New patients, civilians and soldiers, arrived, waiting to show their ailments to Kasanka. He only admitted people to the hospital when it was absolutely necessary, but people had been made to wait, so their wounds had infected and their diseases had progressed. Soon the patients overflowed to a secondary building in the rear of the campus. Kasanka gathered the entire staff to discuss the problem of overcrowding.

"We have so many new patients. We may not be able to keep the soldiers separate: the Zimbabweans, the Congolese, the Rwandese, the Mai-Mai. We will pray about what to do. The hospital must be a place of peace. It must treat everyone. But we must find a way to prevent the war from coming to our hospital."

Bishop and Ilunga Mutombo Build Despite the War

> "Shaky Congo Peace Pact Grows More So"
> *The New York Times*, November 12, 1999

> "Build houses and settle down; plant gardens and eat what they produce. Marry and have sons and daughters; find wives for your sons and give your daughters in marriage, that they may have sons and daughters. Increase in number there, do not decrease."
> Jeremiah 29:5-6

Kamina, Haut Lomami District
September through December 1999

Bishop inhaled deeply, filling his lungs with the humid joy of wet, furrowed earth after the rain. As if before his eyes, the young beans deepened their green and straightened their backs, rising from their hills. Bright reds and yellows of fabric dotted the fields, where workers hoed and harvested. He rejoiced to see so many people earning money, fed, sheltered. He had always said, God had blessed Katanga with nine months of rainy season, rain like manna from heaven. Now the fields were green, Kamisamba Farm, giving birth. Kamina, the ghost town, was coming to life.

Bishop knelt beside the end of the row and took the leaves of the plant in his fingers. Every plant, its nutrition and its growth, revealed a miniature system within a nourishing environment of soil, air and light. But someone must plant the seed. Likewise, the church's work tilled the Kamina economy—much money circulated despite the withered banking and trade in Katanga. Even more than at Kamisamba Farm, someone must be the gardener.

During all of his years as a bishop's assistant, Ntambo had developed connections with the United Methodist General Board of Global Ministries in New York City. Now, those relationships saved lives. He could rely on UMCOR. They were the first to come in when the fighting stopped. *Go to the agencies for relief*—UMCOR served war-torn areas in ways congregations could not.

But, he had learned, the denomination in the United States was changing. American congregations liked to give money directly, to build their own relationships. He thought, *they like African congregations more than their own general boards and agencies.* So he took his cue from the American missionaries who solicited congregational support. *Itinerate, build support for mission. Go to individual congregations for the two thousand dollar items. Paint the picture they can see—churches, parsonages, fishponds, Bibles. Bicycles, for Congolese, like a 747 airplane. Make the comparison, they get it.* And he quickly learned, *Americans care about women. For every man who receives a bicycle, the wife must have one, also. And the widows.*

Since becoming a bishop, he could also interpret the needs of the Congolese church to an entirely new group—his colleagues in the Council of Bishops. *Go to Bishops for schools and orphanages, the ten thousand dollar items. Speak so the people in Kamina come alive before their eyes—they will lead their Annual Conferences to become the peoples' friends.*

He had learned what kinds of stories to tell, what visions of the future to discuss, which audiences understood the potential of which cause.

The monetary gifts of Christians had breathed life into the feeble economy in Kamina. The Methodist church had become Kamina's biggest employer. Teams of Congolese people cultivated the fields, removed the stones, fired the brick, constructed the buildings, fed the workers, cared for the children, all for a small monthly pay of thirty US dollars.

The work evangelized the community faster than months of sermons could. Looking for employment, for songs to sing, for a way to grieve their lost relatives, for hope, villagers and the displaced crowded the dirt pews of the congregations. Once the drums began, children danced in the aisles.

* * *

Kendabantu School, the first primary school to be built of fired brick, became Ilunga Mutombo's new project.

By the time Faustin drove the truck through town, the villagers already knew that Bishop planned to build a school from durable materials. But when would he begin? The church truck, lightly laden, had become a familiar sight, rumbling food and people to and from Kamisamba Farm. But the truck laboring — its bucket heavy laden with fired brick, bags of cement and sheets of tin roofing; workmen hanging from its rim by their arms with their toes perched on the lower ledge—this heralded the celebration that was about to begin. As the truck groaned its way through town, children shrieked, adults clamoured to the doors of their huts, and soon, villagers of all ages followed its path to the construction site.

Ilunga Mutombo, the project director who had cramped his own back extracting the very first stones from Kamisamba's fields, shouted to his workers. Two young men scrambled nimble as antelope up the side of the truck bucket and yanked the large cotter pins out of the door. It clanged to the ground, and the workers began to unload the bricks, the cement, the tin roofing, helped by some villagers. *All of the building supplies have arrived, unspoiled. Now, to keep them from being looted in Kamina.* Ilunga Mutombo pushed the ugly thought from his mind and concentrated on the hard work of organizing the construction materials.

He measured the walls, and the masons began to outline their work.

Several churches and parsonages had already been completed. Townspeople knew that a construction project created community entertainment. Some women brought food; others balanced jugs of water on their heads and offered drinks to the construction crew and the crowd alike. No one thirsted under the hot sun. Men sat in the shade of trees and told stories of how the mud brick school was originally built, comparing the difference between the engineering of mud and fired brick. The crowd remained past sundown, and Ilunga Mutombo himself slept at the site.

* * *

The skeptics niggled like thorns in his flesh. "Don't you know, there is a war, your materials will be stolen."

"So we need to build quickly, because once the cement holds the bricks together, neither the cement nor the bricks can be taken. Once the roof is secured to the building, no one will go to the effort to loot it."

But the skeptics had voiced Ilunga Mutombo's greatest fear.

Representatives in the church office in Lubumbashi nearly six hundred kilometers away had purchased the fifty kilogram bags of cement and eight-foot sheets of tin roofing—valuable items, much desired. They had transported them to the church's walled compound, protected them till the train arrived, purchased passage, loaded them on the train, and guarded them en route to Kamina. *A risky plan, but necessary. Could have gone the way of the bicycles that should never have been sent to Kabalo.*

In September 1997 Bishop had purchased a shipment of bikes for Tanganyikan pastors and their wives and brought them by train safely from Lubumbashi to Kamina. Then the war broke out in Kalemie, and the executive committee had debated whether to send the bikes to an inland city in Tanganyika, Kabalo.

"People from Tanganyika are coming to Kamina," Ilunga Mutombo had argued. "They can receive their bikes when they arrive."

"By that time, the bikes will be the property of people in Kamina," the displaced Tanganyikan district superintendents retorted. "The donors expect the bikes to be given to the church in Tanganyika, and those pastors need the bikes. The church in Kamina may not usurp the gifts intended for its sister, even if she is distant and suffers some fighting. And it cannot appear that Bishop favors Kamina. Transparency produces trust."

The superintendents won the argument. The bikes were loaded on the next train, and a guard was sent. The train sputtered along its way, and, in the meantime, the rebels took Kabalo. The train stopped short in Kitanda. Refugees looted every bike.

Ilunga Mutombo shook the image out of his head, returning his attention to the present skeptics.

"The war will come to Kamina. The school will be destroyed by the fighting. Why bother? Why not leave things as they are?"

"It's Bishop's vision: durable buildings for a durable Congo. Our children will be educated in this very school. Our prosperity is here to stay."

Each day, the masons worked, the walls rose, the community sang and danced. No one disturbed the materials meant for Kendabantu School.

* * *

Bishop rose and dressed when it was still dark. Already, the supplicants had arrived at the door of his compound, a line of twenty-five people, mostly women, seeking his attention.

"I plead your mercy, Bishop, a job for my husband in your construction projects."

"I beg your grace, Bishop, school fees for my oldest son at the new Kendabantu School."

He satisfied what needs he could. Then, he and Nshimba prayed over his morning sorrow—turning away most of the people with only a kind word and a blessing.

Those seeking food and clothes had queued at the depot. The lines before dawn in Kamina stretched like a puff adder lying in wait, momentarily docile but potentially dangerous.

As streaks of orange light reflected from the clouds on the horizon, Ilunga Mutombo arrived at Bishop's door, and they joined the early morning undulations on Kamina's dirt paths. Women trekked to the brewery for water, and men strode toward Kendabantu School or Kamisamba Farm to work. Bishop expected his employees to begin by six o'clock during the cool morning breezes. When he passed a late arrival sauntering on the path, he stopped the man and tapped the watch on his own wrist. Bishop imposed a demanding work ethic, a full day's work for a full day's pay, one US dollar. Many others coveted a tardy man's job.

Bishop and Ilunga Mutombo surveyed the work. The walls of Kendabantu School had risen; the men were ready to attach the tin roofing.

"Well done, Ilunga Mutombo."

"*Wafwako*, my Bishop."

They walked on, ready to meet the executive committee at conference office.

"*Wafwako*, my brothers and sisters. Kendabantu School has given the people hope."

"*Eyo-vidye,* my Bishop. But if I may have the floor."

"Kahunda, the floor is yours."

"Where there is hope, there is also danger. In the bush, people know that Kamina offers food, clothing, maybe even a job. We have already registered nearly ten thousand displaced, but we can only employ five hundred. Too many people, too many expectations could create a riot, could get us killed. Tschimwang Muzangish has a proposal."

"Tschimwang?"

"Building projects outside Kamina, perhaps Kabongo, Kitenge."

Bishop thought, shook his head. "Not building. Too risky. But depots for relief distribution, perhaps. Our central depot in Kamina, with satellites in towns closer to the war. Places where the trains run or food, clothing, and medicine can be trucked. Tschimwang?"

"As we increase our crops at Kamisamba, we will have food to feed the displaced in Kamina and still send to other cities. And perhaps you can appeal to UMCOR for additional help."

"You are right. Tschimwang, develop a distribution plan. Ilunga Mutombo, can we increase our construction in Kamina, so we can employ more workers, maybe eight hundred by the new year? Start the new sanctuary at Centre Ville church, so the people have a beautiful, durable, dignified place to meet. But for the next project—perhaps Umpafu, in the rural area."

"It's a good plan. If we have depots in outlying cities, people who are still in the bush from Tanganyika will remain in those villages. It will be easier for them to have food, clothing, and medicine nearby, and it will not be so easy for the rebels to take those towns if the civilians remain. Especially if Zimbabweans have camps, like in Kabongo and Kitenge. We can work with the superintendents to develop depots there."

At the height of the Luba empire in the middle 1800s, Kamina had been the hub of a crossroads, like Washington D.C. As it was once, Kamina could rise again.

Mama Suzy Arrives in Kabongo

> "Congo's Leader Promises Cooperation with Mediator in Civil War"
>
> *The New York Times*, December 12, 1999

> "(Love) bears all things, believes all things, hopes all things, endures all things."
>
> 1 Corinthians 13: 4-6.

Kabongo, Haut Lomami District
December 1999

Dr. Kasanka sprang to his feet at the sound of the whistle and stood as close to the tracks as he dared, craning his neck to see the incoming train. *This train, bringing his new wife to Kabongo!* Soon, the engine brought the passenger cars to a grinding, chugging, dirty halt. Suzy's face was pressed to the window, searching for him. Kasanka's sister watched over Suzy's shoulder with equal intensity. Kasanka grinned and hurried to the steps of their car, ready to reassure them by his immediate presence.

He remembered his first sight of Kabongo, this rural bush town, so different than the cosmopolitan cities in the south of Congo. *It will not be easy for her at first.*

Suzy and his sister appeared at the door of the car, pushing and pulling the overstuffed, red-and-blue-checked vinyl bags that crowded their feet. Kasanka's assistant jumped to the upper step and nimbly passed the bags one-by-one to Kasanka, who caught them and let them drop them to the ground. He reached to steady Suzy and his sister as they descended the steps.

"*Wafwako*, welcome!" Kasanka nuzzled her cheek with a kiss and hugged his sister-in-law.

"*Wafwako*." Once more, Kasanka embraced Suzy—this time tightly, almost pressing the breath out of her. But when he finally released her and they turned to walk through the depot, Suzy wrapped her arm around his back and snuggled him close to her. He happily slid his hand along her waist, resting it on her hip.

* * *

Despite his devotion to his work, Kasanka had been impatient to bring Suzy to Kabongo so they could begin their life together. Instead of her image in his mind, warning him of possible danger, he desired her bodily presence, comforting him as he faced real tragedies. They had married in April, and she had graduated from secondary school in August. But her father would not allow her to travel alone. War or no war, he insisted, Kasanka must free himself from his duties to return to Likasi to accompany his wife on her first train travel. And a family member must accompany her for a time so she would not be alone in a new place while the doctor worked in the hospital. Until Kasanka could fetch her, Suzy's family expected her to remain with them.

The time had come.

In December Kasanka rode his motorbike from Kabongo to Kamina and then travelled to Likasi by train. He reunited with his wife, packed her belongings, and boarded the return to Kamina with Suzy and his sister. They had good seats, but the train lumbered along, hesitated, and broke down. The journey took nearly a week. Suzy never showed distress. In the night, while others slept, they whispered to one another.

"I'm afraid. I have never lived away from my family. But I am glad we are together."

"I am selfish. I want to live with you as my wife. But it is good that my sister has come, so that you have someone to help you when I am busy, at least in the beginning."

He held her close, remembering how shocked he was when he first arrived in Kabongo, such a backward town. And now, soldiers roamed the streets. He only hoped that once she saw it, she would stay. And they both knew—if Suzy found her new home unbearable, Suzy could return with his sister to Likasi.

* * *

As Kasanka wanted to prepare the house for Suzy's arrival, he drove to Kabongo, leaving the two women to travel a few days later on the train. The ride to Kabongo, unlike the trip to Kamina, was short—only a day and a half. *Much easier,* Suzy thought. *A good omen.*

Kasanka and his assistant were waiting when the train arrived. Kasanka's assistant leapt to the bed of the truck, and Kasanka lifted the baggage to him. The assistant sprang to the ground and opened the rear door, so the women could climb into the back seat. Kasanka crawled onto the rear bench next to Suzy. "We will see a bit of Kabongo and then go to your new home."

Suzy looked past his sister and out the window as the truck rumbled down the rutted road through a lane filled with hedge-lined compounds. *What is this place I have come to? No walls around the houses. Grass roofs, mud huts.*

Kasanka squeezed Suzy's arm, pointing out the window. "Here's the market." Then to the driver: "Stop for a moment." The aide paused the truck but kept the engine firing so it did not stall.

Suzy had enough time to see that several merchants had spread produce on pieces of cloth on the ground; a few kept chickens in boxes. The women looked at each other, long, tenuous looks. Kasanka noticed their reluctance, put his arm around his wife, and squeezed her tight.

The truck continued on. In a minute they paused before the green metal gate of the concrete-walled compound surrounding the old mission houses where

Congolese doctors and nurses now lived. A guard opened the gate. Suzy sighed with relief.

The truck stopped inside the yard. Kasanka jumped out, swung the door wide, as if to create a grand entrance. He held Suzy's hand as she slid from the seat.

She landed lightly on her feet. Stepping away from the car, she stopped before the full view of the house and stood stock still, signalling to Kasanka that she was not ready to go further. He paused, watching her, as she scanned the building. She forgot him as she concentrated on gathering impressions of her first home as a married woman. *Small. Durable. A tile roof. White concrete with green shutters. A long, low porch all the way across the front. Substantial.*

Suzy remembered Kasanka again, holding her hand, waiting patiently for her reaction. She turned to him and smiled. "OK."

They mounted the three concrete steps and Kasanka led her into the living room. Now, she was aware of him watching her as her eyes swept the room, and she squeezed his hand. Then she ignored his gaze and evaluated the furnishings.

A couch with Swiss doilies draped over the head rests, worn on the armrests, but sturdy legs. Two matching chairs. A floor lamp with a bulb, no shade. *Sparse. Tired. Not at all homey, except the lace, a bit feminine, a woman's touch.* In the kitchen, a sink and electric refrigerator and stove. *How much electricity? A backup generator?* A full jug of water by the sink. *No running water. Must be hauled each morning. By whom? Where from?* Some pots and pans. Pineapples, bananas, rice, soft drinks on the shelves. *Enough to cook and preserve food.* In the bedroom, a double bed, sheets neatly folded under a mosquito net. Another bedroom, a single bed for Kasanka's sister. Here, also, linens and mosquito netting. *Comfortable, safe.* The bathroom with a western stool and bathtub. Water in a basin in the corner with a bucket to flush the toilet or bathe. *Hmm. A luxury. The house of a missionary doctor.*

"Fanta?"

"Please." Suzy returned to the living room and sat quietly with her sister-in-law, struggling with her emotions. This was it—a house that she needed to make into her home, comfortable enough, but in a foreign, barren place. She fought against the tears coming to her, feeling her regret. *I missed the doctor, but I didn't mind staying with my family.*

He returned with two bottles of soft drinks, handed one to her and one to his sister. He looked at length at her stricken face. "We will make it our own."

He has read my thoughts. It is good he understands me. "Do you have friends here?"

He gulped. "Not many. The staff at the hospital. Many church members fled when the war came. The nurses, Chaplain Masengo and the mayor have stayed.

The new people at the church are displaced, with their own problems. Some soldiers attend. But at the church—they are good people."

Her belly constricted, fearful of her loneliness and of the sacrifice she would need to make to join her beloved husband.

* * *

The next day Kasanka went to the hospital early, and Suzy and her sister-in-law unpacked Suzy's belongings. In addition to her clothes, she had brought the staples she thought she would need: tea and bath towels, kitchen utensils, soap and shampoo, oil, salt, flour. Then they walked to the market where they were able to purchase some *linga-linga*, a live chicken, and rice. They wandered among the people, displaced and soldiers, undisturbed.

That day the house had electricity, so they butchered and stewed the chicken and boiled the rice and spinach. The sisters ate their portions together, as Kasanka worked till after dark at the hospital.

When he came home, his place at the table was set. He walked through the front door, closed his eyes and inhaled, smelling the oil and chicken that lingered in the air. *I have dreamt of this for so long.* He embraced his wife. "I know it was a long day. I will try to be home earlier. But I love you so much, and I am so glad you are here." Suzy tingled from her toes to her head and returned his embrace.

* * *

A man replenished the water each day before dawn. At least Suzy did not have to do that. Suzy and her sister-in-law ventured further into Kabongo, purchasing food and other supplies. On occasion, Kasanka walked with them. On the night before the train to Kamina was due to return, Kasanka's sister asked the important question:

"Are you comfortable here? Do you want to come back to Likasi with me?"

"I am not at ease. But I do not want to disappoint Dr. Kasanka. And I *want* to live as his wife. We have decided—I will go back in Kamina for my studies in two months. When I am not in school, I will come here."

"All right then."

Suzy had chosen her future, travelling the Jericho road between her studies in Kamina and her doctor in Kabongo.

Pastor Nyengele Emerges from the Bush

> "U.N. Says War Affects Poor Children in Millions"
>
> *The New York Times*, December 12, 1999

> "Love is patient; love is kind; love is not envious or boastful or arrogant or rude. It does not insist on its own way; it is not irritable or resentful. It does not rejoice in wrongdoing but rejoices in the truth. It bears all things, believes all things, hopes all things, endures all things."
>
> 1 Corinthians 13: 4-6.

Kitenge, Haut Lomami District
December 1999

The young rider burst into Pastor Kabongo's hut, breathless.

"*Wafwako*, Pastor Nyengele is coming to Kitenge with three people!"

"What? Nyengele of Manono? Are you sure?"

"Yes. We heard it in Malemba when we went to buy fish. People there talked to him. No food left in Kabumbulu. He came to Malemba with forty people, and they divided into families and went their own way. He wanted to take the train, but they warned him. Too much fighting between Malemba and Kitenge. He decided to walk the long way around."

Two hundred and fifty kilometers. The last leg of a long journey, zigzagging through the bush. "They'll be tired and hungry. Collect four riders with bicycles to meet them on their path and bring them to Kitenge. Call the women, prepare food for their arrival. We must receive them as honored guests."

Pastor Kabongo lowered his head to his hands, tears of joy welling up behind his eyes. *His wife's father—the revered Pastor Nyengele, the founder of the Methodist church in Kitenge, missing since the rebels took Manono, now found alive!* Nyengele had begun so many congregations around Kitenge that, when he moved on to a large parish in Manono, Bishop had appointed Pastor Kabongo superintendent over a new district, largely made up of Nyengele's churches. *He and his party must be made comfortable. But after months in the bush, will he be well? Certainly hungry, thin, perhaps ill.* So many refugees, already in Kitenge, so little food. Still, the people will offer what they can for their beloved pastor.

In 1998, when the superintendents were meeting in Likasi and the war broke out, Pastor Kabongo had openly challenged the idea that the war would reach Kabalo, much less Kitenge or Kamina. *Never believed it would come inland, never thought it would last so long. So wrong.* Now, 17,000 Zimbabwean troops camped in Kitenge, and displaced people fled toward safety in their shadow. Pastor Kabongo had received thousands of guests, and every single survivor was important. But to receive Nyengele, his father-in-law and mentor, filled him with overwhelming gratitude.

* * *

Pastor Kabongo heard the rustle on the road, the singing, the shouts, the ululations. His wife, Bwalya, shrieked and ran out of the yard. Kabongo followed, grinning broadly. He arrived at the lane in time to see Bywala lean over the bike bearing her mother. She hugged her, rocking her side to side, not letting go. Then, a thin man in tattered clothes slid from the fender of a second bike. Kabongo embraced his mentor. He felt his skeleton, smelled his dusty skin— the saturated odor of a man long not bathed, not newly sweated. A living perfume. So good. For a long time Kabongo held Nyengele, so grateful for the heart that still beat within his bones. Then Bwalya hugged her father and Kabongo, his mother-in-law.

Bwalya had stoked the fires in the yard of their parsonage. She had boiled *bukari* on one and roasted bits of meat on the other. She led her mother and father by the hand. "We have prepared some food, the best we could. We begged some meat from the army."

Nyengele turned to Kabongo. "You have a large military force in Kitenge. How are your relations with them?"

"Good. Some of the soldiers come to church, Zimbabwean and Congolese."

"In my church in Manono I had Mobutu's soldiers and civilians. Till Kabila came, then the soldiers fled."

Kabongo led Nyengele to the *air kabongo* chairs by the door to the parsonage, and Bwyana brought them plates of *bukari*. Soon, all the new arrivals were breaking off balls of dough and sopping up the stew. The guests ate slowly, as they hadn't eaten a full meal in a very long time.

"Of course, we did not know if you were alive. Tell me your story."

"We fled from Manono on May 8, about five hundred of us. Many children were separated from their parents when the rebels came. We left together. Every day more died, once twenty in one day. Especially the children. In Kijuki we were about two hundred. We stayed in Kabumbulu for three months, cultivating for villagers, receiving food, until all the food was gone. The last forty people divided and sought help in different places where they felt comfortable. So we began with five hundred, ended with forty. Now we are four."

"Did you have trouble at the barriers?"

"We walked through the bush around the barriers, very quietly, slowly. We did not approach any soldiers, too dangerous."

"Do you have any word of other Methodists?"

"Pastor Kichibi travelled with us for a while, then took his own road. Still trying to find his family."

"It is so good to see you. You'll only be here three days. The train is coming, and we'll travel to Kamina for the executive committee meeting. I am sorry, we have no clothes here. But in Kamina the church has a depot."

* * *

When Nyengele arrived at the executive committee, Bishop, who had become plump on his trip to America, engulfed Nyengele, a wisp of a man who had lessened to a scarecrow. "*Wafwako, wafwako*, you live!" After a long embrace, Bishop led Nyengele to the table. "Nyengele, we want to hear your story."

Bishop clutched Nyengele's hand till he finished, tightening his grip at various points to express his sympathy. "Praise God, you and your family are safe. We take care of all of you, here in Kamina."

Bishop turned to the executive committee. "Here is the man we need." To Nyengele: "We are discussing extending the depots to six areas beyond Kamina: Kitenge, Kabongo, Budi, Kitanda, Ankoro, Malemba. Are you well enough to help us do that? That is my wish. But first, you will go back to Kitenge to bring your family to Kamina."

"I am ready."

Mama Suzy Returns to Kabongo

> "Foes in Congo Appeal for U.N. Peacekeepers"
>
> *New York Times*, April 10, 2000

> "My soul glorifies the Lord, and my Spirit rejoices in God my Savior, for he has been mindful of the humble state of his servant."
>
> Luke 41:46-48

Kamina and Kabongo, Haut Lomami District
April 2000

Suzy stood in the train depot in Kamina, grimacing. Around her, people trying to secure seats on the train to Kabongo chattered in high voices and milled to and fro. Her prospects of traveling to Kabongo to see her beloved husband seemed bleak. In the windows of the passenger cars, Suzy could see that people were jammed several to a seat intended for two; others stood in the aisles leading to the doors. She would have to search for a person willing to forgo a seat for payment, a person who actually had a seat—and quickly—as the train was preparing to leave. As she tried to make a plan, she adjusted the shift that rested over her expanding abdomen. Five months pregnant, she had given up wearing a *kikwembe* over a month earlier.

After two months in Kabongo, Suzy had returned to Kamina to begin her education in law. On this, her first school vacation, she was eager to return to her home to her husband. They were thrilled by her first pregnancy. Either she had to find a place on the train, or they would not see one another for several months more.

As she examined the faces through the windows, searching for a possible entry, a Congolese soldier approached her.

"Lady, why are you not inside?"

"I can't take such a crowded train in my condition. I'm pregnant."

"I have a compartment reserved. You can travel with me."

A chill ran up Suzy's spine. When she purchased her ticket, she had been advised that travellers rode passenger cars and cargo cars. "Do not take those. There, the soldiers who are assigned to escort the trains often rape women." Suzy was determined to avoid all soldiers.

Suzy remained silent, avoiding his gaze. *It would be better to remain at home.*

But then she felt a sharp pain, the pangs of disappointment. *Perhaps he just wants money.* During the war, soldiers made the law; they often reserved seats that they resold at a profit.

He seemed to read her thoughts. "Come with me. You can see there are already others in my compartment. I will help you. We must hurry." He lifted her suitcase and turned toward the train door.

Suzy looked through the windows of the passenger car and saw couples, seated together. *I will not be alone with him.* She followed as he wedged his way through the passengers, asking that they make room for the pregnant lady behind him. When they did not move, he drew his billy club and beat his way to the door. Suzy followed.

When they reached the compartment, he asked his passengers to rearrange the way they were seated. "She's pregnant so let her sit over there, by the window, on the side with only two people."

She offered him money, but he refused. "You will soon have a baby to feed. Keep it."

For three days the train stopped and started. Despite the care of her host, Suzy felt each jostling and lurching of the train in her tummy. She sat upright, leaning against the window to sleep, cramped in a compartment with people with who spoke little, closing her eyes to envision the face of her beloved doctor who awaited her. Thirty kilometers from Kabongo, the train halted once more.

The conductor poked his head into the compartment. "Curfew! Trains may not enter or exit Kabongo after dark for security reasons. We will be parked here till morning."

Suzy groaned. A third night sitting up on the train—unthinkable.

She opened the window to let some of the night air into the compartment, leaned against the window, and closed her eyes. Then she sat bolt upright.

"Suzy, Suzy!" *The doctor's voice!* "I'm here, here!"

The doctor entered the compartment, grinning. Suzy rose and stumbled over the feet of the other passengers, until she hugged her husband.

"We were told that the train would be waiting overnight here, so I came on the motorbike to get you."

Suzy withdrew from her husband's embrace and turned toward her host. "This soldier, you have to thank this man, he has been so kind and helpful to me. If it weren't for him, I couldn't have gotten on the train. You need to pay him something. He has taken nothing."

"Here, you deserve something for assisting my wife."

The soldier shook his head. "No, I'm not asking for payment. I did it for free because she was very vulnerable. I just wanted to assist her. You need to be going."

"*Wafwako.* You are a good soldier, and you have been so kind to me."

"*Wafwako.*" The doctor and the soldier shook hands.

Kasanka lifted the bag from overhead, and he and Suzy disembarked the train. Suzy seated herself side-saddle on the back of the doctor's motorbike, the bag strapped behind her. Her arms wrapped around her husband's chest, her body swayed with the jostling of the bike over the bumps in the dirt road. She pondered the generosity of the Congolese soldier; he did not fit the military stereotype she had assumed.

Within an hour, she contentedly entered the threshold of her own home in Kabongo.

* * *

Suzy woke with a start—the noises in the distance repeated themselves, and she realized they were gunshots. She shook her husband's arm.

"*Docteur,*"—a good Congolese wife, she always addressed him by his formal title— "I hear gunshots."

"Yes, it happens every night. Don't be afraid. They don't come here." He hugged his wife protectively, glad that she was lying in their bed in his arms.

But Suzy did not sleep. In her previous months in Kabongo, she had not heard shooting, nor did such a sound break into the night in Kamina.

I think the war is getting worse here.

She did not wander far from the house, especially alone. She crossed the road to the hospital and visited the wounded soldiers. But increasingly, she feared that her husband would be caught in a cross fire, even if the war did not come to the hospital.

* * *

She was visiting patients at the hospital ward when her husband approached her. "You said you wanted to watch me perform a Caesarian. I have an emergency now. Follow me and do what I tell you."

Suzy had asked to watch a surgical delivery as her husband performed so many. He often talked about how this procedure saved women's lives. She wanted to observe him at work, delivering a baby who otherwise might have died.

He nudged her into place to wash her hands, and she followed him into the surgical theater.

"You have a person ready to give blood if needed?" Kasanka asked the nurse.

"Yes, her husband."

Kasanka began the procedure and soon slid a baby girl from the incision in the woman's abdomen. He cut the umbilical cord and delivered the placenta, while his nurse monitored the mother's vital signs.

Then the nurse frowned. "Doctor, she's in trouble."

"Yes, I can see that she's bleeding too much. She needs blood. Go get her husband to donate."

But shortly, the nurse returned. "He refuses."

"What? How could you let me begin a C-section without a blood donor?"

"He agreed. But he has changed his mind and left the hospital."

"What about another member of the family?"

"They have also refused."

Curiosity about her husband's surgical ability had brought Suzy into the theater, but now she saw the human drama that surrounded her husband's medical practice in the bush. Rural people did not understand western medicine, even as they used it; their taboos and associations made them afraid.

Suzy looked at the tiny, healthy infant and thought of the days and nights of tender care, the sacrifice that only a mother is motivated to provide. Without her mother, how would this little girl survive?

"I will donate. You know I am a universal donor."

Kasanka and the nurse turned toward Suzy with a start. But Kasanka's face beamed with approval. "Let's start."

Together, the three saved the life of the woman so that her baby might live.

* * *

Secretly she wished her husband would practice medicine in Kamina. Patients needed him there. But she also knew all of his reasons to stay in Kabongo. She could recite them by heart.

"I know you are doing important work. But I still worry about your security."

He reassured her with more confidence than he felt. "I'm safe. They know I'm a doctor and that I heal people."

She nodded, but still, she feared.

Two weeks later, the church truck from Kamina brought medical supplies to the hospital. Sorrowfully, she loaded her bag into the truck and rode back to Kamina to continue her studies, praying for the safety of her husband.

Bishop Ntambo Recruits a Music Leader

> "Mandela's Next Job: Trying to Cool One of Africa's Hottest Spots"
>
> *The New York Times*, January 13, 2000

> "Make a joyful noise, all ye lands,
> Serve the Lord with gladness:
> Come before his presence with singing."
>
> Psalm 100: 1-2

Lubumbashi, Haut-Katanga District
January 2000

The thought roused Bishop from his musing. *A good music leader. To raise their spirits. To build morale.*

* * *

Guy Mande Muyombo awoke, sweating. He had had a very strange dream. In it, his friend, Jean-Claude, a lawyer, came to his uncle's house in Kalubwe, an upscale neighborhood in the big city of Lubumbashi, where Guy was living.

"I've just been talking to Bishop Ntambo. He wants to see you immediately."

That Methodist Bishop is a pesky guy, Guy thought. *I have already told him, no! I will never go to Kamina. I am through with rural living. I have a degree in civil engineering. I have ambitions. I will get a good job with Gecamines, and if not with them, with another mining company. I am applying for every job that looks promising, and one will come through. I can keep selling cars for the dealership in the city to make ends meet in the meantime. I do not plan to live the life of poverty in a backward town.*

Guy loved music, singing and composition, and he had worked his way through the civil engineering program at the University of Lubumbashi as the lead singer in the gospel band, Epiphany. The group had built such a reputation for gathering a crowd in Lubumbashi that, when Laurent Kabila became president and launched the new Congolese franc on September 26, 1998, they were invited to sing at the Central Bank. They had played at churches and weddings all around Lubumbashi, performed frequently for groups like the Full Gospel Fellowship, and sang nearly every Saturday afternoon for Aglow, the evangelical gathering where the wives of the most important businessmen in Lubumbashi met for worship and praise.

Those women really take care of the band, nice food, good money! I can live like this, while I wait for a good job.

The leader of the band, however, had had other goals for his future. He wanted to further his education in Cameroon and raise money to take his family along. So, without telling the band members, he marketed his electric keyboard, guitars, and drums—and Bishop Ntambo bought them for $3000. Then Bishop Ntambo contacted all the remaining members of the band, and they auditioned for him. He offered them jobs for a short time at his rural outpost, Kamina. Two musicians, the best guitarist, Delpah, and a singer, Kasongo, accepted the invitation. But not Guy. He had performed for five exciting years with Epiphany, and he loved music. But Epiphany was disbanding, and Guy had other ideas.

* * *

Bishop's villagers were a music-making people. On Sunday mornings the musicians arrived first and called the congregation to worship through drumming and singing—their rhythms, echoing throughout the village, drew people to the sanctuary for the next hour until the service of worship actually began. Their hollow logs beat the African time, sometimes to a frenzy. They sang in *a cappella* voices and danced. Ntambo himself couldn't carry a tune. For a Luba, he didn't even dance that often, though he stepped lively when drawn into the gyrating circle. At best, he liked to conduct the music of a band as it blared from his car radio, waving his arms and grinning. But he understood the importance of music for his people.

Music played a central part in evangelism. He had wanted to encourage people to attend his congregations, and music extended the best invitation. But in the current tragedy of the war and the displacement of so many of his established congregations, music also became a form of pastoral care. Music communicated hope; many displaced people, like Mama Alphonsine and her children, had renewed their spirits during flight through singing. Music was so important to them that, one might even say, they survived because they could sing.

Every Saturday and Sunday when Bishop was in Lubumbashi, he invited church choirs and gospel groups to perform at his home. Like a sports recruiter, he videotaped their performances and watched the replays, scrutinizing the participants, discussing the merits of the musicians with close friends, determining

his top draft picks. He wanted the best choir, the best instruments, the best com-
poser, the best gospel music for his church in Kamina.

Whenever I see this one young man perform, I know I need him for Kamina.

* * *

Guy sat in the living room of his uncle's house, waiting for his aunt to make
breakfast. He tapped his fingers on the arm of the couch, watching television.
She can be so slow. But then he tried to calm himself, to find his patience.
Living here, at least I am in Lubumbashi where I have opportunities. The life
at his uncle's served as a good transition—as a college graduate, he was out
from under his parent's supervision at their home in Likasi. After experiencing
the freedom of university life, he was not ready to return home. But he hated
having to plan his schedule around his aunt's cooking. He wanted what he
couldn't afford—his own living quarters.

Then, the door opened, and his friend, Jean-Claude, entered.

"Hey, man!" They greeted, slapping each others' palms high in the air.

"I've just been talking to Bishop Ntambo. He wants to see you immediately."

Guy dropped his hands to his side, became suddenly serious, and sat hard
on the sofa. "What do you say?"

"I've just been talking to Bishop Ntambo. He wants to see you immediately!"

"It's strange. Last night I dreamt of you coming here, saying exactly that to
me. Exactly that."

"He is in his office and asked me to look for you today."

*Is the dream a prophecy, a way of God's speaking, something to take seri-
ously?*

That Monday morning, Guy and Jean-Claude boarded the bus and rode to
the center of Lubumbashi. Guy knew that this visit with Bishop Ntambo might
be different than the others, all because of a dream.

* * *

"Bishop Ntambo has offered me a job training his choir and teaching at his
college. He has bought my train ticket for Wednesday and his treasurer offered"—Guy gulped hard— "fifty dollars a month." The stipend was nothing,
barely enough to live on.

His aunt spoke first. "Everything good has a humble beginning. You might
complain about the money, but you never know what God has in store for you.
You have your money and you have your job."

A little flicker of gratitude toward his aunt sparked in Guy's heart. *She understands me.* "That is what I thought, after my dream. I'm at peace with this decision."

But his uncle pounded the arm of the chair, hard. "You are quitting. If you are patient, you will get work with good pay. You are throwing away your education. Yes, it's a hard time, the war and all, but still, you're young and talented. A fine position will come through."

Guy's stomach flip-flopped. *What if everything his uncle said was true?*

"And, we must call your father."

On the phone his father was emphatic, angry, even more so than his uncle. "Are you crazy? There is nothing in Kamina. You are throwing away every opportunity you have worked for!"

Word quickly spread throughout his family, and on Tuesday, one by one, his siblings arrived at his uncle's home, determined to stop their brother from destroying his future.

"How will we ever see you, all the way in Kamina?"

"Papa and Mama do not want this. You need to respect their wishes."

"You are talented, our hope. You are betraying the family."

* * *

On Wednesday morning at seven o'clock, Guy lay in his bed, meditating. His bag was packed, but he was paralyzed with indecision. Everyone in his family was against him, except his aunt. He had trained to become a civil engineer, but so far, no job, so he worked as a part-time car salesman. He was an established gospel singer, and God's presence in his life erupted through his music. But had God really been speaking to him in the dream, through the sense of peace he felt? Would God ask him to make a decision that was so despised by his family? What was this gospel-singing anyway—was it entertainment, a way to please people who had little else to do, or did it offer a faith to live by, a guide for the big decisions in one's life? With no experience, how did he know that this strong sense of guidance he felt truly came from God?

He looked at his watch. Seven-thirty. The train left at eight.

At seven-forty, his uncle came to his door. "If you are going to take this train, you need to go. I will drive you. You have twenty minutes."

Guy took his uncle's offer as a moment of human cooperation with divine urging. "I'm coming."

His uncle drove fast through the streets of Lubumbashi.

When they arrived at the train, the whistle sounded and Guy immediately heard his name. Bishop was standing on the steps of a passenger car, waving wildly. "Guy Mande, here, come here, this car! You are late! The train is leaving!" *Bishop, Mama Nshimba, on the train, also? I didn't know!* Conflict and shame—disobeying his family, reneging on Bishop—niggled his conscience but did not have time to re-root in his soul. Someone reached for his bag as his uncle pushed him onto the steps. With a great grunt, the wheels of the train began revolving and the engine pulled the passengers, willing, unwilling, and undecided, from the station. He fell into his seat next to Bishop, across from Mama Nshimba and her sister, closing his eyes with relief. A close call. The timing, Bishop's voice, the hand reaching for his luggage—again, it seemed that God was speaking.

* * *

In Likasi the train stopped for two hours. Guy saw his father and mother waiting for him on the platform. Guy turned to Bishop. "I need to talk to my parents."

His father's face was angry, his words heated. "Is this why you educated yourself in Lubumbashi? This music was an avenue to your career in engineering, but it's not your future. And you are going to work for $50 a month? Go back to Lubumbashi, back to your uncle's. Look for a real job. You are throwing away your future."

People stared, and every time Guy began to speak, his father launched a new tirade until his father's words were spent.

I cannot say to my father, I think this is what God wants me to do. He will not understand.

Quietly, Bishop had exited the train and was waiting for his moment. Guy noticed him standing behind his father. "Papa, meet Bishop Ntambo."

Bishop circled around and extended his hand. "You have a fine son, a talented man." He shook his head for emphasis. "He reminds me of my own son, Gaston. He's a pilot who flies medical missions in the bush. He got his pilot's training in America and is currently in the United States doing his mechanic's training. The church has provided him wonderful opportunities."

The features of Guy's father's face softened, so Bishop continued.

"I'll take good care of your son in Kamina. His music and his teaching will be real gift to the church. If he does well, I'll watch for other opportunities for him. I have a *large* set of contacts, in Africa, in Europe and in America. Kamina will not be his last stop. This job is only a beginning."

"I hope it will be as you say." Then turning to Guy and offering his hand, his father conceded. "All right, son, go with my blessing."

* * *

At the next stop of the train, Tenke, at five in the morning, Guy heard the singing before he saw it.

Bishop stood. "Come with me."

Guy followed Bishop to the steps of the train and faced the swaying, clapping, ululating church choir. All of the women, dressed in matching choir *bikwembe,* all of the men, outfitted with matching shirts, waved at him as they sang. Two girls stood with green boughs of leaves, wrapped in paper, ready to present Guy with a welcome bouquet. The choir finished and Bishop spoke.

"Today we are grateful for our new choirmaster and teacher, Guy Mande Muyombo. You'll all have opportunity to learn from him. He'll compose, direct our choirs, and build our music. He'll teach our children at the college. Welcome him, please."

The district superintendent responded. "Guy, we are pleased that you have agreed to be a musician among us. As you can see, we have many, many good singers and dancers in North Katanga. You will see us all again at Annual Conference in July, if not before. And we look forward to your leadership, building our evangelism."

The young girls came forward, bowed, and presented him with the green leaves. "Feel free among us."

"Do you have words to say to them?"

Guy stood still, dumbfounded. Finally, he stuttered a few words. "Thank you, I am glad God called me to be with you."

At each stop—Luena, Bukama, Kabondo—the train's arriving groans were drowned out by the drums and the singing of the choirs. Bishop introduced him, the district superintendent welcomed him, the girls greeted him, and people brought food. At each stop, Guy felt more like he was part of the community.

The engine labored as it began its ascent into the mountains. The villages were few, the vegetation lush, the valleys deep. The trip through the south Katangan towns had provided a time of embracing the people of the church, but now, the hours through the mountains provided Guy moments of pulling into himself, a cocoon in which to allow his life to metamorphize, hidden and protected from the emotion of the welcoming choirs. The train rose, peaked, and then began a gradual descent onto the plateau beyond. When he caught sight of Kamina sprawled before him, he was ready to emerge. The thatch-roofed huts, the palm-lined streets, and the people waiting to sing and to welcome him—he arrived with a new identity, a new community.

At the train station, the choirs sang, someone grabbed his bag, and Bishop's car took them to his residence. There, in the backyard, the choir had already set up the instruments and the band was ready to play.

"You need to hear this singer," Bishop told the waiting crowd. With that, he handed Guy the familiar microphone. Guy cleared his throat and sang, loud and clear.

Bishop Befriends the Imam

> "U.N. Faces Big Challenge in Any Congo Peacekeeping Mission"
>
> *The New York Times*, January 31, 2000

> "I am going to bring it recovery and healing; I will heal them and reveal to them abundance of prosperity and security."
>
> Jeremiah 33:6

Kamina, Haut Lomami District

January 2000

Bishop stood before the entrance to the new Centre Ville Church, watching the workers apply bright green paint to the external stucco. *The architects created such a beautiful design, the engineers such a solid structure. I could never have imagined it.* The engineers had poured a concrete slab, upon which they built the church's wooden frame. Then the masons enclosed the sanctuary in fired brick, leaving ample windows for ventilation. Simple but graceful, three arches lifted twenty feet above the wooden entrance double-door. The green and cream colors accented the church's yard of grass and sand. *Elegant, warm, inviting. Peace to all who enter. Next dry season, when Conference meets in Kamina, we celebrate here—in this beautiful church and its lovely yard.*

"Bishop?"

He jumped, started, then smiled. "Imam Hatari."

"*Salam alekum.* Peace be with you."

"Amen."

"Amina."

"We have seen the improvements you are making in Kamina. We want to help, in the name of the Prophet Muhammad, His Name Be Praised. Tomorrow our women would like to provide the food and water for your laborers."

When Bishop came to the church at mid-morning, sure enough, the Muslim women of Kamina had stoked their fires in the church's side yard. Their voices chattered over their work. The wood fire, roasting vegetables, herbs, and rice created a fragrant haze that hung in the trees. Bishop approached the Imam.

"You are very generous, Imam. Praise Jesus, Praise Muhammad."

"You are a man of God, to be respected."

"You have always honored me, Imam." *Yes, you have many hungry children. But they do not steal food from my yard.*

The Imam called to the workers to eat. They placed their paint brushes in the cans to keep them wet and pliable, covered them with plastic sheeting, and queued in the yard by the fires, ready to be energized for the afternoon's work.

"Bishop, we eat first." The two religious leaders strolled to the serving table with platters laden with food, and the Imam picked up two plates, handing one to Bishop. They moved a few feet to the shade of a tree, bowed their heads, and silently thanked God and Allah.

Bishop mixed the rice into the vegetables and took a spoonful. "Very good. Thank you. What can I do for you in return?"

"Nothing at the moment—the women have all done a good deed which accrues to them this day in heaven. But we will follow your example and build a mosque. Perhaps then I will ask for a good deed from you."

"Building inspires the people. I want to encourage you."

Some weeks later, the Imam approached Bishop in his office. "Bishop, *Salam alekum*. We have most of what we need for our mosque, but we lack ceiling tiles."

"I believe we have some we can give to you."

"In the name of Allah, Praise to His Name, *Wafwako*."

* * *

Ilunga Mutombo strode into Bishop's office, prepared to give his usual report on supplies on hand, supplies en route. But Bishop asked, "Can we spare ceiling tiles to give to our Muslim brothers and sisters?"

Ilunga Mutombo's eyes grew wide. "We have some tiles left from the church." His voice tone dropped a half note, and his words chugged, like his truck. "But they are so expensive. We...*our men* trucked them from Lubumbashi at great expense and effort. We can use them on the next project."

Bishop shook his head. "The mosque needs them now. Think what is happening. We build durable brick churches and parsonages to build up the church. People say, 'great church,' and we get a good reputation. We become the biggest employer in Kamina. The Imam sees us. He is not jealous, but says to himself, what they are doing is good and I can do it, too. We live with the Imam for a long time, but we do not work together, until we build the school. Now, the Imam becomes excited about rebuilding Kamina, and he wants to build one more durable brick building for the people, the mosque. Construction is bigger than the church, and relationships are bigger than the church. It's always better to support people, not to rebuke them when they are following our example. The church serves all the people, whether they are members or not. God goes where God wants, is not confined to the church."

Ilunga Mutombo smiled, caught the meaning of Bishop's words, then glowed. "I see your point. Bishop, you are wise."

"Please visit the Imam, find out what he needs, load your truck and take it to him. In the name of Jesus, we want to encourage him."

"I will do it this afternoon."

Pastor Ndalamba is Trapped

"Congo's War Triumphs Over Peace Accord"
The New York Times, September 18, 2000

"For this I will lament and wail;
I will go barefoot and naked;
I will make lamentation like the jackals,
and mourning like the ostriches.
For her wound is incurable."

Micah 1:8-9

Kamungu, about thirty kilometers west of Kabongo, Haut Lomami District
September 25, 2000

The Mai-Mai leader and the Congolese Army Colonel stood face-to-face, nearly nose-to-nose, and their voices rose. "You are not needed here," the Mai-Mai shouted at the Colonel. "We can protect this village. We can protect all of the villages! Disarm and go home."

The Colonel's voice raised, loud and fierce. "We are the government soldiers! We are here on the authority of the President. And we are concerned with you Mai-Mai, the trouble you make."

The ugly conversation engulfed the center of the village. Pastor Ndalamba, his wife, and his children heard each word, and all eyes of his family were upon him. "This conversation is not going well. Take the road to the river, as if you are fetching water. Carry nothing unusual with you—just pretend you are going about your business. I will find you later." His wife nodded, and a moment later, the family slipped from the rear of the hut, unobserved by the Mai-Mai and soldiers whose attention was focused on the angry speakers in the village.

Ndalamba stepped from his hut and approached the Congolese officer and the Mai-Mai leader.

"I am the Methodist pastor. Christ be with you."

"*Wafwako,* Pastor Ndalamba."

"*Eyo-vidye.* You sound so upset! Let's see if we can resolve this peacefully."

"Pastor, go back to your hut. We have our orders from our commander—clear the area of Congolese soldiers, who are harassing the villagers."

"Preposterous." The Congolese commander spat.

"You are people who follow tradition," Ndalamba said to the Mai-Mai. Nodding to the commander: "Go to the village chief, as tradition demands. He will judge what to do."

* * *

In September of 1998 Ndalamba had graduated from his studies at the seminary in Mulungwishi and was appointed to serve in Kamungu. It was a parish in the bush, but an old, faithful one. He was excited—he had studied hard for three years and was now well-versed in Bible, church history, theology, and pastoral studies. He felt prepared to care for the current parishioners and to bring others to believe in Christ. He arrived in Kamungu with his entire library, the books he had so carefully read and notated in seminary, eager to teach his studies to others and to refer to the books as needed. He was prepared to be the local scholar, the theologian-in-residence—to teach, to preach, and to evangelize.

He and his family had only been in Kamungu for ten days when the word swept through the village that the Rwandese army was advancing toward Kabongo and the villagers fled. He took what volumes of his irreplaceable library he could. A parishioner who admired his books offered to take the rest to his farm for protection. The parishioner caught up with his pastor in Kabongo.

"I could not carry all of them, so I dug a hole in the floor of the parsonage and buried them to protect them from looting."

Several weeks later, they were reassured: Congolese soldiers and their Zimbabwean allies had secured the area, and it was safe to return to Kamungu. They trudged the thirty-five kilometers back to their parsonage. They unearthed Ndalamba's books and stared, dismayed.

Ndalamba's precious books, so carefully guarded through the years of seminary, had not been looted but had been eaten by termites.

For the next three years, the pastor led worship and ministered among the people. Villagers and Congolese soldiers attended worship. The Congolese soldiers created their own choir, and they lounged at Ndalamba's parsonage, finding it a refuge from the military camp. Friendships grew. But the pastor, his wife and his children lived with their suitcases packed, ready to flee on a minute's notice, as waves of fighting came and went.

As the threat from the Rwandese waned, the danger from the Mai-Mai rose. In Kabongo territory, the Mai-Mai chief Maccabee was advancing toward Lenge. Traditional chiefs who did not cooperate with the Mai-Mai had been killed. Even Methodist pastors were threatened—some lost children or spouses. One person's flesh had been fried and circulated in the village. Churches and schools had been burned. Only the unexpected happened; everything was out of control. *Our parents' life under Mobutu was difficult,* Ndalamba mused, *but they never lived with constant threat like this.* Twice, Ndalamba and his wife left their hut and headed toward Kabongo, only to be turned back by his friends, the Congolese soldiers.

"Pastor, where are you going with your family—and your goat?"

"Many in the congregation have left. I must follow them to Kabongo."

"We cannot let you do that. There are still people in neighboring villages. When they know that the pastor has fled, they will become discouraged, and they leave all of the villages to be occupied by rebels."

"But few of my parishioners remain!"

"You must set an example. You must stay. We cannot let you through."

And so, the pastor, his family, and his goat were turned back to the village and caught in the tensions between the Congolese army and the Mai-Mai.

His intellect, his faithfulness, and his hospitality had made him beloved among the civilians and soldiers alike. But now, he and his family were hostages of the respect he had earned—confined in a village where, he believed, Christ was poised to fight in mortal combat with the Devil. And the Devil came in the guise of the Mai-Mai.

* * *

When the Mai-Mai commander Maccabee camped in Lenge, townspeople, members of the church and others, gathered together.

"We must find a way to convince them. Stay in Lenge, away from Kamungu."

"They won't agree. But they must be urged: come to Kamungu, if they will, without fighting against Congolese soldiers."

"We must send a delegation—not church and community leaders, they are too threatening—but brave messengers who will persuade them."

"Who will go?" The villagers looked from one to another, without speaking. Finally, one church member volunteered, then another, then a member of the community. Ndalamba prayed for their safe journey. And then, he waited.

The delegation returned. "Maccabee is sending his secretary and other Mai-Mai to meet with the Congolese soldiers."

Shortly, a group of Mai-Mai strode into Kamungu.

* * *

The Mai-Mai had already killed village chiefs in Kabongo District. Ndalamba knew that this meeting could end in violence. But culture and custom demanded that the village leader mediate. The crowd of hissing men turned toward the hut where the chief waited, his royal staff, the sign of his spiritual power, in his hand. Ndalamba strode a few steps back to the door of his hut and watched.

"This disturbance cannot invade this village. The Congolese soldiers must go back to their barriers, and the Mai-Mai to their camp."

The warriors crowded the chief, leaning into him. "We have orders from *our* commander, Maccabee: Clear the area of Congolese soldiers. They are harassing the villagers."

"What villagers are asking you to do this?" The Congolese commander growled.

"The ancestors of our commander Maccabee know best."

"Then call your commander, and let us talk to him."

And with that, the entire entourage tromped from the hut of the chief.

The Mai-Mai raised Maccabee on the ham radio, and the traditional chief requested that he withdraw his warriors to his camp. But Maccabee only reiterated what the Mai-Mai leader had been saying: the Congolese army should hand over their guns and leave the protection of the village to the Mai-Mai.

The Congolese officer stood his ground. "We are the representatives of the government here in Kamungu. We cannot give you our guns. We have government orders." He handed back the microphone of the ham radio.

* * *

Ndalamba heard the pop and reply of pistol shots. The battle had begun.

Ndalamba rolled as far beneath the bed as possible, as if he could disappear into the wall of the hut where he could not be found. The explosions of larger, faster gunfire filled the air. His hands pressed to his ears, he felt his heart pound hard in his chest. *It is truly the last day for me.* Closing his eyes tight, he prayed for his wife and his children, asking God to guide them safely toward Kabongo and the Zimbabweans.

The gunfire continued, but no one entered his hut. When quiet came, Ndalamba wriggled from beneath the bed and fled through the back door toward the path to the river. He did not look back and had no curiosity about the dead or wounded. *My family at the river—let them know that I live—let me find them before we are hopelessly separated in the bush.*

When Ndalamba and his family were reunited, they fell into one another's arms, weeping with relief. But his wife was inconsolable. "We have lost everything, our garden, our goat, our clothes, our home—all of our belongings! We will starve."

Ndalamba's heart wept within him. Outwardly, he remained strong. "Don't worry, we started with nothing. God will provide." The next day they began their trek to Kabongo, sleeping in the open, huddling against the cold nights, avoiding the barriers, hoping for assistance when they arrived.

Bishop Ntambo Preaches at Kamina Military Base

"U.N. Peacekeeper Gives Council a Gloomy Briefing on Congo"

The New York Times, March 29, 2000

"When he entered Capernaum, a centurion came to him, appealing to him and saying, 'Lord, my servant is lying at home paralyzed, in terrible distress.' And he said to him, 'I will come and cure him.' The centurion answered, 'Lord, I am not worthy to have you come under my roof; but only speak the word, and my servant will be healed. For I also am a man under authority, with soldiers under me; and I say to one, "Go," and he goes, and to another, "Come," and he comes, and to my slave, "Do this," and the slave does it.' When Jesus heard him, he was amazed and said to those who followed him, 'Truly I tell you, in no one in Israel have I found such faith. I tell you, many will come from east and west and will eat with Abraham and Isaac and Jacob in the kingdom of heaven, while the heirs of the kingdom will be thrown into the outer darkness, where there will be weeping and gnashing of teeth.' And to the centurion Jesus said, 'Go; let it be done for you according to your faith.' And the servant was healed in that hour."

Matthew 8: 5-13

Kamina

January through March 2000

"A Zimbabwean officer, Major Sungura, a chaplain and soldiers came to the office. All Methodists. Their commander, General Mugoa, wants to meet you," Kahunda reported.

Bishop mulled what he was hearing. A small hope rose in his heart. *Perhaps, through the church, a door opens, a good relationship with Kamina Base for the people of Kamina.* Then he sobered. *Or one that brings suspicion, more rumors.*

The Methodist Church was building its reputation in Kamina. The care for displaced people, the construction projects, the employment, the relationships with Muslims—people were thinking well of the church. Established congregations were growing—new congregations were forming.

A relationship with Kamina Base could backfire. Townspeople hated soldiers. Some villagers and government officials distrusted Bishop's frequent trips to America and thought he must be CIA. But the Zimbabweans provided Congo's best protection. A relationship with the Zimbabwean military might actually help the Methodist Church in the government's eyes, even if the villagers looked on with distrust.

Bishop remembered the words that Martin Luther King, Jr. had repeated in so many of his speeches: "the moral arc of the universe is long but bends toward justice."

I take the risk.

"I will invite their entire delegation for dinner at my house. John, write it now on my letterhead, in English, so I can sign."

* * *

Bishop Ntambo prepared for General Mugoa's arrival as if he were hosting a state dinner. He and Mama Nshimba carefully discussed the menu.

"By tradition, a goat must be procured."

"Bishop, where do we get a goat?"

"OK, not a goat. Then chicken and dried fish. Cabbage, beans and rice from Kamisamba Farm. Something from the agricultural projects."

Mama Nshimba hired some women to help, and they cooked for two days. Bishop planned the seating. He and General Mugoa would sit side by side in the middle of the table where they could talk, with the Major and the chaplain rounding one end and Kahunda and Tschimwang observing from the other. Bishop had decided what he wanted to communicate.

After opening formalities, they talked about the war.

"We appreciate the protection of the Zimbabwean army. The villagers know that where you are, they will be safe. Oh, the western newspapers say you are here for the gold of Congo—but there is no gold in Kamina! You are here for the people. You have brought us stability."

The General nodded. "Your construction projects, they are strengthening the Congolese resistance. It's important that the villagers stay in place and do not leave Kamina to the rebels."

"We have begun three schools and next year we will begin a university. It is a sign that the people have a future. God is smiling on Kamina."

"Perhaps you could come to Kamina Base as a chaplain, to preach?"

"I am ready." Bishop nodded vigorously.

"We want to encourage your projects. We'll find a way."

"Please, come back to my house, any time. Use my house as a place to relax, to get away from the Base. My wife and I, we are happy for you to come."

And so it came to be that General Mugoa visited regularly at Bishop and Mama Nshimba's home.

After the General and his delegation left, Bishop, Kahunda and Tschimwang took precious bottles of Fanta to the *payotte,* where members of the cabinet waited to hear what had happened and to celebrate the occasion. After the delicate dance of the dinner with the General Mugoa, retelling the story and laughing with happiness provided relief. In the moments between joking, the men could hear the clatter of dishes as Mama Nshimba and the women cleaned up the kitchen.

* * *

Bishop Ntambo looked his most distinguished self in a purple clerical collar and dark blue suit. A large contingent accompanied Bishop—Kahunda, Tschimwang, Nyengele, and John Mutombo, to translate from English to Kiluba, rode in the cab. Guy Mande, the musical instruments, and fifteen musicians, men and women, piled into the truck's bed.

Faustin, the chauffeur, headed northeast. On the outskirts of Kamina the dirt road to Kabongo turned north, but the macadam road to Kamina Base, built by the Belgians in the 1950s, stretched straight another fifteen kilometers. The asphalt of "Mobutu's Belt," as the locals called it, had broken in ragged fragments on either side, narrowing it to three-fourths of a lane. Faustin balanced his trusty truck with one wheel on the pavement and one wheel on the dirt shoulder some six inches below, so that it rumbled along on an angle, nearly scraping its frame on the ground. The steering wheel shook, and Faustin gripped it till his knuckles turned white.

At the gate to Kamina Base, Zimbabwean guards in ochre berets jumped to their feet with their rifles drawn, surrounding the car. Faustin rolled down the window, and Bishop leaned forward so that his clerical collar was in full view.

"I am Methodist Bishop from Kamina, here to see General Mugoa," Bishop announced in English.

"We're expecting you. He's at the main building."

The road wound through palm trees and savannah bushes, past huts and concrete houses, by Congolese soldiers in maroon berets lounging about, and across the top of a ridge that afforded a wide view to the slopes of the countryside. There, a long, sweeping white concrete building three stories high, with imposing pillars and twenty or more building-length steps approaching the doors, announced itself as the primary administration building. Congolese and Zimbabwean guards stood at attention. Faustin parked the truck, and the delegation approached the soldiers to request entry.

General Mugoa himself came to greet them. "Bishop, good to see you!" He offered his hand and Bishop shook it, heartily.

"And you!"

"Come in. The chapel is this way." He turned down a hall with Bishop's delegation following.

* * *

At choir rehearsal, Guy Mande and his musicians had discussed the best way for Congolese Luba Christians to speak to Zimbabwean Shona Christians through song. The cultural image of the Luba warrior led the people to identify with many Old Testament stories, especially those in which God is strengthening the community for a just war. For decades Luba Christians had circulated many songs with lyrics about warfare in the Old Testament, and Guy selected one that set the story of Gideon from Judges 6:11-18 to a traditional Luba melody.

The choir drummed their rhythms as the Zimbabweans filed into the chapel. The guitars introduced the melody, and the vocalists began the worship service. The congregation clapped with anticipation; the music had excited them.

Then, the story of the centurion was read in English and Kiluba. Bishop stood, his Bible in hand. He looked with great seriousness at the congregation, his eyes riveted on those of his audience.

"You Zimbabweans, you are like the centurion, the foreigner. You come to Congo, your sick servant. You have General Mugoa, a man of authority, one who has faith. He says to Jesus, help the sick servant, the Congolese nation. And you see, your faith is healing Congo. The rebels are negotiating, and the war is coming to an end. Now is the time for faith in development, for peace. Please continue to help the Congolese nation."

The room stilled until Bishop's sermon ended. Murmurs rippled through the congregation, then shouts of "Amen!"

Then General Mugoa stood. "And now, let us eat together!"

* * *

Kahunda followed Bishop and the General out of the chapel, immersing himself in the chatter of soldiers and civilians. As he reached another doorway he paused. What? The smell of chicken and fish frying! And then, entering the long white mess hall, he saw the platters on the banquet table piled high with chicken, fish, rice, relish and *linga-linga*. He grinned. Such a pleasure! He had rarely eaten chicken or fish since the war began.

He filled his plate with the delicacies. Then, he reached for a firm, spongy ball of... *bukari*? It squished. He looked at the white substance that had plastered itself to his hand and shook it onto his plate. Then, swiping the Zimbabwean *basa* with his forefinger, he seasoned it with *linga-linga* and licked. *Very good!* He sucked at his fingers, leaving no trace of food.

Placing his plate on a table, he seated himself on a bench. *What luxury!* He feasted his eyes, examining every morsel of the golden crust of the fried chicken leg and thigh. He bathed his nose in its fragrance. Finally, he lifted the chicken with two hands, bit off a piece, closed his eyes, and chewed. This day, this day only, he filled his stomach.

* * *

Meanwhile, the Zimbabweans had invited the highest ranking Congolese officer, Colonel Shilungu, to the service and to the feast. When the Zimbabwean General excused himself for a moment, the Congolese colonel approached Bishop.

"You are doing so much construction. My office, here at Kamina Base, it's in shambles, hard to clean up. The army has nothing. What do you think, Bishop? Could you help us with some paint and cement for my office?"

"I am ready!"

* * *

A few months earlier, Bishop would not have believed the scene he now watched.

Ilunga Mutombo's workmen passed fired bricks from the truck bed, hand over hand, adding them to the already large stack. Nearby, some Zimbabwean soldiers stirred concrete, and others—armed not with guns but with pickaxes—were digging a hole as long and deep as a large man. But this was no grave. Rather, it was the latrine for the Katuba Parish, the school and the church. As General Mugoa had promised, he brought his engineers. They designed the latrine and Mugoa donated the cement, the paint and the labor. Now Bishop watched the construction, pondering its possible meanings.

The villagers of Kamina and the displaced people stayed in Kamina because of the construction projects and because of the Zimbabwean army. They resisted the rumors that encouraged them to flee. Durable, fired brick buildings, a symbol of stability for Congo.

The latrine is healthy. But a positive relationship between the townspeople and the Base? Soldiers who encourage the villagers' hopes, dreams, needs—their future—rather than destroying them? Zimbabweans, showing Congolese soldiers how to behave with good will towards townspeople? Maybe Congolese soldiers will change their behavior, protect Kamina rather than loot and rape. Maybe good comes for the villagers. Maybe.

An African latrine, an enclosed building with a concrete slab with openings to pee into or squat over, had rarely offered so much possibility.

Doctor Kasanka Reconciles Soldiers and Mai-Mai

> "DANCE REVIEW; Driving Evil Spirits Away with Song and Pulsating Rhythm"
>
> *The New York Times*, September 20, 2000

> "You prepare a table before me in the presence of my enemies;
> you anoint my head with oil; my cup overflows.
> Surely goodness and mercy shall follow me all the days of my life,
> and I shall dwell in the house of the Lord my whole life long."
>
> Psalm 23:5-6

Kabongo, Haut Lomami District

September 2000

The aide swung wide the door to the maternity ward and waved to Kasanka at the far end of the room. "Doctor, emergency!" He strode quickly between the two columns of thirty side-by-side iron cots, whose frames revealed bare, unprotected metal beneath fragments of white paint, worn from decades of use. He approached Kasanka, waiting till he was close enough to speak without creating anxiety in the room full of new mothers. "Badly wounded Mai-Mai."

Kasanka lowered the *kikwembe* cloth over the belly of the woman whose C-section incision he was examining. He patted her hand. "It looks fine. You'll go home soon."

Kasanka turned, walked through the ward to the hall and inclined his ear toward his aide.

"A commander, bullets torn through the flesh of his arm, bad. His charms did not protect him." Kasanka looked hard at his aide; the aide smiled for a split second, then regained his serious, professional composure.

Kasanka's heels clicked in the corridor, announcing his arrival. In the examining room sat a Mai-Mai warrior, dressed in animal skins, necklaces, arrows and spears, accompanied by a Zimbabwean soldier in military fatigues

The warrior supported his left arm with his right, blood soaking a cloth, dripping to the floor.

"I'm Dr. Kasanka, the head of hospital and surgeon here. May I examine your arm?"

* * *

In Kamina Bishop roused and dressed at three a.m. He sat in the dark in the velour overstuffed chair in his living room, trying to make sense of the reports he had been receiving on the ham radio—of Mai-Mai militias terrorizing villagers around Kabongo in his home territory.

Voices in his mind wrestled with each other. *Kabila had been right to encourage the Mai-Mai! Now it's all wrong. The Congolese army is weak and corrupt, filled with ethnic conflict.* The corners of his mouth drew into a deep frown.

To augment the Congolese military, Laurent Kabila had promoted the development of civilian militias in Kabongo territory. He had even sent an emissary to talk about self-defense to the rural people and offered some training and weapons. When villagers fled, Mai-Mai militias stayed put and helped to defend Congo, so the land was not vacant and easily occupied by rebels. When the Rwandese attacked, the local Mai-Mai fought alongside the national Congolese army and its allies.

But soldiers identified only weakly with the army. Under Mobutu, the Congolese soldiers had served as the mercenaries of a dictator; the army had no identity of its own as protectors of a country. So when Kabila became commander-in-chief, loyalty to those who spoke one's own language prevailed over fidelity to a united Congo. Congolese soldiers resented being deployed to areas of Congo beyond their home territory, to defend people whose languages and dialects they did not speak. Without loyalty to the local villages, they easily looted the Luba villagers for food.

Kinyarwanda-speaking soldiers from Eastern Congo, Lingala-speaking soldiers from Kinshasa, in Kiluba-speaking Katangan villages. Not good. Those soldiers must be the ones who rape Luba women in the countryside, who loot our villages. Certainly, our people live by traditional values of not stealing and not taking another's wife. Why would a Luba destroy the life of another Luba person?

When Congolese soldiers turned on Luba villages, looting what they had, the Mai-Mai fought the Congolese soldiers, not only the Rwandese. But the Mai-Mai, in turn, sought food and payment from their neighbors.

Those Mai-Mai follow the same rationale as the army: 'We protect you, so feed us.' The villagers run out of food, the Mai-Mai attack the villagers. Luba destroying Luba. How can it be? But it is. And then the Mai-Mai got greedy— they discovered they could loot maize from villagers and ship it to Kasai for a profit. One looting of villagers for profit led to another.

Villagers knew that the Zimbabwean, Namibian, and Angolan armies provided security. Where they had large forces, as in Kabongo, it seemed that civilians were safe. But their fates had turned: as the Lusaka agreement took hold and the Zimbabweans, Namibians, and Angolans withdrew, the villagers were at the mercy of the Mai-Mai. Mai-Mai had even set up military-style road blocks, preventing commerce.

The Lusaka deal included a United Nations peacekeeping force, MONUC. They had already arrived in Congo. *But those peacekeepers will be busy in Kinshasa and the Kivus. They'll leave Kabongo alone. For the rural Katangan villagers, I see no real security—anytime, anywhere.*

And all of them—soldiers, militia and civilians—sat beside one another in Methodist congregations for for singing and worship. Pastors reported that Methodist children were being recruited into the Mai-Mai.

If they were true Christians, they would repent, stop killing people. How to help those Mai-Mai give up their charms? How to help them become Congolese, loyal to the president? How to get food and medicine to places like Kabongo?

Bishop rubbed his temples, trying to relieve the headache that crept across his forehead.

The society he was creating in Kamina—the durable brick homes and churches, the farm for crops and agricultural training, the employment for so many people—gave hope to the villagers and displaced. With so many people in Kamina, rebels didn't try to take over. But the word from Kabongo showed how fragile the peace in Kamina really was.

And so, he was driven to one prayer: *God, blessed are the peacemakers, let us be peacemakers.* He prayed, repeating the phrase, over and over.

Bishop could face the horror in his mind and petition his God in the pre-dawn hours. But as the sun rose, supplicants queued at *his* door. Now, they waited. Placing his hands on the arms of his chair, he pushed himself upright, opened the door to his house, signalled to the guard to release the lock to the compound, and allowed the first woman in line to approach. Then he received her plea for school fees for her children and offered her encouragement, blessing, and money.

* * *

In Kamungu the Congolese soldiers had fought with Mai-Mai, and they captured an important prisoner: the secretary to the militia's commander, Maccabee. He was badly wounded. He would have been shot by the Congolese soldiers, except that the Zimbabweans insisted on a new policy regarding prisoners—that they be handed over to the Zimbabwean army and treated as prisoners-of-war, rather than killed. So a Zimbabwean soldier was assigned to bring the warrior to the hospital for medical care.

In Kabongo Hospital Kasanka operated on the arm of the commander. His muscles had been lacerated to the bone; he had lost much blood. When the Mai-Mai regained consciousness, the Zimbabwean soldier listened as Kasanka proposed the treatment.

"You need to stay here where we can observe you for infection. I have given you some anaesthetic—you will also need antibiotics. You are lucky. We have the medicine you need."

And then, he took a deep breath and implemented the decision he had made with Chaplain Masengo and the medical staff. First, he addressed the Zimbabwean.

"We are running out of beds in the ward. Until now, we have tried to keep different forces in separate rooms, Zimbabweans and Congolese in one building, Rwandese in another. But we are too crowded."

He looked directly into the eyes of the Mai-Mai warrior. "Now, in this hospital, each of you is a patient, not a warrior. We will do our best to heal your wounds. But you will have to cooperate with the others in your ward."

The Mai-Mai listened, too much in pain to respond.

The Zimbabwean soldier murmured to the Mai-Mai. "This is our field hospital; he is our doctor. Do what he says."

Then, Kasanka pointed toward a man who had entered the room. "Here is our chaplain, Pastor Masengo. He will pray for you. And he will remind the others that they, too, are patients, not here to fight you or one another. You will remain here in the surgical theater until he has talked with each one."

* * *

Pastor Masengo entered the ward of soldiers. He paused between the first two beds.

"How are you feeling today?"

"I have less pain."

And to the patient in the bed beside, "And you?"

"I need to see the doctor. I am not better."

"I will tell him. Now I have something I need to talk with you about. Until now we have had patients in this ward who have fought on the same side, and their enemies in a different building. But we are too crowded. We must place combatants in whatever bed is available. Shortly, we will be bringing a wounded Mai-Mai to this ward."

The patient who was not getting better struggled to rise and rest his upper body on his elbows. "I will kill him. The Mai-Mai attacked my family, my village. He deserves to die."

"Have you hurt God's creatures in this war? Do you need God's forgiveness?"

The soldier lowered himself, staring at the ceiling, not looking at the pastor.

"This Mai-Mai may have done horrible things—we do not know. But he is a human being, like you are. He must face his misdeeds, as you must. He deserves God's forgiveness, as you do. And here, you are not enemies—you are both patients in need of a doctor."

Masengo waited, silently, until the patients relaxed with acceptance. He prayed for their healing. Then he continued to the next two beds.

Fifteen times, Masengo spoke to wounded soldiers, explaining that from now on, Mai-Mai, Congolese, Rwandese, Zimbabwean, Lingala-speaking, Kiluba-speaking, all patients would recuperate in the same ward. He heard their reactions and, as God put the words in his mouth, preached his gospel.

* * *

The hospital provided medicine, but not food.

The Mai-Mai lay in his bed. Initially, the pain had blocked his desire to eat. But when the wife of the man in the next bed brought cassava and fish oil, the Mai-Mai felt his hunger. He turned his head and his eyes traced her movement as she broke off bits of cassava dough, wiped it in the gravy, and placed it in her husband's mouth.

She glanced at the man watching her and quickly returned her attention to her husband. Still, the Mai-Mai stared.

The husband turned his head toward the one who was fixed on his wife. All of the husband's suffering was concentrated in his gaze. The look of the Mai-Mai in the next bed softened and deepened, revealing his agony.

"Mama, give a bit of cassava to the new patient beside us. He has no family to bring him food."

His wife looked shocked, then quizzical. "Papa, I am here to help you get well. Not the Mai-Mai."

"Here he is only a patient without family. Please feed him."

She hesitated. Then, without speaking further, she broke off a piece of cassava, wiped it in the gravy, and handed it to the new patient in the next bed. She continued in that way, alternating a piece of cassava on the tongue of her husband and a portion in his neighbor's hand.

* * *

Masengo had spent much time in the ward, talking, observing. The patients chatted, told stories, sang songs, even laughed with one another. Now Masengo crouched low by the bed of the new patient.

"I have prayed for your health. You are getting better?"

"Yes, it's a good place to be."

"Then I need to speak seriously to you. Your charms did not protect you. And the people here, the ones you are fighting, they are human beings, like you are. They love their mothers, fathers, their children, like you do. Give up your charms, and put down your weapons. The foreign soldiers will leave; you do not need to continue this war against your own people. Let me tell you about Jesus Christ. He, not your charms, will save you."

* * *

Kasanka stood at the door of the ward of soldiers, surveying the experiment created by necessity. *Every person is God's creature, and every creature in danger needs a doctor.*

He had hoped for quiet, no fighting. But what miracle had happened? They had made a little reconciliation, at least in the hospital. The patients talked with one another, saw each other as people. And Kasanka was pleased that Chaplain Masengo had converted the new patient. He had renounced the Mai-Mai and handed over his charms.

As other wounded arrived, whatever their affiliation, he now made the same introduction to the ward: "Here, we only have patients, no enemies."

Raymond Mande Attends the United Methodist General Conference 2000

"RELIGION JOURNAL; Repenting Racist Acts and Recalling Genocide"

The New York Times, May 13, 2000

"He replied, 'It is not for you to know the times or periods that the Father has set by his own authority. But you will receive power when the Holy Spirit has come upon you; and you will be my witnesses in Jerusalem, in all Judea and Samaria, and to the ends of the earth.'"

Acts 1: 7-8

Cleveland Convention Center, Cleveland, Ohio
May 2-12, 2000

Dr. Raymond Mande, a color-coded map in his hands, tapped the back of the chair on the edge of each row as he loped along the edge of Section A, nodding his head, counting in French, *seize, dix-sept, dix-huit.* There. He paused and peered down the row. Soon, he would occupy one of the seats reserved for the sixteen delegates from the North Katanga Annual Conference in Row 17. He looked up—the four Tanganyikan/Tanzanian delegates were across the aisle in Section B, one of the four quadrangles on the floor of the Cleveland, Ohio Convention Center. Then, he scanned the thousand empty seats, imagining them filled with delegates, mostly from the United States, but also from Europe, the Philippines, and Africa. He had been waiting for this moment for months. He was determined to make a difference for Congo.

* * *

A year earlier Mande had sat in his office in the English Department at the University of Lubumbashi, poring over Bishop's copy of *The United Methodist Discipline,* preparing himself to be a delegate to the United Methodist General Conference. Mande, who worked as a part time lecturer at the University of

Lubumbashi and a part time assistant to Bishop Ntambo, had written his English literature doctoral dissertation on an African interpretation of metaphors in the work of Henry James. After such thought-provoking complexity, the language of the *Discipline* seemed simple, even mechanical.

But when he came to a section entitled "The Social Principles," he sat up straight. The paragraph that caught his attention began: "We believe war is incompatible with Christian teachings and the example of Christ…" So the church had an official statement on war.

Now, he read analytically, pondering its meaning.

He moved on to the procedural instructions for General Conference. Then he got an idea. He was proud of his ability to uncover the subtext of a work of English literature—but a literary critic could also be an author.

When he was scheduled to assist Bishop, he hustled up the three flights of stairs to the United Methodist floor, a spring in his step. Nodding to his colleagues, he wound his way through the church quarters, a dingy maze of rooms. At the far end, Bishop's office looked out upon Lubumbashi's main square and the intricate, peach-and-dirty cream pillars and balconies of the dilapidated Park Hotel. The office was filled with light from the tall windows, and Bishop sat at his desk, reading reports.

"Bishop, even though it's my first time to be a delegate, I think I can talk to the people about the war in Congo. It says that petitions can be sent by groups and Annual Conferences but also by individuals. With your permission, I would like to write a petition."

"Great idea. Most of the delegates are from the United States. The US can stop this war"—and then he clicked his fingers high in the air for emphasis—"like that."

* * *

Mande gathered his thoughts, waiting to write till he had clarity about what he wanted to say. Then, he crafted his first draft very close to the final words:

(Title)

General Conference lead in finding solutions to stop war in Congo and aid Congo United Methodists financially to help refugees

(Body)

Whereas war breaking out in the Democratic Republic of Congo has caused death, wiping out families, causing a flow of refugees, and displaced people; and

Whereas Rwanda, Uganda, and Burundi troops have imposed this war on the Congo, thus occupying half of the country and recruiting Congolese making them rebels; and

Whereas Western countries and the United Nations Security counsel are aware of this situation, and no condemnation has been charged against the invading countries; and

Whereas these occupation troops are killing, wiping out villages, burning, violating women, that's infecting them with the HIV virus; and

Whereas the United Methodist Church believes in international justice; and

Whereas there is a way for the church to take a lead in chaotic situations like the one going on in the central region of the African continent,

Therefore, be it resolved that the 2000 General Conference of the United Methodist Church take a leading step in finding solutions intending to stop this war.

Be it further resolved, that the 2000 General Conference send two petitions, one to the United Nations Security Counsel, and the other to the U.S. Congress, with the only subject: STOP WAR IN THE DEMOCRATIC REPUBLIC OF CONGO.

Be it further resolved that the 2000 General Conference assist the United Methodist Church in Congo financially to help face the many problems related to refugees, displaced people and community development.

What more important work could the conference engage?

A month before the General Conference was due to begin, Mande received his advanced copy of the *Daily Christian Advocate*. He sat down to read. It became clear that the debates would be dominated by discussions about whether gay and lesbian people could become United Methodist clergy, by Americans' repentance for slavery and other forms of racism, and by how the church should be organized—all issues emerging from the American church. Many resolutions focused on social issues in the United States, and if he read them as he read *The Turning of the Screw*, through Congolese eyes, he would have had to rewrite most of them. Like the document about gun control—what about the guns that were supplied to Rwanda, Uganda, and Burundi that were killing Congolese people?

Then, on page 1150, he found his petition exactly as he wrote it.

* * *

Once in Cleveland, Mande felt invigorated by the opening formalities and worship. But he also felt impatient, as he sat through hours of words upon words. *The moment is coming to ask the conference to invest in stopping the war in Congo.* Then, the plenary was disbursed to smaller legislative sessions.

Mande walked the halls, checking the room numbers and the signs, looking for his committee, Church and Society.

When he found the room, he sat, listening to the chatter of the delegates as they entered, thirty or so people facing the front of the room where the chair of the session and the secretary sat. *Did they know what important business they had to do?* The officers quieted the room, and soon he heard familiar words—outrage about war and violence, determination to bring peace. But no one mentioned Congo.

He raised his hand.

"Please."

He stood. "My name is Raymond Mande Mutombo Mulumiashimba, and I am a professor from North Katanga Annual Conference. Thank you for giving me the floor." He took a deep breath. "We are discussing peace and war in so many places, but not in my country, Democratic Republic of Congo." Then, with hope rising in his voice, "Could we discuss the petition I submitted since we are talking about the violence in other places, like Sierra Leone?"

He watched the chair of the committee. It was as if minutes passed, until he heard, "This committee is not concerned with that petition. It has been assigned to the Central Conference committee. It will be dealt with there."

Numbness crept down Mande's hands and feet. *Why not here? Did this Church and Society committee care about peace and war everywhere but in Congo?*

"I don't understand." Mande clenched his fists, and his mouth tightened into a straight line. "I left my country to be part of this delegation, and I belong to the population of Congo. It does make sense to me that we discuss what is happening and that this conference should invest itself in finding an end to the war."

"It's just that your petition is part of a different committee's docket."

Mande did not know how to counter their response. He felt a burning in his chest, the rising flame of grief. "But you are discussing violence and peace! If the conference will not invest in this situation, then there is no international justice in the United Methodist Church for the people of Congo."

He sat down hard in his seat, and his eyes blurred with tears. The writing, the sending, the waiting, the anticipation, the hope—for what? He lowered his head, his shoulders began to shake, and then he began to cry. But he was not the only one so touched. Another delegate from North Katanga, Pastor Mut-wale, who was assigned to the same session, walked across the room and sat in the empty chair next to Mande, gripping his hand. Mutwale, too, began to weep.

Mande and Mutwale sobbed in chorus, and then, like an orchestra that adds background swells to an opening melody, the room filled with the sounds of scraping, pushing, and footsteps. Mande could not raise his head, but he felt hands on his back and his shoulders and heard people praying in whispers. Then a woman with a strong, deep African-American voice began to sing. And so it continued, until Mande and Mutwale lamented all they had seen—churches burned, congregants murdered, women raped, children made into soldiers, fam-ilies divided, displaced and impoverished.

As he dried his eyes with his hands, Mande lifted his head and felt strong arms around him, pulling him slightly upright.

"We will help you. Where is your petition?"

He showed them the *Daily Christian Advocate*, page 1150.

"Can you write with a computer?"

"Yes."

The chair of the session gestured to a person hovering at the edge of the room, where the staff of the General Board of Church and Society sat. "Here, he will help you make it into a document for the plenary."

* * *

When the General Conference was over, Mande sat in the Cleveland Hopkins airport, waiting to board the plane for Johannesburg. *The conference DID invest itself in Congo!* He smiled, thinking of all that had transpired. The delegation from the Central Congo presented a resolution describing the effects of the war and the need for United Methodists to plead Congo's case with President Clin-ton, the United States Congress, and the United Nations Security Council. A day later Mande's own resolution was referred to the General Board of Global Ministries and the Board of Church and Society for action. Bishop Felton May from Washington, D.C., who minced no words of protest, set up a Congo com-mission, and all three Congolese bishops—Ntambo from North Katanga, Onema from Central Congo, and Katembo from South Congo—spoke. And then they called on Mande for his statement—and again, he asked the assem-bled to take steps to bring peace to Congo.

Mande savored his most important moment, rolling the image over again and again in his mind. He had spoken to a delegate who promised to help, a pastor from a large church in Washington, D.C., who also served as a chaplain to President Clinton. The delegate listened carefully as Mande told him the whole story of the invasion of Congo. "Please tell President Clinton we the people of the Congo need peace. This war of aggression has ruined the Congo with killing, women raped, and devastation. If President Clinton simply says a word to Rwanda and Uganda, the war will stop, as we know President Clinton is a man of peace."

Mande had made his first trip to the United States with great anticipation and returned to Congo, filled with hope.

John Mutombo Opens the Guesthouse

> "Security Council Demands that Rwanda and Uganda Leave Congo"
>
> *The New York Times*, June 17, 2000

> "...for my house shall be called a house of prayer for all peoples..."
>
> Isaiah 56:7

Kamina, Haut Lomami District

July 2000

"Bishop, here is the proposal: make the former missionary house into a guesthouse. The Adventist doctors who used to visit the missionaries would like to be able to stay there. But they would like to pay. What do you think?" John Mutombo's soft quizzical drawl, the slight tipping of his head, his tentative, open questioning—he made Bishop smile. *John connected quickly—the right man for public relations.*

The church owned the compound in question, which had been built during the era of the late Bishop Wakadilo and stood on the corner of two streets, the last in a row of four such homes where the American and Swiss Methodist missionaries had previously lived. Built of white-painted concrete and brick, it was considered one of the best lodgings in Kamina. In the riots of 1991 and 1993 it had been targeted, but not by Congolese soldiers—rather, by gangs of youths who joined the soldiers: they believed the missionaries had the best loot in town.

Outside, its peaked roof rose above the brick border walls where colorful geckos raced up and down, back and forth. Orange birds-of-paradise edged the front porch, and the porch roof lined the entire front of the house. A large mango tree and palm trees dotted the side yard. A second, smaller auxiliary guesthouse graced the back of the property, offering a similar porch, two bedrooms and a bathroom.

Through the screened front door one entered the combination living room and dining room. A conversation pit of overstuffed, brown-flocked love seats ringed a coffee table, and the large windows provided ventilation when the blue floral curtains were drawn back. The formal teak table seated eight comfortably and the china cabinet provided a side bar for buffet serving. A small front room off the living room provided John an office. The small central hall off the dining room led to two bedrooms with closets, a bathroom with a western stool, sink and bath tub, and the kitchen with a large pantry, refrigerator that operated when there was electricity, and cabinets full of china dishes, pots and pans. The kitchen connected to more utilitarian, airy, open rooms: a workroom for laundry and food preparation, a carport, another bedroom, and a screened-in porch. In all of these areas, staff of the guesthouse could do their work, out of sight, but with opportunities for socializing with one another and their own visitors.

The former residents, whom John had helped to evacuate to Zambia in 1998, had decided to retire and return to the United States. Bishop did not plan to bring new *wuzungu* to Kamina after the war: several talented and trained local Congolese persons stood ready and in need of their jobs, especially now, after so much displacement had destroyed the livelihoods of so many local church leaders. Mama Nshimba had looked over the furnishings of the house, chosen the ones she thought should remain, and Bishop had paid the missionaries. The house truly belonged to the indigenous church now.

Bishop immediately saw the opportunity. "Yes, we can make this house for guests. I'd rather they don't pay—we just offer hospitality. But talk with the financial officer, Pastor Disu."

Disu agreed with John that the guesthouse should accept payments. "If they pay something, we can purchase new beds and mosquito netting for the two bedrooms. And they want to pay. We can open an account for you, and with the funds, you can pay salaries and maintain the house."

So John and Disu agreed that the guesthouse should be self-supporting.

"I will tell the Adventists they can stay."

* * *

Such a guesthouse required a staff—watchmen to guard the gate, boys to sweep the yard, women to clean the house before the guests arrived and after they left. More employment for the people of Kamina! The Adventists were pleased, and the word spread. Within a year, guests from other non-governmental organizations—Crossroads and World Vision—arrived. Government officials used it as a place to host their guests. The guesthouse, its staff, and its proprietor began to thrive.

The guesthouse had opened its eyes to see, its ears to hear, its nose to smell—but it would hold the confidences shared there close to its heart, until the time came to tell its story.

**North Katanga Annual Conference and Congo Central Conference
Convene, 2000**

> "As Peace Mission Deteriorates, U.N. Sends an Envoy to Congo"
>
> *The New York Times*, August 15, 2000

> "For just as the body is one and has many members, and all the
> members of the body, though many, are one body, so it is with
> Christ…if one member suffers, all suffer together with it, if one
> member is honored, all rejoice together with it."
>
> 1 Corinthinans 12:12, 26

Kamina, Haut Lomami District

July 2000

The overstuffed sofa in the *payotte* of Bishop's concrete house in Kamina
seemed to the woman like a billowy luxury after the hard, damp dirt of her
makeshift hut in the bush. She sat side by side with Bishop, the plump cushion
firmly cradling her body. She was comfortable, but not comforted. She could
not look at Bishop; rather, her eyes were focused on the floor between her feet,
where her toe traced a crack in the cement.

Bishop gazed at four additional tear-swept church leaders, three men and
one woman, who sat on the sofa to his side. He never became accustomed to
the changes wrought by displacement: he last saw these church leaders looking
robust and muscular. Now, their shaggy clothes hung around their skin that was
drawn tight over their bones.

A block away, the Annual Conference was gathering under a canopy of palm
branches that had been constructed over the yard of the Centre Ville Church;
Guy Mande and the choirs' music, punctuated by the women's ululations of
greeting, wafted through the screened windows. But the Annual Conference
could sing and wait. The five had left their makeshift homes in the bush and
walked overland a full week to attend Annual Conference. They wanted to talk,
Bishop, to listen.

As Bishop inclined his ear toward to woman seated by him, the sounds of
Annual Conference faded from his hearing, replaced by her heavy breathing
and occasional deep sighs.

"I am so glad to know that you are alive," Bishop murmured quietly. "Speak
when you are ready."

She glanced at him briefly, then looked back at the crack on the floor. "It
began with the war of the *Banyamulenge*, near Kalemie. If they found a man,
even if he is a baby, they will kill him. If they found a woman and she is pregnant, they will kill her. That is why we wanted the Mai-Mai movement, to protect the people from the *Banyamulenge*."

She stopped, rubbed her toe along the crack once more. Bishop squeezed her hand but waited patiently, without speaking.

"We hadn't eaten for three days. I was walking from the village to town to find food. I didn't know that the Mai-Mai had set up a barrier on the path, and that they didn't want people to come to the barrier.

"The Mai-Mai came to fight with the *Banyamulenge*. Then they found me. They said, 'Why are you taking our path?' They did not care about my answer. They said, 'Put this woman in the house. We will fight, and then we will come and kill her.' But God is with his people. I was able to run away."

Bishop sat, a silent, reverent witness to the woman's story. But he had to wonder: Had she been molested? It happened to so many women. He did not want to ask, to breach her privacy. But she told him, almost as an aside.

"Now, I am a useless Congolese woman."

She sobbed, and her shoulders shook. Tears formed in Bishop's deep, dark eyes. He gripped her hand, reassuring her of his acceptance. *There are no useless women,* he thought. Yet Luba tradition rejected women who were barren or violated. *She is fortunate that her husband remains by her side.*

When she composed herself, Pastor Kayaputa, the district superintendent from Manono, who was seated on the sofa, changed the subject. "For many months we were in Ankoro. The Congolese soldiers and the Mai-Mai continued to fight. We said, 'We have left our homes. Now, here, we are like displaced.' We said, 'We as the church have a voice. Let's go and meet those people together.' We tried to intervene. We invited the chief commander of the soldiers and the chief of Mai-Mai, as you say, the Bandama, and we sat together and we talked to them till they agreed to stop fighting, and we signed some documents. The fighting paused, but then it began again. Finally, when the time for North Katanga Annual Conference came, we said, 'let's go.' So we came together."

Bishop nodded with gratitude. "You have risked yourself for peace. I am so glad to know you are safe." Then, he frowned. "Where are your children?"

"We have left them in the bush where we were living."

"You and your families have served Christ and the church well. I will give you money—when the Annual Conference is over, you will fetch your children. North Katanga will provide shelter, food, clothing, education, a church to pastor. God will bless you here in Kamina."

"*Wafwako,* our Bishop, our Papa." The men rose, smiled, and, one by one, placed their left hand on their right forearm, shook Bishop's right hand enthusiastically, and turned toward the door. The women wept tears of pain and joy, and Bishop patted them on the shoulders. "God be with you, my sisters."

Then the women followed their husbands out of the door of the *payotte* and made their way to the joyous music-making of the Annual Conference.

* * *

Now, it was time to greet his colleagues with pleasure. Bishop donned his black robe over his purple clerical collar and western business suit and stepped into the morning sun. Beads of sweat from heat and anxiety broke on his face as he walked the block to the church. It was a special Annual Conference—he had served as Bishop for four probationary years, and this conference, according to the custom of African Methodism, would recommend him to the Jurisdictional Conference for re-election for life. He approached the milling, singing crowd that gathered under the canopy of palm leaves that had been constructed over the yard of the Centre Ville Church.

Wafwako, Wafwako. He shook the hands of the pastors in the procession and then greeted his guests. The Muslim Imam, the Zimbabwean general, the Congolese colonel from Kamina Base, and the king from Kinkunki, *Kasongo Nyembo*, had joined the procession behind the district superintendents. Now that Bishop arrived, the celebration could commence.

Bishop Sends Women to Africa University

> "Death Toll in Congo's 2-Year War is at Least 1.7 Million, Study Says"
>
> *The New York Times*, June 9, 2000

> "The Lord GOD has given me the tongue of a teacher,
> that I may know how to sustain the weary with a word.
> Morning by morning he wakens my ear
> to listen as those who are taught."
>
> Isaiah 50:4

Kamina, Haut Lomami District

June 2000

She perched on the edge of her chair in his *payotte*, the young woman with golden skin and delicately braided hair that swirled toward a spiral on the top of her head. Bishop, too, had slid forward in his seat. Twice before they had sat here—she, plaintive but eager, sharing her dreams for her future, and he, compassionate and encouraging, but responding with the routine words of a benefactor evaluating a supplicant's request for a scholarship. He, saying, "School fees, yes, but no pocket money or living expenses." She, expressing her appreciation. With his sponsorship she had attended *Institut supérieur pédagogique*, the local teacher's college, and then the University of Lubumbashi to study English.

Before, she had always sought his assistance, but this time was different. He had asked her to come to hear his very important proposal.

"I've watched you develop for many years now. I believe you could become a fine pastor."

A pastor? She frowned but said nothing.

"We have already sent five men to Africa University to study for the ministry. Now, I want to promote some women. But I don't want you to go because you owe me anything—only because you want to."

Her heart leapt as she realized the opportunity he was offering: she had graduated from school and had no job. Nor was she married.

"I would love to attend Africa University. But to become a pastor? I've never thought about that."

Then, Bishop raised the stakes even higher.

"Perhaps from there you will be able to go to America to study."

Her frown bent into a slight smile, one she could not control. *To study in America! The dream of so many African men! But for her, a woman? To study in Zimbabwe? Or the United States?*

"Of course, I will talk with your parents."

"Yes, please."

But they both knew that her parents would respond as the typical village African does to a leader who holds the reins to their children's future: *She is your child. You are free to make any decision about her future that you want.* Bishop had become her social father.

* * *

He also had his eye on another talented and intelligent young woman, a cousin. He had known her since she was born, and they had bantered together like an uncle and a niece. As he became a community leader, he pondered her future. She had been less eager to continue education and more interested in getting married and having children.

"Not yet," he had insisted. "First, you finish your education." He was convinced of her intelligence, her talent. He saw women like Hillary Clinton and Margaret Thatcher becoming leaders in the world. *I want her to be one of those, not a woman whose husband is educated but she is not.* He believed that she, too, could be a fine pastor, and he wanted to send her for study at Africa University.

* * *

Africa University had been established by the United Methodist Church in 1990 to provide university-level study. Bishop Wakadillo had nominated the first five North Katanga students, all men. The Annual Conference agreed to provide their tuition if the students paid for their passport, student permit, transportation, and pocket money. But the Bishop's death delayed their plans.

When Bishop Ntambo was elected, the conference asked: what about the men who were supposed to go to Africa University? But it was the year of the war against Mobutu: people were frightened and money was scarce. The war delayed their plans once more.

Over the next year Bishop argued, "Young leaders are critical." He convinced the Annual Conference to provide the additional money for passport, transportation, student permits, and fees—if the students and their families could provide the pocket money.

So North Katanga sent the first five men to Africa University.

* * *

Now, Bishop's changing view of women's roles was taking shape. He looked at his wife with pride. He knew that she could welcome any visitor, high rank or low, to their home, and they would leave happy. *Even a white man!* Cooking and cleaning for *wuzungu* offered different challenges than entertaining even high ranking Congolese—but Nshimba knew how.

He and Nshimba had come from village life where she, as a woman, was educated only through primary school. She had participated in the home economics education for pastors' wives when he got his B.D. at Mulungwishi Seminary. He had pressed her to cook for special guests; she thought he asked too much; he knew she was right. She was feeding and raising their six children; he travelled frequently; she already had too much work to do. But when she became Mama Bishop, the entertaining intensified; furthermore, the women looked to her as their leader. She had helped to organize the orphanage and the feeding program for children. Bishop Ntambo and Nshimba had decided to employ widows in the orphanage, even though Luba culture traditionally shunned women who were barren or no longer child bearing. The work of women was essential to relief, to caring for displaced children and families.

As a pastor, he had been astonished to encounter the women leaders in the church. Luba women had always occupied positions of trust, even with the king—cooking food that they knew was pure, advising him spiritually and politically—and women supported him as pastor. But Pastor Ntambo also observed women in the church who were leading activities in their own right. Like the president of Kipindano, the United Methodist Women—she acted with power, even more than some men. So many women were talented, but the church didn't use their gifts. They were forgotten as women. *And why? We are losing out. Once we put those people into a very good position, they can produce very high things for the benefit of the church, as well as the nation.*

And he had thought about his five daughters, four of whom had stayed in the United States after the war. He had had to face the question: *Who will they become if I die?* So he committed himself: *I want my girls to enjoy marriage but to be independent. My girls, they will fall in love, but I don't want them to depend 100% on the pockets of their husbands. I don't want them to boast about*

*money to their husbands. If tragedy comes—if her husband falls sick or dies
and she is alone, I want her to have resources to care for the children. To make
that possible, they need an education. And it's the same for all women— for
now I don't see men as superior.*

*No. One day, we will have a General Secretary of the Board of Global Min-
istries who is a woman. We will have a president who is a woman. So this is
what I want for you.*

It was time to send women to Africa University.

Pastor Nyengele Distributes Relief in Kamina

"RELIGION JOURNAL; Back from Africa with a Cry for Help"

The New York Times, September 16, 2000

"For the Lord your God is God of gods and Lord of lords, the
great God, mighty and awesome, who is not partial and takes no
bribe, who executes justice for the orphan and the widow, and
who loves the strangers, providing them with food and clothing.
You shall also love the stranger, for you were strangers in the
land of Egypt."

Deuteronomy 10: 17-20

Kamina, Haut Lomami District

August 2000

*My hardest time, first thing in the morning—to face the displaced people who
are so desperate, so afraid that we will run out of food and supplies.* By four
o'clock in the morning, Pastor Nyengele heard the first footsteps and muffled
voices outside the door to his durable brick parsonage near Kamina Military
Base. He rose in the dark, prayed, and ate his bananas and peanuts, fortifying
himself for the day. By the time he finished, waves of people wandered restlessly in his front yard. Under the morning stars they flooded the lane leading
to his house and swelled onto the road beyond—perhaps four hundred people
in all, a roiling sea. The depot, where the distribution occurred, was ten kilometers away, down the road called Mobutu's belt and Kamina's dirt streets. But
newly arrived displaced had heard that *he* was in charge of the depot, so, following the Luba tradition of supplication, they sought *his* door each morning.
Displaced guests who had been in Kamina longer, who had learned how the
distribution occurred, were simultaneously queuing at the depot. They would
be served first.

Nyengele appeared at his door, placed a chair in front of him, and stepped
upon it so he could look over the crowd. Steadying himself, he stretched his
arms and hands toward the anxious, bedraggled people. He raised his voice to
its highest pitch, as if preaching to a large congregation. "God bless you. I know
you are hungry. This is only my house. We have nothing here to give to this

crowd. Everything is at the depot, several kilometers away. I will leave to walk there in a few minutes; you can follow me. To receive food, you must be registered as a displaced person. You will be placed on a list of other people like yourselves and told which day your group is served. This week we will distribute on Monday, to the large families, on Tuesday, the small families, on Wednesdays, the single people, on Thursdays, the orphans. Some of the large families are already lining up at the depot. If you let me pass safely, you will be given supplies on the day to which you are assigned. Please spread the word to those down the road."

He stepped down from the chair, backed into his hut, closed his door and listened to the rising din, the conversation rippling out to the street. They had to realize that they would only receive food if he could walk safely into Kamina. When the chatter began to quiet, he opened his door, stepped into the yard and then the street, and began the long walk to the depot, with several hundred people filling in behind him.

The police guarded the depot at all times. When Nyengele arrived, the police unlocked the door. He entered and gazed at Tschimwang with relief. He had survived the most stressful part of the day.

Nyengele and Tschimwang had been colleagues in Manono, pastors in the same district, and each was displaced from his home but in a very different way. Nyengele had heard the gunfire, watched a child gunned down on the street and killed in cold blood, and suddenly found himself leading a band of children through the bush. Tschimwang had left Manono in February 1999, in order to prepare for attending a meeting of the General Board of Global Ministries in the United States. During that time his family took up residence in Lubumbashi. So he was out of the country on May 8, 1999 when Manono was overtaken by the rebels and Nyengele fled. When Tschimwang returned to Congo, he had lost his home in Manono, but his life had not been threatened.

Bishop had said, "Stay in Lubumbashi with your family. You're from Tanganyika and know the people, and you've just made contacts at Global Ministries. You organize support for the displaced." So when the churches could no longer provide for their guests, Tschimwang developed a conference-wide system for relief. He negotiated with UMCOR for payments, worked with the treasurer to purchase food and medicine, and arranged to transport the supplies by train.

But now Kamina had nearly 10,000 displaced guests—far more than Tschimwang had ever imagined. The organization of relief, especially in outlying depots, required his presence in Kamina. Leaving the purchasing of supplies in the hands of Bishop's assistant in Lubumbashi, Dr. Raymond Mande, Tschimwang moved with his family to Kamina in order to supervise the distribution. Now, he and Nyengele, colleagues who had such different experiences of displacement, began the day early, in exactly the same way.

* * *

"People are starving in Kitenge. We need to ship to depots in outlying areas, as we have been discussing."

Pastor Kabongo spoke with authority. Now that he had been promoted to district superintendent in Kamina, he had a new sense of responsibility in Bishop's executive committee. But Kabongo remembered his church members in Kitenge with great angst.

"UMCOR sent $10,000 and, *Programme alimentaire mondial,* let's see—" Pastor Kahunda, the former superintendent who was now Bishop's assistant in Kamina, looked at his notes, furrowing his brow, narrowing his eyes to read from his careful handwriting on the ledger. "The church treasurer has purchased a container of rice, beans, flour, salt, oil, clothes, soap and medicine. This shipment should arrive by train within the next two weeks. It will replenish the central depot. I think we have enough in storage to make our regular distributions until then."

Pastor Tschimwang nodded. "We have plenty of need among the displaced people here, but I agree—we must begin shipments to the secondary depots." Tschimwang turned the page of the ledger and ran his finger down the columns of numbers that registered their current displaced guests. "Kitanda. 800 men, 600 women, 1081 girls, 881 boys. We can truck some of the food there. We need to be sure that each of the outlying depots gets food on a regular basis, so that the people will not need to come to Kamina."

"Yes. If they stay, it helps to secure those towns. It's too difficult to absorb more displaced people here."

Nyengele's heart beat loudly in his ears, and he flushed with sorrow, thinking of the people who still roamed the bush. *His parishioners in Manono, his parishioners in Kitenge!* When he boarded his family on the train to Kamina with tickets paid for by the church, he knew that he, as a religious leader, had been given a privilege that might mean the difference of life or death. Average church members did not receive that opportunity; they stayed in their villages or made their way by foot. Their security was enhanced by the presence of Zimbabwean soldiers, but food was scarce. For so many, remaining in the bush could mean *the end,* unless supplies arrived on a regular basis.

"Will we be able to send some food to Kitenge?"

Tschimwang nodded. "Soon."

"Good." His relief, for the moment, assuaged his guilt.

* * *

The whistle blew and the train pulled out of sight. A man leaned from the door of a boxcar, waved, and then disappeared inside. Nyengele, Kabongo, and Tschimwang watched until the train rounded a bend and disappeared into the low-lying trees of the savannah. They smiled at one another, soberly. Two years earlier, the bicycles intended for the church in Tanganyika had been looted—this train now carried the first supplies since that shipment to six towns at the war's front: Kitenge, Kitanda, Budi, Kabongo, Ankoro, Malemba. Tschimwang had taken advantage of the railway's offer of free passage for humanitarian supplies; at each stop, the district superintendent would organize unloading and distributing. Nyengele, Kabongo, and Tschimwang knew that people faced starvation if they did not receive help. And they easily imagined the long, anxious lines of desperate displaced people who would soon awaken the district superintendents in these towns from their slumber.

Bishop Ntambo Speaks Before Kabila the Son

> "Congo Leader Reportedly Dead After Being Shot by Bodyguard"
>
> *The New York Times*, January 17, 2001

> "Then Paul stood in front of the Areopagus and said, 'Athenians, I see how extremely religious you are in every way.'"
>
> Acts 17:22

Lubumbashi, Haut Katanga District
February 2001

Who had assassinated President Laurent Kabila, father of Joseph Kabila, on January 16, 2001? Many groups were motivated to do so—Rwanda, who had lost Kabila's allegiance and become his arch enemy; Laurent Kabila's disgruntled child soldiers, his *kadogos,* who were unhappy with their pay and privileges; Angola, displeased that, after supporting Kabila against Rwanda, Kabila had allowed UNITA, Angola's revolutionary group, to support itself with profits from mining operations in Congo; Lebanese businessmen, who operated in the shadows of mining operations. Mystery shrouded the murder, but clarity quickly emerged over the result—the presidential cabinet chose twenty-nine-year-old Joseph Kabila to lead the country. And Kabila the Son, as he would soon be called by local Congolese, quickly showed that he was no puppet of his father's administrators—rather, he had his own agenda. He extended himself to the United Nations, to the United States, and to leaders among his own people. Now, on his first visit to Lubumbashi, he had asked the governor of Katanga, Ngoy Mukena, to invite three bishops to lead the welcome celebration: the Lutheran officiating, the Catholic preaching, the Methodist speaking.

Bishop Ntambo leaned against the wall in his office in Lubumbashi, staring mindlessly out of the window. He barely noticed the people who jaywalked between the cars that braked and honked down one of Lubumbashi's main streets—rather, he was muttering words, trying them out in his mind and on his tongue. His assistant, now *Doctor* Raymond Mande, now a professor of English literature at the University of Lubumbashi, sat at Bishop's desk with pen in hand, correcting, writing, crossing out. Occasionally he suggested a different phrasing and Bishop nodded. Then Mande wrote again, inserting new words on the margin of the paper. Shortly, Mande exited the office, displaced the office administrator from the one computer, typed the manuscript of Bishop's speech, and returned to the office. Bishop was still staring out the window, mouthing words, practicing phrases.

Bishop rarely wrote a sermon or a speech word-for-word, preferring instead to elaborate a theme with stories that he easily remembered. But in important preparations such as this one, he consulted with the literature professor, talking through the ideas and depending upon the scholar's careful sense of language.

Mande shuffled his typed papers into order, handed them to Bishop, and Bishop read what they had written one more time. His mind wrestled with key words. *L'autonomie*—that was safe enough, a word Kabila the Father had often used. *L'honnêteté*—was he now pointing fingers? *Abandonner la corruption et les commissions pour la transparence*—dare he be so bold, so forthright?

Then he decided. The occasion—a celebration welcoming the new President, Joseph Kabila, to Lubumbashi—called for honest vision. He would speak forthrightly about his hopes for a new Congo. *The governor will censor the speech in advance. If I'm too bold, he'll change it.*

Bishop called a courier to take the text of his speech to the governor. A day later the speech was returned—approved.

* * *

When he preached, Bishop Ntambo looked into the eyes of his audience and read their reactions as he spoke. He had never addressed a political assembly before, nor had he met the Governor or Kabila the Son. But now he stood before them, speaking from his heart about the qualities of government that would allow the Congolese people to flourish. He spoke with authority and passion, but he knew, even as he spoke, that the two dignitaries had a mixed response. The President had risen four times to applaud, while the Governor sat still, shaking his head. Watching them while he spoke, it was as if the hall grew dark and silent: only their reactions mattered. When he took his seat, he felt exposed, as if the leaders could now mock his naked soul.

Late that afternoon, after a thunderstorm had cleared the humidity from the air, Bishop was relaxing in the living room of his compound, a Fanta in hand and a cool breeze occasionally drying his wet brow. The telephone rang, and the voice of the Governor jolted Bishop from his contentment.

"Why did you say that? What kind of speech did you read? The President is very angry with what you did. You destroyed my career."

"What?"

"I want to see you and your speech in my office, day after tomorrow." The phone clicked and the line died. Bishop moaned. His hands shook as he returned the receiver to the cradle.

Nshimba, wiping her hands on a towel, came to the doorway between the kitchen and the living room and stared at him. "What happened? You are white like a *muzungu*."

He repeated the conversation. Their eyes locked, knowing, troubled. They did not need to speak their fears: they both knew that a person who threatened a politician's career in Congo risked his life.

"I want to call Dorothy." Nshimba's grown daughters were her source of comfort, and she often called each, one after another. Their daughters had sought permanent asylum in the United States during the war. Nshimba repeated the conversation to her eldest, who lived in Indianapolis.

"Let me speak to Papa. Now. Papa, you are in danger, more than when you fled from the Rwandese. Go to Zambia. Buy a ticket. Come to us."

Bishop closed his eyes and drew a deep breath. "If I run now, where to? For what? How do I return to my country, my people?" He looked at Nshimba, saw fear on her face, tears in her eyes. He felt torn, stricken, as if a trail through the bush had suddenly disappeared, leaving him no path to follow. "Other times, it seemed wise to leave. But where to flee from a Congolese politician? He has connections. If he wants me dead, he can kill me, anywhere. Just a matter of time."

"But if you are out of the country, you won't threaten him."

"Perhaps. But I have just been re-elected for life. How can I forsake my people?"

His decision had been made. Nshimba took the phone, and Ntambo walked the few paces through the night to his *payotte,* leaving her to be calmed by her daughters. *We discussed it: if I became a bishop, some people would hate me. I could even be poisoned.* He looked up and pondered the dank heavens.

Compared to the shimmering, full beauty in the northern hemisphere, the stars of Congo's southern sky looked dim. Even under a cloudless sky, their remote, scattered spots of light marked a lonely existence.

* * *

The next day, around three in the afternoon, Bishop was resting in his *payotte* when heard the long squeak of the compound's metal doors and the steady hum of a quiet automobile engine. A slight crunch of sand and gravel announced that the car had stopped. A creak signalled the closing of the doors.

Strange, the guards did not announce a guest.

Bishop rose and peered through the screen. A black Mercedes limousine had slid quietly through the gate. *A very expensive car. My life is finished.*

He exited the *payotte* and approached the car. Two people, a man and a woman, very well dressed in formal, authoritative black suits emerged from the rear seat. *Bodyguards?* The driver remained in the car.

"Hello."

"Hello, welcome."

"Do you speak English?" the man said.

"Yes."

"So do I. How are you, Bishop?"

Bishop relaxed hearing the man's tone, his question. He called to his teenage son inside the house. "Nkulu, can you open the door for our guests, please?" To the man: "I'm okay. Please, come in."

"Bishop, congratulations."

"For what?"

"President Kabila sent us to commend you on your speech." For this, for this, for this... the two visitors ticked off the main points of the speech, the keywords, praising the vision Bishop had proposed. . . .

Bishop could see a clock behind them. *They have been talking about my speech for fifteen minutes!* Like Mars when it orbits close to Earth, Bishop's star now seemed unusually large and glowing.

"But, we have brought something—not for you, actually, or even for your church, but for the cathedral where the service was held." The woman pulled an envelope from her purse. "President Kabila's bodyguard prevented him from putting his offering in the plate. So he has sent it to you, to add to the rest."

Bishop's head began to spin. A donation, after a worship service, from a President? It was unheard of. If Mobutu left without contributing, he took his money with him. Then Bishop's anxiety and excitement gave way to panic. *How to have proof if someone later accuses me of taking a commission?*

"Thank you. So generous. Please thank the President. And I will take it to the cathedral, to be sure it is deposited in the account. But first, let us take a picture." His voice rose to a commanding tone that he rarely directed toward his wife. "Nshimba! Nshimba! Bring the camera!" Bishop stood by the emissaries from the President. They smiled, and Bishop held the envelope where it could be clearly seen. Flash! Bishop blinked hard, mostly in disbelief.

* * *

The next day he entered the Governor's office, confused and anxious, to discover that the Catholic and Lutheran bishops were also present. The Governor smiled warmly.

"Bishops, your eminences, I believe you have begun economic development projects—yes, I'm told your churches have built orphanages, schools, and hospitals. They are important to the economy of the Democratic Republic of Congo. Please, tell me all about your projects…first, would you care for Fanta?"

The Governor's demeanor had changed. Ntambo waited, but the Governor never mentioned the speech.

A few months later, Kabila the Son called Bishop Ntambo to meet with him. A Bible lay on the President's end table.

Bishop's speech had resonated with the new President. What did Bishop think about Kabila's five-point strategy for Congo's development? *First, the government must secure the peace, and that will not be easy, but after that…*

Chapter V

The Mai-Mai Continue the War— Peacebuilding through Networking and Conflict Mediation (January 2001-September 2004)

Historical Introduction

Joseph Kabila had proved to be a more willing negotiator than his father. Several events provided the foundation for the Global and All-Inclusive Agreement that formally ended the war on December 16, 2002.

The United Nations had launched an initial peacekeeping force, MONUC, in November 1999. It increased its presence in subsequent years. The United Nations also authorized an expert panel to investigate illegal mining that perpetuated the war. Between June 2, 2000 and October 23, 2003 the panel documented an increasingly formal system of illegal mining that had the sophistication of organized crime. The Inter-Congolese Dialogue in Sun City, South Africa met from February 25, 2002 through April 12, 2002. It provided a political framework for a transitional government that would serve until elections could be held.

The people of Katanga, however, were now consumed by the war of the Mai-Mai militias. As the international soldiers withdrew and the government did not have military or civic control, these paramilitary groups increased in power. They formed a loose network under leaders who also fought against one another. So Mai-Mai signatures on the All-Inclusive and Global Agreement meant little to local Mai-Mai in Katanga.

While international attention focused on political developments and militias operating in the Great Lakes region, powerful Mai-Mai militias in Katanga filled the vacuum left when Congo's allies withdrew. In villages surrounding Kabongo, the Mai-Mai devastated the lives of people more than the Rwandese war of aggression. The war of the Mai-Mai, as local people called it, required sustained relief efforts from Kamina since internally displaced people could not return to their homes. In order to "feed my people" Bishop's development and relief projects continued with intensity, even as governmental and religious leaders tried to persuade the local Mai-Mai to lay down their arms.

Pierre Kapata Joins the Mai-Mai

"Doubts on Whether Kabila's Son Can Lead Congo"

The New York Times, January 21, 2001

"But while he was still far off, his father saw him and was filled with compassion."

Luke 15:20

Nkombe, thirty-five kilometers beyond Kabongo
January 2001

Nineteen-year-old Pierre Kapata stood still, gazing in wonder at the activity around him at the Mai-Mai paramilitary camp just outside the village of Nkombe. At eleven-thirty a.m., before the noon-time ritual, men sauntered around the camp dressed according to tradition—red headbands, traditional bows and arrows made from sticks, stones and feathers, and necklaces laden heavy with charms that communicated the wearer's rank and power. Soon, after the ritual bath was complete, he, Pierre Kapata, would don the attire of the Luba Mai-Mai warrior. He would become a patriot, joining the other men—and some women—who were defending the villages from the Rwandese military and Congolese soldiers. Such an opportunity! His heart filled with gratitude and pride. Surely, his father, the Methodist schoolteacher in Nkombe, who had opposed his decision, was wrong about the Mai-Mai.

Pierre had become intrigued with the idea of joining the militia during conversations with his school friends. They said the camp just outside Nkombe was governed by the greatest of Mai-Mai warriors, Chinja-Chinja, who had attracted six thousand followers. He had become powerful within the well-established Mai-Mai movement in Malemba territory, some distance to the east, and his power stretched beyond Nkombe. Yes, other leaders ruled nearby territories—Gideon protected villages east of Malemba; Maccabee led the militias to the west, closer to Kabongo; Kebe Konkeka ruled thirty-five hundred warriors further south. But in Nkombe, Pierre could protect the village of his family and learn the skills of the militia under the guidance of warriors trained by the mighty Chinja-Chinja.

Before coming to the camp, he had been recruited by a friend who had talked to a friend who had gotten the information from one of the militia members. The Mai-Mai, he was assured, honored traditional Luba values—do not loot your enemy, do not take the wife of another person, do not engage in unjustified violence. He would call on his *own* family's ancestors for guidance, to be empowered by his *own* family's charms and contribute their power to that of the militia.

The militia movement deep in the interior of Katanga had countered the threat of the Rwandese "high speed guns" and the easy purchase of Congolese military loyalties. Initially, militias fought with sticks and the tails of hippos, and they called on their traditional charms to protect them from the bullets. Eventually, they were able to lift guns and ammunition off the bodies of the soldiers they killed. Militia leaders also discovered that the army's enlisted men—disillusioned, undisciplined, and hungry—were easily persuaded to defect to the Rwandese. The militias even accused Congolese officers of collaborating with the Rwandese to such an extent that they had sold to Rwanda "all of Katanga, Kamina Base, and the lucrative Kapushi copper mines." These traitors were not "true Congolese"—therefore, in the eyes of the Mai-Mai, violence against them was justified.

By the time Pierre joined, the Mai-Mai were emerging as a staple part of village life in rural Katanga.

* * *

"No one at your rank sees Chinja-Chinja," Pierre was told. "He conducts his ceremonies in private, near his own lodging, protected by soldiers at many barriers. He is very careful not to display his charms. But he prays when the sun is highest, and during that time, lower officers will take you to bathe in the water. When we are fighting, you will cry 'Mai-Mai, water-water.' The water will create an invisible barrier against the bullets of guns."

Pierre listened attentively, but he did not need the explanation. The teacher was simply restating Luba tradition.

"Our charms are more important than guns. Your ancestors may guide you to power in plants and herbs, and, if so, you carry those. But sometimes the ancestors tell us to gather power from people in the villages, or from soldiers, in another traditional way." Pierre knew that meant killing a powerful person and eating his flesh or removing breasts or genitals, male or female, to make a charm to wear. "This is how our ancestors will protect us against bullets. Now, you smoke this marijuana, and you drink Nituko, this alcohol. You will like it. Then you bathe."

As he prepared for the noon ritual, an inviting, sweet cloud hovered around Pierre. His head tingled with well-being, and joy filled his entire body. As he washed, he was confirmed in the power the officers had promised—he could indeed face bullets without fear. Surely, he was invincible against the machine guns of his future opponents.

After the ceremony, he rested with the other initiates and prayed to his ancestors, seeking their guidance for making his charms. During this prayer, his conscience niggled—his Christian father, who did not drink any alcohol or smoke marijuana, would not like some parts of the rituals the Mai-Mai performed.

* * *

Days passed. With the other recruits Pierre made traditional bows and arrows, cutting handles from trees, shafts from the bush, and bowstrings from the skins of animals caught in the camp. He watched the more experienced Mai-Mai. They wore military uniforms and carried machine guns—clearly they had killed enemy soldiers who were threatening civilians.

Some nights he slept in the village with his family, but mostly he lived at the camp and learned its particular rituals and taboos. Ceremonies occurred at dawn, midday, and sundown—walking anywhere was prohibited at noon. When they roasted a chicken, they were allowed to eat its flesh but not to break its bones. When they caught a fish, they ate its body but not its head or tail. They could not eat manioc directly from the river. Pierre did not understand the reasons for these things, but he absorbed the rules and did not challenge his teachers.

Women roamed the camp and they, too, were prepared for war. Pierre and his friends sat under the trees at the edge of the clearing, admiring them, choosing their favorites. Sometimes the women and the men flirted with one another, but more contact than that was taboo: it was forbidden to have sex while the sun was up.

* * *

His officer and a few of the more experienced warriors gathered with the recruits. "We have been chosen for a special mission. Our group is growing, and we need more space. We will go to the chief in the next village to ask for land. We conduct our ceremonies at dawn, smoke and drink, and then we go."

During the dawn rituals Pierre could hear the voice of his father: "the Mai-Mai live differently than we do."

Some of the men and women dressed in their traditional clothing, others in military fatigues. Each carried his or her most trusted charm, and a few wore necklaces that showed the dried breasts or genitals of people whose power they had absorbed. The party was a large group, perhaps twenty-five in all, when they approached the hut of the village chief. The chief and his family greeted them in the yard of his compound.

"*Wafwako.*"

The experienced leader spoke. "*Wafwako.* We are Mai-Mai from Nkombe who come as your friends. You own land at the edge of our camp, and we need more space for those who have joined us. We are here to ask you to give us your land."

"Why're you recruiting more Mai-Mai? Peace is coming."

"Your village still needs protection."

"*Wafwako*. But *I* am charged with protecting my village, and that includes keeping the peace. It also includes preserving the land so my village can cultivate."

"*We* can cultivate for your village."

The chief gripped his staff tightly and held it steady in front of him. "We will consult our ancestors."

The Mai-Mai leader shrugged. "We will return in an hour." He turned, and the recruits followed, withdrawing to the edge of the property.

The leader stopped and turned, and Pierre and the other followers inclined their heads toward him. "Chinja-Chinja has sent word from his ancestors: this village chief must cooperate, or we must kill him and his whole family. He is powerful, but we can overcome him. If he denies us, it is justified to shed blood."

The Mai-Mai, holding themselves higher than the traditional leaders? Pierre was shocked, but a voice inside him warned, *be careful of their power.* He knew better than to allow himself to show disrespect for what the leader was saying. Shortly, they returned to the hut of the chief.

Before sundown, the Mai-Mai leader was multiply victorious: he had acquired the land and the chief's charms, had absorbed his power, and was leading the new recruits back the Mai-Mai camp. He led his band, whooping with excitement. Pierre walked at the very back, his eyes focused on the path beneath his feet, lifting his head to utter an occasional shriek.

* * *

On their next mission, the recruits battled with Congolese soldiers. That night, some of Pierre's friends laughed and strutted through the camp in the uniforms and guns they had confiscated. At sundown, one of the recruits boasted to Pierre. "You watch. I've learned how it is done."

When his favorite woman crossed the camp, the young man rose and scampered to her side, nudging her and laughing to attract her attention. He drew close to her and with his left hand he grasped her upper arm, stopping her from going further. They murmured between them, and then he nuzzled her neck. She shook her head and tried to draw away from him. But Pierre's friend gripped her arm tightly and he pressed his chest closer to her back. The woman cried out sternly. Then Pierre watched his friend as, with his right hand, he quickly removed his newly-acquired gun and rubbed it against the woman's hip. She stiffened, and his friend used his gun to caress her waist, then her side, then her shoulders, until his arm was firmly around her. He guided her out of Pierre's view, into the shadows at the camp's edge.

Is he violating the Luba value: "Do not take another man's wife?" Pierre wondered. No, Pierre justified. She is young, and perhaps she has not been claimed by another man. Still… it seemed wrong. Again, he heard his father's words: "The militias are soldiers. They will not live as you have been taught as a Luba or as a Christian."

A sickness grew in the pit of Pierre 's stomach, and he wondered why he wasn't feeling well. Perhaps the cooks had broken one of the many food taboos.

The next few afternoons Pierre took his dinner and slept at the hut of his father. But he was back in the camp in time for the dawn ceremonies.

* * *

Only a few weeks had passed, but Pierre had seen enough. He perched at the door to his father's hut on the *air kabongo* chairs to have an important conversation.

"You were right." Pierre had thought so much about what he had to say that he did not hesitate. "I was wrong. I wish I had listened to you. I don't like living with the Mai-Mai. Their ways are not our ways."

His father's lips smiled but his eyes grew dark with concern. "Will you be coming home for good?"

Pierre shook his head. "No. I can't leave the camp without endangering you. They have made it clear that any 'traitors' will be killed—they and their entire family. And they believe that only they are right—they cannot accept advice or dissent—I have heard it, over and over, with my own ears. So I will continue to go between our home and the camp, much as I have been doing. I will eat here as often as I can. I will hang back from their activities and observe. But I will not rape women, as they do, and I will avoid killing, even though I will have to participate in their raids." He shifted his gaze and looked directly at his father. "I promise."

His father's smile drooped, but his eyes acknowledged Pierre 's dilemma. "I suspected as much. Do what you must to be safe."

And so Pierre began three unhappy years with the Mai-Mai.

Bishop Ntambo and Raymond Mande Prepare for American Visitors

"Who Runs Congo? The People, New Leader Says"

The New York Times, April 15, 2001

"Seek the welfare of the city where I have sent you into exile, and pray to the Lord on its behalf, for in its welfare, you will find your welfare…For surely I know the plans I have for you, says the Lord, plans for your welfare and not for harm, to give you a future with hope."

Jeremiah 29:7

Lubumbashi, Haut-Lomami District

April 2001

Bishop sat behind his desk in his Lubumbashi transit office, his face lifted expectantly, waiting for his assistant, Raymond Mande, to absorb his words. Mande stood at the window, staring at but not seeing the market on the public square and the Park Hotel, pondering the news Bishop brought to him.

"We will have visitors from America. My friend Bishop Ken Carder will come with a delegation, maybe even eleven people. They will help to dedicate the churches and the schools that we have built in Kamina. But we have much to prepare."

Mande turned toward Bishop. "You are taking a risk."

"Yes, it is a risk. But I am very"—Bishop tapped the desk for emphasis—"very proud to show them what we have done."

"Then it will be. What do they want, and what do you want?"

"They are being sent by the Council of Bishops to see how North Katanga has used money from Hope for the Children of Africa fund. Money given for schools and orphanages. We will dedicate Kinkunki, Mitwobwe, Dean Scott, Katuba parishes and Kendabantu and Umpafu schools.

Bishop leaned forward on his desk, staring at his folded hands, and spoke pensively, almost talking to himself. "You know Americans, they have their own way to evaluate things. Americans give you $2000, they want a report in detail. They go to the grocery store, they buy things, they get receipts. But that's not the way things go outside of America. You have nothing. You feel so much pressure. You don't want to feel like a thief, but the people outside will not understand you that you didn't steal. The Americans won't ask, but I see it in their eyes. So we will confirm that the money which they sent has been used they way they wanted."

Bishop ended his murmurings, looked up and matched the gaze of his colleague, with his attention focused. "What do I want? Blessings for my people. To show that we have brothers and sisters who are caring about us from the outside. It will be a spiritual comfort for them to find out that American church is gracious—that it is a church that reaches beyond itself, in the name of Jesus, to people who are really suffering. Through American people it shows us as a church how lovely we are."

Bishop paused, but Mande said nothing. He could see his leader was still thinking and knew that Bishop had more to say. "The war is finishing. People are still so afraid. Now, if Americans visit Kamina—it will say to the whole town, no one is going to kick us out. It will build great confidence in people to stay settled instead of running, expecting always that war is coming. They will say, 'If Bishop Ntambo is able to continue building, if he is able to bring Americans here, no war will reach us.'"

Then Bishop sighed deeply. "But you know what people say. Bishop Ntambo is CIA." He tilted his head and laughed. "The Catholics are so proud of the Vatican. But people will see—*this* is the superpower, the strength of United States of America. The church. We will show the Congo government the United Methodist Church can bring American money to do good in North Katanga."

Bishop stood, ready to depart. "You need to do all the preparations, all the logistics, beginning with the government. And the first concern is security—transportation, food, lodging."

Mande nodded pensively. "We will prepare carefully, reduce the risk."

Mande grasped the vision, could write it when the time came. For now, he had to organize, like preparing to clear a big shipment through customs. One or two missionaries or visiting staff from international agencies who were used to travelling in Africa—that was one thing. A delegation of first time, short-term visitors—Bishop's foreign donors? Mande understood at once: they will require a different kind of care. The stakes for Bishop and for Kamina couldn't be higher.

* * *

Mande wrote letters, provided information, filled out forms, spoke to officials he knew. He wanted no room for surprises—no chance that something could go wrong, like the day that he and the Swiss missionaries had ended up in the Ndola prison. All of the government and military officials needed to know who was coming, where they were going, what they were doing.

Bishop's mind birthed the way the trip would unfold—a polished example of Congolese hospitality with no detail for the visitors' comfort unattended. Mande ticked off the necessary negotiations. "I have talked with immigration at the airport—they can wait in the VIP lounge while we process their entry into Congo. We have clearance to purchase transit visas at the airport. And I think I have found a safe airplane to fly the team into Kamina."

Chartering a plane to transport the delegation—this decision required more wisdom than any other part of the preparation. Bishop could not guarantee the safety and comfort of an American delegation on a Congolese train. The country's political situation was not yet stable enough to bring the church's Cessna 172 back to Congo. A competent pilot, a safe airplane, large enough for eleven people? Mande had inquired among his government contacts, found private individuals with airplanes, and did research on safety records.

"Here is the plane I propose. A Russian cargo plane. The delegation won't have to sit on the floor. The plane will have webbed lawn chairs for their comfort." He and Bishop discussed the charter company that Mande believed could provide a safe flight, including an evacuation if someone became ill.

Bishop agreed and then added an additional precaution: "I talked with Colonel Schumungu at Kamina Military Base. I told him, 'High level American visitors coming in for four days. If fighting happens in Kinshasa, if there is danger, if we need to flee them, can you fly them out of Kamina?' We have good relations, easy communication. If necessary, Kamina Base will help."

* * *

And cooking? Kamina had local, cheap food, mainly cassava and dried fish. As far as Bishop was concerned, nothing appropriate for western visitors. He knew Americans had weak stomachs. *Their chicken is so soft, you can break the bones. They eat cheese. Salad. Even mushrooms. Mostly uncooked food. We eat cooked food. All the vegetables we have are cooked. All the fish we eat is dried. We have no refrigerator. We just put our food away today, tomorrow it smells, but we just eat it, it causes no problem. Our cassava, for white people, it's very strong. Instead, they eat potatoes, very expensive. Carrots, just for white people. If people were farming carrots, all of it was to sell to white people. We grew up knowing such kind of things.*

But Mama Nshimba made a list—eggs, bacon, white bread, vegetables, beef, chicken, potatoes, carrots, spaghetti, coffee, tea, sugar, milk—everything to be purchased in Lubumbashi and flown into Kamina with the team.

Then came the news: Bishop Carder, delegation head, had had a medical emergency. The new leader was Bishop Morris and his wife—African-Americans.

Bishop smiled, recognizing a different opportunity. "We will welcome them home. And cook them some African food."

Prophet Mechac Makes Peace with Mai-Mai

"U.N. Delegation, off to Africa, Sees Glimmer of Hope in Congo"

The New York Times, May 16, 2001

"Now he had to go through Samaria. So he came to a town in Samaria called Sychar, near the plot of ground Jacob had given to his son Joseph. Jacob's well was there, and Jesus, tired as he was from the journey, sat down by the well. It was about the sixth hour. When a Samarian woman came to draw water, Jesus said to her, 'Will you give me a drink?' (His disciples had gone into the town to buy food.) The Samarian woman said to him, 'You are a Jew and I am a Samaritan woman. How can you ask me for a drink?' (For Jews do not associate with Samaritans.) Jesus answered her, 'If you knew the gift of God and who it is that asks you for a drink, you would have asked him and he would have given you living water.'"

John 4: 4-10

Kaboto, beyond Kabongo, near Lenge
May 16, 2001

"I have received a new instruction from God," the Prophet Mechac told his secretary, Pastor Mutalala. They stood in the shade of the tree by the substantial brick-and-concrete hut that served as Mutalala's *bureau,* the place where he made meticulous notes about all of the Mechac's activities. "I have heard, 'Blessed are the peacemakers.' Please record it and announce it to the community." Mutalala noted the revelation in the Prophet's book of records.

Word spread. When the Prophet's followers at Kaboto heard the news, they crowded into the meticulously swept, wide-open sandy yard beside the church. Their singing invoked the Spirit of the God of the Living. The Prophet's words floated into the crowd.

"To be God's peacemaker—what does God want from me? From us? I will invite the Mai-Mai leader Maccabee to meet with me in a neutral village, Kansumba." His followers applauded with approval.

Afterwards, Mechac faced Mutalala in his carefully whitewashed *bureau,* the window shutters closed for privacy and concentration, dictating the exact words of the letter to Maccabee. "I, Prophet Mechac, a servant of Almighty God, invite the Mai-Mai Commander Maccabee to meet me in Kansumba to discuss how peace may come to Congo."

A courier departed. A few days later, he returned with Maccabee's reply: "I will meet Mechac."

Mechac chose Mutalala, his legal representative, and other advisors to accompany him. And he also contacted the local police commissioner—a small cadre of policemen would always travel with him to meetings with the Mai-Mai.

* * *

"You are now counted in the government, and you will play a role." In this way the Prophet Mechac had heard the voice of God at the prayer meeting in Munyungi, back in September 1996.

The 1996 prophecy had come to pass within a few weeks. Some years before, forty-two Rwandese businesspeople had settled their herds of cows on the fertile pastures of the Haut Lomami district near the Prophet's village of Kaboto. They had lived as good neighbors, selling milk and beef to the nearby villagers. When Laurent Kabila and the Rwandese turned their attention to Katanga Province in their effort to overthrow Mobutu, the dictator feared any Rwandese who might aid Kabila in the center of the country. The local government officials warned the businesspeople that Mobutu was sending soldiers to kill them. The businesspeople sought sanctuary in Kaboto, and the Prophet and his people agreed to protect them.

How can I allow God's creatures to shed blood in my land, which God has made holy ground? It is better that they kill me first. Mechac met the soldiers, dressed in the green fatigues and leopard caps of Mobutu's army, outside his village.

They had never seen such a face as Mechac's: oblong and soft-lined with a beckoning smile and eyes that expressed absolute calm. *This man is not at all afraid, they realized; his spiritual connection to the other world is absolute. He cannot be bought or shaken.*

Mechac spoke with a gentle authority that communicated complete confidence in divine guidance. "God revealed to me that you were coming. The Holy One has sent me to tell you that these Rwandese will give you no trouble."

"We have our orders from Mobutu!"

"Your human boss is old and frail. Almighty God lives and reigns forever! He is speaking to you through me. And God is the ultimate authority to whom you will answer."

The soldiers had been warned by the people: Mechac is a man of God. Disregard him, and you will be cursed.

What to fear—the lingering grasp of Mobutu, or the zeal of the God of the Prophet Mechac? The soldiers departed, leaving the Prophet to release the businessmen to the protection of God.

* * *

Mechac was dressed in his carefully ironed light brown suit and matching shirt. He focused his attention on the meeting to come and never noticed how he tossed and jumbled in the front seat of his truck. His closest followers crammed the truck's interior; the police rode on the truck's bed.

Maccabee, Mechac knew, would conduct ceremonies prior to entering, soliciting the protection of his ancestors during the meeting. Nearing Kansumba, the Mechac's party stopped for their own prayers, but Mechac did not seek to contact family members who had died.

"You are the Holy One, the God of the Living. You are the One who gave me my short life on this earth, and you will welcome me into your arms when I return home. You have guided me with visions and revelations all my life. I enter this village to be a peacemaker according to your will. May I be your vehicle, may my mouth speak words inspired by you, may my countenance command respect for your ways. May your will be done." Having finished his prayer, he was filled with confidence inspired by the Holy Spirit. He took up his walking stick and, followed by Mutalala and other carefully chosen assistants, finished his trek to the village.

As custom required, they first approached the hut of the village chief who welcomed his esteemed visitor.

"Please, we are here to talk with Maccabee and his followers about how to bring peace to this area. Maccabee has agreed to a conversation in this village. Could you send a messenger to Maccabee? Tell him I have arrived? First, we will have a prayer meeting—Maccabee, his companions, and your village are invited. Then, Maccabee and I will talk."

And so, the chief sent a courier with the message. Mechac waited calmly, expecting Maccabee and his followers to appear. Instead, the courier returned. "Maccabee refuses." So Mechac worshipped with the chief and his villagers. "May John 4: 4-10 come to pass in this village."

On the next day, another courier travelled to Maccabee with the message, "You and your followers are invited to a prayer meeting and to a discussion about peace. You, yourself, must come—not just your representatives. It is God's will."

* * *

The next day Maccabee arrived, surrounded by his followers. They blocked the entrance to the village so that anyone who entered or exited had to pass through their guards. They had adorned themselves with all of the power they believed in—their charms, their spears, their animal skins, their human fetishes. They stood with their rifles slung across their abdomens.

When the police saw the symbols of power that adorned the Mai-Mai, they lowered their eyes and shifted their feet. Mechac saw their fear.

But Mechac had seen all of these artifacts of power during his seventy-three years in the rural bush. *Exactly as I expected.* Mechac greeted Maccabee with a gentle smile, offering his hand, taking Maccabee's in his own.

God's Almighty Presence exuded from the Prophet; the aura of the Holy surrounded him. *Their guns and charms are silly against the Power of the God of Jesus Christ,* he thought. *The Mai-Mai and the police are so afraid.*

"*Karibu,* Maccabee. Before we talk, we worship God."

And so, under a giant mango tree, in the open-air compound of the chief, the assembly finally gathered—Mechac and his party, Maccabee and his followers, and villagers. Music reverberated as Mechac's followers and the villagers roused the Holy Spirit in song. Then, the Prophet read John 4: 4-10.

"I have received a vision based on Jesus with the Samaritans and the Galileans. Jesus, through his Prophet Mechac, is in an African village, with Mai-Mai on one side, and soldiers on the other, reconciling them. You are involved in the fighting, so this message is for you, also. Let us talk about how we can bring peace to our land."

Mechac began his first discussion with Maccabee, right there, with the Mai-Mai, the Prophet's followers, and the village listening.

"Maccabee, you are the children of God. I come to you as your spiritual father, one who loves his children. Let us bring peace to this area."

"Both of us want peace."

"You, the Mai-Mai, are a particular movement for a particular time. You are fighting against the government. And the government is here for the long term."

"Yes, what you say is true."

"The government is able to fight you, to win. You will suffer. If you want to have peace here, you cannot hold guns. You must surrender your arms to the government."

"We Mai-Mai are civilians who have organized to fight the rebels. The government is fighting the same rebels. We have the same purpose. But the government soldiers don't accept the Mai-Mai as their companions in the fight. So as you are standing in the middle between the Mai-Mai and the government soldiers, would you tell them to accept the Mai-Mai?"

"I can give them your message. But you must surrender your guns."

"No, you tell them why we continue to fight. When the government soldiers see a Mai-Mai, they follow him everywhere, to beat him, to kill him. So we keep our guns. You tell them we are both fighting the same enemy; they should accept us."

"I can tell them. But you must give your guns to the police commissioner and his officers who have come with me—show a tangible sign of your good faith." The Prophet's spiritual power, gentle but determined, and surely of God, shone from his face.

Maccabee relented. "I belong to the government. I am working for the government. Prophet Mechac, we'll give you the guns we have with us today."

"Put them here."

The police formed one line, Maccabee's followers the other. The Mai-Mai laid the rifles between them. A photographer took a picture.

"And Baba Mechac, I will go back to my village and organize a prayer meeting. Will you come and pray for our people and for my village? And there, we will give you other guns."

It did not surprise Mechac when Maccabee finally acquiesced. It was the will of God.

* * *

Shortly, thereafter, Maccabee did invite the Prophet to Maccabee's village, Kisula, for worship and prayer. As in Kansumba, Mechac, his followers, and the police visited. True to his word, Maccabee did surrender more guns. When they concluded the meeting, Mechac and his entourage visited smaller villages—Musau, Nyembo, Mpasa—to pass the word of peace and encourage young people not to join the Mai-Mai.

Bishop Ntambo Dedicates Churches

"Front Line of U.N. Effort to Take Guns from Children"

The New York Times, July 15, 2001

". . .the crowd gathered and was bewildered, because each one heard them speaking in the native language of each. Amazed and astonished, they asked, 'Are not all these who are speaking Galileans? And how is it that we hear, each of us, in our own native language? Parthians, Medes, Elamites, and residents of Mesopotamia, Judea and Cappadocia, Pontus and Asia, Phrygia and Pamphylia, Egypt and the parts of Libya belonging to Cyrene, and visitors from Rome, both Jews and proselytes, Cretans and Arabs—in our own languages we hear them speaking about God's deeds of power.' All were amazed and perplexed, saying to one another, 'What does this mean?'"

Acts 2:5-12

Kamina

July 2001

The sun had not yet risen, though a soft glow muted the stars and transformed the black sky to indigo. Bishop sat on the screened-in porch behind the guesthouse with the staff, rehearsing details, making sure that everyone understood.

"Today, our visitors land in Lubumbashi. Tomorrow, in Kamina. Now what do we do to please our guests?" He looked from one to another to be sure he had their attention. Of course, he did: this staff was handpicked as the most trustworthy, the ones who would be closest to the delegation.

"These Americans live differently from us. If we grew up in a poor family, we don't worry about cleaning. They like it clean. That's American, *wuzungu*. So we make it clean. Sweep, wash the floors, make sure all is ready."

They nodded but did not speak.

"Mama Sila, have you arranged for water to be delivered to the outdoor tank early every morning?" Mama nodded.

"Good. During the daytime, be sure that the barrel in bathroom is full, that the small bucket is always at hand to flush the toilet or for them to wash their hands and face." Again, those facing him nodded. The staff toileted using the latrine in the backyard that required none of this labor. They hauled water only for cooking and drinking. But the delegation would use the inside bathroom with a western stool and sink that required manual flushing. The staff understood the difference.

"They need boiled water for cooking and for coffee and tea. Well boiled. Bottled water, only, for table. We do not want anyone getting sick."

"These Americans are used to electricity. Be sure they have candles and matches when the lights go out." The staff had melted the bottoms of candles and stuck them to cup saucers; they were ready.

"Take care of yard. Guests don't like snakes. Sweep every morning."

"Watch over food. They don't like rats. For us, no problem. We just kill, eat the rats." He laughed. "For them, it's big problem! Keep rats out of house."

"Mwilumba, John Mutombo and Raymond Mande will translate the group speeches, but stay alert. If you see a need for translation for individuals, step in."

"Every morning early we meet at my house to review how things are going."

* * *

That night Bishop called Mande to hear about the delegation's arrival. How had they reacted? Mande reported that they seemed pleased to be met planeside and taken to the VIP lounge. A bit surprised, perhaps, when Mande offered them bottles of Fanta and requested their passports. Quiet and nervous when they were driven through the Congolese soldiers who guarded the airport, but interested in Lubumbashi. Bishop Morris and his wife had been taken to Bishop's house for the night's lodging; others were checked into the Park Hotel. All was well.

The next day at five a.m. the staff gathered at the guesthouse to report on preparations. Bishop decided to add a final reminder.

"You are all trustworthy. But, the temptation to steal is there. Guard the visitors' suitcases. Lock their rooms. A guest may open his suitcase and leave money about, and we all know the importance of dollars. Papa Jerome, Papa Kongolo"—now he spoke to the men to sat at the green metal door next to the driveway, everyday, announcing guests— "guard carefully. Be sure no one gets into the house to steal. If a guest has money stolen, he will go out with broken heart, and we will lose our value in relationship."

They were ready. They left for the airstrip where the whole community was gathered.

* * *

The atmosphere at the hanger by Kamina's dirt airstrip was electric. Choirs rehearsed, clapping, beating their drums. Bishop saluted the rifle-bearing soldiers who lounged in the shade. Mama Nshimba chatted with women and children from the orphanage. Onlookers pushed their faces against the broken chain fences.

By the time the plane rumbled onto the landing strip and chugged to a halt, the singers and drummers had filled the air with rhythm and harmony. The pilot lumbered down the steps and and turned to raise a hand to steady the passengers. As they appeared on the plane's steps, they stood still, mesmerized by the choirs. *Yes, I'd hoped for this reaction!* Bishop and Mama Nshimba had to walk toward the visitors to get their attention to greet them. The introductions and the music lasted many minutes, and when the singing quieted, Bishop presented the visitors formally to Kamina in Kiluba, while Dr. Mande translated. Bishop called two girls in school uniforms who presented a newspaper cone full of green leaves and welcomed the delegation in English. More speeches. The visitors responded. More translating, now English to Kiluba. Finally, the team invited the delegation to climb into the trucks they had hired to bring the Morrises to Bishop's house and the others to the guesthouse.

* * *

The next day, Ilunga Mutombo, the manager of the Kamina depot that distributed building materials, arrived early at Bishop's door. They grinned, laughed, shook hands, and hugged each other. Today, the townspeople, the traditional chiefs, the religious leaders, the government officials, and the American visitors—the whole assembly—would know the dedication of the people who had built the churches and parsonages of Kinkunki, Mwitobwe, Dean Scott, and Katuba and the schools Kendabantu and Umpafu. Everyone would know the talent and commitment of the local church leaders. What dignity, what happiness!

The Congolese looted life can give way to the stable life of fired bricks, Bishop mused.

Despite the baking heat, Bishop and the clergy were bedecked for ceremony in black academic robes and bright red stoles. Streaks of sweat shone through Bishop's hair, creating a glistening halo as he and Mama Nshimba walked toward the truck. Bishop climbed in the passenger seat with the American delegation. Ilunga Mutombo and more men piled into the flatbed. Men in their best business suits mounted motorbikes or bicycles, women in brightly colored *bikwembe* rode sidesaddle behind them. The entourage crept slowly toward Kinkunki, attracting the attention of every villager it passed.

Forty-five minutes later they arrived in front of the church. As the driver parked, Bishop felt the vibrations of the drums arising from the earth and heard the congregation singing.

Bishop climbed from his car with the Americans at his side and motioned to the engineers and workmen to join them. They walked hand-in-hand toward the congregants, followed by the other dignitaries and then the rest of the conference delegates. The Kinkunki parishioners, all the while singing and swaying, parted, creating a path toward the strip of ceremonial white ribbon that indicated the place where the dedication would be performed. The dignitaries approached and stopped before the *sherehe kamba*; the congregation crowded in behind them.

Bishop turned toward the assembly.

"Are you happy?" he shouted.

"*Wafwako!*" They responded. The women ululated.

"Today, let us thank the Lord! When I became your Bishop, you were worshipping outside. On my next trip to the United States, I talked to American congregations. I said, for two thousand dollars you can support a new church with a parsonage, a Bible, a fishpond and a garden, and a bicycle for the pastor. This church was made possible with help from our brothers and sisters in congregations in the United States. Now, we dedicate this church and parsonage—named for the village of our own king, Kinkunki."

He turned to Pastor Kabongo, the newly appointed Kamina district superintendent.

Kabongo rose. "On behalf of this church, we thank you, Your Excellency, Bishop Ntambo. We thank the donors who have made this church possible. We thank the workers who have built it. We entrust this church to the guardianship of its members. This is a place of pride and care, a place where we will build the lives of our families. It is not a place for children to throw stones and be destructive. This is our church. We will remember the donors in our prayers." He nodded to the traditional chief.

King *Kasongo Nyembo* raised his mahogany staff, the symbol of his reign, and spoke in the Luba metaphor of the hunter. "Our ancestor, Kiluwe, the hunter, came to this land, searched through the bush, and found the beast that fed the people. For that, he was blessed. He was like the lion, the best hunter of all. Now, Bishop is like the lion among us, leading his pride. Like Kiluwe, like the lion, he has led you, the people, to find the beast. The fruit of your hunting is the church, the first one in Kinkunki. This church will play an important role. It will be a place for weddings and large gatherings. Now, despite the heat or large storms, these celebrations will take place. You have impressed me. I have plenty of land; maybe you will build a clinic, a school. Feel free, you are welcome."

Kasongo Nyembo nodded to Bishop.

"Praise God!" Bishop shook the air. He turned to Kyoni, the district commissioner, representative of the governor, who spoke the concluding word.

"Long time, we did not see people building. No activity. No economy. I express the joy of governor at seeing the Methodist Church building. Stable churches—for a stable society."

A woman stood by with a knife in one hand and a glass of water in the other. Now the commissioner took the knife and cut the rope. Then he took the glass, sucked a large mouthful of water, and spit forcefully on the ground, on each side of the entrance. The men cheered and applauded, the women ululated. The crowd began to swarm toward the cars to proceed to the next church.

Nearby stood the engineers, masons, and Ilunga Mutombo, who by now had been nicknamed De Depot. De Depot extended his arms and looked at his hands, cupped toward one another. Hands, a man's greatest asset. The lines had become deeper, the calluses had formed on his palms. Overwhelmed with gratitude, he thanked God for his hands, then walked toward Bishop and hopped aboard the flatbed of the truck.

* * *

One morning a few days later, Bishop collapsed into his favorite chair in his living room. The community had gathered, they had dedicated the churches and schools, and the delegation had left for Lubumbashi in the company of Dr. Mande. No problems, no illnesses, no political instability, no mishaps. Soon, they would be on their way back to America.

Suddenly, Bishop felt very, very tired. His head dropped and he slept deeply, the choirs singing their Biblical songs in his dreams.

Pastor Kora Distributes Relief in Kitenge

> "WORLD BRIEFING: Africa: Rwanda: Former Allies Hold Talks"
>
> *The New York Times*, July 7, 2001

> "He humbled you by letting you hunger, then by feeding you with manna, with which neither you nor your ancestors were acquainted, in order to make you understand that one does not live by bread alone, but by every word that comes from the mouth of the Lord."
>
> Deuteronomy 8:3

Kitenge, eighty kilometers north of Kabongo
July 2001

The train whistle blew, rising from the bush grasses like the forlorn cry of an endangered feline longing for companionship, signalling its immediate arrival at the widened spot of red clay that served as the Kitenge depot. *A rare sound, a rare sight, once familiar,* thought District Superintendent Mujinga Mwamba Kora. He rose to his tip-toes, craning to see, a bit impatient. He expected this train from Kamina to Kitenge to bring a shipment of food—maize, oil, salt, milk, sugar—that he, his pastors, and his Roman Catholic colleagues would distribute to hungry civilians. Soon, the engine, followed by a long line of box-cars, came into view.

* * *

In August 1998 Pastor Kora, a new Mulungwishi Seminary graduate, had been assigned to an area outside Kitenge to begin a new congregation. Villagers responded eagerly, and a church formed quickly. But when Rwanda invaded Congo and war reached Kabalo, the people of Kitenge fled in many different directions. Kora and his family trekked eighty kilometers to the North Baluba District of Kabongo territory. By January Kora's conscience poked and prodded, leaving him no peace. He felt he had deserted his church.

"How does a pastor, a shepherd, abandon his flock?"

He grieved. At the Holy Spirit's bidding, he chided himself. Finally, in January 1999 he confided in his wife.

"I am a pastor. I must return to Kitenge and see what has become of the church."

Alone, he picked his way through the dirt and bush, back to Kitenge. But all of his church members had fled. Still, he beat the railway track, calling anyone who might hear to come to worship. Perhaps his members were hiding in the bush, waiting for a signal from their pastor.

But Congolese soldiers, rather than former parishioners, wandered into the church, filled the benches, and began to sing. Kora preached.

That week, Kora visited the encampments of Congolese soldiers in Kitenge. *If Congolese soldiers are now the new residents, then I will be their chaplain.*

"I'm happy to teach, preach, and pray with you. Where you living? I will visit you in your villages."

But when he tried to make his way down the paths to the huts of his members, he was stopped by Mai-Mai warriors.

"You want to pass? Then you pay us in salt, in oil, in maize," the warriors told him. "Whose side are you on? Congolese soldiers, or Mai-Mai? Show your loyalty."

"I'm not a soldier, I'm not a Mai-Mai rebel. I'm a pastor. A United Methodist pastor. You need God's protection. You need God's salvation. I came now to preach and to see other church members who are here."

And when Kora didn't meet Mai-Mai, he met Congolese soldiers.

"Where you come from? You meet Mai-Mai? Where are they?"

"I'm not a rebel. I'm a pastor. I'm not a politician. I'm doing Good News to those people, even to you as a soldier. I am trying to worship God here. I'm preaching, I'm praying for you."

Every time he walked to the villages, the same conversations, the same stories. But God guided him, and he was always respected as a man of God. He was never harmed.

* * *

Kora's ministry was so successful that he was appointed to replace Pastor Kabongo as district superintendent in Kitenge in July 2000. Kabongo had left him thirteen circuits of congregations and no Mai-Mai.

Now, in July 2001, Kora waited by the train tracks, eager to receive and distribute a shipment of supplies to Kitenge. He had divided the town in two—east and west—and planned to take portions of the load to a church in each area that would serve as a depot. He knew he could be mobbed, as people were desperate. He had prepared the people and hoped they would remain orderly.

* * *

The whistle of the train announced that one container of supplies had arrived, designated to help the registered displaced people till September. The church recognized the signal; the townspeople heard it, also. So did the Congolese soldiers and the Mai-Mai. For the next forty-five minutes, chaos reigned.

Mai-Mai ran through the streets, dressed in charms; the footfalls of Congolese soldiers pounded the paths as they, too, rushed into town, dressed in fatigues and armed for battle. Villagers heard the rapid fire of guns and the screams of soldiers. Townspeople fled while Mai-Mai and Congolese soldiers fought one another. Kora hid with others in the bush, some seven kilometers from Kitenge, until the sound of battle ceased.

Kora wound his way through the paths that led to Kitenge, listening for the guns, feeling for vibrations. Nothing. He found his way to the Roman Catholic parish. He and the priests had been good colleagues. They had talked regularly about the social life of Kitenge and about how they could cooperate on development projects when the time came. Two of the priests had fled, but one remained.

"I agree; you cannot leave the food at the depot or hide it at your home. It will be looted. Bring it here—our walls are more secure and we will try to protect it. We can call a scout, and we will try to bring as much of the food to the parish as possible."

For the next three days, they trudged the paths, loading bikes, carrying the precious, life-giving foodstuffs through the quiet town.

The Catholics guarded the food well. Over the next three weeks, the townspeople who returned from the bush would have had nothing to eat. The church provided maize, sugar, oil, and salt, appeasing a bit of the villagers' hunger.

Prophet Mechac Mediates Between the Colonel and Maccabee

> "Peace Talks to End War in Congo Finally Begin"
>
> *The New York Times*, October 17, 2001

> "For a child has been born for us, a son given to us;
> authority rests upon his shoulders;
> and he is named Wonderful Counsellor, Mighty God,
> Everlasting Father, Prince of Peace."
>
> Isaiah 9:6

Malemba, one hundred kilometers east of Kabongo

October 15, 2001

Prophet Mechac looked down the line of faces, Congolese military on one side, Mai-Mai on the other, watching for any emotions he could discern. Colonel Chipola, the commander of Kamina Military Base, and his soldiers sat at attention along one wall of the long room; Maccabee and his warriors perched stiffly on their blue plastic chairs, facing the Congolese officers along the other wall. As their mediator, Mechac sat at the head of the two lines: from there, he watched the stony, unrevealing faces for moments of hot anger, disdain, fear and flickers of the desire for peace.

Colonel Chipola had approached Haut Lomami Commissioner Kyuma and the Katangan Vice-Governor Jacques Mayumba to discuss the increasing activity of the Mai-Mai in Katanga Province. The Sun City peace process could not pacify Katanga if the Mai-Mai continued to terrorize the countryside. Yet neither the military nor the emissaries from the government had reduced the Mai-Mai threat. The spiritual leaders like Prophet Mechac seemed to make some progress. Mechac had established a relationship with the Mai-Mai leader Maccabee, and, for almost three months, peace had held. If the spiritual leader facilitated the conversation between the army and the Mai-Mai, perhaps the leaders would listen.

* * *

Colonel Chipola had invited Prophet Mechac to Kamina Military Base to quiz him about his negotiations with Maccabee. "So how are you effective with Maccabee? How do you approach him? What arguments do you use? How are you able to convince him to surrender his guns?"

"All we do is guided by God and based in prayer. Of course you, as the military, cannot do that."

"So what would you suggest we do to bring this Mai-Mai threat to an end?"

"I cannot be a messenger for you. You, the Congolese military, must talk directly with Maccabee and his Mai-Mai. You must learn to trust one another. Only then will the fighting stop."

"So will you lead a conversation between Maccabee and his Mai-Mai and the Congolese soldiers?"

"Of course. I want to bring peace to this land. And yes, I am willing to extend the invitation to Maccabee. He will feel more secure if we meet in Malemba."

The Colonel's convoy arrived in Kaboto, picked up Mechac and his delegation, and they, together with the Congolese military, chugged across the dirt paths to Malemba to meet with Maccabee. The moment of negotiation had arrived: the governor and the military on one side, the Mai-Mai on the other, and Mechac in between.

* * *

Mechac stood and prayed, then, "We will begin by giving his excellency the governor the floor."

The Governor rose. "We are from two different areas of the province, but we are children of the same country. The country belongs to all of us. Why should you just continue killing one another? The time has come to work together, to bring peace to the country."

"Peace is our goal, also."

"Mai-Mai have long been part of Congolese society. We can accept living with you. But we do not want you to carry guns."

"We protect the villages. And from Congolese soldiers! How can we do that, if you carry guns and we do not?"

"There are many ways to provide protection. Guns are not the only answer."

And around and around they went, arguing over whether, when and how the Mai-Mai would lay down their guns.

Finally, Maccabee agreed once more to put down his guns.

But the Mai-Mai threat was not yet over for Katanga.

Pilot Gaston Returns to Missions in Congo

> "WORLD BRIEFING: Africa: Rwanda: Charges of Plunder in Congo Denied"
>
> *The New York Times*, November 24, 2001

> "As they came near the village to which they were going, he walked ahead as if he were going on. But they urged him strongly, saying, 'Stay with us, because it is almost evening and the day is now nearly over.' So he went in to stay with them. When he was at the table with them, he took bread, blessed and broke it, and gave it to them. . . . That same hour they got up and returned to Jerusalem; and they found the eleven and their companions gathered together. They were saying, 'The Lord has risen indeed, and he has appeared to Simon!' Then they told what had happened on the road, and how he had been made known to them in the breaking of the bread."
>
> Luke 24: 28-35

Lubumbashi

November 2001

Gaston Ntambo shuttered as he peered sideways through the windshield of his Cessna 172. Villagers hovered between the concrete walls of the roofless, bullet-pocked hangar at the Manono airstrip, the lines of their gaunt faces etching their images into his psyche. *The people, they look like they just came through the woods, the shoes, the clothes, worn out, as if they had been living in a hole, dirty, smelly, no soap, for a very long time. Their skin—stretched over their bones with malnutrition and suffering.* Some people had stayed throughout the war, some had reappeared from the bush, and now they stood, solemn faced, their hands waving, as if pleading, *Wafwako, farewell, please return.*

They had not seen a civilian plane in a very, very long time—especially one overflowing with gifts for them. Gaston had packed medical supplies into the plane's every crevice, filling even the co-pilot's seat. The villagers had emptied the plane and had grinned, however weakly, as they built tall towers of boxes on the landing strip.

In town en route to the clinic, Gaston was shocked by the rubble of what had once been Manono. He delivered the supplies to a shattered medical center, where nurses still tried to care for the sick. *Manono is what they call their home, so they try to make an effort.*

Gaston's displacement had been so different than that of the people he had left behind. He and his family had spent the war years in Michigan, USA, where he had completed his airplane mechanic's training. In late 2001 the church had decided that it was safe to return the planes to the DRC, and he had been appointed as a home missionary. By flying he brought hope—even miracles—to ill and suffering destitute people.

But, he still had to fly with caution. Some inland villages had fire spots. He did not want to fly into places where rebel fighting continued, and now the Mai-Mai had become troublesome. He also dreaded the other enemy—disease—especially a cholera epidemic. *The pastor who comes to unload the plane, the one who wants to shake hands, might be a carrier of killer germs.*

But he flew with faith in his mission. Strange visitors had come, and he believed that Jesus hovered very close to his side.

* * *

In 2001 Gaston and Jeanne had returned to Lubumbashi, encouraged by the church to make the medical mission service, Wings of the Morning, self-sustaining. *Buy a farm for the church, create an income stream for the medical flight ministry—others had done it in Zambia.* He researched a fine farm and paid the seller $70,000 in cash. Within days, a powerful man had challenged his claim to the title. Gaston was shattered, and he laid bare his soul to Jeanne: *How am I going to explain to the denomination that I just spent $70,000 buying a farm that was not for sale? And how am I going to give that money back? Will they ever forgive me? Will I lose my job because of this?* He told no one else.

The sun was barely streaking the sky on Tuesday morning when his household sentry knocked at his bedroom door.

"Three men and one lady here to see you."

"Too early, way too early." He hugged the pillow to his cheek.

"They say they have a message for you. From God."

He rolled over and groaned. "I'm coming."

Reluctantly, he forced himself out of bed. *People don't just walk in with a message from God. If God wanted to talk to me, he would appear in my dreams.*

At the gate he stood face-to-face with the four messengers.

"You must be Mr. Gaston."

"Yes, it's me."

"We heard your name when we were praying. We got a word from God, and we came to see you immediately. We will give you the message, and then we will continue with our business."

Clearly, they wished Gaston no harm, and he wanted to be kind. "Come to my *payotte*." Gaston led them under a thatched roof and indicated chairs where they should sit.

They did not hesitate. "You are going to have a solution to the problem of the farm that you are having right now."

Gaston sat upright, wide awake, shocked. "Say that again?" No one knew about his dilemma over the farm except Jeanne.

"We have a message for you about the problems with the farm."

"Let me get my wife." And soon, with Jeanne present: "Can you start all over again so she can hear what you have to say?"

"First, God knows the problem you have with the farm. Before the end of this week, the situation is going to be over with. Second, you're building a house and a church, and we learned that you used all your money. And God says, he will find a way for you to finish your house quickly. Third, the farm you are going to buy will never be used for anything else. And it's you who are going to keep using that farm."

Even with Jeanne present, verifying what he was hearing, Gaston sat, dumbfounded, not knowing what to say.

"What church are you from?" They described a church that was very easy to find—a red tent, no roofing.

The visitors rose to leave. Gaston and Jeanne stumbled over their words, found their etiquette. "May we offer you some money?"

"No, we aren't here for money."

"At the very least, take $20 for your transportation."

After they left, Gaston and Jeanne sat together, shocked into silence.

Later that week Gaston casually asked Bishop, his father, about the church. *I know it, they have no roofing, only a red tent— if the wind comes they will all get wet.*

Like Mary and Elizabeth, Gaston and Jeanne pondered these things in their hearts, but the visit did not change the terror Gaston felt at the threat posed by the powerful men.

* * *

On Thursday night Gaston received a phone call from a government official in charge of land titles.

"Some men have brought a complaint about the title to a farm you say you bought. Would you come with your paperwork to my office tomorrow morning at eight o'clock? Just come by yourself."

This is it. The end.

The next morning Gaston dressed in a white shirt and tie and gathered his papers. But when he entered the government office, he discovered he was underdressed. His accusers—three men and their lawyers—were already seated, dressed in formal dark business suits.

The government representative greeted him. "Your papers?"

Gaston presented his papers to the official sitting at his desk.

"And yours?"

His powerful challengers did the same.

Gaston avoided the eyes of the men. For ten minutes of uneasy silence the government official read.

Finally, he laid the papers flat on his desk and raised his head, looking straight at the well-dressed team.

"You have no claim to this land."

"Do you know who you are talking to?" one of the men screamed angrily.

"I am not going to take land that belongs to the church and give it to you."

One of the lawyers jabbed a pointy finger at the official as the six rose to leave. "You're going to get what's coming to you!" The door slammed behind them.

The official turned to Gaston. "They are trying to steal from you. Don't worry about it, it's over, I already signed off. Take your papers and good luck to you."

Gaston sat stunned, not believing what had just happened. He, himself, never spoke. The official did all the fighting, had stood down powerful men and put his job at risk, it seemed, just to be honest.

* * *

After three weeks with no further disturbance, Jeanne and Gaston decided to repay their reassuring visitors. *We'll buy them some roofing material so they can get their church started.* So they went to red tent in the early morning and waited until the church members finished their prayer meeting. Finally, the pastor gave them his attention.

"We had visitors who came from you and brought us a message. We want to thank them because so far, everything they told us has come true."

The pastor looked at them, a strange look on his face. "We don't have that program here."

"No, no, no. It can't be anywhere else, they gave a very good description!"

"Another church near here, our neighbors, maybe it's them."

Gaston and Jeanne went to the second church, the same story. The messengers could not be found.

Gaston had been brought to a stronger faith: God truly did walk by his side.

The Traditional Chief Neutralizes the Mai-Mai Power

> "Congo Peace Negotiations End Without Accord After Seven Weeks"
>
> *The New York Times*, April 20, 2002

> "When the righteous are in authority, the people rejoice; but when the wicked rule, the people groan."
>
> Proverbs 29:2

Ngoy-Mwana

Sometime in 2002

The chief of Ngoy-Mwana, a group of seven villages deep in the bush, glided down the path from the forest toward his central village, Kamome, his gait filled with grace. Chief Kanda-Fwanyinwabo had followed Luba tradition carefully, honored his gods and his ancestors, and hearkened to their guidance. His ceremonies had filled his mind, his brain, his body with the sweet smoke of transcendent peace. As he reached the edge of his village, his spirit yielded to a more finite sense of humility. He was deeply grateful for the intimate connection he had cultivated over the years with his deities and ancestors. They were his closest relations, more than any earthly beings. This oneness expressed itself in his love for his villagers.

As an earthly being, the chief communicated his spirituality to his villagers in many ways. His meticulous appearance exuded the dignity that his gods conferred upon him. He always wore his leopard-skin cap and carried his carved mahogany staff, symbols of his responsibility for the peace of the community. His body was that of an elder statesman, supple and lean; he dressed in carefully sewn and pressed shirts and trousers. His bearing exuded a quiet wisdom and determination that could not be found with every chief.

And now he gathered his primary ministers around him. "We have had many interactions with the Mai-Mai, some good, some troubling. A young boy came to kill me yesterday. I have sought my ancestors' advice about what kind of action to take. We must deal with him and the others from this village who have fallen under the spell of the Mai-Mai. It is time to neutralize their power."

The men nodded: when the chief spoke, so it would be done.

* * *

The chief's villages lay on the outskirts of Kamina territory, two hundred and fifty kilometers north of Kamina. During their rise to power, the Mai-Mai leaders who came to dominate the area, Maccabee and Chinja-Chinja, did not venture this far—rather, their emissaries recruited young men from the villages.

Some years earlier, the leader of a small band of Mai-Mai approached the chief, speaking gently. "Chief, you know that the Rwandese are moving in this direction, but the army is not stationed here, and there is no one to secure your villages. We have come to enlist young boys to protect our goods and our families. Send those whom you choose, bring them for rituals, and they will watch over your villages."

They spoke reasonably, as if they were making a kind offer. And indeed, Laurent Kabila's envoy *had* visited the villages, asking them to organize Mai-Mai throughout Katanga to augment the regular army. The emerging militias had made such an offer to a neighboring chief who had accepted it, and a defense around his villages had been developed.

But even watching the good outcome nearby, Chief Kanda-Fwanyinwabo had his doubts. As one charged with traditional government, he was free to make up his own mind. He gripped his royal staff and sat for a moment in silence, feeling its power. *He* had received the white lime; *he* was responsible for peace in his village.

The chief had five younger brothers in the national army. *You should be coming to ask me to give you people here to release to the army. The war is in the east. Why can't you go there? Instead you come here where there is no war?*

Before I would let them go with you, I would go into the forest for some days, invoking my deity—I would come with all my power and wash my people with the power we bring. Then nobody would be killed from here.

He did not need the Mai-Mai; he could protect his people.

He was a chief of many thoughts but few words. "I have considered your offer. I appreciate your endeavor, but, no, it is not necessary for my group of villages."

* * *

Months later the word circulated: the Mai-Mai have gifts for the chief who recruits young men for the militias.

Gifts—no, bribes! And once the Mai-Mai enter, the chief must collaborate with them. I cannot sell *my people. I am not here to accept war. I do not want to kill, to see people dying.*

Again Chief Kanda-Fwanyinwabo said no to the Mai-Mai.

* * *

By the time the Mai-Mai approached again, Chief Kanda-Fwanyinwabo had become suspicious of their tactics. They seemed to want the power of the chief without the responsibility—and they had killed five chiefs in village groups outside Kabongo in their quest.

As the chief, I am forbidden to kill. I am the one who takes care of the insects, the animals, the birds, the water, the fish, everything made by the Creator. I have the power, and I know where I get my spirit. But if I start negotiating with the Mai-Mai, I will show them where my source of power is, where the deities are, how to do devotions to them. When the Mai-Mai has my power, he feels secure. People will not see him, and he will perform so many miracles. But he will come to me when I am absent-minded and kill me.

"My answer is the same as it has always been. No."

* * *

Finally, the Mai-Mai attacked the village. But their power succumbed to that of the chief.

They tried to force us. They were thinking we could not resist. But their fetishes kept falling. Their charms were left on the ground. Every Mai-Mai attack disintegrated.

Even so, the Mai-Mai had successfully recruited young men from the village. And one such recruit was sent to kill the chief. But the chief's spiritual power neutralized the Mai-Mai's will.

The chief approached the elders of the village with the recruit. "This young man followed the Mai-Mai, but he has learned that their power does not hold. Please, take him to the village, marry him to a wife. He must take responsibility for her livelihood, have children, and develop a stable life."

It was time for the upstart, would-be warrior to grow up. Adult responsibilities would save him from the Mai-Mai.

* * *

But there remained the problem of all the other young men who had been recruited into the Mai-Mai.

"It is time to end the Mai-Mai threat in our villages. We will go hut to hut through all seven villages, find the young men who have become part of the militias, and take their charms and their fetishes. We will make sure they marry. They will not use their power against me or my villages."

After the chief and the elders finished their work, the chief stored all of the collected charms and fetishes in his house for safekeeping. There they remained.

I have gained their respect. They will be happy with their wives and forget the Mai-Mai.

Guy Mande Makes Hydraform Bricks

> "Struggling to End Africa's World War"
>
> *The New York Times*, August 2, 2002

> "Therefore do not worry, saying, 'What will we eat?' or 'What
> will we drink?' or 'What will we wear?' For it is the Gentiles
> who strive for all these things; and indeed your heavenly Father
> knows that you need all these things. But strive first for the king-
> dom of God and his righteousness, and all these things will be
> given to you as well."
>
> Matthew 6:31-33

Kamina

April through August 2002

Guy Mande stood with his back to his students, writing math problems with
bits of chalk on the blackboard, intently focused on his task so they could not
see his embarrassment. He felt ashamed. He had been complaining about the
difficult living conditions in Kamina—the dilapidated mud huts and leaky
thatched roofs, the monotonous food, and the lack of transportation. But as class
began, he heard his students comparing stories—some biked over two hundred
kilometers from Kabongo, avoiding soldiers, and others rode nearly eight hundred kilometers from Manono, carrying cooking oil—just to get an education
at the *Institut supérieur pédagogique*. Compared to them, he had not sacrificed.

That evening, he scolded himself. He had had so many more advantages
than the students who perched on rounded and crumbling mud brick benches in
his classroom. They tried to learn without writing utensils, paper or books. After that, he focused on what he could give to his students and forgot what little
he was earning each month. He committed himself to match his sacrifice to
theirs. As he immersed himself, he discovered that he loved teaching.

* * *

Guy had been summoned by Bishop to his home; now he sat on the edge of an
overstuffed chair in Bishop's outdoor *payotte,* waiting, quizzical. Bishop
opened the door, stooped and entered, looking straight at Guy, his eyes twin-
kling. *What kind of mischief could Bishop be conceiving now, involving me?*

Bishop sat back, comfortably. "You have an engineering degree, so in addition to teaching and leading the choirs, I want you to oversee making bricks."

Guy nodded. He knew the brick-making operation at Kamisamba Farm, the
hollow brown scar in the green field near a large termite hill. He had seen the
crews packing termite dung into a form and firing it in a kiln. After that, the
bricks were stacked, ready to be transported to the site of the new churches and
parsonages.

But Bishop had not finished. "We have a new venture: building with hydraform machine. It's new technology developed in South Africa. In Mozambique we bishops saw houses made with these kinds of bricks, very strong. GBGM will purchase two machines to use here, as test for Congo. And…"—now Bishop's eyes danced— "…you will need to go to South Africa with a team of Congolese and missionaries to learn to use hydraform machine and to bring it back to Kamina. We hope to build much stronger bricks than before."

Guy threw back his head and laughed, imagining how he would tell his father: *my job in the backward church requires me to apply for a passport!*

* * *

Guy and his team pushed with all their strength as they hitched the bright yellow fifteen hundred and sixty kilogram hydraform machine to the rear of the truck. The men jumped onto the truck's bed, from which they watched the machine behind them as the driver jostled and bumped, squeaked and creaked across the town's red clay rutted roads. When they came to the low-slung buildings of Lupandilo Nursing School, they eased the machine onto the edge of the field near the large trees that spread their branches for shade. Already, they had positioned yellow jerry cans of water and bags of cement with part of the crew nearby, standing ready.

Dry season had settled over the land. Still, around Guy's soul, towering thunderstorms and thick bolts of lightning threatened. He felt exposed, without a place to hide. The crew spoke in short, tense sentences, revealing their anxiety as the townspeople crowded near the large yellow machine, then shifted their positions to make way for Bishop's special invitees: the town administrator and the district commissioner, the Muslim imam and the Catholic bishop, the Zimbabwean general and the Congolese colonel. They stood in the front row. Now, in front of all them, Guy and the team were expected to demonstrate the new machine. Bishop had broadcast the news far and wide that the church was bringing technology that would produce stronger bricks than the kiln at Kamisamba Farm.

Soon, it would be time to test the mixture of sand and clay, to blend the local materials with cement, to push the button and watch the bricks arise from the machine a few seconds later—*and do it right the first time, to build the town's confidence.*

When the time came, the crowd quieted, straining to look over each other's shoulders. One of the workers filled it with earth and added water to separate sand from clay. Perfect. Another worker shovelled the correct amount of sand and clay into the wheelbarrow. Guy added a measured amount of cement and mixed. They globbed it into the well of the machine. Bishop stepped forward to push the button. A few seconds later the machine produced a brick like a chicken lays an egg. Presto! The women ululated, the men cheered and applauded. Happy chatter bubbled throughout the crowd.

One of the workers placed the brick on the ground to begin a pile that could be sprinkled with water for the next fourteen days, helping the bricks to set and dry to their maximum strength. Now, Bishop invited each of the dignitaries to step forward, push the button, and create a brick in just a few seconds.

Later, in Bishop's *payotte,* they discussed the second machine that remained in Lubumbashi. "We are a pilot project. Leave it in Lubumbashi. The other conferences may want to use it. Perhaps we can even set up a shop and sell bricks to make money." Guy suggested.

"The church shouldn't make a profit from its projects," Bishop protested.

"Right now you are raising a lot of money in America. That won't last forever. How can we make construction sustainable?"

"We will see. We are the church." Bishop believed in God's providence through radical human generosity, American, European, and Congolese. "Don't worry about the money," Bishop had been known to say, even when he had none and his family hungered. He applied these tenets personally and professionally, and so far, his system had worked. He did not worry, even when those around him did. So one hydraform machine remained in Lubumbashi, waiting for its call to mission.

Meanwhile, the team in Kamina moved the machine to Umpafa, near Kamisamba Farm. The dirt provided a perfect mix of sand and clay, and a nearby river offered a steady supply of water. With a built-in generator, the machine ran even when general electricity failed. So twelve workers, many of whom had never been able to go to school, camped at the machine, running it day and night. They proudly earned the steady salary of fifty dollars a month. They learned the craft of construction on the job.

The sight of the men, camped around the yellow machine in the soft glow of the moon and the stars, gave the project a nighttime halo. Morning brought more people—men, youth, even women of the churches—walking from the horizon toward the site, bundles of food on the women's heads, tools in all their hands. The bricks for their churches and their parsonages were being produced, and the people came ready to work! After protecting their food in the shade or in the church, they lumbered into the fields and set to work, scraping, shovelling, wheelbarreling, moving the topsoil toward the machine.

Together, they developed momentum, and soon, the team and its congregational volunteers produced a thousand bricks a day.

* * *

One thing led to another. "Bishop, if you want our engineering office to function, we need instruments."

"Make a list." The construction team sat at the table, brainstorming. On his next trip to Lubumbashi Guy purchased the equipment, and then they went to work. With a small laptop and home software, the team designed churches of different sizes, parsonages, schools, and even a university.

The buildings had to be furnished. "Bishop, we can purchase furnishings from the brewery, $1900." When Guy closed the deal with the brewery's CEO in Lubumbashi, the discussion turned to music. The brewery offered to provide the truck, the gas, and payment whenever the band played a concert.

Meanwhile, some townspeople grumbled to Bishop. "How can we be the church and have our musician riding around in a truck that advertises the brewery?"

The church became embroiled in heated debate, for and against.

"The truck only advertises Gino, the brewery's soft drink, and you all drink it. It's ok," Bishop decreed.

* * *

"Bishop, we can purchase the cornmeal factory next to the carpentry shop for $35,000. People can bring their corn. We can grind it and sell it to support our other ministries."

"If it will help us feed the people, yes, but not to make profit."

* * *

The heady scent of eucalyptus and faint smoke, the particular fragrance that welcomes people to the abundance that is peculiarly African, filled the air. Success seemed to overwhelm itself. The church now employed eight hundred people; even more received food and clothing. War was ending; peace surely neared. Prayers had been answered.

Morning after morning, Guy prayed, first as a member of a prayer group, then leading for a whole month. He was asked to preach. His pastors, Pastor Kasembwe and Pastor Umbadolo, vouched for him to Bishop. "He is not only an engineer and a singer but a preacher. Send him for studies."

Oblivious to the conversation among his elders, Guy followed his daily routine: at four-thirty or five a.m., attend morning prayer, at five-thirty bike to Kamisamba Farm in the dark, singing. More prayer, go to the brick site, then to the school to teach, and then to the office in the headquarters in the afternoon. One day, in one of their meetings, Bishop made the proposal: "Do you have a vocation to be a pastor? If so, I can send you to Africa University in Zimbabwe. You will learn English and complete your theological studies."

Guy threw his head back and laughed, his face settling into a grin as he thought of the forthcoming conversation with his father.

Pastor Kora Hears a New Word at Annual Conference 2002

"Rwanda and Congo Sign Accord to End War"

The New York Times, July 31, 2002

"Then I heard the voice of the Lord saying, 'Whom shall I send, and who will go for us?' And I said, 'Here am I; send me!'"

Isaiah 6:8

Kamina

July 2002

Usually, Pastor Kora wriggled and squirmed as he sat in the flimsy blue plastic chair during the long sessions of Annual Conference. They were designed to hold someone half his weight. But today, he sat stock still, unaware of his discomfort. He had been appointed district superintendent, replacing Pastor Kabongo, in July 2000, and he regularly encountered Congolese soldiers and Mai-Mai who followed the most powerful warlord in the area, Chinja-Chinja. The words spoken by Colonel Shinba Mulongo, the chaplain from Kamina Military Base, seared his heart like a perfectly thrown spear, as if the colonel had spoken in private directly to him.

"This is the church's time. Only God can deal with the war between the Congolese soldiers and the Mai-Mai. You pastors, you are the people of God who have the divine spirit, the power to intervene. So talk to them if you can. But be careful how you approach them. They do not want to take advice from anyone but their ancestors. Have the courage that comes only from Christ, but do not risk your life."

He knew his time would come.

Raymond Mande Visits Texas

"War is Still a Way of Life for Congo Rebels"

The New York Times, November 21, 2002

"The one who had received the five talents went off at once and traded with them, and made five more talents."

Matthew 25:16

Texas, USA

November 2002

In Texas, USA, Dr. Raymond Mande stared at the television set of his host family. The news anchor proclaimed that the United States had cornered Osama bin Laden and would soon capture him. *A rare environment. The Americans are living with their own vulnerability, their own threat, their own enemy, their own war. They are trying to find their own sense of power. How do I conquer their spirits with compassion for the suffering in Congo?*

Mande had been invited to Texas by one of the Americans who visited Kamina to dedicate churches and schools, a physician who had asked, might Kamina benefit from the services of a visiting medical team? If so, would Mande be willing to come to Texas to speak in hospitals and churches about Kamina's needs?

Mande welcomed the invitation. On his previous visit to the United States for the General Conference in 2000, he had arrived in the middle of the night, attended the twelve days of the conference, and left the following day. He had formed his impressions of Americans by what he had experienced inside the Cleveland Convention Center. He was eager to meet them in their own homes, their own churches, and their own hospitals—to discover their spirit beyond the floor of the General Conference. If he understood Americans in their own world, his work might be more effective.

Bishop was enthusiastic. "The first time I went to America to talk in churches, I expected to go to New York, Washington, all the places you hear about. But no, they take me to little churches in Indiana, all around. And I'm troubled. I think, why am I doing this? But I learned: it's the teachers and the farmers, giving five dollars a week, who support the mission in the church."

With Bishop's blessing, Mande had landed at the Dallas, Texas airport. After Mande greeted his host, he phoned his family to say that he and Mande would be at their home soon. Mande joked, "Just tell them, 'the diplomatic parcel has arrived.'" But his words had serious undertones: he hoped to be a good ambassador for his country, his bishop, his people.

* * *

The next day Mande visited the first of several hospitals where he met a flurry of new, indistinguishable faces, doctors and nurses, people who his host thought might be interested in travelling to Kamina. They had studied up on Congo and asked questions he had anticipated about the new Congolese president, Joseph Kabila, the war, security and danger. But one question surprised him. A gentleman with gray hair and a wrinkled face spoke. "I'm retired. Do you think an old doctor like me can be of some use in Kamina?"

Mande had an immediate answer. He knew that doctors like Kasanka had improvised during the war, but as the crisis lessened, they were eager to develop their skills. "Sir, you will treat people, but you can also teach our young doctors. You will share with the people of Congo, not only the patients but also the medical professionals, to give them hope."

* * *

Mande's visit had progressed from the white-and-glass hospital walls glittering with the reflection of blinking technology to a long car ride through the tan, blowing grasses of Texas ranchland that baked under a blazing sun. His first host had handed him off to his second, a pastor who had also been part of the delegation to Kamina. As they glided down the highway in the pastor's swift, smooth SUV, the pastor wanted to know what kind of project his church could do in Kamina. Mande threw out some possibilities. A drill for a well? A church and parsonage? Nothing fit. Mande pondered the lights of the dashboard and then his gaze settled on the pastures outside the car window. *Land in Texas, land in Congo.*

After buying Kamisamba to cultivate, North Katanga had purchased Lewji Farm, one with hills for livestock to graze. Bishop had envisioned a herd of cattle from which the cows and calves could be distributed to country families.

"The land is good for livestock. People in the Congo raise chickens. But they have large families. You sell a chicken; they give you 2 dollars. But with 2 dollars you will not provide all the needs for the family. Now, if people can be initiated into raising cows, this will help. If the church has cows, within 3 or 5 years, we start distributing to families. So each family will have cows of its own, within ten, twenty years. So there will be cows everywhere for families, and that will solve this problem of poverty. If there's a way to raise money for purchasing cows. . . ."

"Yes! A herd of 1000 cows. Texas is the place of ranches. It's a project people can understand. All right, in the service you won't preach. I know the questions people will ask—I'll ask and you answer."

When the time came, Mande stood in front of the congregation of four thousand people.

"This congregation knows what your bishop is doing to build churches and parsonages and feed displaced people. What difference might *cows* make?"

Americans like to hear that people are being empowered.

"Cows will help people to solve the problem of poverty. Instead of relying on the chicken, which is not significant in terms of income, they can raise and sell cows, which will provide food and livelihood." More clapping, cheers.

"Now. The time has come to make you into a real Texas cowboy. Here's the initiation. Do like me. *He haw!*" the pastor crooned.

"He haw!" Mande cat-called. The congregation hooted.

"At the first service, you got your cowboy boots, at your second, you got your cowboy belt. Now, here's your hat." The pastor plopped a ten-gallon straw hat on Mande's head. More guffaws, more clapping. "And what you do with your hat, cowboy? You pass it for an offering." The pastor quickly removed the hat from Mande's head and placed it on the pulpit. "Now, c'mon up here. Let's help our cowboy get his herd of cattle."

The congregation began to sing, and Mande nodded at the people as they passed by him to drop money in the hat. *Come help. Men, women, even children.* A little girl clutched her purse and dropped a coin into the hat. *This is American spirit, roused for Congo.*

The pastor proclaimed: "This is only the beginning for the herd for our cowboy. The campaign will continue. He will go back to the Congo, and we will send the money to him."

A few months later a DHL delivery appeared at Mande's Lubumbashi door. Mande signed for the yellow and red cardboard envelope and tore open the flap. He gasped, and then he called Bishop Ntambo. North Katanga now had the funds to purchase the herd: the church in Texas had sent $33,000.

Even during their own war, American hugs embraced Congo. He now knew something of the excitement Bishop Ntambo experienced as he raised money in the United States. He looked forward to hosting the medical team.

* * *

The church had returned its planes to Congo. For the medical team, Mande did not have to charter a hand-me-down Russian cargo plane with webbed garden chairs—Gaston could fly the team. Coordinating transportation for an American team stressed Gaston, who had to fly to Zambia on a specific schedule for av-gas for the old Cessnas, but it relieved Mande immensely. The checklist of advanced notifications remained, and Mande planned to travel with the team to interpret, to smooth any problems, to negotiate any threats.

The medical team arrived. Since it was so difficult to import pharmaceuticals, they had brought funds to purchase medicine. Mande took them to the drugstores in Lubumbashi. Then, they boarded Gaston's Cessna, arrived in Kamina, and met the Congolese medical personnel.

Bishop had sent the word into the rural area, and thousands of people had arrived to be seen by the team of Congolese and American doctors.

Pastor Nyengele Distributes Relief

"WORLD BRIEFING: Africa: Congo: Officials Suspended"

The New York Times, November 13, 2002

"Then you, together with the Levites and the aliens who reside among you, shall celebrate with all the bounty that the Lord your God has given to you and to your house."

Deuteronomy 26:11

Kamina

November 26, 2002

Pastor Nyengele had mourned the loss of his congregants when Mobutu's army fled Manono during Kabila's uprising; then he had suffered as his congregants, most of them children, died in flight. Now, he had become one of the leaders of relief distribution to displaced people who survived.

He stood in the hall of the Kasingi-Noseke distribution site and looked from one table to the next. The wooden desk nearest Nyengele held the ledger of registered displaced people. Twenty-six of these, who were paid 2900 Congolese francs for their day's labor, had organized the rations that were due to be distributed to two hundred and seventy-five families. One worker stood by the pile of sacks of corn flour; another held a cup to scoop dried beans from the bulk container; a third had stacked boxes of oil, which would be divided cup for cup between small groups; the fourth manned a large bag of salt. Others replenished supplies or spelled the distributors.

All was ready. Nyengele nodded to the policeman, and the first hungry supplicant walked through the door. From this moment in the morning until sundown, the displaced presented themselves to Pastor Nyengele, registered, and received their share.

It was a day like many yesterdays, a day like many tomorrows.

Today's distribution offered sixty kilograms of flour, ten kilograms of beans, four and a half kilograms of oil, and three quarters of a kilogram of salt. Unless the displaced had a garden to cultivate or found vegetables in the bush, this ration alone kept a displaced family alive for thirty days.

Once a month, at the end of the day, when all of the families had received their share, Nyengele himself stood up and took his place in line. One of the workers registered him, and he received his allotment to take home to his family.

Supervising the distribution site, Nyengele aimed to be transparent—all registrations and distributions occurred in the open so people believed they were dealt with fairly and riots would not break out. The name of each adult to be served appeared on a preprinted list, in order to avoid duplicate distributions.

Every day, he prepared the log to send to UMCOR, World Vision and the World Food Programme.

It was a thankless job. Nyengele's memories of gleaning food in the bush remained strong, and he was amazed by the ingratitude of many of the displaced. They grumbled ongoingly.

"It's not enough."

"But it's something."

"I have an orphan living with me now—more mouths to feed."

"Must be registered." Nyengele turned his back. *But you have something! And you could say, Wafwako!*

Day after day, from sun up to sun down, Nyengele supervised the distribution of aid until November 6, 2003, the day the program ended.

Prophet Mechac Denounces the Underground Economy

"40 Nations in Accord on 'Conflict Diamonds'"

The New York Times, November 6, 2002

"Is not this the fast that I choose:
to loosen the bonds of injustice,
to undo the thongs of the yoke,
to let the oppressed go free,
and to break every yoke?"

Isaiah 58:6

Kaboto, March 2003

Prophet Mechac's lips formed a tight line. Like the fire of God on Mount Sinai, a righteous, white-hot anger filled his body, but it did not consume him. Rather, it tempered his determination.

"I have prayed with these people and talked to them. I have tried to teach them as a spiritual father. But they have betrayed God and the people they serve. They cannot be allowed to get away with what they are doing to innocent villagers. The time for talking with them has passed. I will proclaim their sins to all; I will denounce their misdeeds, even if they kill me."

The conversations between the Mai-Mai and the Congolese soldiers in October 2001 had worked well. They had stopped their fighting; around Kaboto and Kabongo they could be seen, talking together, laughing together. Then in June, the harvest time, the Prophet saw trouble once more.

The Mai-Mai and the Congolese soldiers had developed an underground economy. The Mai-Mai stole the harvested food from the villagers. They sold it to the soldiers or they traded for guns and ammunition. The soldiers looted the food and possessions of the same villagers and then they traded their booty with the Mai-Mai.

"The Mai-Mai is a good movement gone wrong—gone wrong because of power, drugs, guns—but, also, because of greed," the Prophet told his followers. "They have taken on the ways of the military, looting at will not only to survive but to enrich themselves. That is why—despite all of our efforts—the war of the Mai-Mai and the Congolese soldiers against the villages continues."

And he warned his followers: "Jesus died for one purpose: to save people. And I am ready to die to save our villagers from harm—that's better for me than to stand aside and do nothing while villagers are threatened, injured and killed. I'm not afraid of Mai-Mai or Congolese soldiers. What can they do to me? They can take away my earthly life, but not my presence with God."

The Prophet denounced the economy of the Mai-Mai and the Congolese soldiers from village to village.

* * *

The Prophet, his leaders, and their families had retreated to Lenge for a prayer meeting. They followed Jesus' custom of finding a quiet place, and usually, they were not disturbed. But today, a breathless man burst into the room.

"Prophet, Prophet! Chinja-Chinja is in Kaboto, in your own hut, waiting to kill you!" The man had ridden his bicycle as fast as he could, across the dirt roads from Kaboto to Lenge. In the past, Chinja-Chinja had occasionally visited Kaboto but he had not threatened the Prophet.

"*Wafwako.* You have ridden far to warn us. But be calm. You are safe. Tell us what you know."

The man shuddered and then looked directly at the man of God. "Chinja-Chinja came into the village silently, from the rear. He took over your house. Some of his followers went on to wait for you at the bridge. They told us, 'Today we will go home with the Prophet's head!' Over and over! Many people heard it."

Everyone in the room began to murmur, filling the room with concern.

"Prophet, you cannot go back to the village."

"We need to find a place where you are safe."

"First, I will pray for the people who are in the village." The Prophet bowed his head. And when he finished, all of the eyes of the men in the prayer circle focused on him.

"We will go back to Kaboto immediately."

"But you may be killed!"

"Yes, but what of the people who have followed me because of God? I can't leave them to face Chinja-Chinja alone. Some of you will come with me, and others stay here with the children. Let's go."

* * *

Prophet Mechac and a few members of the prayer meeting tromped through the trees, down the dirt road, toward the bridge that crossed the brook that formed the perimeter of Kaboto. Their footfalls rustled on the road, alerting the warriors that they were approaching. The Mai-Mai had dragged a tree across the road—a military-style barrier—to prevent access to the bridge. As the small party neared, the warriors drew their guns, bows and arrows, and traditional spears. But Mechac did not pause—he walked steadily toward the commander of the armed warriors, who was aiming the barrel of his gun directly at Mechac's chest.

The commander howled at them. "Today, you will die!"

The concrete houses and thatched roofs of Kaboto lay a kilometer behind him, down a long, empty, dusty road.

Mechac spoke in a soft voice. "Where is Chinja-Chinja?"

"Waiting for you at your own house!"

"Let us through. I will meet him."

And then, as if a spiritual force had intervened, the rifle that had pointed at the Prophet's chest lowered until its nose became buried in the sand.

"Today, I will *not* die," Mechac thought to himself.

* * *

Chinja-Chinja met Mechac outside his hut. The warrior wore his khaki t-shirt and red culotte—the dress he wore when he was determined to kill—yet his demeanor was not threatening. Mechac placed his left hand on his right forearm and stretched out his hand. Chinja-Chinja did the same, and they shook, looking each other in the eye. Then Mechac invited the warrior into the house. *His power has been neutralized.*

"I did not come here for you," Chinja-Chinja told Mechac. "I am here to attack the soldiers from Lenge and Kitenge."

"Oh?"

"Yes, the soldiers told me to visit you, to tell you that you shouldn't have denounced our politics. They don't like that. They said, 'if you kill the Prophet, no one will know what we are doing.' But we are here to attack them."

"Why?"

"They have said, 'we have salaries, you fight for nothing. If you loot the villages, we can buy.'"

So that was their rationale.

"They have said, 'Sometimes you have to provoke trouble. If you create a disturbance that gives you a reason to protect the villagers and demand payment.' Then we trade. It's the way we make money. But you know, I also protect the villagers from the Congolese soldiers."

Their local economy had been revealed by Chinja-Chinja himself. They did not fuel the war by illegally mining minerals, as in the eastern Congo, but they sustained the violence by stealing food, using a similar system. The ones without money loot food and sell it to someone else, and the ones with money find someone else to steal it and then they buy it from the thieves. They all added their footprint to the same pattern—the Mai-Mai, the Congolese soldiers, other African armies, politicians, and businesspeople with multinational corporations.

* * *

Once the Mai-Mai retreated from the village, Mechac's leaders gathered. "God has worked a miracle today. Chinja-Chinja has lost his power."

Chinja-Chinja had become the commander of six thousand men. He had been selected for this success by the evil spirit of the lake, the *megwishi*. Had the Satanic power that dwelt in Chinja-Chinja been broken?

The leaders chattered a moment with one another, and then one spoke. "Yes, we have seen different ways that this happened."

"We heard the report of the people who saw Chinja-Chinja approach the village. He was on his bicycle. But he fell as he approached the village. It seems he fainted. He had a charm that he held in his hand, a skin with knots and strings in it. But when the bicycle fell, the charm dropped and fell apart. He rose, and then he fell a second time."

"When he reached the Prophet's house, he had the skin with strings, his hand power. He just put it on the ground. He said, 'I have lost important powers today.'"

Mechac's leaders nodded with approval.

From the time in which Chinja-Chinja came to kill the Prophet, the Christians in Kaboto believed that Chinja-Chinja's power began to decline.

Doctor Kasanka Drives Among the Hutu from Kamina Base

"U.N. Says Congo Rebels Carried Out Cannibalism and Rapes"

The New York Times, January 16, 2003

"I lie down and sleep; I wake again, for the Lord sustains me.
I am not afraid of tens of thousands of people
who have set themselves against me all around."

Psalm 3:5-6

Kabongo to Kamina
April 2003

Kasanka's gaze roamed back and forth, back and forth. First, he glanced through the jeep's windshield at the refugees who surged toward him, crowded between the thick forests that lined the two-lane dirt road from Kamina toward Kipukwe. Women trudged on foot with packs on their heads and backs; men pushed bicycles loaded with their possessions; and many men, women and children held rifles. Then, Kasanka lowered his eyes and glanced sideways across the driver's hands on the steering wheel, trying to read the black numbers on the speedometer. The needle barely touched fifteen kilometers an hour with forty more kilometers to reach Kamina. The jeep's progress seemed agonizingly slow under the late afternoon sun.

And so he travelled: trying to watch for trouble among the refugees without staring at them, and studying the odometer, grateful for every rotation of the dial to a new number.

Kasanka had been invited by the government to attend a medical workshop in Kamina. Polio had again erupted, and the World Health Organization had organized a country-wide campaign to coincide with the National Day of Vaccination. The political parties and their military counterparts had agreed to a truce while non-governmental organizations vaccinated children. But the western NGO's groups could not access areas controlled by a patchwork of powers, such as Kabongo District, that jockeyed back and forth between the Congolese army and the Mai-Mai. Kasanka and his three medical students hoped to help find a way to bring the polio vaccinations to hard-to-access areas of the DRC.

* * *

The crisis had occurred when, during the days before the workshop, six thousand Hutus were expelled from the environs of Kamina. Paul Kagame's Rwandan government had long insisted that it had invaded Congo in self-defense against many militant Hutus who lived in refugee camps just over the border near Goma. To pacify Rwanda, the Congolese government had resettled many on the grounds of Kamina Military Base. When space became crowded, some moved into *Quatre-vingt-deux*, a neighborhood in the civilian city of Kamina. Well away from the Rwandan border, they could not be accused of trying to overthrow the Rwandan government from a place of safety in Congo.

But the solution did not satisfy many in Congolese government. It was never clear who in the Congolese army or the government had secret allegiances with Rwanda. If Rwanda took Kamina Military Base in the center of the country, the DRC could not be defended. As long as the Zimbabwean Army was stationed there, Kamina Base was safe. With the Zimbaweans now gone, the Rwandan Hutu could potentially strike a deal with Rwanda's Tutsi government and sympathizers within the Congolese army, leaving Kamina Base vulnerable. In this context, the DRC reversed its earlier decision and expelled the Hutu, forcing them to return to either Rwanda or Burundi.

Hearing this unwelcome news, the Hutu of Kamina Base knew that their lives and their futures were uncertain. They requested medicine at the base hospital for their difficult journey ahead. When a physician and a nurse refused, the Hutus became enraged. They killed the doctor, the nurse, and some Congolese soldiers.

Now, a long queue of refugees from *Quatre-vingt-deux* joined those from Kamina Base on the road from Kamina to Kipukwe. For the first time, the population of Kamina heard the whirr of helicopters over their city, as the government dropped pamphlets throughout the area, asking the villagers to allow the Hutus to pass through the bush without harassment. The atmosphere on the road was electric, as if it could burst into flame at any time.

As Kasanka's jeep neared, the wayfarers stepped aside to let it pass. But then they filled in the road behind the jeep so that it was surrounded. Kasanka knew that every action mattered—the way he and the truck's passengers looked at the people surrounding the jeep, the way the driver eased the vehicle through ochre-puddles without splashing the passersby.

* * *

Kasanka and his party had left Kabongo for Kamina without expecting trouble on the road. As they neared Kipukwe, Congolese soldiers stood before the car, waving. They had met one more roadblock, engaged in one more negotiation. But the soldiers insisted that the road to Kamina was too dangerous to pass. Finally, they were invited to spend the night in Kipukwe at the home of one of the solders.

At one a.m. Kasanka was awakened by a knock on the door. Through the doorway he heard an animated conversation between the Congolese soldiers— the word "doctor" leapt through the doorway.

What did they say? What could they want now? Kasanka rose, pulled on his trousers, and walked to the living room where the soldiers were gathered.

"Doctor, we need your jeep. Some Rwandese Hutus are killing people. We need to catch them before more die."

Always, the soldiers have eyes on the car. It was urgent to save lives, but he couldn't allow the soldiers to take the jeep by themselves. "If my driver agrees to drive you."

* * *

When the driver arrived back at the house at ten the next morning, he reported that the situation was truly dangerous. Then, while the driver slept, Kasanka contemplated their next move. If they failed to appear in Kamina, the vaccinations might not occur in Kabongo. That too meant more death, more disability, more suffering.

At four p.m. Kasanka decided they could wait no longer. They left Kipukwe, hoping to arrive in Kamina by sunset at six p.m. The jeep wove its way through the crowd of Hutu refugees. Its passengers held their breath, but they were not detained. At the junction of Mobutu's Belt the crowd of refugees thinned. The driver turned away from Kamina Base, believing the danger had passed. But nearing the outskirts of Kamina, they were stopped again, this time by a policeman.

"Where are you coming from?"

"Kabongo."

"Did you meet the Hutu?"

"Between Kipukwe and Kamina, all along the way."

"There is no way to enter into Kamina. We are not certain all the Hutu have left. But your business is important. You will need to come with us. Leave your jeep at the police headquarters, and we will take you to your destination."

* * *

In the workshop, the strategy emerged. Three groups could doom the process of vaccination: the military, the Mai-Mai, and the African indigenous churches who taught their members not to use western doctors. If the leaders of each of these groups could be persuaded of their importance to the process, if those leaders would promote the vaccinations with their followers, children's lives might be saved.

Kasanka and his team drove back to Kabongo with a new mission: to explain the process to the army, the religious leaders, and the Mai-Mai commander, Chinja-Chinja, in order to engage their cooperation and make them feel important to the success of the vaccination program.

But Dr. Kasanka was becoming restless. He had served through the dangers of the war and learned all he could at Kabongo Hospital. He needed a new experience, and Suzy wanted to continue her education in law. Once this program ended, he decided, he would tell Suzy he was willing to move his family back to Lubumbashi.

Pastor Kora Hosts Chinja-Chinja

"World Briefing: Africa: Congo: Punishment Vowed for Rapists"

The New York Times, January 27, 2004

> "So he set off and went to his father. But while he was still far off, his father saw him and was filled with compassion; he ran and put his arms around him and kissed him. Then the son said to him, 'Father, I have sinned against heaven and before you; I am no longer worthy to be called your son.' But the father said to his slaves, 'Quickly, bring out a robe—the best one—and put it on him; put a ring on his finger and sandals on his feet. And get the fatted calf and kill it, and let us eat and celebrate; for this son of mine was dead and is alive again; he was lost and is found!' And they began to celebrate."
>
> Luke 15:20-24

Kitenge

Last week in February 2004

District Superintendent Kora stood, touched his right forearm with his left hand, and extended his right hand toward the Kitenge Administrator, Paul Domier Dombe. "My Administrator, I will make arrangements with the pastor of Yordono Parish. You invite the Mai-Mai and the Congolese soldiers. I know my bishop. It will be his wish and his prayer. He will want the church to serve this way." Around them stood the other pastors and the traditional chiefs of the local villages, some nodding slightly with approval, some murmuring, others stone-faced. When he let go of the hand of the administrator, Kora turned, wound his way through the rickety benches and chairs of the administrator's office, and, once outside the building, strode purposefully past the sky blue and gold colors of the flag of the Congolese nation.

This particular Tuesday in February the village leaders—Roman Catholic, Seventh Day Adventist, United Methodist, Pentecostal and traditional chiefs—had been sitting for an hour, hearing the administrator's plea, discussing his plan, preparing themselves for the dangerous mission that the Kitenge administrator had set before them.

"We cannot continue with this violence. We need a neutral place—a church—where the Mai-Mai and the Congolese soldiers, traditional chiefs and government, and religious leaders can meet to discuss peace."

The administrator had approached the three Roman Catholic priests but they demurred.

"We cannot accept without permission of our bishop. When those Mai-Mai come, they may destroy our church. The responsibility will be on us."

District Superintendent Kora had risen to his feet. He remembered the words of Colonel Shinba Mulongo, the chaplain at Kamina Base, at Annual Conference: *The church must get involved.* Now, his voice boomed with bold authority. "I can accept the invitation. We have Yordano Parish. It's a good place to talk about peace. I will tell the pastor that this meeting will be in his church on Saturday."

Kora's determination had inspired the others, and in the end, each one committed to support the meeting.

* * *

Yordano Parish church stood in the middle of Kitenge. Everyone knew the large, orange mud-brick structure with doors that swung wide, windows that allowed an occasional breeze, and moveable benches that sat two hundred. A canopy slung from an outer wall, supported by tree branches for beams and uprights, shading the groups that gathered in the open air on benches or around tables.

Kora poked his head into the sanctuary, found no one, and circled the church. He discovered the pastor seated under the outdoor canopy, reading his Bible and enjoying a respite from the afternoon sun.

"*Karibu!*"

"*Jambo.* Let's sit."

Kora straddled the end of a bench. "I have an important meeting to discuss with you. It will be held at your church on Saturday." As Kora described the commitment he had made, the pastor's eyes grew large with fright. He sputtered as he spoke, and his words tumbled out rapidly.

"Pastor Kora, I agree, it is better to have that meeting. But those people will destroy our church. Maybe you will be killed. *You* can choose to be with those people! But not me. Myself, I will not be with you." Silence. Then, "Did you talk with Bishop?"

Kora shook his head. "No." Then he gazed at the pastor directly and spoke firmly. "But it is our time. We are suffering from the problem of security in our village."

"Yes, I agree. But I will stay in my home praying for you."

"If that is your wish. But tell your people—we will be here on Saturday."

As Kora left, the sun was setting. When he entered his parsonage, balls of *bukari* lay on a plate on the table. The children had eaten; Kora's wife awaited him. But he did not touch the food—instead, he blurted out his story.

She gaped at him, her mouth wide open. *My husband has risked his life so many times, returning to Kitenge after the family fled. He meets Mai-Mai on his way to visit Congolese soldiers who attend his church. Is he testing God?* The Luba proverb flashed through her brain: *nso kahandjile mayo abidji—* swimming in the same stream, an eel cannot escape for two seasons.

Her voice was shrill, with an edge of panic. "Pastor, *why* did you agree to do that mission?"

His voice rose. "I'm a pastor! What can I do when people are fighting? I need to separate them and seek peace for those people."

"You have already taken too many risks. This time you can be killed!"

Kora shook his head, emphatically.

"No! God saved me in the lake. God saved me during the coup. God saved our children when I was absent. How can I leave and give up? When I'm running away, my sheep are killed. Children are killed. Women are raped. Now, what can I do?"

Again, silence. Kora's black eyes—watery, mystical, spirit-filled—pored deeply into his wife's, and her gaze held his, at first fierce and defiant, then softening, finally accepting.

"Yes, I know God will be with you, like when you fell from the boat." Then she hesitated and glanced at the ground before her eyes met her husband's once more. "But I will stay in my house, praying for you."

*   *   *

Kora had been standing in the boat, a fishing net in his hands. As he lost his balance and fell, he felt the edge of the gunwale of the *pirogue* bite into his leg. Then the hard surface of the water slapped his body, as if spanking him for his mistake. But soon, the lake relented, offering a gentler welcome—a splash, a gurgle—and then, down, down—he billowed in the water, feeling the water push against his flailing arms as he sank. Something dug into his flesh and he opened his eyes—limbs of a tree that had fallen and now lay underwater. He grabbed a branch and held it tight. The water had now enveloped his legs, his torso, his arms, his head—if only he knew how to swim.

Suddenly he felt a force from below, pushing him up, up, up. He released the branch and broke the surface of the lake, sputtering, splashing, hearing the shouts of his companions in the *pirogue*. He felt their hands grasping his, pulling him to safety.

He lay on the bottom of the boat, panting, his eyes closed, his cool wet clothes clinging to his body under the baking sun. It was a while before he could breathe normally. But over and over he relived it—the rush of water pushing him back toward the surface, back toward life.

Surely, he had been rescued from death in the lake by the very arm of God.

*   *   *

One hundred and twenty Mai-Mai followers of Chinja-Chinja and fifty Congolese soldiers lounged outside Yordano Church, some protected by the canopy, others braving the hot noon sun. They talked in small groups—but all stood ready with arms to defend their leaders inside. Thirty police in blue uniforms wandered in twos and threes among the guests, observing them, wary of any action that might create unrest.

Inside, Administrator Dombe stood before the assembly of nineteen leaders, appealing to their common interest. "People are suffering in your area—no soap, no food, no salt. You Mai-Mai, without salt you cannot eat, you cannot live—but you cannot come to town to shop without Congolese soldiers stopping you. You Congolese soldiers, there is no food in Kitenge, but you cannot go to the rural areas to glean or to purchase food without Mai-Mai attacking you. And all of the rest of you, and all of the other villagers—you have no security. Like this, we will become nothing. Without peace, our nation is finished. Today, we must find a solution, to live together, to eat together. But before we discuss how to make peace, we will listen to Pastor Kora. The government is sponsoring this meeting, but he is our spiritual host, and he will preach the word. Pastor Kora?"

Kora rose and took his place at the pulpit. Next to him, on a table, rested the Bible and empty cross, representing Jesus' resurrection. Directly in front of him sat Chinja-Chinja, the wiry Mai-Mai commander who had established his headquarters outside Kitenge.

He was dressed in soldier's fatigues and boots. Kora had met Chinja-Chinja four or five times when he had trudged over the lanes to the huts of parishioners who lived in Impele and Kaloko and Nkombe. Chinja-Chinja had demanded Kora's loyalty to the Mai-Mai, and Kora had told him each time, "I am not a Mai-Mai. I am not a Congolese soldier. I am a United Methodist pastor." Chinja-Chinja had finally respected Kora's spiritual neutrality, going so far as to send Mai-Mai to protect church meetings in the rural villages.

Chinja-Chinja was flanked by nine of his followers. They wore army shirts, civilian trousers, animal skins wrapped around their hips, hats with large feathers, and necklaces that bound together the charms and powers they had captured. Their spears and guns lay on their laps.

The Congolese Army Major Mwamba and two soldiers in green and maroon uniforms sat at attention on the benches, fingering their rifles. Three policemen in their blue uniforms hunched over the pistols on their laps. The traditional chief of Kitenge clasped his hands around the carved mahogany staff that signified his royal power. The head Catholic priest carried his crucifix, the sign of Jesus' death.

Kora swallowed hard and prayed. *What word will be accepted by the Mai-Mai rebels and the government soldiers and the police? I don't want to preach and then have a problem. I don't know, but You as God can empower.*

He stood still in the pulpit—but his memory flashed to walking, walking, walking, when Laurent Kabila led the coup against Mobutu. The war had threatened his village, and Kora had plucked his way through bush and path one hundred and thirty kilometers, alone, to safety in Kaniama. He did not know which combatants he might encounter in the road. He had prayed, *God, take my life in your hands*. He had felt no fear, only God's presence. And now, the same calm, divine friendship steadied him. He lifted the Bible. He began to read to his congregation, Luke 15:11-35, the parable of the prodigal son. Then he spoke.

"We are like the son who is lost. All of us, Mai-Mai, Congolese soldiers, even pastors—we are all sinners. We have sinned against God and against our neighbors—we have harmed the people who are our relatives and friends in so many ways. That is why we need God's mercy to have peace in this country, in this village, in the villages surrounding Kitenge. But I praise God: we are here, in this room, in peace with one another. God has heard the ones who are praying for this meeting."

And then he sat.

Chinja-Chinja spoke first. "Thank you, Pastor. I understand that I'm a sinner. And that I make mistakes. Now, I need to repent and to seek for reconciliation."

And then Major Mwamba spoke for the Congolese soldiers. "Pastor, we thank you. We were waiting for this kind of word, a message to be together. Even as government soldiers we made mistakes against those people, the Mai-Mai."

The discussion continued. After some time, the Administrator, Major Mwamba, and Chinja-Chinja appeared together at the door of the church to announce to the crowd outside: "We are reconciled. We have come to an agreement to remove the barriers from the roads and to travel freely from village to village." And they spread the word: the next day at the stadium the Administrator, Major Mwamba and Chinja-Chinja would make a great announcement.

Bishop Preaches at General Conference, 2004

"Hopes and Tears of Congo Flow in Its Mythic River"

The New York Times, April 21, 2004

"The fear of the Lord is the beginning of wisdom; all those who follow his precepts have good understanding. To him belongs eternal praise."

Psalm 111:10

April 29, 2004

Long rows of tables stretched across the floor of the Pittsburgh Convention Center in Pennsylvania, USA, where the nearly thousand delegates to the 2004 General Conference sat. Eighteen Congolese delegates from Bishop Ntambo's episcopal area should have occupied one section, but many of their seats remained empty—most of the duly elected, very poor rural people had been denied visas. They had been unable to prove their economic ties to Congo, so they could not satisfy the American embassy in Kinshasa that they would return to the DRC when General Conference concluded.

That poor woman who walked two weeks to get transport to Kinshasa. She was the one whose absence Bishop most grieved. *We are teaching democracy, and then the Americans deny her a visa.*

But Raymond Mande, Mama Nshimba, and Gaston Ntambo—the only three delegates whose visas were approved—now waited with anticipation. Mande felt, oh, so proud. Very soon, *his* bishop from North Katanga, *his* spiritual leader would speak in front of people from across the world! There, from that podium, Mande would hear *his* voice, *his* English in the local accent of North Katanga. He would see with his own eyes the dignity, the respect of the church for his Bishop.

While he thrilled with excitement, Mande also felt the weight of stone in his heart. Bishop had developed an increasingly international profile. He had been appointed chancellor of Africa University in Zimbabwe and interim bishop of Nigeria, positions in which he had sought to calm the tumult of African ecclesial politics. Here, the international church politics of the General Conference, and the pressure on Africans to side with different groups of Americans and Europeans, hung grimly in the hall. The Americans and Europeans were divided over the participation of gay and lesbian people in the church. The side seeking restrictions had lobbied Bishop to take a public stance against homosexuality in his sermon. But he, like the other African bishops, continually struggled to bring the strife in Africa into view.

As always, Mande and Bishop had discussed the dynamics of the sermon and Mande had sought to put Bishop's mind into words: *How to focus the people on God?*

Now, Bishop rose to speak, looked over the audience, and smiled.

> Dear brothers and sisters in our Lord Jesus Christ,
>
> I will open today's sermon with a French saying: *"La langue, c'est le pouvoir."* That is, "Language is power."
>
> I am wondering in what language am I to address you. Some are certainly willing to hear the Queen's English, with some Texan or Spanish accent. But my English will be Ntambo's English with Ntambo's accent.
>
> You know, when I was struggling with speaking English, a friend of mine from Ethiopia gave me some comfort by confiding to me that "The English language was born in England; it grew up in America; it got sick in India and inevitably died in Africa." This means that I will speak to you in English made in Africa.

Sometimes, Americans are very kind with me. One day I entered one of your thousand restaurants. A waitress came to me and asked me a funny question. What she said was, "What kind of dressing do you want on your salad?" It was a scary question to me because so far what I knew about dressing, it was dressing my son or daughter. I never learned how to dress salad. So English is still difficult.

To come to the point of the day, I would first like to thank the General Conference; for through your prayers and support, peace is in process now in the Democratic Republic of the Congo, which is my home country, in Angola, Liberia, Sierra Leone, Ivory Coast, Rwanda, Uganda, Burundi, and most of the African countries which have been engaged in war.

I want to thank the General Conference for the event of Africa University. As chancellor of Africa University, I would like to confirm that the dream is alive. With this accomplishment, let me quote for us 2 Corinthians 8:11, which reads as follows: "Now finish the work, so that your eager willingness to do it may be matched by your completion of it, according to your means."

I am thankful to the Council of Bishops for Bishops' initiative "Hope for the Children of Africa." We have a saying in Africa that "you can steal everything from me but you cannot steal my education." Education is so meaningful to our people that Bishops' initiative program has a meaningful impact in the future and development of African nations.

We are thankful to all the agencies of the church for their continued support to the churches of Africa. These kinds of actions can be translated about the church as being a church which cares with love and compassion to build a broken world. It is a church which brings unity among the nations, to say a church which follows the teaching of our Lord Jesus Christ. Our pains were your pains, our joy was your joy and our vision as Africans was your vision.

The most important thing that this church has done to me was to lead me to know Christ as my personal Lord and savior from the pagan family I was in.

A ripple of applause spread through a portion of the audience.

One woman from Russia was asked, "What does the United Methodist Church mean to you?" Her reply was, "This is the church which led me to know Jesus Christ." Let me tell you the United Methodist Church is a church which has served as a cornerstone in the lives of people, bringing them to Christ: Yes for fear of God.

To come to our passage of Psalm 111:10 we proclaim: "The fear of the Lord is the beginning of wisdom; all those who follow his precepts have good understanding. To him belongs eternal praise." Our target point is fear. Of course, there is fear and fear.

The fear I am alluding to is not the fear like the one I felt when I was asked to take place in a solo flight. It is not the fear of war or instability. It is not the fear to go to the jungle. President Franklin Delano Roosevelt once said: "There is no bad thing than the fear of fear." It is not this fear that I am speaking about. The fear that makes the appeal of my sermon is the fear like the one of David: the fear of God.

"He said to his men, 'The Lord forbid that I should do such a thing to my master, the Lord's anointed, or lift my hand against him; for he is the anointed of the Lord.'" (1 Samuel 24:6)

A second illustration of David's fear of God reads:

"So David and Abishai went to the army by night, and there was Saul, lying asleep inside the camp with his spear stuck in the ground near his head. Abner and the soldiers were lying around him. Abishai said to David, 'Today God has delivered your enemy into your hands. Now let me pin him to the ground with one thrust of my spear; I won't strike him twice.' But David said to Abishai, 'Don't destroy him! Who can lay a hand on the Lord's anointed and be guiltless? As surely as the Lord lives,' he said, 'the Lord himself will strike him; either his time will come and he will die, or he will go into battle and perish. But the Lord forbid that I should lay a hand on the Lord's anointed. Now get the spear and water jug that are near his head, and let's go.'" (1 Samuel 26:7-11)

David feared the Lord; that is why he spared the life of Saul. He had all the power to kill Saul, but for fear of the Lord, he did not. David had his army; he has even King Saul's spear and water jar. He has all the rights to kill King Saul, but for fear of the Lord, he did not do it.

The fear of the Lord to you and to me is to please God and not God to please us.

When we live in infidelity, there is no fear of the Lord;

When we hate others or practice tribalism, by killing one another, we are not in the fear of the Lord;

When we live in hypocrisy, we are not in the fear of the Lord.

When we miss to accomplish our responsibility and duty toward our children, we are not in the fear of the Lord;

When the church has not accomplished its mission toward the people of the world, we are not in fear of the Lord.

When the church fails to identify the sin as seen to the church members, it does not live in the fear of the Lord;

When the church or the nation fails to identify and meet the needs of the hungry people and the disinherited, and when the nations have the means to finish poverty and hunger but do not act accordingly, there is not fear of the Lord. We can illustrate with Franklin Delano Roosevelt as he says that: "I see one-third of a nation ill-housed, ill-clad, ill-nourished... The test of our progress is not whether we add more to the abundance of those who have much; it is whether we provide enough for those who have too little."

The rustling in the room quieted.

The Lord requires us to say "no" to sin.

I like eating spicy and hot food. It turns in the end by giving me stomachache. When I tell my wife about it, she keeps reminding me that I should learn to say "no" to spicy food. That is true. The church should learn to say "no."

My conversion is worth mentioning. I am coming from a pagan family. My grandfather was a witch doctor. We were worshiping idols. I said no to the practice and gave my life to Christ. It is a duty of the church to say "no" to oppression, racism, injustice and so forth.

This is a generation well-equipped to win the people to Christ for example in communication, evangelism can be done from drum in the African village up to the CNN; new books are getting printed daily; yet we still have people who have not heard the message of Christ. Thousands of ministers do not have Bibles to preach the word of God. We have lists of missionaries waiting; the General Board of Global Ministries' hands are tied because the church is claiming not to have money to hire the missionaries to do the work of the Lord.

We have local churches which are losing members day after day, but we have no one to make efforts to bring them back. This is not the fear of the Lord. Of course, God is love, grace, compassion and forgiveness, but God is also a judge, and the judgment is ahead of us for you and me.

I cannot end my sermon without illustrating with Martin Luther King [Jr.]'s words of devotion to God. Let us quote Luther King: "And I leave the word to you this morning. If any of you are around when I have to meet my day, I don't want a long funeral. And if you get somebody to deliver the eulogy, tell them not to talk too long. Every now and then, I wonder what I want them to say. Tell them not to mention that I have a Nobel Peace Prize; it isn't important. Tell them not to mention that I have three or four hundred other awards; that's not important. Tell him not to mention where I went to school."

Applause rose from different areas of the room.

"I'd like somebody to mention that day, that Martin Luther King Jr. tried to give his life serving others. I'd like for somebody to say that day, that Martin Luther King Jr. tried to love somebody. I want you to say that day, that I tried to be right on the war question. I want you to be able to say that day, that I did try to feed the hungry. And I want you to be able to say that day, that I did try, in my life, to clothe those who were naked. I want you to say, on that day, that I did try, in my life, to visit those who were in prison. I want you to say that I tried to love and serve humanity.

"Yes, if you want to say that I was a drum major, say that I was a drum major for justice; say that I was a drum major for peace; I was a drum major for righteousness. And all of the other shallow things will not matter. I won't have any money to leave behind. I won't have the fine and luxurious things of life to leave behind. But I just want to leave a committed life behind. And that's all I want to say… If I can help somebody as I pass along, if I can cheer somebody with a word or song, if I can show somebody he's traveling wrong, then my living will not be in vain. If I can do my duty as a Christian ought, if I can bring salvation to a world once wrought, if I can spread the message as the master taught, then my living will not be in vain.

"Yes, Jesus, I want to be on your right side or your left side, not for any self reason. I want to be on your right or your best side, not in terms of some political kingdom or ambition, but I just want to be there in love and justice and in truth and in commitment to others, so that we can make of this old world a new world."

This church has to engage day and night in the prospective of the fear of the Lord. The day we will meet the Lord we will be given the crown of victory. As a church, let us stand all of us and proclaim: "The fear of the Lord is the beginning of wisdom."

Mande breathed with relief. None of the delegates had liked the whole sermon, except, perhaps, the three who made up the North Katanga delegation. Many would disagree with various parts. But the mood in the house was respectful. Bishop had walked a tightrope, pointing upward the whole time.

Prophet Mechac is Arrested

"Warring Militias in Congo Test U.N. Enforcement Role"

The New York Times, April 11, 2004

"How long, you people, shall my honor suffer shame? How long will you love vain words, and seek after lies? But know that the Lord has set apart the faithful for himself; the Lord hears when I call to him."

Psalm 4:2-3

Kaboto to Kime
May 24, 2004

Even before dawn villagers were lining up at the door of the small hut, and by the time the doctors from *Médecins sans frontières* arrived, the queue formed a snake that stretched for nearly a kilometer around the village.

Kaboto had grown during the war. Mechac's followers had settled in permanent huts in Kaboto, along with schools, chapels, and gardens. Interspersed with his followers were internally displaced people who had sought refuge in his community, and various others, who for some reason or another had camped around Kaboto. The population had swelled so much such that MSF had begun to provide a weekly clinic in the village.

The physicians from MSF, known to Mechac as Gabriel Riselli and Frances Bush, with Mr. Mark, Mr. Luke, Mr. Fred, and Madame Unique, set up their travelling clinic. They prepared to treat sick people—people with malaria, people with malnutrition, people with diseases of the foot—all the kinds of illnesses that were rampant in the bush among the displaced and the poor, alike.

MSF had begun their clinic when the soldiers streamed over the bridge. Two brigades, four thousand in all.

* * *

Mechac walked to the door of his hut and peered toward the horizon that marked Kaboto's entrance. He saw soldiers flowing over the narrow bridge. They formed an ever-widening river, rushing toward the center of the village. They immediately expanded into a flood of uniforms and guns, their boots pounding the earth. Trucks dotted the tributary like large, slowly moving boulders or other debris.

The villagers gawked. They were queued at the medical hut—a crooked line of human heights, like scrawny tree lines between the bush and the forest—and they did not move, afraid to lose their coveted place. Other villagers joined them, staring at the soldiers.

Trouble, for sure.

The Prophet waited till the head of the brigade neared his hut. Then he walked out of the door and extended his hand toward the commander who seemed to be in charge. The commander shook it.

"*Wafwako!* What brings you here?"

"We have word that there are Mai-Mai here who we can question."

"Mere children! Child soldiers recruited by Mai-Mai, very low level. They have renounced the Mai-Mai and become Christians. They do not threaten you."

"Perhaps they have valuable information. We want to meet them, right here, in this yard, in front of your hut. Where are they?"

But it was an unnecessary question. Already the soldiers were trickling into the line, asking questions of the villagers, identifying children and youths, and pushing them toward the yard in which the commander stood.

"We are a holy village! An orderly people of God! This is not a place to mistreat children."

"We need to find out what they know."

Soon, the yard teemed with children. Some parents cried out, but mostly, the children were orphans, separated from their parents, so adults stood and stared. And when their prey were assembled, the soldiers began taking their names and loading them onto the backs of trucks.

* * *

A night later headlights appeared over the Kaboto bridge, and the sound of an engine called villagers from their huts. By the time the army truck halted in front of Prophet Mechac's house, it was surrounded by a milling, angry mob.

One of the Congolese commanders stood atop the truck. "The Prophet Mechac is a person who knows much. He must come with us."

But the crowd surrounding the truck shouted back. ""What do you want with him? He is a man of God!"

"You will not take the Prophet from this village!"

"Not in army trucks!"

"Not in the night!"

"You will be stricken dead!"

Mechac's followers did not back away. They were determined to protect him, to prevent the army from taking him from the village.

Outnumbered, the soldiers swung back into the cab of the truck and sped away.

* * *

The next day another army truck arrived at Mechac's house. The traditional chief of Kaboto and his son sat in the front seat. An officer and the chief's son approached the people surrounding Mechac's house and spoke politely.

"We have a message for the Prophet."

Nothing seemed amiss. The crowd remained quiet, and Mechac came to the door of his hut.

"*Wafwako*. Now, what word do you bring?"

"You and the traditional chief and his son are requested for a meeting with army officers at Lenge, this afternoon. They are waiting for you. We will bring you."

"Oh?"

"They want to hear your opinion about how to bring peace between the government soldiers and the Mai-Mai."

"Peace is what we seek, so I will go."

* * *

Mechac was seated in the cab of the truck, a place of honor for a guest, a place where the army had control.

The driver came to a fork in the dirt tracks that served as a road, where green scrub bush divided the path. Instead of turning toward Lenge, he swerved in the direction of Kime, where the Congolese soldiers were based.

* * *

The soldiers at Kime Military Base had clearly been expecting an important prisoner. They had thoroughly cleaned a room in a substantial concrete house, made sure the Prophet had a comfortable chair and washed linen on a mattress and bed. They treated him as a visiting dignitary, except for intense security:

three soldiers guarded Mechac in his room, three immediately outside the door, and three at the entrance to the house. Clearly, they considered him a flight risk. Mechac left the room only to relieve himself. In these moments he was treated as an honored guest: the soldiers allowed the elderly spiritual leader his privacy. They endeavored not to humiliate him. Nor did they interrogate him about the Mai-Mai, as he assumed they would.

* * *

The soldiers allowed visitors.

Mechac's ministers visited and brought news of happenings in the village.

"After you were taken, the police commissioner remained with us. The soldiers surrounded the village. But they have not disturbed us."

The doctors from MSF also found Mechac in his cell. "We are talking with the military, vouching for you as a good man who wants the peace of the people, who is not siding with the government or the Mai-Mai."

Along with Mechac Kaboto's traditional chief had been incarcerated. But the chief's son was free, and he visited Mechac in his cell. They sat in the concrete room, and as the Prophet Mechac prayed, the young man began to shake and sob. And then he shrieked loudly, so all the soldiers could hear.

"I am responsible for everything that has happened—the arrival of the soldiers, the removal of the children, the arrests. You have disrupted the economic transactions between the soldiers and the Mai-Mai, and for that we planned to kill you. But I realize that you are guilty of nothing. I have set myself against a holy man. I see myself for what I am. Let them kill me rather than you."

And then the son of the traditional chief began to publicize his treachery far and wide, about every plan he had developed with the soldiers and Mai-Mai. He named all the people who were included in that plan.

Shortly thereafter he was arrested as a madman, a fool. But still, Mechac remained incarcerated.

Mechac's visitors told him that the doctors and nurses from MSF had met with the territory commissioner and other politicians, advocating for him. A few days later the soldiers came to release him, and he went back to Kaboto. The Prophet and his community credited MSF with saving his life.

North Katanga Annual Conference 2004

> "The Saturday Profile; Rescuing Victims Worldwide 'from the Depths of Hell'"
>
> *The New York Times*, July 10, 2004

> "Blessed are the peacemakers, for they shall be called the children of God."
>
> Matthew 5:9

Kamina

July 2004

The Annual Conference in Kamina drew people from near and far—in addition to Kamina's inhabitants, pastors, their families, and church leaders bicycled from congregations located in the bush. Displaced people, believed to be dead, appeared. Many expected the trip by bicycle to take two days—but they arrived at the conference three, five, even seven days late, and reported that it had been difficult to make their way through the Mai-Mai checkpoints. Some stories from the newly arrived guests greatly saddened the conference; the church lamented and mourned members now known to be dead. They heard tales of churches attacked and burned, of supplies of cement and tin roofing stolen.

But they gathered the news, grieved the dead, sang and danced in celebration over those who appeared, and prayed for those who had been lost.

In 2004 the committee who prepared for the Annual Conference travelled with Bishop to Kamina Base to visit General Nyembo. He requested the opportunity to speak to people who had come from all of the areas where the Mai-Mai were operating, as well as from the areas safe from Mai-Mai presence.

* * *

General Nyembo stood beneath the canopy that protected the assembly from the blazing sun.

"For many of you, I am confirming what you are experiencing in your own communities. For others, I need to emphasize that the situation your brothers and sisters are facing is truly grave, and the church must get involved.

"The Mai-Mai people are our children. They are our young brothers and sisters, sons and daughters. They are your church members. Many choir members are Mai-Mai.

"If we continue to conduct military operations against the Mai-Mai, we will kill many of our own children. We will kill the church and kill our communities. We don't want to do that. We need to hear their grievances. And since so many of the Mai-Mai are your relatives and your members, you may be called upon to help."

Bishop spoke after the General. "God can only answer our prayers if we become God's vessels. Pastors, go home and prepare your congregations. Preach on the beatitude, *blessed are the peacemakers.* Speak to your people. Prepare the church not only to pray but to risk their lives for peace throughout our land. We do not know how or where, but our opportunity will come."

Everyone in the conference experienced the fragility of life; the decision to live, itself, meant enduring the vulnerability to extreme suffering from malnutrition, disease, or violence. People yearned for peace and stability. Bishop's instruction fell on willing ears. Still, to encourage the congregation to take risks in the few moments in which congregants felt safe—well, then, peace, security, what could it mean?

Pierre Kapata Leaves the Mai-Mai

> "WORLD BRIEFING: Africa: White Rhino Numbers Cut in Half"
>
> *The New York Times*, August 7, 2004

> "For this son of mine was dead and is alive again; he was lost and is found!"
>
> Luke 15:24

Nkombe

July 2004

Pierre and his father perched on the *air kabongo* chairs in front of his father's hut, etching a makeshift map between them in the dirt. A larger stone signified the Mai-Mai camp near Nkombe where Pierre still reported every dawn, and smaller pebbles and lines in the dirt marked possible locations of government soldiers. Pierre's father heard rumors in town, and Pierre, in the camp. Together they sketched what they pieced together about Mai-Mai and Congolese positions. Government soldiers, they postulated, were poised within fifteen kilometers of Nkombe. An attack seemed imminent. Pierre's father nodded grimly.

"I believe the Mai-Mai are weakening. Your chance to escape will come soon."

If he deserted the Mai-Mai, Pierre knew he could not risk returning to his family immediately. They agreed: the nearest sanctuary lay in the village of Prophet Mechac.

For the last three years Pierre had been trapped in a charade, outwardly loyal to the Mai-Mai, inwardly watching for a moment to escape that would not jeopardize his family. He had joined the militia in the euphoria of believing that he could protect his parents and younger sister from the excesses of government soldiers, but soon he realized that he had compromised his own beliefs. The

Mai-Mai sought to overthrow the traditional chiefs—drugs, guns and power had gone to their heads.

For the next three years, Pierre had watched the Mai-Mai recruit village boys, mostly between nine and fifteen years of age. Had Pierre warned them away, the new enthusiasts might not have listened anyway—and he would have risked the lives of the family he had sought to protect. Once inducted and ritually bathed by leaders, the boys knew something of the Mai-Mai's ceremonies. To protect this power, the boys were taught the consequences of desertion. A band of Mai-Mai leaders would visit the deserter's family, demanding payment for the boys' knowledge of Mai-Mai secrets and power: *Pay two goats and 75,000 Congolese francs–or be robbed, or beaten—or even killed.* Pierre's conscience could not allow his actions to make his parents and younger sister vulnerable to the Mai-Mai. So he and his parents held the secret of his false loyalties close to their hearts.

* * *

Even as a Mai-Mai, Pierre attended his parents' church, and his participation assisted his pretense. Early on, Mai-Mai leaders had visited the village pastors, just as they had the village chiefs: *Allow the Mai-Mai to come to your church, to sing in your choirs. Then we will defend you.* At first, the pastors and their congregants readily agreed, and Mai-Mai and villagers worshipped the Christian God side by side on the wooden benches under the sanctuary's thatched roof. As Mai-Mai from villages outside the Groupement demanded food and supplies from the locals, the pastors and their congregants, too, were trapped—some pastors who resisted the Mai-Mai had been beaten and even killed. When Pierre and other young men sang in the choir at the church, the Mai-Mai leaders approved: he was solidifying the church's loyalty. Secretly, he had a moment of freedom from deceit—he could sing what he really believed.

Pierre also noticed the way that Christian language had infiltrated the Mai-Mai. The leaders in charge of ritual bathing, while using their charms and calling on their spirits, invoked God with words that they had picked up in church: *if God is willing, you will be protected.* And they called on the Christian Mai-Mai to entreat their God for power on their behalf as Mai-Mai warriors: *You people, you need to respect your deities.* Mai-Mai leaders affirmed the power of the Christian God, a supernatural presence that only intensified the power of their traditions.

* * *

Pierre's battalion of Mai-Mai had camped at Mukako village, in the Groupement of Nkombe. In the moonlight the Mai-Mai had bathed and conducted their rituals. The morning dawned bright, and when the attack came, they were groggy and disorganized.

Machine gun popping, boots crashing, rifles firing, trees rustling—the racket came from every direction, and Pierre knew that the government soldiers had surrounded the Mai-Mai. *Mayhem. Cover in which to escape.*

Pierre gazed toward the sun and its arc and calculated the direction toward Kaboto, the village of Prophet Mechac. If he could crawl through the underbrush, avoiding both Mai-Mai and government soldiers, he might be able to reach safety.

A young boy whirled from the impact of a bullet and he collapsed. Minutes passed. The fighting was littering the ground with bloody bodies, dead and wounded boys. *His friends!* He groaned in anguish, and tears came to his eyes. Such a battle—never had he seen so many Mai-Mai or government soldiers killed. But then he focused on his father and his mother and his sister—he must survive for them. He wriggled through the bush, picking a path where the gunfire had quieted, and finally, the gunfire and the dead bodies seemed to be behind him. But still, he heard rustlings in the bush, saw shadows behind the trees.

When he arrived on the path that led to the Mechac's village, he joined a steady stream of boys who had taken their opportunity to escape from the Mai-Mai.

Chapter VI

Kamina Hosts the Mai-Mai Peace Conference
(September 2004)

Historical Introduction

The countrywide election promised by the Global and All-Inclusive Agreement could not be held until ballots could be distributed in the countryside. The Mai-Mai controlled the roadways in large portions of the country, including rural Katanga. After many attempts to negotiate with Chinja-Chinja, Maccabee, and other Katangese Mai-Mai leaders, the government turned to the churches in Kamina to conduct a conference with all of the necessary actors present: Mai-Mai, traditional chiefs, military leaders, religious leaders, government officials, and civil society. It was a process inspired by the Inter-Congolese Dialogue, but with different participants and religious, rather than political, conveners. The power of spirituality in Congolese culture was recognized as a factor that could unite those who held a variety of different beliefs.

As a spiritual leader, Bishop Ntambo realized that he needed to honor the leaders who agreed to come to the conference. The Mai-Mai leaders, traditional chiefs, and others observed food customs that signified their esteem—with specific requirements about what to eat, where to eat, and who could prepare food. "To feed my people" became a task of reconciliation, by providing the means to eat with dignity.

Bishop Ntambo Receives the Phone Call

"Thatcher's Son Held in Failed Africa Coup"

The New York Times, August 26, 2004

"As he rode along, people kept spreading their cloaks on the road. As he was now approaching the path down from the Mount of Olives, the whole multitude of the disciples began to praise God joyfully with a loud voice for all the deeds of power that they had seen, saying, 'Blessed is the king who comes in the name of the Lord! Peace in heaven, and glory in the highest heaven!'"

Luke 19:36-38

Kamina
around September 1, 2004

The recently appointed governor of Katanga Province, Dr. Kisula Ngoy, sat in the leather chair behind his desk in his private medical clinic in Lubumbashi.

The furnishings of his office reflected his profession: as a physician whose private clinic served those who could pay, he valued an environment that spoke to both the means of his clients and the excellent care he could provide. Once his patients drove into the compound, they stepped into the aura of first class medicine—cheery, clean, neat, functional surroundings. They entered the yellow-painted stucco building, checked in with the receptionist who sat behind sliding glass window doors, and waited on comfortable chairs that ringed the room. When the doctor was ready, a receptionist appeared at the door and called the patient's name, beckoning them into one of the series of examining rooms, each with blood pressure cuffs, thermometers, other basic medical equipment, chairs by the desk at which the nurses or doctor sat to interview the patient, and a paper-covered examining table. Dr. Kisula Ngoy's private-pay patients were reassured by the ethos of the clinic—they knew they were receiving Congo's best medical care, diagnosis and pharmaceuticals.

This morning, however, his mind did not roam the details of medicine. Rather, he contemplated his challenge: pacification of Katanga. The Congolese government controlled only part of the province. By Lake Tanganyika the Rally for Congolese Democracy (RCD), the Rwandan-backed political party, still occupied territory—those forces should be withdrawn by political agreement. But the Mai-Mai in the interior? Especially Chinja-Chinja and his followers? The militias posed a different problem.

Some Mai-Mai militias had been included in the Inter-Congolese Dialogue, had signed the Global and All-Inclusive Agreement that ended the war, and now had roles in government or the army. But their signatures did nothing to pacify Katanga. No structure linked the Mai-Mai as a political entity with a central communication or command. In fact, far from following each others' lead, different militias became competitors, even adversaries. Chinja-Chinja, for example, had originated as part of Maccabee's followers. But he had challenged Maccabee's power and now commanded an even larger force in a portion of the province adjacent to that dominated by Maccabee.

Some Mai-Mai had murdered traditional chiefs and government and military emissaries who had sought to negotiate with them. But they lived by supernatural beliefs. They feared and respected spiritual power. So far they had refrained from assassinating religious leaders like Prophet Mechac.

The governor had talked it over with his ministers. Their best chance for success in rural Katanga lay in a Mai-Mai peace conference patterned after the Inter-Congolese Dialogue but led by a religious leader. It required representatives from all sectors—government, military, traditional chiefs, civil society, and local Mai-Mai. But who could lead such a conference? What about Bishop Ntambo and Bishop Kalala, the Methodist and Catholic leaders in Kamina?

* * *

The cell phone rang at Bishop Ntambo's house in Lubumbashi. Governor Ngoy!

"Bishop, we are considering how to bring peace to Katanga. People have suffered in two wars. Now, we need a conference, and we have chosen you to host it. All people, including myself, will come to make peace in our area."

Bishop sparked with curiosity, genuinely intrigued. "Which people, whose area?"

The governor sounded matter-of-fact but determined. "People from Kalemie, Kabalo, Lubumbashi, the whole of Katanga, will come to Kamina."

"That was my dream and my hope, because people have been suffering. But who will participate?"

"Key Mai-Mai leaders, prominent military leaders, soldiers, police, chiefs of villages, *Kasongo Nyembo*, government administrators, religious leaders— all of the people who are important to bringing peace."

"How many people?"

"120."

"How to feed them?"

"We ask you to feed them."

"How to lodge them?"

"We ask you to house them."

"How do we transport them?"

"We ask you to provide transportation."

"How to be in touch with them?"

"On the side of government and civic leaders, we will contact them. But on the side of Mai-Mai, we ask you."

The importance of the invitation, the confidence of the government in his leadership and the weight of the responsibility landed on Bishop's heart but bounced off with a lightness of step. He thrilled with excitement. *We are the church, and we will be doing reconciliation.* The task was enormous. But after years of talk, Bishop was ready for action.

Pilot Gaston Prepares to Fly Officials to the Meeting

"Change Africa's Borders"

The New York Times, September 5, 2004

"A dispute also arose among them as to which one of them was
to be regarded as the greatest. But he said to them, 'The kings of
the Gentiles lord it over them; and those in authority over them
are called benefactors. But not so with you; rather the greatest
among you must become like the youngest, and the leader like
one who serves. For who is greater, the one who is at the table or
the one who serves? Is it not the one at the table? But I am among
you as one who serves.'"

Luke 20: 24-28

Lubumbashi

September 2004

Gaston bent low before the flat end of the twelve-foot-round circle of gray steel,
swung wide the door, squeezed past the first control yoke into the far seat, adjusted the joystick on the second set of controls, and pushed the button to begin
the flow of electricity. The computer screen lit, for a moment showing the
wavy, four-box-colored logo; then it faded briefly and came back to life showing the names of major airports around the world. He clicked on "Atlanta Harts-
field" and the flat large screen in front of him blazed. He sat before the runway
of the busiest airport in the world, as if ready for take off. His homebuilt flight
simulator allowed him to practice flying any airplane he wanted, anywhere he
wanted, even to teach a student to fly, right in his own backyard in Lubumbashi.
As he glanced at the list of airplanes from which he could choose, he hesitated.
He relaxed into the pilot's seat and closed his eyes.

He had felt his best friend settle into the seat beside him, and they needed to
talk.

"Ok, so there's this guy at the landing strip. He's probably waited there all
day, nothing to do, and when I land, he has to show people how important he
is. He comes up to me, 'I have to inspect everything in the airplane. You might
have to pay something.' 'What are you talking about, I'm here to bring medicine and fly sick people.' But no, he wants to push his weight around, just a
village version of the Lubumbashi guys who wanted to make trouble about the
farm. So I say, 'Look, you leave me alone so I can do what I came to do, or I'll
tie you up like a criminal and take you back to Lubumbashi in the plane and
turn you in to the police.' He tries again, and I say, to the crowd, 'Go get me a
rope.' I have to threaten him, but it's the only way he'll respect me. You know,
no one pushes me around—not the little big guys, and not the big little guys.
Finally, he goes away."

Gaston pauses, just for effect.

"I do what I have to do, and then I find him. I apologize. 'Sorry, I'm just stressed. I shouldn't have said that. But you need to leave me be next time.' When I fly in to the airstrip the next time, he's like my best friend."

Satisfaction. He's handled it well. He waits, listens. No disagreement from his friend.

"Ok, we've talked about humility a lot. I work with so many people at all the landing strips, and it's a balance—I need their respect and their help, but I don't want them to idolize me because I'm an African flying a plane. They have to be comfortable enough to approach me, to tell me, hey, you have a flat tire.

"But it's such a fine line. The guys who work for me, all of their work is equally important to making this little plane run. I want them just to call me Gaston. No titles, no Papa Gaston. But they can't do it. So they finally decide, they just call me Boss."

He listens. No admonitions, no advice. So he broaches another subject, one they had already discussed, and his friend had given him the sign he'd looked for.

"Yes, I want to be humble in my attitude. But what about that Mercedes? You know I needed a car. I told you, $6800, I could have the money together in about three months. I knew I could fix it, and have a really snazzy car like I never thought I'd have. Some people say a missionary shouldn't drive a Mercedes at any price. But it didn't sell, and the asking price even came down. It was the sign we agreed on. Thank you for guiding me. It's sitting in the driveway now."

Gaston sighed with satisfaction. Then he reported on another incident, one where he needed no guidance.

"Another mining company has offered me a job at four times the salary I get right now. I was a little bit tempted, but I turned them down, again. They would have taken over my life, had me flying three flights a day, and for what? To fly minerals? Rather than people? No high salary can pay me enough to give up being used for your miracles."

It was all prologue to the real issue where he sought confirmation for the decision he was ready to make.

"People are dying from the war of the Mai-Mai. I can't fly medicine to them. I can't fly the sick people out. This conference—can it bring an end to the Mai-Mai problem like my father hopes it can?"

He paused, waiting for confirmation.

"I think I can save more lives by supporting the conference, bringing the officials from Lubumbashi and Kinshasa, transporting Bishop, the governor, the commissioner, the other officials, than I can in the same time flying medical missions."

He listened, felt for any reservations that the presence in the simulator might communicate.

"But I won't fly the Mai-Mai. Too much potential for trouble if the plane lands in the territories they control."

Any admonition? No. He felt a strong sense of affirmation.

"Please, Jesus, be present with my father as he guides this meeting. Keep him and the entire meeting safe."

Again, he waited. All was dark, quiet, harmonious, peaceful. A sign that he and the one he followed, the one to whom he increasingly turned to guide his every step, concurred.

Then, the sense of a presence in the cockpit faded. He opened his eyes, looked down at the list of airplanes on the simulator, and chose a 747.

* * *

Government leaders needed to get to Kamina by plane. Gaston knew he played an important role in the conference his father was planning. But he was part of the infrastructure, and logistics alone could not produce success. He trusted his father and the Spirit that lived in him.

He knew his father could feed the conference, much the same way he had fed his family.

The boy Gaston lived with his mother and sisters in Luena. His father had been gone three or four months, planting churches. Most days the family ate boiled cassava leaves—it barely kept them alive. How much Gaston hated the tasteless scrub that filled their stomachs to take away the pain! His skin tone, and his mother's, his brothers' and his sisters', had paled from their monotonous diet. On the day his father returned home, there was nothing to eat, not even boiled cassava leaves.

"We have never gone hungry in this house, and we will not go hungry today." The man Gaston could hear his father's words, fresh as if he had spoken them aloud, here and now.

But as a boy, he had grumbled. *What, you're a magician? What you gonna do?* But he dared not speak his thoughts aloud.

"Gaston, quick, go get my Bible. Get the hymnals."

Why are we singing? Because we are hungry. Because my father says we have to.

So they sang. And they prayed. And they began to have some fun. And they heard an old metal wheelbarrow in the distance, coming closer and closer. Soon, one of his father's parishioners who worked for the mines in Luena stood before the door with a sack of corn and a chicken. "I have two sacks of corn today, so, I brought one for my pastor and his family."

That day, they ate better than they had before, the first protein they had had in months.

He also knew his father could calm a lunatic, like he had in Labudi.

He could see the man in the village, roaming the streets, acting crazy. Then the man approached Ntambo. Ntambo did not shy away; they became friends.

My father did a strange thing: he locked himself in a room with the man for three days. In his mind's eye the man Gaston could see the closed door to the hut, imagine his father and the lunatic inside.

And when they came out, the man seemed normal. He took a job, married, had children and lived in the village. The rumors began that the Methodist pastor had the power to heal.

Recently, a government official, not a Christian, flew in the plane to Kamina to meet with his father. The man Gaston witnessed what had transpired.

"I came to ask you to pray for my election." And Gaston's eyes widened as he watched his father holding a Bible, standing in front of the kneeling man. It was like when they were children: his father knelt to pray, and his mother knelt to pray, so who were they, as children, not to humble themselves before God? And they had heard unusual words, like *kumgwanbanzi,* words they rarely heard growing up, native words with more power than any name for God in English.

All small steps, leading to this great one. God-willing, his father could lead this conference.

Kamina Prepares for the Mai-Mai Conference

"CLASSICAL MUSICAL DANCE GUIDE: Simba Yangala, a professional African dancer from the Democratic Republic of Congo, will perform…"

The New York Times, September 17, 2004

"Then he took a cup, and after giving thanks he said, 'Take this and divide it among yourselves; for I tell you that from now on I will not drink of the fruit of the vine until the kingdom of God comes.' Then he took a loaf of bread, and when he had given thanks, he broke it and gave it to them, saying, 'This is my body, which is given for you. Do this in remembrance of me.' And he did the same with the cup after supper, saying, 'This cup that is poured out for you is the new covenant in my blood.'"

Luke 21:17-21

Kamina

September 2004

Bishop and Raymond Mande sat in Bishop's *payotte*, anticipating the conference's organization.

"Mande, I brought you here so I could ask your opinion. What will make this conference succeed?"

"Bishop, take your pastoral role. Receive all of the groups who come. Some you will know. Others will come because of your reputation. Receive them at your house. Hear their complaints. Listen to them. But don't bring them together until they have already made agreements. Then, it will be ok."

* * *

Bishop sat with his organizers: Pastor Kabongo, the Kamina District Superintendent; Pastor Tschimwang, Pastor Kahunda, Pastor Nyengele, and Ilunga Mutombo, who had organized the displaced people and the depot. Now, he needed their administrative skills again—first, to think about the food.

"I've called UMCOR. They will send $10,000."

Ilunga Mutombo spoke. "We can use the stores of corn flour we have here in Kamina for feeding orphans and displaced people and then order replacements from Lubumbashi."

"Yes, but we need to treat our guests with high hospitality, *high* hospitality! Chicken and goats and fish—they must be fed well. No beans and rice, no termites."

"It's expensive to feed so many people that kind of food for five days."

"But we must follow Luba tradition—to communicate respect through the food they are offered. Treat them as dignitaries. The food they receive will tell them that we are their servants, that we sincerely want the best for everyone, that we do not care to overpower anyone. We will extend our generosity and good will, and we will ask them to meet us with theirs. We can do that best by feeding them a royal banquet."

* * *

Pastor Nyengele stood before the gathering of displaced pastors. They looked expectant, ready to hear about their role in the upcoming Mai-Mai peace conference.

"We don't know exactly which Mai-Mai will appear—look for people you knew from your former congregations. You are the conference chaplains. Behind the scenes, keep them calm. If they react or get emotional, talk gently. Take them aside, listen to their complaints. Tell us if they feel overlooked or unimportant. Do not argue with them. And then, if you find the right moments, a time when they are open, help them commit to peace. Find out what they need to feel comfortable enough to disband their groups."

Murmurs of approval broke out among the pastors. So many of them had former parishioners who had become Mai-Mai—they knew them, they knew their ways. All they had learned through their pastoring as the war grew, all they learned through their displacement, might now become important in this risky endeavor to make peace.

* * *

Governor Kisula visited. He and the District Commissioner, Kyoni Ngoy, met with the commander of Kamina Military Base with the message: the Mai-Mai are coming. The District Commissioner made announcements on the radio: "Kamina will hold a peace conference with Congolese soldiers, Mai-Mai, government leaders, facilitated by all the religious leaders. Please stay calm."

Kamina bustled with excitement, curiosity, anticipation—and the sense that danger approached.

Where is Chinja-Chinja?

"Another Triumph for the U.N."

The New York Times, editorial, September 25, 2004

"Then Satan entered into Judas called Iscariot, who was one of the twelve; he went away and conferred with the chief priests and officers of the temple police about how he might betray him to them."

Luke 22:2-4

Kamina to Nkenke, beyond Kabongo
September 2004

In Kamina delegates to the conference were arriving at the green metal gate of Bishop's house. Soldiers in uniform, government officials in their business suits, traditional chiefs with their carved staffs, influential Mai-Mai wearing necklaces of fetishes—the power of prepared but restrained force had never been so open in Kamina. New groups appeared hourly, and, heavily armed with rifles, spears and bows and arrows, roamed the streets of the peaceful town.

As the Mai-Mai arrived, Ilunga Mutombo, Pastor Tschimwang, and Pastor Kahunda greeted them. "Welcome to Bishop's house. We will register you; please wait here in the yard, and soon, Bishop will receive you."

Hour after hour, Bishop heard the Mai-Mai's complaints: they had responded to Laurent Kabila's call to defend the villages against the Rwandese aggressors, but they had never been paid by the government. They always had to live as the military often lived: demanding food from the villagers' harvest. They had no other possibilities for jobs, no opportunity to attend school, no hospital when they became sick. Bishop heard their complaints, prayed with them, and took their sorrows onto himself. They bore their suspicions openly. With each who came, Bishop created a strand of trust like a filament of a spider's web, a slim connection from the Bishop's heart and soul to the place of passion and hunger in each leader.

In the living room of the Methodist guesthouse, Bishop Ntambo and the conference organizers perched on the brown faux velvet overstuffed chairs with doilies on each headrest, intently focused on their task. Coffee, milk, sugar, peanuts and bananas lay on the china cabinet at the end of the room, just beyond the teak dining table. Mama Sila had filled a tray with china cups and saucers and had brought food and drinks to the coffee table. The nourishment had been welcomed, and now, small caramel-colored puddles of coffee, cream and sugar settled in the bottoms of the cups and on the saucers.

The religious leaders, Bishop Ntambo and Prophet Mechac; the Kamina district commissioner, Mr. Ngoy Kyoni; the Governor's representative, Mr. Ngoy Kitwa Scholler; and a representative of the government in Kinshasa—were reviewing the preparations for the conference. An important participant was missing.

"Bishop, you have not heard from Chinja-Chinja? If he and his people do not participate, anything the others agree to will unravel. After all this work, all this money, all this risk, the conference will be a failure."

Bishop Ntambo, who had been charged with inviting the Mai-Mai, squirmed in his seat.

"We need someone to go to Chinja-Chinja to persuade him to attend."

"Mechac has had the most experience with him."

"But Chinja-Chinja knows that Mechac can neutralize his power. It will be too threatening. Your district superintendent—Pastor Kabongo? Isn't he from Kaloko, Chinja-Chinja's village?"

"He is the one!"

Bishop Ntambo shook his head. "He might be killed. He has a young family."

Prophet Mechac raised his head and spoke with authority. "We started with God. We want God to lead us. And we hope God will help us, as he will help you lead this meeting. And God will help Kabongo collect Chinja-Chinja."

Bishop Ntambo sighed deeply. "You are right." He stepped to the front door and called to one of the guards who lounged by the green gate at the front of the compound. "Send someone to bring Pastor Kabongo to us."

* * *

The screen door on the front of the guesthouse creaked on its hinge as Kabongo slid through the door. He stood quietly as the august leaders finished their discussion. The room stilled quickly and all eyes turned toward him.

"We have an important mission to discuss with you." Bishop looked directly into the eyes of his district superintendent. "Chinja-Chinja and his representatives are not here. If he does not come, the conference will be a waste of time. We need someone to go to Nkenke where Chinja-Chinja now lives, someone who he might trust, someone he has known but with whom he has no recent dealings, a neutral person. . . ."

Kabongo knew where Bishop was leading. "And that someone is me." Kabongo looked around at all of the waiting faces, their tight mouths, their concerned looks. "Yes, Chinja-Chinja and I are from the same village. I know him; he knows me."

Even as he spoke, Kabongo's mind raced ahead. The Governor had sponsored this meeting, but he was not present in the room. If Kabongo were killed in a mission for the Governor, the Governor should be responsible for the care of his wife and four children.

Bishop's eyes searched those of his younger colleague. "Will you go?"

"I am ready. But I could be killed. Before I go, I want to speak with the Governor. And I need someone else to go with me, so that if something happens to me, there is witness who can tell you how I died."

* * *

It was only a block to Kabongo's parsonage, usually a short, brisk walk down a dusty lane past familiar houses. But today, the few paces were filled with a kaleidoscope of images of what the next twenty-four hours might bring—the rough jumble by motorbike over the rutted red dirt roads, slowing the bike to approach military-style barriers, guns and arrows pointed at him, ready to be released within seconds.

When he told his wife about his mission, her eyes grew wide with fright and she clasped her hands to her mouth as if to ululate. But she did not speak.

"Anything can happen. That guy can refuse to come to Kamina and kill me instead. But as a pastor we are required to save people. Please, understand. You are in the church. The church will take responsibility to protect you and to take care of my children."

"I do not want you to go. But if you do, pray with Prophet Mechac first. His prayer will keep you safe."

"I will."

Kabongo returned the guesthouse where the leaders still waited.

"Prophet, my wife will agree if you pray for me."

"Let's pray." Kabongo knelt before Mechac, and he placed his hands on Kabongo's head, appealing to God to protect him. When Mechac finished, Kabongo stood.

Mechac warned him. "Do not spend a night in Nkenke or any village under Mai-Mai control—if you do, you will be finished."

* * *

He revved his motorbike and soon pulled alongside the hut of a young teacher from Kendabantu School. He had seen that Désiré Mbuya showed great faith. His presence could strengthen their journey.

"Hey, too much is going on here. I am going to my village near Kabongo to see my family. Do you want to come?"

The young man accepted the invitation. It was now five p.m. on September 24, a few days after the vernal equinox, so the sun rose directly in the east and set twelve hours later in the west. The thunderstorms had passed, but a few hours of light remained. Time to travel. They headed out Mobutu's belt, the macadam road that led northeast toward Kamina Base, and shortly, turned north on the dirt road that led to Kabongo and beyond, to Kaloko.

After about twenty kilometers, the evening sun became twilight, and Kabongo stopped the bike. "We will pray." He parked the bike, went into the bush, knelt, and silently poured out his heart to God. *Why me? Normally it should be someone else who would go to collect that guy. I know him. I know he will kill me, just as he did the others who went to advise him. Why me?*

The prayer quieted Kabongo somewhat, and he rode on, but over and over again, fear rose and overtook him. And as he biked he began to pray without ceasing, muttering his words. *Why me?* Finally, he heard the voice of his partner from the back seat.

"Why do you keep saying the same prayer, over and over? Are you afraid?"

Methodist leaders had travelled this road many times during the war, delivering medicine or relief to Kabongo and outlying villages. The Congolese army accompanied them for security, but still, they took many risks. Disgruntled soldiers, Mai-Mai, and bandits roamed here, ready to rob or solicit commissions from businessmen. This time, Pastor Kabongo knew, a different, grave danger lay beyond the town of Kabongo. He was not ready to confess his mission to his companion.

They spent the night in Kipukwe under the stars. Kabongo prayed as he dozed and dreamed. As the sun rose, so did the pastor, with a new confidence. The night had absorbed his fears.

* * *

The motorbike rounded the town of Kileo and neared a village about eighty-five kilometers before Nkenke. People came to gawk, to see who was coming toward their village.

"Where to?"

"To Nkenke, to visit my family."

"No, no, no! Don't you know? Chinja-Chinja stays at that village! Have you seen a car, a bike, anything coming this way? Don't go."

"But I must go, I must."

They passed through the village, and then Kabongo slowed the motorbike. The time had come to tell Désiré Mbuya of their mission. Kabongo twisted on the bike, so that he could see the face of the teacher.

"We are going to collect Chinja-Chinja."

"No!"

"Look, I know him. What I know, if he decides to kill me, he won't kill you. He only kills officers or leaders, people with roles of responsibility. I have brought you so that, if I die, you can tell people in Kamina how I was killed."

"You should have told me."

"You wouldn't have come."

* * *

As they neared a village called Kalulu ka Mbayo, they approached a military-style barrier. They slowed the motorbike and were met by Mai-Mai guards.

"My name is Pastor Kabongo. I'm a Methodist pastor."

"Oh? Where are you coming from?"

"Kamina."

"Hah! Why are you coming from Kamina all the way up here? So you can learn how we are living here? So you can go and inform people in Kamina?"

The guards turned their attention from the travellers and argued, angry, among themselves. "They should not pass."

"We will kill them."

"They are no good."

"What should we do with them?"

We are finished now.

"Call our master, our chief."

As the Mai-Mai commander approached, Kabongo recognized him as Chinja-Chinja's younger brother, Kuyela.

"Papa! *Wako!*" Then Kuyela ordered his guards, "Don't do anything to them. I know him. He can come to the village with me."

Kabongo and Désiré Mbuya followed to Kuyela's hut where they could talk in private.

"Who has sent you here? People don't come here. You're in danger."

"I have been sent by the governor, the Methodist bishop, Bishop Ntambo, and the district commissioner to see Chinja-Chinja. I think you heard that there is a conference in Kamina on peace. We sent an invitation. Why didn't you come to Kamina?"

"We're afraid. Those people, we know them. They want to catch people, to arrest Chinja-Chinja and myself. Why did you agree to be involved in a situation like this where they want to arrest us? You're against us!"

"No, if I were against you, I wouldn't come here. Where is your brother, Chinja-Chinja?"

"He is far from here. This is the first barrier, the first group of Mai-Mai. You have to pass the second, the third, the fourth, to come where Chinja-Chinja is."

"I want to go to see him."

"Ok, but be ready. Anything can happen."

Kabongo's heart pounded in his ears. A second time, he thought, *I am finished now.*

"As you have come with this young man, he is going to stay here. You will go with one Mai-Mai."

"I won't go with someone else, Kuyela. I want to go with you."

Kabongo turned to Désiré Mbuya and spoke in low tones. "Do not eat meat if they offer it to you. Just say, I only eat vegetables and fish." And, leaving the young teacher behind with the Mai-Mai soldiers, Kabongo took Kuyela onto his motorbike and they continued to Nkenke.

The Conference Opens

> "Congolese Roots Now Helped by Hip-Hop"
>
> *The New York Times*, September 30, 2004

> "Then he withdrew from them about a stone's throw, knelt down, and prayed, 'Father, if you are willing, remove this cup from me; yet, not my will but yours be done.' Then an angel from heaven appeared to him and gave him strength."
>
> Luke 22: 41-43

Kamina

September 2004

Bishop Ntambo had not slept. He slipped from the back door into the side yard under the palm trees. There he paced, his body casting shadows in the bright moonlight. His yard, where, like Jesus in Gethsemane, he was alone with his God and his fears.

Why did I allow that young man to be sent to Chinja-Chinja? And why did I agree to hold this conference in Kamina? All of the charms, all of the weapons. We have not had them here before. Someone will be killed—it's just a matter of time, just a question of who it will be.

Overcome by his guilt, his tears flowed, and he slowly fell to his knees.

We will fail. God, why me? Why did I accept to do this? The fight is coming. We will end with people to be killed.

He cried until his tears ran out. And then he rose, obliged to face the rising day.

* * *

Raymond Mande sat in the back of the large lecture room at the Roman Catholic Church, observing the groups who now perched on the benches where normally, worshippers sat. The various groups of Mai-Mai, army, traditional chiefs, and religious leaders huddled together with their own kind. He knew that at this moment, all could be lost.

Bishop had shown him the speech that District Commissioner Kyoni had originally written, outlining his grievances against the Mai-Mai. He had listed all they had done wrong: attacking villages, raping women, eating human flesh, even threatening his life when he sought to meet with them. Mande, the artist of words, had approached Kyoni.

"Are you sure this is the right time to accuse them? Why not just welcome them, make them comfortable? You have brought them to this city—congratulate them for attending."

"I'm angry at them! Perhaps you can write such words."

So Mande wrote the words of appreciation with which the district commissioner now opened the conference. "Our city, Kamina, is pleased to welcome you. We are glad that you are have come. Let us turn our hearts toward peace."

Then Governor Kisula Ngoy took the floor. "We are here to bring peace to our land. Let us introduce the good people who have come to this conference." And the morning continued with each group introducing who they were and where they came from.

"I am from Kamina Military Base…."

"I am the Roman Catholic priest of the parish…."

"I am the chief of the village…."

"I am from the government...."

"I am observing…."

They listened carefully, and then, Bishop Ntambo and Bishop Kalala led the group in prayers.

* * *

Chief Kanda-Fwanyinwabo, the chief of the village Groupement Ngoy-Mwana who had resisted the Mai-Mai approaches in his territory, sat on his bench, observing the proceedings. He wore his leopard cap and carried his carved ebony staff, and he commanded respect through his appearance—his impeccably creased khaki shirt and pants draped his lean body. He, as chief, sought ancestral power through traditional ceremonies. He disdained Christianity as white man's religion. But as he watched Bishop Ntambo, a warm admiration spread through his body. He felt the thrill of hope.

He had seen the worst: Congolese soldiers on one side, Mai-Mai on the other—each coming to the village, each accusing the villagers of conspiring with the other side, each attacking the same people and their families. So many innocent people had been caught in the middle of this horrible war. It was time for this killing to end.

Bishop Ntambo, he practices white man's religion, completely different from traditional ritual. But he is God's messenger. The power in him is not physical but supernatural. He has the power to unite with traditional people and Christians, the good people and the bad ones, and he will succeed in bringing us together. Perhaps his Spirit has laid his hand on us to be successful.

* * *

And Bishop explained the plan: "You will begin with conversation. I will return to my home and the Governor to the guesthouse. If you need to talk to us, you will find us there."

The participants were divided into small groups and instructed to explain to each other why they thought the conflict was occurring, what they proposed as a solution and how the government might assist them. Each person had the opportunity to speak.

As Bishop and the governor left, Raymond Mande observed the hall. Conversation rose like a giant storm—thunder and lightning crashed from voices in different parts of the room. He sought to calm his anxiety. *Trust. That some in small groups could take a pastoral role. That the Mai-Mai, the soldiers, the government officials could speak fiercely but not become violent. That they could bring their grievances out of the hall to Bishop and the Governor. That they could focus on solutions.*

The storm continued, with different groups coming and going to speak to Ntambo and Kisula. By the end of the day, the stormy weather in the hall seemed to be abating.

* * *

That night Bishop slept with more confidence that the conference would actually remain peaceful. He knew that Mande had been right. His pastoral role, and that of the pastors whom Pastor Nyengele had commissioned as chaplains, held the key to success. *When they are divided, we will use all wisdom to bring them together. I am their servant; I offer humble understanding, appreciation; I won't condemn them.*

The Mai-Mai had made clear their claim. *We fought for our country, we were never rewarded. We request to be recognized, to share something.*

Kujatalala ekwabana biya. 'You will eat peacefully, when everybody received his portion of the share.'

Pastor Kabongo Approaches Chinja-Chinja

> "FICTION: Fire Eaters, Flying Ants, and Joseph Conrad"
> *The New York Times*, September 26, 2004

> "In his anguish he prayed more earnestly, and his sweat became like great drops of blood falling down on the ground."
> Luke 22:44

Nkenke

September 2004

"Stop here."

Kabongo's motorbike, with Kuyela riding on the rear seat, chugged to a stall. Kabongo stretched out his legs in an A-frame to brace the bike.

Kuyela breathed hotly into Kabongo's ear. "I will perform the necessary ceremonies to enter the village. Wait here. Do not follow me."

"I'm here on the bike." Kabongo faced resolutely forward, staring down the dirt road toward Nkenke village, occupied by Chinja-Chinja. The bike leaned slightly as his passenger slipped off and fled into the forest.

In not too many minutes he heard footfalls and felt the slight vibration of Kuyela remounting the rear of the bike. "We'll go now." Kabongo lifted his foot and revved the engine. They puttered slowly down the trail until they reached the barrier that blocked the entrance to the village.

The Mai-Mai sentries stood. To Kuyela: "Why are bringing him here?" Without waiting for a reply, to Kabongo: "What's your name? And on a motorbike?"

Curious Mai-Mai villagers came running to the barrier. One of the onlookers spoke from behind. "He is from this village! We know him." Kabongo looked into the assembly and recognized the familiar faces of people whom he had lived near as a child.

"I have come to speak to your chief. Where is Chinja-Chinja?"

But the guard demanded to know more.

"Before I tell you where he is, who are you?" He pulled a notebook and pen from his pocket and wrote down Kabongo's name.

"Why do you want to see Chinja-Chinja?" The sentry continued to write.

"Who is your wife?"

"Who are your children?"

"What village are you coming from?"

"Who has sent you to see Chinja-Chinja?"

"Why do they want to see him?"

Then he shoved the paper in front of Kabongo. "Sign here." *Nothing else to do*. Kabongo signed.

"If something happens to Chinja-Chinja, you are responsible. You, your wife, your children and your village will be burnt."

The picture of his family, his parsonage, and Kamina formed in his mind. They had become collateral for Chinja-Chinja's safety.

* * *

Kabongo followed Kuyela and the sentry through the village of mud huts with grass roofs to one that looked like every other, except that Chinja-Chinja's officers, dressed in the uniforms of Congolese soldiers with rifles slung over their shoulders, guarded the yard. Kabongo recognized Chinja-Chinja's father, who greeted him warmly. Then, Chinja-Chinja, also uniformed but unarmed, emerged from the hut.

"Papa, *wako wako.*" Chinja-Chinja smiled.

"*Eyo-vidye.*" Kabongo grasped his right forearm and extended his hand, grinning.

"Let's sit outside." He motioned to chairs in the side yard. They sat, with the soldiers lounging about.

"You must eat something."

Kabongo felt hungry but also repulsed. *Not red meat that might be human.* "*Wafwako.* I can have chicken or vegetables—no cow or goats."

"It will be. Now, why have you come to see me?"

"I didn't come on my own. I have been sent by the Governor." Chinja-Chinja's face tightened. "He is in Kamina, waiting for you. The district commissioner is there. Everyone is there, except you. So everybody needs you so that they can bring peace to our land."

"I want peace. That is our purpose. But we have to protect this area around Kabongo, even from Congolese soldiers."

"If you are not going to Kamina because you are fighting, think again. This is your chance for *recompense.* You were organized by the government, but you have fought for nothing from 2002 till now. You should go and speak to those people. Say to them, 'I fought against rebels and now I need you to pay'. Military soldiers have occasional salaries, but you have nothing."

Chinja-Chinja nodded. "You are right. But I am afraid. I have killed people. Especially Congolese officers. Kamina Base has many soldiers. Even if I took all my warriors from here to Kamina, we're nothing before all of them."

"The soldiers are part of the conference. The governor will ensure your safety. They will not harm you."

"If you can guarantee that I'll be safe, I can leave here. But my warriors will stay here. If I go there and something happens to me, as you have signed here, you will be killed, you, your wife, your children and people from the village where you now live."

"OK, I take those kinds of risks. But, I need you to go to Kamina. You can choose your transportation. If you want to go by plane you have to move from here up to Kabongo. If you want to go by car, they will send a car up here to bring you."

"Ok." And then he paused. "Who else is there? Did you meet Bakanda Bakoka? Is Bakanda there?"

"Yes, he is there."

"And from Musau, Maccabee, is Maccabee there?"

"No, but he has sent representatives."

"So I can send some people."

"No, don't send people. They want you."

"I will go with you only if my spirits are behind me. Now, I must consult my ancestors. Let me take your motorbike."

Chinja-Chinja straddled Kabongo's bike, revved it, and vanished into the bush, the chug of the motor quickly fading. The next two hours, Kabongo fidgeted as he waited with Kuyela, wondering what Chinja-Chinja's ancestors would advise. Would they reverse Chinja-Chinja's decision, even advise him to kill Kabongo?

* * *

Finally, Kabongo heard the motorbike and Chinja-Chinja, singing. He stood and waited patiently to hear the decision. Soon, Chinja-Chinja rode into the village, laughing, exuberant. The Mai-Mai men cheered and women ululated, welcoming him. Chinja-Chinja stopped the bike, his followers crowding around him.

He announced to the crowd: "I will go to Kamina! My ancestors will protect me."

Kabongo heard, sighed, and relaxed. Chinja-Chinja approached.

"I'm ready to go. I will go by car."

"The car will come tomorrow."

"Here are the conditions. Tell them: I don't want to see a gun in the car and I don't want to meet any soldiers on the road who say, 'Stop, we want to make a check.' Tell them. And I want three people in the car, only: one representative from the governor, one from the district commissioner, one from the church."

"I'm sure they will agree."

"Will you spend the night here?"

Kabongo remembered Mechac's admonition. *Do not sleep there.* "I must leave now. I need to reach a place where I can call Kamina. I hope to make it beyond Kalulu before midnight."

It was very late when Kabongo and the Désiré Mbuya reached Lenge, a village more than sixty kilometers from Chinja-Chinja's stronghold where they could spend the night. They went immediately to the ham radio and called the district commissioner, using a code that could not be deciphered by soldiers who might be listening.

"Your sister is very sick. She cannot make it. Would you please send a car to collect her tomorrow?"

"We cannot send a car till you are here."

They took a short rest and rode on to Kamina.

* * *

They arrived at the guesthouse in Kamina at six a.m. The Governor met them. "Can you tell us the news from Chinja-Chinja?"

Kabongo said, "Yes, the general is a very good guy. I was received with respect, treated as a man of God. I was not maltreated along the road, not even insulted. He has agreed to come, with terms. 'I don't want to see a soldier in the car, no checkpoints, no guns. I want three in the car, that's all." Kabongo paused, then added. "And I'm very very thankful to my God because I was afraid I would be killed."

"Do you think if we send a car and some people inside, he will kill them?"

"No. But, if something happens to him, he will attack me, my wife, my children, and my village. Please, can you protect me by giving him security?"

"We'll do our best."

Your best must be good enough.

The Governor Negotiates with Chinja-Chinja

"Friends Matter for Reclusive Creature of African Forest"

The New York Times, October 12, 2004

"Then afterward I will pour out my spirit on all flesh; your sons and your daughters shall prophesy, your old men shall dream dreams, and your young men shall see visions."

Joel 2:28

Kamina

September 2004

The Mai-Mai had made clear their claim to Bishop and the Governor. "We fought for our country, but we were never rewarded. So we live as the military does, paid by the people. Sometimes they do not like to give us our due. So we need to be recognized, to share something."

"And you will concentrate on jobs, on economic development, on education, if you are given assistance?"

"What jobs?"

"You can take military training, be integrated into the military."

"Fishing on the River Congo, agriculture. The church has training at Kamisamba Farm."

"The government can provide hoes and hand tools for you to cultivate."

"We can exchange your guns for bicycles."

"But you must stop your other activities: take down the roadblocks, eliminate checkpoints where you are collecting things from people. Do not harass the population."

* * *

When they returned to the plenary, the decisions had already been made: government would provide garden tools and hoes for cultivation, bicycles so people could take their crops to market, and schools and clinics in the rural areas. In return the Mai-Mai would disassemble their roadblocks and disband their members.

* * *

King Kayamba listened to the report respectfully, but skeptically. Yes, it was wise to listen to the Mai-Mai, to reduce their power. But to give them all these things? He shook his head. *No, they cannot be trusted. They will rise again. The chiefs will need to continue to be prepared to deal with them.*

His own villages had fought against the Congolese soldiers with Bakande Bakoka. But once the threat was over, he had led his people back to their villages. Kayamba had become suspicious—he suspected that the new militia leaders wanted to become like kings. They continued to make trouble. Just this year, in April, he had captured some Mai-Mai and sent them to Kamina Base to be punished.

These people pretend, they say they are convinced, but when they go back, they will repeat the same old thing.

And, Chinja-Chinja had not yet arrived.

Chauffeur Hubert Drives Chinja-Chinja

"Juveniles and the Death Penalty"

The New York Times, October 13, 2004

"Now on that same day two of them were going to a village called Emmaus, about seven miles from Jerusalem, and talking with each other about all these things that had happened. While they were talking and discussing, Jesus himself came near and went with them, but their eyes were kept from recognizing him."

Luke 34:13-15

Nkenke to Kamina
September 2004

"Hubert, some people coming to the conference are very tired, so you will go to collect them. When you have prepared the car, go to Bishop Ntambo. He will give you instructions."

Hubert, the chauffeur for the Roman Catholic Bishop Kalala, received the request from his spiritual leader without a second thought. "Yes, Monsignor. I've been at the garage servicing the Land Rover. It's in good shape. I'll clean it"—Hubert always made the interior gleam— "and be ready."

Within the hour, Hubert arrived at Bishop Ntambo's office. There, his esteemed passengers waited: Mr. Ngoy Kyoni, the district commissioner from Haut Lomami, and Mr. Ngoy Kitwa Scholler, the governor's representative to Kabongo District.

Bishop Ntambo introduced them. "Gentlemen, you will be in good hands with Hubert! He is Bishop Kalala's trusted driver, a good Catholic. Hubert, you will be travelling to Kabongo."

"Welcome, gentlemen. This way."

Hubert asked no questions. He often drove officials on important business as a favor bestowed by Bishop Kalala. A professional driver and mechanic, Hubert maintained discretion—he only needed to know the destination to be sure he had enough fuel and parts to make the trip. Kabongo? Three hundred and eighty kilometers, round trip, through thunderstorms, puddles and mud? No problem.

They had already travelled for a full day when Ngoy Kyoni directed Hubert through Kabongo to the road north. When they arrived at the military barrier at Kime, Hubert pulled the Land Rover close to the checkpoint. He rolled down the window, and the Congolese army's guard peered into the vehicle, staring at each passenger. Then he smiled. He recognized the district commissioner at once.

"Your excellency, Commissioner Ngoy! *Wafwako!*"

Ngoy Kyoni spoke tersely. "We are going to Nkenke to bring Chinja-Chinja and his party to the peace conference in Kamina. When we return, be prepared for us: it is *essential* that your soldiers do not stop us, question us, or search us. You know the car. You yourself must direct your soldiers—otherwise there could be trouble. Your commander at Kamina Base and the Governor—this is the governor's representative, Ngoy Kitwa—" Ngoy Kyoni nodded to the man in the next seat— "want Chinja-Chinja to attend the conference in Kamina without an incident."

"We know. We will be sure you do not have trouble here."

Hubert's chest tightened as he heard the conversation between the commissioner and the guard. *So that is the errand in Kabongo district! To that place. So many people go there without returning. They end up by dying.*

Ngoy Kyoni nudged Hubert. "Drive on. We cannot lose time." Hubert put the Land Rover in gear and pressed the accelerator.

Someday, I am going to die. I have already accepted this responsibility from Bishop Kalala. I am committed. I will not be afraid.

Whatever his bishop asked, it was his duty to perform.

* * *

The sun rose as they drove among the thatched roofs of the houses of Kamungu, expecting to see the hustle and bustle of village life at dawn—women drawing water or taking crops to market, men selling firewood. But no, strangely, the travellers saw none of the usual activity. Puzzled, they drove into Kamungu to consult the Methodist pastor, Mudimbiyimadi.

"Going to Kaloko? To find Chinja-Chinja? Really dangerous—all of the villages between here and there controlled by Mai-Mai. This one was ruined. You can't cross by car either to Kitenge or to Kalulu. I would advise you to go back to where you came from."

The governor's representative agreed. "What else can we do? So many government emissaries have been killed, even before they neared any of the barriers where Pastor Kabongo negotiated passage. He is known here. On a motorbike, he had more flexibility to go around the barriers. We will not get through. It is better that we go back."

Ngoy Kyoni shook his head. "No! I'm the commissioner of the Haut Lomami, and I'm known. Pastor Kabongo risked his life to negotiate with Chinja-Chinja, and now everyone is waiting for us. It's our best chance for success. We *must* proceed."

Pride prevailed over common sense, fear and the prospect of shame. So Hubert wove the Land Rover onto the road and picked his way through ruts and puddles to the first barrier at Kalulu, the one where Kabongo had encountered Chinja-Chinja's brother.

* * *

Hubert slowed the car when he saw the Mai-Mai sentries.

"What you want here?"

"I am Ngoy Kyoni, the commissioner of Haut Lomami, and here is the governor's representative, Ngoy Kitwa. Your chief, Chinja-Chinja, is expecting us to pick him up to take him to Kamina for the peace conference."

"Oh, yes, Your Excellency, we have heard! If you are going to Chinja-Chinja, we should go with you." And Mai-Mai opened the car doors, shoved their guns and arrows toward the center of the Land Rover, and filled the seats behind the driver and his passengers.

* * *

They arrived at Nkenke at seven a.m. The visitors stopped at the parsonage of a Pentecostal pastor who could play a mediating role; he sent a messenger to Chinja-Chinja. Soon a group of Mai-Mai emerged from the bush and surrounded the car.

Ngoy Kyoni knew rural people; he understood that they had been taught from the time they were small to trust only those who spoke their own language. Kinyarwanda-speaking Rwandans, Congolese who spoke other languages and dialects—those were taken as enemies. So he spoke in Kiluba, making it clear that the people in the car were one with the Mai-Mai, not soldiers or emissaries from a linguistic group in another part of Congo.

"I am Ngoy Kyoni, and he is the governor's representative, Ngoy Kitwa. Hubert, our driver, is from the Roman Catholic Church. We are awaiting your chief, who asked that we three—from the district, from the governor, and from the church—travel with him to Kamina for the peace conference. So let's be united, to bring peace to our land."

"We have been waiting for you! We are glad you have come! We have prepared chicken!"

And soon some Mai-Mai appeared, bearing pots, a sign of welcome to the visitors. They offered a piece to the passengers and then to Hubert. He picked up the chicken leg, looked at it, and bit gratefully. And he began to chat with them.

"How do you survive? How do you eat?"

"We cultivate, we purchase supplies in town."

"But we don't want soldiers here because soldiers are the ones who disturb people."

Then a Mai-Mai came, leading a live goat, handing the rope to Kyoni Ngoy. "We bring you this sign of welcome."

Hubert sat patiently, overhearing, watching his surroundings. Twice more, delegations appeared, talked with the officials, and left to bring word to Chinja-Chinja.

* * *

The crisp thwack of drums, clapping and singing floated from the trees toward the car—a choir appeared like a spiritual forward guard, announcing the arrival of a crowd who now emerged from the wood. They surrounded a small, wiry man dressed casually in an African shirt. His face was coated with *impembe,* the dust of the white lime. He carried a small suitcase. He loped toward the car in the midst of the singers—the women and men around him pranced to the music. It was four p.m., and Chinja-Chinja had arrived.

So this is the famous Chinja-Chinja. Hubert jumped to his feet following the example of Ngoy Kyoni, who had risen and now stood straight with his eyes on the Mai-Mai commander, communicating dignity and respect. Chinja-Chinja's people halted before the officials and the car. They continued singing.

Hubert furrowed his brow, watching. The Mai-Mai leader, the master of all the surrounding villages, gazed at the district commissioner, the highest government official in the area, unflinching. They seemed like lions who meet on the plain, wary, communicating through their posture, their eyes, and their pacing, until they establish which lion will dominate and which will submit. Now, these rulers of the bush eyed one another, negotiating their power, timing the right moment to speak. Within a few seconds Ngoy Kyoni had communicated his acquiescence to Chinja-Chinja's leadership. But he also established his own dignity, his right to negotiate.

"Your Eminence, Pastor Kabongo came to speak with you. We are here to take you safely to Kamina where you can help to bring peace to our land."

"I will take one wife who will cook for me. But I have four other wives who will need money while I am gone. You must pay for them if I am to leave."

"We are prepared to provide sustenance for your family while you attend the meeting."

Then Chinja-Chinja turned to face his singers. "I am going with them to the meeting to meet the leaders over there, as Pastor Kabongo has come and convinced me already."

He turned to Ngoy Kyoni and stood still, expectant. The district commissioner gave him money that he then distributed to his wives.

* * *

"The driver and the car must be spiritually prepared. Otherwise we can't enter. Driver, sit in the car."

Hubert was a professional chauffeur. He was prepared for almost everything he would meet on the road. Expressionless, he did as he was instructed. The mighty Chinja-Chinja and his followers began circling the car, washing it in the bloody, sticky charms they had prepared, painting it with bold red-brown stripes. When they finished, they opened the car door and dumped the remaining fetish on Hubert. Hubert sat motionless, receiving their ritual without complaint. Then, Chinja-Chinja's bodyguard, who was travelling with them, spoke through the window into Hubert's ear.

"*You* are the one who is taking him. You have been prepared, according to the guidance of our ancestors. They have offered their safe passage. So if anything happens, *you* are responsible. *You* will be killed."

Then the bodyguard turned toward Ngoy Kyoni and Ngoy Kitwa. "There are seven of us—Chinja Chinja and his wife will sit in the front seat. I will sit in the second seat by the door. His father will sit next to me, and then the three Mai-Mai soldiers. You will sit in the rear seat. Now, we will take our seats. You first, to the back."

* * *

The Mai-Mai rolled and lit their marijuana, and its sweet smell mixed with the sickly stink of bloody charms. Chinja-Chinja had been muttering some sort of words, some kind of incantations.

Now he spoke in Kiluba. "Stop the car." More muttering. "I will not go with you to Kamina. I will walk." He opened the car door, and he and his wife got out. The rest of his entourage followed.

Hubert glanced over his shoulder as Ngoy Kyoni also squeezed his way out of the back seat of the Land Rover. "Stop! Let's talk. Chinja-Chinja, you are the master, the greatest of the respected Mai-Mai. If you do not come to Kamina, everyone will miss you. And you cannot walk there in time. We will only arrive for the last day. Please, please come back in the car with us. Let us proceed. We have arranged for your safety. Guaranteed."

And then, discussion, murmuring, more conversation outside the car. Finally, Chinja-Chinja turned his wife back toward the car. The soldiers filed back into their seats, his wife sat next to Hubert, and Chinja-Chinja took his place.

Hubert put the Land Rover in gear, released the clutch, pressed the gas, and the car inched forward. And then, the Mai-Mai began to sing. And they lit more marijuana.

Hubert felt tingly in his head and happy in his heart, and his mind wandered. But he brought himself back to the road in front of him. He rolled down the window and took a long draught of fresh air. Then he steeled himself—he must allow the revolting smell of stale sweat, damp blood and marijuana to become normal. He focused carefully, determined to do his job: safely traversing the ridges and ruts that could bring disaster, even tortuous death, on the Jericho road between Kabongo and Kamina. The lives of his passengers, and his own life, were in his hands.

As the Land Rover approached the checkpoint at Kime under moonlight, Hubert gripped the steering wheel, hoping that the soldiers would follow their instructions. The soldiers saluted but did not try to stop the car, and the driver relaxed his grip.

Then Hubert pressed the hardy vehicle deep into the bush, into the lush green-black shadows of the river valley at Samba village, the burial place of Luba kings. He traversed the road where it narrowed to a one lane, a mud dirt path, sheltered by a canopy of bush leaves, a tunnel pierced only by the beam of the headlights. Finally, he arrived on the open savannahs that surrounded Kamina. Now the moon barely showed as it hung low to the horizon, awaiting the sun.

At three-thirty a.m. they arrived ten kilometers from Kamina, and Ngoy Kitwa called the Governor. "What are our instructions? Where do we take Chinja-Chinja?"

"Do not bring him to us. Take him to Bishop Ntambo."

Bishop Ntambo Receives Chinja-Chinja

> "The Listing; PERFORMING ETHNICITY"
>
> *The New York Times*, theater, October 29, 2004
>
> "But they urged him strongly, saying, 'Stay with us, because it is almost evening and the day is now nearly over.' So he went in to stay with them. When he was at the table with them, he took bread, blessed and broke it, and gave it to them. Then their eyes were opened, and they recognized him; and he vanished from their sight."
>
> Luke 24:29-30

Kamina

September 2004

Bishop had had another long night, talking with the various participants, hearing their concerns, telling them the final meeting was not yet ready to begin. He got a few hours' sleep, but still, he was awake in the living room when his cell phone rang. At the sound of the ringtone, Nshimba, sleeping fitfully, arose. She entered the living room, where Bishop's elderly Mother waited, praying.

"Yes, Governor." Pause. "Bring him here. I am ready."

Bishop closed his phone. "Be prepared. Chinja-Chinja has arrived, and the governor has instructed the driver to bring him here."

Nshimba and her mother-in-law stared at each other, fright in their eyes. Then Nshimba put a hand on her husband's arm.

"You be safe. We will go to your mother's house. We will pray for you there."

Bishop's mother had a house a few blocks away. Bishop nodded, squeezing her fingers. "The guard will escort you."

* * *

Bishop heard the chug of the Land Rover's engine and strode out his door. His sentries had already cracked the gate, but now they hesitated.

"Open it wider, so they can pull in." The car rolled into the yard but did not turn off its engine. The bodyguard had already jumped from the car, his gun drawn, ready to fire at anyone who threatened. Ntambo's sentries froze in place.

But at the sight of Bishop Ntambo, Chinja-Chinja's voice boomed within the car. "I don't want you to hurt anybody at this house. And I don't want you to smoke any marijuana here." He opened the door and stepped from the vehicle.

"Kambo, Grandpa. *Kambo,* would you pray for me?"

"Grandson, welcome to my house." Bishop's eyes twinkled with a warm but serious smile. The muscular Chinja-Chinja stepped into the yard and knelt before Bishop, his head almost level with Bishop's belt. And Bishop placed his hands on the younger man's head, praying in Kiluba.

When Bishop concluded, Chinja-Chinja looked up. "We are not going to get peace unless you people of God are involved."

"Amen."

"I believe in God. I'm not fighting for human beings. I'm fighting for justice, for dignity. I'm defending Kabila. Kabila has brought peace to us. The people are destroying the good will the man has given us. I am on the side of the president. I am a soldier of God. I am going to defend Kabila, to protect our own people."

And when he finished, he rose. Bishop said, "Please, you, your wife, your father—come into my house. The soldiers can remain in the yard. My sentries will close the gate." He raised his voice to the guards: "And admit no one to this house unless I have called for them." He turned, led the way to the door, opened it, and beckoned them into his living room. "Please."

Each one, Chinja-Chinja, his wife, his father and Bishop settled themselves into seats in Bishop's living room. Then Chinja-China spoke. "I have responded to your invitation."

"I congratulate you, and I thank you."

"I know these people, what they are thinking of me. Tell them, if they want to cause trouble I'm ready to fight with them, here."

"No, they do not wish to hurt you. I will take you to your own house where your bodyguard can take care. You can have good security." Bishop smelled the Mai-Mai leader, his sweat, his charms, his smoke. "Do you need anything? Do you need to bathe?"

"Yes, I want to bathe."

Bishop showed him to the bathroom, giving him towels and some time. Meanwhile, he called Nshimba. "You can come back. You are safe. We must eat." Then he called Kabongo. "Please, come to greet your brother Chinja-Chinja."

* * *

Chinja-Chinja was still bathing when Kabongo arrived. Bishop met his colleague in the yard.

"Where will we house him? We don't want to mix him with other people. Otherwise anything can happen."

"The second dormitory in the orphanage. If Mama Mujing moves the children into the first house, and he and his people are in the second house, it will be secure. There will be no one to provoke them."

"Please, go to Mama Mujing and ask her to move the children into the first house. But first, come greet him."

* * *

Mama Sila rose before dawn. The guesthouse provided a central meeting place for the leaders of the conference—it needed to be spotless. Bishop wanted fresh coffee, roasted and ground from the nuts of the trees planted at the orphanage. And hot water for tea. And peanuts, bread, pineapple, bananas—always something for the leaders to eat if they were hungry. For days they had met in the living room and in the side yard, men with serious tones of voice, sometimes anxious, other times angry, occasionally soothing. Mama Sila monitored the mood, more so than the words. And to enhance an atmosphere of good will, she cooked and cleaned, provided plentiful snacks, and assisted the chef, Papa Dona, brought from Lubumbashi to direct the cooking.

The hinge on the screen door creaked as it swung open to admit Bishop. Mama Sila heard Bishop's footfalls and prepared a tray of china cups, sugar and milk. She turned, stopped, saw Bishop and his guest, heard the china rattle a bit, and balanced her load. She looked down, so as not to stare. It was he, Chinja-Chinja. In her house. She steadied her hands as she walked across the dining room and placed the items on the coffee table in the living room. Between them. Bishop on one side, Chinja-Chinja on the other. She, in the middle, they, only a foot to either side.

"*Wafwako, Mama Sila.*"

"*Eyo-mwa.*" Mama Sila turned, and unable to stop herself, glanced quickly at the face of the one so feared, and looked away. She hurried to the kitchen and busied herself with her work, listening for the tone of the voices in the living room, like a mother who monitors the sounds of her child in another room while she goes about her housework.

* * *

Shortly, a horn honked at the compound gate.

"It's the Governor's car."

Again, the hinge creaked, and Governor Kisula Ngoy and District Commissioner Ngoy Kyoni entered the guesthouse living room. They took seats.

Bishop introduced the governor. "Coffee, Governor?"

"Thank you. Chinja-Chinja, we are pleased that you have come. We have been talking with the other Mai-Mai leaders, hearing their concerns. And we have made agreements with them. We would like to make similar agreements with you."

Chinja-Chinja nodded slightly.

"We have decided, one, that the Mai-Mai need our economic support. The Mai-Mai who live near the water will be supported in fishing, and those who live inland will be supported in farming. That way, they will have food and livelihood. Do you agree with this first decision?"

Chinja-Chinja shrugged his shoulders. "Yes, of course, how can I not agree with that?"

"And if the Mai-Mai have their livelihood in agriculture and fishing, they will not need to ask the villagers for their fish or for the contents of their gardens. So the Mai-Mai leaders will order their followers to discontinue the harassment of villagers. Do you agree?"

Chinja-Chinja nodded.

"And checkpoints on the road will be dismantled. That will end." He paused. "And if these things are fulfilled, do you agree to stop fighting? Do you agree to give back arms, uniforms, other kinds of objects you have collected from soldiers?"

"I will give back everything if we can remove those Congolese soldiers from Kabongo and Malemba. If there are no soldiers, I can give my word, everything I have."

"Good." The Governor smiled.

But Chinja-Chinja did not return the smile. "But, you know, all this takes time. I have 6000 men. What am I to do with them? How will they live? There is the question of *recompense, compensation.* We have fought but not been paid."

"Yes, we know all the Mai-Mai want to be paid for what they have contributed."

"And we need a school and a health clinic. I have some soldiers who are sick, they need some medicine. We need food, we need salt, because we are living in the bush. Those people are ready to stop fighting but how can I send them back to their families empty handed? I need something to give to them, like exercise books for those who want to go to school, bicycles for those who want to travel to meet with their families. Things like that."

"Yes, we will give you money to support your people."

They had a document ready for him to sign.

The meeting had gone well. In a short time, the Governor and the District Commissioner left.

Then, Pastor Kabongo arrived. "We have made your accommodations ready at the orphanage. It is just across the street from here. I can take you and your family and your soldiers there now."

* * *

Mama Alphonsine was still in her hut in Katuba Parish with her children when she heard the news that Chinja-Chinja had been taken to Bishop and then to the guesthouse and was now being lodged at the orphanage. She immediately stopped what she was doing and prayed for Bishop, for Mama Mujing, and for the children. She included a prayer on her own behalf—she was due to care for the children during the night shift. The cell phone had rung, and she had been warned. *All the children have moved to the rear dormitory. Enter through the back door. And do not cross the courtyard, especially after dark.*

That afternoon, as she walked from Katuba to the orphanage, she imagined all she had heard about Chinja-Chinja. The evil things he did. The killing, the mutilations, the charms, the rituals. Her biological children could remain safely in their hut in Katuba parish. But the orphans! The fierce protectiveness of her motherly instinct quickened her pace. But she was not prepared for what she saw the next morning.

In order to draw water for the children's breakfast, she had to walk around the outside of the front dormitory to the well in the front yard of the compound. And there, she encountered a Mai-Mai woman. *A very dirty woman, a woman wearing charms.* As Aphonsine worked the handle of the well, the woman boasted, "I am the strongest! There is not a man here who can stand and fight with me!" Alphonsine shuddered and skittered back to her side of the compound as fast as she could, trying not to slosh water from the bucket. Still, some splashes slipped over the side. The outside of the bucket was wet when she arrived at the rear dormitory.

Alphonsine whispered to Mama Mujing. "Have you seen her?"

Mujing nodded, her eyes focused on the onion she was chopping.

"Have you seen her powerful charm?"

Mujing nodded again and diced the onion carefully.

"Isn't it sad? What about love, and mercy, and all the ways we care for children? These are the things that go with being a woman. But to brag about fighting and killing—it's contrary to what we should hear from her."

"Such a woman could do anything. We will pray for the children's food, that our God will keep it safe."

As days went on and Alphonsine caught glimpses of Chinja-Chinja and the woman, she asked herself, which was worse? To imagine the evil he had done, or hers?

During the next week, when she walked back and forth from Katuba parish to the orphanage, villagers stopped her. Had she seen him? What did he look like? Curiosity held the hand of fear, skipping down the lanes of Kamina, pulling some near, pushing away others who fled till the conference ended.

Hubert Returns Chinja-Chinja to Kalulu

> "We've Seen the Enemy and They are ...Who, Exactly?"
>
> *The New York Times*, October 17, 2004

> "While they were talking about this, Jesus himself stood among them and said to them, 'Peace be with you.'"
>
> Luke 24: 36

Kamina to Kalulu

September 2004

No one, including Pastor Kabongo, wanted to accompany Chinja-Chinja back to his village. But Hubert had seen him around Kamina and had interacted with him. *All has gone so well.* He felt reassured that nothing dangerous would happen. *Compared to the first time, this will be relaxing.* Chinja-Chinja and his followers must have agreed: when time came to return, they had no need for charms.

So Hubert proceeded, driving at night with Chinja-Chinja and his retinue, singing, telling stories, joking and laughing along the way. At six a.m. they arrived in Kalulu, the village of a thousand Mai-Mai living in thatched roof houses surrounded by palm trees.

Chinja-Chinja and his party emerged from the car. At the sight of them, Mai-Mai ran toward the car. The men shouted and the woman ululated. "Chinja-Chinja, our king, lives! He is home!"

News travelled. Mai-Mai filled the space between the car and the hut. They welcomed the travellers, leading them toward the village. Chanting. Singing. Beating drums. Dancing. The ground shook. The great confusion evolved into a joyous celebration.

"Hubert, stay with us! Spend the night!"

When Hubert told his wife that he was, again, driving Chinja-Chinja, she pled in fear—"Do not spend the night!" So as the followers of Chinja-Chinja smoked and drank and celebrated, Hubert slipped into his Land Rover and slid onto the road in the direction of Kamina.

Kebi Konkeka Disbands His Mai-Mai Warriors

"Foes of the Death Penalty Making Gradual Gains in Africa"

The New York Times, October 20, 2004

"In the last days it will be, God declares,
that I will pour out my Spirit upon all flesh,
and your sons and your daughters shall prophesy,
and your young men shall see visions,
and your old men shall dream dreams."

Acts 2:17

Late September 2004

Kebi Konkeka, a Mai-Mai commander whose name meant "pulverizing in a crucible, like a woman crushes cassava into flour," sat alone in his hut, pondering the report he had just heard from the delegates he had sent to the peace conference in Kamina. He himself did not attend, as his ancestors had warned him to stay away. But the word had spread—Maccabee had sent delegates, Bakande Bakoka was there, Chinja-Chinja was coming—so Kebi Konkeka sent his leaders. He needed to hear first hand, from his own people, what was happening. As soon as they returned to Kipusha, his stronghold outside Kabongo, they described the government offer.

"The war has finished. The government says, we would like Mai-Mai and soldiers to be one, so that we can have peace in our country. So we are going to do this: Mai-Mai will not operate, Congolese army will not operate. We are going to integrate, create one army."

"Wafwako. I will consult my ancestors and let you know what we will do next."

Kebi Konkeka commanded many warriors—not as many as Bakanda Bakoka, Maccabee, or Chinja-Chinja—but enough to make him a strong Mai-Mai commander. He controlled his territory. But the balance of power was shifting. He could gain much by taking a command in the Congolese army.

What would his ancestors advise? He stood, resolutely, to walk to the forest to divine their will.

* * *

In the forest Kebe Konkeka reviewed his militia's whole history and placed his current dilemma before his ancestors.

Elders had called a meeting with those who were strong in the village: let's make a group that can be against these people. With ritual washing we will create a traditional barrier around us; when the Rwandese attack the population, we will arrest them. So we resisted the invasion of Katanga.

Then the defense of villages became offense against Rwanda. They started arriving at Kipusha, outside Kabongo. We started attacking them. They came with sophisticated guns. We fought them with sticks and bows and arrows and even our hands. But we kept our traditions: we shouted Mai-Mai and their bullets did not hurt us. Our ancestors kept us safe.

When we captured them, we discovered that all this area was already sold to Rwandese. Yes. Kabongo territory and Kamina Base were already sold.

We attacked them and they ran a little bit. When they retreated, we found Congolese soldiers fighting us! This is how we started, Mai-Mai and Congolese soldiers. And we discovered that Congolese soldiers were looting, doing bad things to the population. We as Mai-Mai discovered that these people are doing such things as they are not true Congolese.

When the war started, we were in one group—Maccabee, Bakanda Bakoka, Chinja-Chinja, Kebe Konkeka. A group went to the border and fought with Rwandese. When they came back, people of other territories came, took the movement their village. We selected strong commanders who could lead their people. Some people were in contact with their ancestors. And so the Mai-Mai spread in Katanga.

Security people came to our group from the government, taking information, and going with it to Congolese soldiers. And we discovered, this security of the government, instead of collaborating with us, it creates a certain kind of conflict among ourselves. So we rejected them, the messengers from the government. We didn't have a prison or a jail. There was no way to arrest them. We had to kill them.

We asked the people from the villages to bring their charms to fight the rebels. But some were doing witchcraft against us. They broke our tradition and our taboos. They made us vulnerable to bullets. So they were the first rebels: we were obliged to fight and even kill, to weaken their charms.

You, my ancestors, were telling us not loot, not to take wife of other person, to be in unity.

We kept the tradition, more important than everything. Now, what should we do?

* * *

Kebe Konkeka stood before his primary leaders. "You reported from the Kamina conference, a plan for peace. Our purpose was peace in Congo, so when I heard that word I was very happy and accepted that.

"I have consulted my ancestors. I am obliged to neutralize the power we were given from them. To become Mai Mai, we drank, we washed our bodies. This created a certain kind of a barrier. So now, before we leave that world, we will have another ceremony. And then, you will return to your families."

They disbanded, as did other Mai-Mai militias.

Chapter VII

Peacebuilding after the Mai-Mai Conference
(October 2004 and following)

Historical Introduction

Many witnesses reported that the Mai-Mai Conference pacified the Mai-Mai threat around Kamina, Kabongo, Kaboto, and areas controlled by the Mai-Mai leaders who attended the conference. Most importantly, the roads and paths opened for commerce, so that villagers could walk and bike freely to sell their produce or fish at market. Bicycle ambulances now brought sick people to hospitals in Kabongo and Kamina without fear of harassment. Mai-Mai from the inland areas of North Katanga integrated into the army and took formal military training or demilitarized to village life. Now, when the world heard about Mai-Mai activity, it mainly arose from the Kivu provinces and the northern Great Lakes regions.

Witnesses differed in their assessment of Chinja-Chinja's continued influence on Mai-Mai activity. Some villagers believed he had mended his ways, but government officials reported that he moved on and attempted to create a new Mai-Mai following. The government could not allow a Mai-Mai problem that had been pacified to re-emerge. In April 2005 Chinja-Chinja travelled to Kinshasa intending to meet with President Kabila. The government arrested and imprisoned him, where he remains at this writing. In retaliation, five journalists were captured and then released by his followers. Some local people believe that he was betrayed.

Meanwhile, work remained for the church in reconciliation and rebuilding of the North Katanga areas. Food continued to be both a potential source of conflict and one that symbolized peace and reconciliation. "To feed my people" carried literal, symbolic, and spiritual meanings.

Reconciling Families and Congregations in Kalemie and Moba

> "Africans Pick Congo Leader, Not Sudanese, For Union Post"
>
> *The New York Times*, January 25, 2006

> "Taking the five loaves and the two fish, he looked up to heaven, and blessed and broke the loaves, and gave them to the disciples, and the disciples gave them to the crowds. And all ate and were filled; and they took up what was left over of the broken pieces, twelve baskets full. And those who ate were about five thousand men, besides women and children."
>
> Matthew 14:13-21

Kalemie and Moba

January 2006

The plane bumped to a stop on Kalemie's landing strip. Pastor John Mutombo, now graduated from Africa University, turned to his partner, Pastor Kitenge Lumaliza Joseph, and tried to offer a reassuring smile that was betrayed by a bit of wrinkle in his brow. *What should they expect next?*

Bishop Ntambo's only detailed communication from the churches in Kalemie in five years had come through displaced persons arriving in Kamina. Kalemie had been targeted by the rebels early on as it was a strategic gem. An area rich in mineral mines, it also offered transportation—the railroad linked to this major port on Lake Tanganyika. After the 2002 peace agreement, the Rwandan army had delayed its departure until the Congolese government gave it an ultimatum. The people had experienced the earliest and latest stages of Africa's World War. Furthermore, Kalemie had been terrorized by four different Mai-Mai groups who occupied nearby villages.

Bishop Ntambo had thought John Mutombo and Pastor Kitenge well suited to make the first post-war contact with the church in Kalemie. John excelled as a pastor and diplomat: he took note of his surroundings before speaking and acting; he listened carefully and spoke wisely. Pastor Kitenge, educated in Kinshasa, offered erudition: he knew history and current events well and could teach on the spur of the moment. From his experiences in the refugee camps in Bukavu, Bishop Ntambo knew the importance of a pastor capable of deep compassion; as North Katanga's religious educator, he also believed in the value of one who could teach. He sent John and Kitenge as his ambassadors, to visit the churches, to hear their stories, and to determine whether it was safe for him to visit in person.

John and Kitenge arrived in Kalemie on one of the first commercial flights from Lubumbashi after the end of the war. Now, some passengers screeched with excitement; in a few minutes they expected to be reunited with family members. Business people stood, silent and expectant; they anticipated negotiating new trade routes for their wares.

John and Kitenge rose from their seats. They crammed into the airplane aisles behind the other passengers, slowly working their way to the open door.

As they peered down the stairs to the crowd waiting on the cracked concrete below, John's spirit leapt. There, waving and smiling, stood Pastor Kalenga Ngombe, John's ninth grade teacher, now Kalemie's district superintendent. John reached the bottom of the stairs and Kalenga grasped his hand.

"*Wafwako, Eyo-vidye!*" John's voice broke with excitement.

Behind Kalenga a milling crowd of gaunt church people danced, hands raised, waving, ululating, singing.

"Where is Bishop Ntambo? We heard he is coming."

"We are his representatives. He will come but not on this trip."

We need to do something. John reached into his pocket, drew out his cell phone, and dialed Bishop's number.

"Bishop, they were expecting you. You need to talk to them." He pressed 'speakerphone' and held the phone facing the crowd.

Bishop's voice squeaked, loud enough for Kalenga and those at the front of the crowd to hear. "These are my representatives, coming before me, preparing for my visit. I am very concerned to hear all about you through them. Be strong, have hope!"

* * *

After several days of listening to the tales of members and congregations, John lay prone in the dark, feeling his own weight, stretching his legs, shaking away the tension. It was as if his body had absorbed all of the stories and now they saturated every pore, congesting his heart with a great sadness. Their words circled round and round in his head, unwilling to depart, to leave him in peace. Behind the congregants' complaints droned the words: *Désolé, désolé.*

Neighbors accused neighbors of betrayal. "Our father was caught by rebels, killed in the presence of children, with *that neighbor there*, spying, pointing. We know who was leading, the one who was giving direction."

Or, fingers pointed at children. "Among the soldiers that came from Rwanda, even *their children* were involved. We saw a boy who was wearing a combat uniform who came to bash our door. *That boy* who came to shoot *this boy* here,"—pushing their son forward— "and came to shoot the husband."

And, parents were accused of protecting children's wartime betrayals. "Because he is mine I support him." And others said, "How can a Christian like him know what his son was doing and defend him?"

As word spread of John's compassion, women whispered of being raped. "The time I was raped *this fellow* came with soldiers and pointed at my door. I saw him, *with my eyes*. The soldiers came and attacked me, and I was raped by maybe ten soldiers."

Many refused to attend church if their neighbors were present. "We like our church, but we don't like *that one*. His son was involved in the conflict; he was Mai-Mai. He's the one who *did this*, who cut *that one*."

"No, we can't talk to *them*."

"We will withdraw, we will not tolerate *such a group*."

And some blamed Bishop and his representatives for not providing tangible assistance. "You are representing Bishop. You come from a part of Congo that did not experience war. What have you brought us? We are suffering. We have nothing, not even enough food to eat."

Many of their conflicts, John realized, were rooted in their poverty. The Congolese church, strained to the limit, had little left to give.

* * *

Meanwhile, Kitenge held public workshops to communicate Bishop's message. "Through Bishop the church is working to unify our country. Here, in this picture, you see Kamisamba Farm: the soldiers are demobilized, they have given away their arms. The church is giving them hoes to cultivate.

"People, we need to live in union and to accept one another, including our differences. And for cities and villages, peace is a project we have in common." Pastor Kitenge, the professor, invoked Jean Jacques Rousseau. "Live freely, live the life of justice and peace with the neighbor. Understand each other, tolerate, forgive."

* * *

As they talked to more and more people, they discovered that the conflict involved not only the church but the entire community.

Inland, around Kabongo, villagers, soldiers, and Mai-Mai fought over the crops. Here on Lake Tanganyika, John discovered that many festering wounds began with fishing. These disputes were magnified by drugs.

"I went to fish with *that person*, I got to know drugs. When I take drugs, I feel no cold. I can see clearly, with strength. Friends smoke with friends. Smokers walk around in groups, ten, twenty. They welcome rebels, soldiers, Mai-Mai as liberators. There is no education, no training, no future—so it is exciting when as a young man you can carry their loads or spy for them. They give you guns and combat gear. You feel powerful. Now, not only are you ready for war, you can settle your personal accounts. 'When I went to buy donuts over there, *that woman* did not give me a lot of money back. Now she will see!' '*That woman*, I liked her, but she did not want me. Now that I have the combat gear, I'll show her!'"

The problems, John and Kitenge realized, might not have anything to do with the war, but the townspeople used the means of war to satisfy their desires for revenge. They had violated women, shot men. And once they raped and killed, they felt that they could do it again.

But now, people had become exhausted by conflict. They were prepared to give up their animosities. Every day John and Kitenge reported to Bishop. People hungered for talk of reconciliation; talk of peace energized them.

Meanwhile, hearing the reports, Bishop called Kinshasa to make sure the government officials were aware of what John and Kitenge were doing. Enthusiasm as easily fueled suspicion as peace. Who knew what was being said, through whom, in what network? He did not want the government in Kinshasa to mistake the activity in Kalemie for a new rebellion.

* * *

As John listened to the people, his sermon began to form. On Sunday morning he told the story from Matthew 26: 36-46 in this way.

"Jesus was in the garden of Gethsemane, enduring his agony, before he was taken to be crucified. The three disciples who went with him had fallen asleep. He wondered, 'Why can't you stay awake to pray with me?' He thought, 'I brought these people for one mission, but they did another one.' And then he saw people were coming to attack him. He said, 'No, there is nothing left do. Let's stand and go together.' Jesus lived beyond the conflict, beyond the disappointment. He looked at his attackers as brothers and sisters.

"I have heard what you people have experienced. War is not such a pleasurable experience. People, your neighbors, your own family—they did such wrong things. But do you follow the example of Jesus? To follow Jesus, say, 'let's stand and go together. Forgive and forget.'

"And Jesus and the disciples went together till Peter was shocked—then he cut the soldier's ear. But Jesus said, 'No, I prepared in prayer, not physically. If it was about power and might, I could ask to my father to send legions. But all I have to do here is to stand with others. To go with whomever, even the one who did wrong things.'"

He and Kitenge had met people with bony faces, numbed agony or fiery anger in their eyes, timid and overly-gripping handshakes. Such suffering! In the call to forgiveness in the church, thirty-six people had come forward, ready to live a new life with their neighbors. The hearts of the townspeople, nearly dead, had been quickened by hope.

At the end of their time in Kalemie the pastors wanted to celebrate communion in the community. But some would have been excluded because of theological differences. So instead, the women cooked, and the community ate peacefully, together. *Kujatalala ekwabana biya.*

* * *

Bishop's call to Kinshasa, the report of his peacebuilders on the ground in Kalemie, and the positive response of the townspeople led to an invitation from the government. Would John and Kitenge sponsor workshops in Moba, so townpeople, rebels, Congolese soldiers, even officials from Kinshasa could talk together? Samba Kaputo, a Roman Catholic and local member of Parliament from Moba and special advisor to Joseph Kabila, offered to be the local host. He wanted to invite everybody—traditional chiefs, military, government officials.

When John and Kitenge arrived in Moba, townspeople sang and cheered, as in Kalemie. Samba Kaputo introduced them to Moba's members of the Ministerial Alliance of Pastors. Leaders of Pentecostals, Baptists, Charismatics, Presbyterians, the Assemblies of God, and the imam, Selemani Mwenye Nvua, all wanted to participate. The religious leaders met and formed a plan for different workshops that each would lead.

While John worked behind the scenes with individuals and families, Kitenge and others taught classes that proposed a vision for the war-torn communities. They agreed: even as the church, they needed to teach people about politics, about the project of building a good society.

On their last day in Moba, the women brought food to church, and that day, everyone ate enough. The townspeople had shared their sufferiing, and little by little, the trauma they experienced was aired. After villagers spoke words of forgiveness, others in the community offered blessings. The choirs from the churches sang. Their roofs still leaked in the rainy season and their children still hungered, but for this day, the whole community feasted, in body and soul. The traditional chiefs presented white lime to John and Kitenge.

* * *

After their long trip John and Kitenge reported back to Bishop. Kitenge held up a book with its hand-drawn cover.

"I'm writing a book entitled *The Christian Sense of Politics*. Here you can see Bishop preaching to the whole nation and the message is the cross. If we understand the cross we can agree to live together"—then he paraphrased Galatians 3:28— "'there is no Jew, no Greek.'"

He flipped though the pages. "John is in this book and he is saying, 'we have the body and the spirit.' We are teaching about health, malnutrition and hygiene. On this page, you see the aspect of development. Soldiers are there, politicians are there. Bishop is stimulating government to promote agriculture. The churches come with all this. People will be busy, each one doing his work. Nobody will create a conflict with his friend. The church is interested in all this, so security is there, and freedom, and when everything is in place, we will have peace."

* * *

John visited his elderly mother to tell her about their mission to Kalemie and Moba. She sat before him, her hands pressed together as if in prayer. "Remember that, before, I was a hopeless first wife, unable to conceive a child. Even though your father's second and third wives had given him children, your father still loved me. And when I was old, you were conceived. You lived, born on Christmas day. And so it will be in Kalemie and Moba—even though all hope was lost and the land seems barren, something new, something special, will rise. It is God's way."

Repelling the M-23

> "Autocratic Leaders Who Improve Their Countries"
>
> *The New York Times,* opinions about Paul Kagame,
> September 19, 2012

> "When the Philistine drew nearer to meet David, David ran quickly towards the battle line to meet the Philistine. David put his hand in his bag, took out a stone, slung it, and struck the Philistine on his forehead; the stone sank into his forehead, and he fell face down on the ground."
>
> 1 Samuel: 17

New York, Ottawa and Washington, D.C.

September 2012

Gazing absent-mindedly at the buildings of Manhattan from the window of his new office at 475 Riverside Drive in New York City, Guy Mande Muyombo, who now preferred to be called by his Congolese name, Mande, pressed the phone receiver to his ear, listening carefully to the report he was hearing from his friend who worked at the United Nations. The journey that began with leading music and supervising hydraform brick making in Kamina had just taken him to New York City. In early August Mande had begun his new position as Executive Secretary for Africa at the United Methodist General Board of Global Ministries.

Preparing for this work, he took care to follow political developments throughout the continent. Now, he had regular contact with all of the African bishops, in addition to Bishop Ntambo, in the crises and opportunities they faced. In his position he vowed to be impartial and not favor the DRC. But he followed Congolese politics in detail, and his contact at the United Nations fed him accurate, inside information faster than any African internet service. The news from eastern Congo caused him great concern. Between March and the end of August the Congolese government and army had been unable to quell the rebellion of the M-23.

In 1998 so many rural Katangans had naïvely disbelieved the rumors of war—certainly, they had thought, the fighting at the border of the DRC and Rwanda could not reach the interior. Before it was over, Africa's World War had devastated two-thirds of the country. When on March 23, 2012, a new group of rabble-rousers troubled Goma, Katangans took the matter seriously. The explosive potential at the border with Rwanda stirred their memories; the ghosts of the years following 1998 haunted their dreams.

Rwanda seemed to be backing the M-23, as the movement was now called, and some in the international community had caught on to Rwanda's pretense. Enough was enough. The Kabila government requested help from religious leaders and civil society—this time, in international relations. A million Congolese had signed a petition pleading for peace. The Kabila government organized a delegation of thirty religious and civil society leaders to present the petition to the General Secretary of the United Nations and then visit their respective contacts in North America and Europe, asking them to become witnesses for peace in Congo.

Bishop Ntambo had called Mande in New York. He would need a point person to organize meetings in New York City through the ecumenical Church's Center for the United Nations and in Washington, D.C through the United Methodist General Board of Church and Society.

Mande thought often of the day he had disobeyed his father who feared he was throwing away his future by moving to Kamina. Mande had followed God, and he had eventually left professional music behind. Instead, he opted for politics. He had finished a Masters degree in Peace and Justice at Africa University in Zimbabwe, completing two theses, one on the church's response to the Mai-Mai and the other on the United Nations. He had returned to Kamina to direct Kamina Methodist University, and, a year or so later, he landed the position at the Africa desk. From there, he carefully promoted the church's social justice activities throughout Africa. He was midway through completing his low residency doctor of ministry degree at Saint Paul School of Theology in Kansas City, Missouri. Now, the politics of the DRC legitimately commanded his immediate attention. He began to call his contacts in church agencies in New York and Washington, D.C.

* * *

Bishop Ntambo's cheerful, enthusiastic voice boomed on Raymond Mande's cell phone. "President Kabila is organizing a delegation of religious and civil society leaders to present the Congolese petition for peace in New York City.

Bishop Djomo, representing the Roman Catholic Church, will lead the delegation. I will represent the United Methodists. Dr. Mande, I have been authorized to invite you, as a university president, to represent civil society."

Much had changed in Dr. Raymond Mande's life since the day he proposed to the new Bishop Ntambo that he could undertake the organization of his episcopal office and then, during the war, organized the shipment of supplies for Bishop's building projects and for displaced persons' relief from his office in Lubumbashi. After the war, he had resigned as the Bishop's assistant in order to become an administrator at the University of Lubumbashi. But he and Bishop Ntambo remained fast friends. Then, he had been chosen as head of *L'Institut supérieur de commerce* in Lubumbashi. There, he had supervised the rebuilding of the campus. His success was known to the government. He had developed the kind of profile that allowed his appointment to such an important delegation.

* * *

Thirty men and women, representing the eleven regions of the DRC, landed in New York in September 2012. The timing couldn't have been worse. The General Secretary of the United Nations, Ban-Ki-Moon, was travelling in Asia. The United States Congress was not in session, as the Democrats were busy at their party's convention to nominate President Barack Obama for a second term. Senator Romeo Dallaire, the head of the United Nations Peacekeeping mission during the Rwandan genocide, had left his usual Montreal office for travel in western Canada.

Still, the delegation presented its petition at the United Nations, and the delegation that remained in the United States and Canada—Bishop Ntambo, Bishop Djomo, Dr. Raymond Mande, Emma Selamani, a representative of civil society from Kalemie, and Mr. Santiti, a Roman Catholic reporter—spoke with groups at the Church's Center for the United Nations, the United Methodist Women's Division, and the Society of Friends in New York. Through their partners at the United Methodist General Board of Church and Society, they presented their case to congressional aides in Washington, D.C. Then they addressed religious leaders in Toronto, and through the ecumenical social justice group KAIROS, arranged for a visit with the Canada's foreign policy office in Ottawa. Everywhere, they repeated their message, passionately, but calmly.

Shortly after their visit to Canada, they were elated to read the statement issued on September 14, 2012 by then-foreign affairs minister John Baird:

> Canada condemns the actions of the armed group known as M23, which is committing horrific abuses against civilians including forced recruitment, summary executions and rape. . . .We are extremely concerned by continuing allegations of Rwandan support

of M23 and urge the immediate cessation of any form of assistance. . . Canada will continue to press regional actors, including
during the upcoming Summit of La Francophonie in Kinshasa, to
protect civilians, including women and children, and to pave the
way for peace and stability in eastern Democratic Republic of
Congo and the Great Lakes region.

Bishop Ntambo, Raymond Mande and Mama Selamani heard this news as they
prepared to travel back to Washington, D.C. There, their pleas to Congressional
aides and the behind-the-scenes work of their partners at the United Methodist
Board of Church and Society had produced a major achievement. Bishop
Ntambo was invited to testify as part of a panel addressing the Subcommittee
on Africa, Global Health, and Human Rights of the Committee on Foreign Affairs of the House of Representatives of the 112th Congress of the United States,
on the subject "Examining the Role of Rwanda in the DRC Insurgency."

In the introduction to the panel Representative Chris Smith, Republican
from New Jersey, noted that in June 2012, the United Nations Expert Panel had
verified that "Rwandan Defense Minister James Kabarebe and other top military officers played a central role in organizing, funding and arming the muti-
neers in Eastern Congo." For the panel, Mark Schneider of the International
Crisis Group and Jason Stearns of the Rift Valley Institute provided data collected by international observers.

Bishop Ntambo provided something different: the passion of a local Congolese leader who had absorbed the suffering of his people by identifying with
them from the inside out. Once again, Raymond Mande had put his pen to work
on behalf of Bishop, co-authoring Bishop's prepared statement.

* * *

Name: Ntambo Nkulu Ntanda

Title: Resident Bishop of United Methodist Church in North Katanga Episcopal Area, Kamina/DR Congo

Date: September 19, 2012

"House Committee on Foreign Affairs, Subcommittee on Africa,
Global Health and Human Rights."

Mr. Chairman and distinguished Members of the Subcommittee:

It is a privilege and honor for me to be invited to your distin-
guished House to witness on the situation of war going on in the
Democratic Republic of the Congo on its Eastern border with
Rwanda. . . .

We did not come to represent the Congolese government nor did we come to declare war on Rwanda. Our approach does not seek to harm Rwanda in any form of action but to denounce its wrong-doings reflected in its constant killings and rapes of our people. For two decades, Rwanda has been attacking the DR Congo, by fabricating all sorts of rebels and militia groups, changing one name to another. The Rwandan regime must stop attacking our country, the DR Congo and our people, especially women, children and young men who are victimized and inflicted any kinds of debasement.

We have come to you Americans because we know who you are: you have power, you have strong voice and have all means to stop this war. You love us as we love you.

. . . . We can picture the tragic 9/11 event in New York. It was atrocity, terror, cries and tears, death, fear and destruction. Many children lost their parents and spouses lost their beloved ones. This situation brought Americans to be united as one to fight the enemy and all acts of terrorism. Seemingly, 09/11 and terrorism are going on every day in the Democratic Republic of Congo. . . .

Our people are in tears; there are cries, killing, atrocities of all kinds and poverty leaving behind orphans, widows, children without education. The situation of the women is catastrophic, no respect of the women who have become the battlefield; women are systematically raped and infected with HIV/AIDS. Some are mutilated, buried alive or inflicted fissures. Knives and rifle cannons are introduced for pleasure in the genitals of the women just as acts of sabotage and debasement of the women. Pregnant women have their womb opened wide with any kind of knife or machete to see the fetus inside. Raped women are rejected by their spouses and by society, they become victims twice in their body and in the community.

We strongly denounce this situation and call for justice. . . .for 800,000 people killed during the genocide in Rwanda, the international community, including America, feels guilty and has given all the means of the world to Rwanda and its leadership, but for the 6,000,000 that Rwanda has killed in Congo there is not even compassion from the international community, including America. Where is justice? We come to ask America to stop this war and to do justice to the DRC and to the Congolese people. We ask

America to stop barbarisms of Rwanda in the DRC, by telling Rwanda to stop. . . .

Peace in the Democratic Republic of the Congo will also be peace in Rwanda and in the region. The people of Congo and the people of Rwanda live together, marry mutually, school together and do shopping together from one side to another of our border. The evil comes from Rwandan Leadership for the reason of evil.

In the name of "The Responsibility to Protect" we demand America to stop this war because it is a nonsense war. If it is minerals that the multinationals want, we invite them to address the Congolese government . . . .It is disturbing that most of these US companies which buy the minerals are dealing directly with the Rwandan regime, knowing that most of the minerals do not have any trace in Rwanda but in the DR Congo. Accordingly, the smart phones are helping fund the wars in the DR Congo and contribute to the killing and raping of innocent children and Congolese women.

As for the genocide that took place in Rwanda in 1994, it was a result of an internal conflict between Hutus and Tutsis in Rwanda. It did not come from Congo. We wonder why Congo should pay this heavy tribute simply because of hosting Rwandan refugees on demand of the UN. So instead of the UN repatriating the Rwandan refugees for national reconciliation or dialog in Rwanda, in the contrary Rwanda attacks Congo and the International community closes the eyes. Congo needs justice as we believe in America and its institutions being defenders and advocacy of justice.

Mr. Chair, as established, the current war that Rwanda is fighting in the Congo is not ethnic-based as suggested before but resource-based.

On this token, we would like to take you back to the bill you passed in this house in 2006 known as "Democratic Republic of Congo Relief, Security, and Democracy Promotion Act of 2006." Through this bill you reiterated the important geo-strategic position of the DR Congo, not only in Africa but the world. You committed yourselves to support the post-conflict DR Congo into a peaceful and prosperous country with strong institutions. We are so grateful for the support you provided and continue to provide in the organizations of our first ever democratic elections and the ongoing peacekeeping efforts through the United Nations Mission for the Stabilization of the DR Congo, which mission we request that it be not only limited to observing but also mandated to intervene any time to protect the population and eradicate the armed bands that bring disasters in the region and help arrest the criminals who find refuge in Rwanda (Bosco Ntanganda, Nkunda Batware, Mutebushi, etc.)

We are grateful for your efforts directed at strengthening governmental institutions and building a strong military in the DR Congo, and for the many American mission programs which are working in DR Congo in the area of health, education, poverty eradication and capacity building programs thanks to USAID.

Certainly, such progress cannot be sustainable if the Rwandese regime continues to destabilize the DR Congo and exploit minerals such as Coltan, gold and killing the rare animal species that the DR Congo has protected (Gorillas, Okapi).

In reference to the Democratic Republic of Congo Relief, Security, and Democracy Act of 2006 in its section 105, it is indicated:

"The Secretary of State is authorized to withhold assistance made available under the Foreign Assistance Act of 1961(22 U.S.C.2151 et seq.), other than humanitarian, peacekeeping, and counterterrorism assistance, from a foreign country if the Secretary determines that the government of the foreign country is taking actions to destabilize the Democratic Republic of Congo."

All evidences corroborate the fact that Rwanda is indeed working for the destabilization of the DR Congo, so why is this provision of the bill not being implemented? This is the cry of the Congolese people, we strongly believe that such a move will push the Rwandan regime to stop fabricating and arming the rebel groups and engage dialog for deep reconciliation within Rwanda.

As religious leaders and civil society, we live at the grassroots level, we see the suffering of the people. The US and the world have the responsibility to protect Congolese people. Rwanda should cease to behave as a spoilt child. We believe in the US justice.

God bless America, God Bless the people of Congo.

Washington, September 17th, 2012

Reporting for the Church Leaders and Civil Society

  Mgr Ntambo Nkulu Ntanda

Record Keeping

Prof. Mande Mutombo Mulumiashimba

* * *

The United Nations General Assembly convened on September 18, 2012, and both President Joseph Kabila of the Democratic Republic of Congo and President Paul Kagame of Rwanda attended. UN Secretary General Ban-Ki Moon organized a special roundtable to review Rwanda's support for the M-23 in the DRC. Pressure against Kagame came from protesters on the street and his traditional allies in the meeting. When he was accused of supporting the atrocities committed by the M-23, Kagame notoriously left the meeting. Shortly thereafter, Rwanda began to withdraw its support, and Goma was freed from rebel control. But the threat of the M-23 slinks around the Great Lakes border, ready to seize its opportunity when the international world turns its attention in other directions.

The Ongoing Work of Constructing Peace

"Congo: Fighters Quit, U.N. Says"

The New York Times, January 14, 2014

"The hand of the Lord came upon me, and he brought me out by the spirit of the Lord and set me down in the middle of a valley; it was full of bones. He led me all around them; there were very many lying in the valley, and they were very dry. He said to me, 'Mortal, can these bones live?' I answered, 'O Lord GOD, you know.' Then he said to me, 'Prophesy to these bones, and say to them: O dry bones, hear the word of the Lord. Thus says the Lord GOD to these bones: I will cause breath to enter you, and you shall live. I will lay sinews on you, and will cause flesh to come upon you, and cover you with skin, and put breath in you, and you shall live; and you shall know that I am the Lord.'"

Ezekiel 37:1-6

Throughout Katanga
January 2014

Gaston paced around the Cessna Grand Caravan, visually inspecting the craft, looking for any possible problem, as he did before every flight. Just six months earlier, after a major fundraising campaign in the United States, the church had replaced the little six-seat Cessna 172 with Gaston's dream—a fourteen-seat, jet-fueled plane. He no longer needed purchase av-gas in Zambia, a process that required visas and permits that consumed time, created anxiety, and produced trepidation when people relied on him. With the new Caravan he had modern instruments and computer capacity. He could transport far more medical supplies and people. Now, just a year and a half after he had flown the plane from the United States across the Atlantic, through Europe, and into the DRC, the upgraded plane and his own training safety record had made him the pilot of choice for an important peacemaking mission. For the sake of peace in Congo, he agreed to do what he had disavowed in 2004: to fly into hotspots potentially controlled by known, newly revived Mai-Mai militias.

His pre-flight routine usually provided him a time of centering, almost a moment of walking prayer. Still, this morning, his spiritual discipline failed to produce calm—his back cramped with tension. His thirteen esteemed passengers included some of the most important political figures in Katanga. His father, Bishop and Senator; Kwum wa Wanza, the president of assembly in Katanga province; Mbuyu, deputy national deputy; Kabongo, minister of health; Kabange, minister of sport; Kabanza Mulalie, minister of mining; Kabalulu, minister of transportation; Kaswashi, two lawyers of high rank in government, and two former governors, among them Dr. Kisula Ngoy.

* * *

In 2000 Bishop Ntambo had found it exciting to dedicate two new schools in Kamina; now, in his role as a Congolese Senator, President Kabila had asked him to supervise the construction of thirty new schools in Haut Lomami District of North Katanga. After the 2006 election, when President Kabila formed his new government, Bishop Ntambo had been elected by the general assembly to serve as Senator from Haut Lomami. With the grudging support of his family and despite criticism from colleagues in the Council of Bishops, he agreed to serve, hoping that from this position he could bring more development to Kamina and the rural villages of Haut Lomami than he could as bishop.

In April 2013 the government funded the construction of 1000 new schools. Bishop Ntambo and the church had been asked to supervise the construction schools in Kolwezi, Kamina territory, Bukama territory, Malemba territory, Kabongo territory, Kaniema territory, schools in villages as remote as Kitumi, Kibumbe, and Muhale, 1000 kilometers from Lubumbashi.

In January 2014 Bishop Ntambo had reported about the project's progress to President Kabila.

"School construction, going well."

Then, the President changed the subject.

"Bishop, I have a concern about our people. The fighting in Goma—those people are near Rwanda. But now my own people are fighting against me. I don't understand why. I can react as a president, ask government officials to arrest those people. Or I can send soldiers, but you know the way they will behave—people will be killed. And I don't like to be blamed or accused by my own people. I want you to take a team to do your best to calm them."

Kabila was referring to the recent uprising of a group of Mai-Mai known as Bakata-Katanga. They had fought in the countryside, and then, on December 31, 2012 and January 1, 2013 attempted a coup in Lubumbashi. Bishop had been at home and had listened to the gunfire in the city. He had worried that the violence could spread.

Now, Bishop felt honored to be asked to organize such an important mission for the President, and he was humbled by the responsibility on the delegation's shoulders. He had to believe in the success of the mission—he did not want to disappoint his President. Ninety-eight per cent of the country had been peaceful for many years. Congo had made progress that should not be reversed.

* * *

The team planned to fly from village to village in search of discontented Mai-Mai, many of whom were Luba, others, Bazila people. The team discussed transportation, and, together, they chose two airplanes—Gaston's, flying the important political figures, and one to follow with staff, bodyguards and supplies.

Gaston landed the team in Kamina and Kabongo: no Mai-Mai. So different than in 2004 when Mai-Mai controlled the Kabongo area. In Malemba they met a small group operating on the boundaries between Malemba, Moba, and Manono and, there, Bishop Ntambo was known.

"You other politicians, you are lying to us, you stole our things. Now, you have a man of God who is with you, and we trust that whatever you are telling us, it will be done."

In the work of reconciliation, to be a bishop is more important than to be a senator.

In Mitwaba, the home of the leader Muzila, who had influenced young people to be involved with the coup, they met four Bakata-Katanga. In Kabalo, the hometown of the Prophet Mukungubila, who had led the Lubumbashi coup attempt, none.

But in Manono, they met four hundred and seventy-five Bakata-Katanga. Here, they uncovered the problem that was giving rise to a new generation of Mai-Mai.

"First, we are fighting because of poverty. We are in the bush—no road, no salt, no soap, no school. How can we survive? Second, the harassment from soldiers. Wherever they go, they burn, loot and that makes people angry. We have to defend ourselves."

The women spoke for themselves. "The soldiers violate women. How can you allow soldiers to rape women and our husbands to look at us like this? We can't accept it. So we agreed with Muzila from Mitwaba who said: the time has come to change this government. Let's fight, kick out Kabila, take over, and when we win we will have prosperity."

Much had changed in the DRC, but in this rural area and others like it, the same problems dominated. The new generation knew the old response: assemble Mai-Mai.

Hearing their familiar pleas, Bishop Ntambo thought, *the work of development, the work of reconciliation walks hand-in-hand. Even 1000 schools, distributed around Congo, are not enough to reach each rural village.*

The delegation promised: "We'll talk to the president so the government can provide schools for your children and jobs for you—perhaps building roads. If we do that, will you stop the Mai-Mai or Bakata-Katanga behavior and return as normal persons loyal to the government?"

The man of God and the politicians had come and had listened. The Mai-Mai and the Bakata Katanga agreed: they had heard "a word of confidence" that the government would respond to their suffering.

* * *

"People are angry because the administration of the province is bad." The radio, the television, and the internet publicized the criticism: the former governor, Dr. Kisula Ngoy, they claimed, had loudly criticised the incumbent, Governor Katumbi Moise. The report of the trip that sought to unify the rural villages now divided the urban leadership. People took sides; accusations escalated.

In the halls of Parliament in Kinshasa, Ntambo greeted Katumbi, but Katumbi asked for a longer conversation. "Papa, Bishop, I need your assistance. I have problem with Kisula Ngoy. I can talk to him in your presence. I want you to come."

A few days later, Ntambo sat with the current and former governors in Katumbi's office. Both felt hurt and angry; both turned to Bishop, defending themselves. Slowly, the emotion dissipated and they began a more conciliatory conversation.

Katumbi Moise turned to Bishop. "This man, whenever I see him, I express all my respect to him. I don't know why he says this. Look what he said."

And then, Kisula Ngoy. "Well, Bishop, I am telling you. This man has great respect for me. Even in a crowd, he will come to greet me. And I have great respect for him. But what he heard from journalists is wrong. The journalists turned around the words."

Katumbi felt insulted; Kisula, misquoted. *They are looking at me now, for my reaction.*

"It's not between you. You have allowed outside people to control your relationship. As a result, look where you are. The way I look at it, you like one another. How many people in Katanga province were selected to become governor? This is divine providence. This is a gift from God, and you have been chosen. And everyone has done a great job.

"You, Kisula, you remember, if today we have peace in this Katanga province, it's your work, what you did with the Mai-Mai.

"You, Moise. You make Katanga province proud. Look what kind of job you are doing.

"In America today, Bush the father, Bush the son, Obama, Ford, Carter, they have a team of former presidents with the current president. The former governor can be your consultant. He can be your adviser.

"Kisula, when you start to speak bad language to this man, remember you were in this position. Whatever you say to him, it will turn back to you. Because you were there."

The mood of the meeting turned. The former governors asked for prayer; they both knelt. The three men shook hands. The shouting ended; a good relationship began.

* * *

Senator Ngoya Bijou had asked for the meeting, and Ntambo readily agreed. She welcomed him, her handshake warm, her eyes gleaming.

"Bishop, thank you for what you have done."

"What?"

"What you have done with Kisula and Moise. You made peace between these two people. This is what we are missing in this country. Because most of the people who go to seek Katumbi Moise, it's just to seek financial assistance. You as a man of God, you did it without any interest, without looking for money, just to make peace. We all say thank you to you. We are looking such kind of leadership in our midst.

"What do you think between Katumbi Moise and Muyambo? So those are key people. Muyambo used to be a minister, a leader of a political party, a very popular, very intelligent guy. He and Moise used to be great friends. They grew up together. Because of politics they started to accuse one another, to insult one another. Muyambo wrote four hundred pages insulting Moise, sharing all the bad things Moise has done in his life. It was a shame. They arrived to the point whether they were looking to kill one another.

"You are a man of God. How can you make peace between Kisula and Moise and not plan to seek reconciliation between Muyambo and Moise? Between Kisula and Moise, it's not as bad as what's going on between Muyambo and Moise. The situation is very bad, and it is not just hurting just them, it is hurting the whole Congo."

Ntambo knew it well. *People were making money from that conflict. They go to Muyambo, 'look look.' They give money, and their secretary uses it to send back stuff underground to the opposition. Moise has radio and television, Muyambo has radio and television. This one insulting the other on TV, national TV. These politicians fight each other in public: it's bad. As if John Kerry and Hillary Clinton were fighting each other. There are people close to starting a war in Katanga because everyone has his militia.*

Ntambo had eagerly accepted the challenge to gather the Mai-Mai in Kamina. Looking back, as the risk had unfolded he had realized that he had been naïve; still, it had been the right thing to do. He had known the consequences of not trying: more and more people would be killed.

He had willingly agreed to meet with Katumbi and Kisula: he had had good relations with both, and Katumbi had requested it. He had the trust of both men and the risk seemed small.

But to insert himself in Governor Katumbi's life, asking him to meet with an arch political rival? He hesitated.

"I don't know Muyambo and Muyambo doesn't know me very well. My main connection with Moise has to do with how we can develop North Katanga. Like building the market or the stadium. I never talk politics with him concerning people."

He weighed the risk. *And this is his primary enemy. He will look at me and think that I side with his opponent. I will lose that relationship with him.*

The risk, too great. "Please, don't ask me to do this. I want to just be the small person I am."

Then, in answer to his denial, it was as if Senator Ngoya Bijou held up a mirror. "I have prayed, Bishop, that you will do something. You are a man of God."

The conversation with Senator Ngoya pursued Bishop Ntambo the next few days. *This is my pastoral role. I'm not there to gain any money or please anybody but to reconcile people. Unless I play my role as a pastor, I am nobody.*

He told Senator Ngoya, "All right, I will try. But if they agree to meet, you must be present."

* * *

Moise and Ntambo had chatted about all their common concerns, like Ntambo's upcoming trip to Japan to address a group of students about peacebuilding. At the end of the conversation, he told the governor about the conversation with the senator in Kinshasa. As he did, Moise's face darkened, then hardened.

I'm in trouble. But having entered the river, Ntambo waded in deeper. "Looking back, you had a good relationship. Today, you fight, people are hurt, Congo is hurt." Then, he appealed to the governor's self-interest. "And in the future, if you collaborate well with this man, you will benefit politically. Two powerful politicians working together, if both parties are willing, they can support one another to win."

Moise agreed, so Ntambo pressed on. "Do you have peace when you are in conflict with someone? I think neither of you have peace. If you reconcile, you free your mind, peace comes, and you can sleep. Otherwise, you are suffering."

Moise doubted that Muyambo would meet with him. But Moise himself had softened. He had opened himself to the possibility of meeting with Mayumbo. "With all my respect to you, Bishop, OK, you may try. If it works, thank God. If not, it's ok. I know my opponent. Good luck. And call me."

* * *

Bishop called Muyambo and made the same arguments.

"Bishop, if this weren't coming from you, I would 'shoot the messenger' because I have received many hypocritical people. But, tell me what you want me to do. Do you think if I agree to meet Moise, he will agree to meet me?"

"Yes, that is what he told me. If you are willing to meet, I can convince him."

"OK, try to call him. I'm not sure he will agree."

Bishop called Moise, and Moise responded with appreciation. "I'm so happy that Muyambo agreed. To prove that, tell him that we will meet at your house!"

Not at his house, at your house! Good news. And calling Muyambo, Bishop reiterated: "Look what your friend said."

"To meet at your house, I agree. Let's meet at six."

* * *

The two political enemies and the two mediators, Bishop Ntambo and Senator Ngoya, settled into seats in Bishop's *payotte*. Moise and Muyambo sat stiff, erect, looking at Bishop and the Senator but not at one another.

This meeting began so differently than the meeting with Moise and Kisula. Bishop assessed the mood in the room. *If I give them the opportunity to accuse each other, I will lose ground. Let me go straight to the point.*

And so, rather than allowing them to air their grievances, Bishop spoke.

He began by reminding them where they began as young men and what they had achieved—their political contributions, their popularity. How blessed by God they were! How God uses chosen people to make peace—and *they* are chosen to make peace in Congo and in Katanga. He reminded them how much they have done for people with construction and development. Then he questioned—what is going on now? Can they see their province, their country, being hurt because of them? Their talents, their gifts, their strength creating hatred and conflict rather than building Katanga? They were losing ground, they were losing money, they were losing relationship.

He testified, watching their faces, timing his words, for about half an hour. When he believed he had hit the mark, he concluded.

"Time has come for you to think twice."

The two prominent men sat, tears in their eyes, a shadow across their cheeks, a vulnerability before one another softening their posture.

"You can ask God's forgiveness. You can ask each other's forgiveness."

And they did.

They swore that they would not make trouble for one another, that they would be friends and brothers, and that no one would come between them. And if someone tried, they could return to Bishop to resolve the problem.

In the rural village, the chief might have celebrated their reconciliation with the white lime; he might have marked the occasion of reconciliation with an axe, scarring a tree as a reminder of their vow. But here, sitting in Bishop's *payotte*, they prayed, securing their promise by offering it to God.

Conclusion

The Peace to Build

"U.N. Envoy Rice Faulted for Rwanda Tie in Congo Conflict"

The New York Times, December 11, 2015

> "The land that was desolate shall be tilled, instead of being the desolation that it was in the sight of all who passed by. And they will say, 'This land that was desolate has become like the garden of Eden; and the waste and desolate and ruined towns are now inhabited and fortified.' Then the nations that are left all around you shall know that I, the Lord, have rebuilt the ruined places, and replanted that which was desolate; I, the Lord, have spoken, and I will do it."
>
> Ezekiel 36: 34-36

Burlington, Ontario and Merrillan, Wisconsin
December 2015

In January 2008 I spent a month in Kamina documenting the story of rural, local religious peacebuilding emanating from the community that surrounded Bishop Ntambo. I decided write in such a way that the witnesses could speak for themselves and that the general, secular reader interested in Africa might meet the people I had encountered. As a scholar I formulated three premises:

- o *that contrary to the dominant image of Congolese people as victims or perpetrators of violence, many Congolese are leaders for peace;*
- o *that many such people live in the rural inland Congo, beyond the usual reach of western journalism, and*
- o *that Christian and indigenous religious motives ground their activities of peacebuilding and lead members of the community to risk their lives for peace.*

Over the next seven years I plumbed the stories I collected on this and subsequent research trips, and I read secondary literature on the war as it began to be published. I derived three overarching conclusions that are not yet part of the scholarly literature on "Africa's World War" in the DRC:

- o *that hunger feeds the conflict in rural Katanga and is underrepresented in the secondary literature as a source of violence in the DRC;*
- o *that Christian and indigenous spiritual traditions motivate local people to engage the dangerous work of peacebuilding. Western, secularized journalists, political analysts and conflict practitioners often bring stereotyped views of religion and spirituality to their interpretation of the culture and frequently fail to respect and explore the potential of this reality; and*

    o   *that the community in Kamina provides a case study of a complex, organic model of peacebuilding that might be replicable elsewhere.*

Both Congolese and western readers of the draft manuscript wanted a conclusion written from my perspective. I struggled: how do I write a conclusion that addresses both Congolese and western readers at the same time?

Ghosts and Spirits

On May 17, 2007 Bishop Ntambo and I sat in the dim light of the TGIF restaurant in the Indianapolis Airport, a tape recorder balanced on the table between us, planning the scope of this project and outlining the story of his community about the work of peace in Kamina. In that first interview, he characterized the Kamina he encountered in 1996 as a "ghost town." More than seven years after that conversation, on November 9, 2014, in my final interview with Dr. Raymond Mande Mutombo at the Renaissance Hotel in Pittsburgh, Pennsylvania, Dr. Mande returned to this metaphor, saying, "Ghost town. I'd say, this Bishop here is Bishop of the ghost town, the ghost people, the ghost city. Which means that the action undertaken for peacebuilding is to change this picture of ghost town, ghost people, into a city coming to life, as reported in Ezekiel 37 when the spirit of God brings the bones to life." I had already transformed my understanding of my role from ghost-writer to spirit-writer, but Dr. Mande now set the whole work of peacebuilding in the context of that metaphor. Bishop Ntambo's first and Dr. Mande's final comments frame this conclusion: In this story of rural Congolese people who transformed their victimhood into leadership for peace, what spirits have quickened the city, and what ghosts do they try to displace?

The Spectre of Hunger

Mobutu left the rural people of Katanga with aching stomachs, but the rise of Laurent Kabila offered new hope for a laden table. Then, when Rwanda and its allies invaded Katanga, villagers buried their possessions and fled for their lives, leaving their fields and their gardens to be harvested by soldiers and internally displaced people who followed. After gleaning food from fields or gnawing on roots and leaves, displaced people arrived in Kamina beyond the war but within the range of strained local food supplies. They ate, but not enough.

    Hunger lopes through these stories, emitting the eerie cries, knocks, and groans common to dead souls who cannot rest in peace. It alights on fields and gardens picked bare; it wanders down paths between villages connected by generosity, threat, demand and honor. It laughs at huts emptied. Works on the sources of "Africa's World War," representing macro-level dynamics in the

Great Lakes region, cite the international profit from trade in guns and minerals and longstanding ethnic hatreds. From a villager's microlevel perspective in rural Katanga, however, the war feeds on the food scarcity around which social practices hover.

Multiple witnesses in this project described a cycle of hunger-based violence that begins with unpaid Congolese soldiers. They ask villagers for food in return for the protection soldiers provide, as is their right, or so the norms of custom dictate. When soldiers return to the villagers day after day and their larders run low, the soldiers' request becomes a demand for the last of what the villagers have. Villagers resist and soldiers attack, looting and doing physical harm. Villagers suspect that some officers perpetuate the practice so they can pocket the money that the government has sent to feed the soldiers.

The idea that soldiers have a right to loot is not unique to the DRC or to Africa but has long existed within the practice of international warfare. It continues to exist where conditions have not created a prohibiting regime. This practice begins a chain reaction that reverberates through other forms of violence in the DRC.

Mai-Mai militias arose in the 1970s as a local defense against the raping and looting of "Mobutu's soldiers" and reemerged in the late 1990's to protect villages, first against the aggression of the Rwandan army and later from the looting by the Congolese military. But the Mai-Mai, too, were unpaid; they, too, told villagers that civilians must provide food in return for "protection"; they, too, conceived for themselves the right to "take" if they were not given; they too developed their own forms of currency in food and looted goods—so much so, that villagers reported that militia activity increased when villagers were harvesting their fields. The witness Mwilumba specifically noted that foreign soldiers allied with the DRC—Zimbabwean, Angolan and Namibian—did not terrorize civilians in this way.

Furthermore, the militias developed military-style checkpoints that offered another opportunity for extorting food. They expanded their power by creating barriers on the roads around Kabongo, places where they could demand payment in kind by villagers taking their food to another town to sell. Commerce halted, and checkpoints became a place of further violence.

Witnesses reported Congolese soldiers' and Mai-Mai militias' opportunism—to hedge their bets against their poverty, they developed relationships with their supposed foes. Early on, Congolese soldiers defected to Rwandan forces and, as tides turned, back to the Congolese army. Later, they developed enough contact with the Mai-Mai that, as Prophet Mechac denounced, an underground economy of looted food and other village goods in the rural bush mirrored the system of stolen minerals and gun trade documented in United Nations' expert reports on the Great Lakes region.

The rural victims of this violence picked their way through the bush, avoiding the major routes manned by soldiers and warriors. They came to Kamina as desperate people. From among them, religious leaders emerged to serve the population distributing aid, even as they, at the end of the day, signed their names to the list of the displaced and collected their own rations. They faced potential violence from those who, like the Israelites wandering in the wilderness, grumbled for food and complained against the local distributors.

These dynamics played out easily in a region where malnutrition was rampant and food scarce. In this context, the spirit of agricultural production at Kamisamba and other farms rises as a counter image. Food produced there fed orphaned children and widows during the war. At the Mai-Mai conference, the leaders built trust with the Mai-Mai by honoring local traditions—including eating together and eating in private—that communicated respect. In Kalemie and Moba, food celebrated the newly reconciled relationships. Experiments in teaching food production at Kamisamba Farm later became a model for projects at Kamina Military Base. Food builds and seals the spirit of trust and goodwill.

When people are fed and live in peace together, the Luba proverb *Kujatalala ekwabana biya*— "you will eat peacefully, when everybody received his portion of the share"— rings true, and the Christian miracle story of the feeding of the five thousand, which includes the eucharistic action of "taking, blessing, breaking, and giving" bread, reveals its foundation in the spirit of satisfying hunger that overcomes the ghost of food scarcity.

The Spirit of Luba and Christian Traditions

Spirituality and religion infuse the culture and lives of Congolese people, regardless of whether they practice indigenous religion, Christianity, or both. They instinctively fear and respect supernatural power; they trust and give authority to spiritual experience. Despite this commonality, people differ in the ways they call upon, think about, or integrate Luba tradition and Christianity. Only when westerners understand that Congolese people relate to the supernatural very differently than do people in secularized societies, yet lack a formal model for integrating indigenous and Christian experience, can westerners begin to conceive of the way *all decisions for violence or peace in the DRC have partial, if not entire, religious or spiritual motivations.*

Luba tradition, especially the role of the guidance of ancestors, enters the story in ways that provide justifications for both peace and violence. Western journalists tend to focus on the (for them, preposterous and magical) Mai-Mai belief that ritual washing provides protection in battle. But it would behoove westerners to understand ritual washing within the larger context of the advice and protection sought by ancestoral guidance. Mai-Mai and Christian witnesses reported that the Mai-Mai battled, participated in peace conferences, and disbanded their troops only if these actions were confirmed in ceremonies in which they received their ancestors' approval.

The interpretation of spiritual experience, in this and other situations, may depend upon the role and maturity of the interpreter. The wise, grandfatherly traditional chief Kanda-Fwanyinwabo, whom the community had vested with the responsibility for peace, is guided by the spirits of his ancestors to reject the Mai-Mai and to claim the young men of his villages from their clutches. But many Mai-Mai are young, under the influence of powerful drugs, heady with guns and power, and challenging both traditional chiefs and the military. Like young fundamentalists of any religion, they believe *they* are the true defenders and their elders have failed to 'keep tradition'. Those whom they deem infidels, the Mai-Mai attack. Indigenous spirituality, like Christianity and other religions, has no one answer to the question, "How does spirituality guide a practitioner's relationship to violence?" But more than in most secularized Christian countries, spirituality is at the heart of the decision.

Bishop Ntambo says of the intersection between Luba and Christian tradition, "It's easy for Africans to be Christians. We already have a deep sense of the Creator and the Spirit. Add Jesus, and we have the Trinity." To understand different forms of Christianity, however, one must ask: which understanding of Jesus Christ is being practiced?

Bishop Ntambo's Christianity follows the nonviolent Christology of Dr. Martin Luther King, Jr.—a fact that complexifies his relationship to 'colonial Christianity.' White evangelical missionaries provided the adolescent Ntambo's opportunity for education and the chance to study American leaders such as King, Franklin Delano Roosevelt, and John F. Kennedy. Out of his commitment to King's version of Christianity, Bishop Ntambo led his followers to embody a non-violent and risk-laden, rather than domesticated, form of Christology. In the words of Pastor Kabongo, as he tells his wife that he has agreed to try to meet Chinja-Chinja: ". . .before going I told my wife that everything can happen but as a pastor we are required to save people." And, as summarized by Pastor Ilgha Ilunga Monga:

> I think as a pastor we got a very big, a great mission, to spread the Gospel of God. . . . It is on the basis of that that we can build peace. Because, we always speak about love but it is still very difficult to experience it, to live it in our daily life. . . . once I see that I am poor and somebody waves money, they suggest to do evil, even to sell my own brother, I can sell. And that happened during wartime, we heard of some commanders who were selling those young soldiers, simply because they were corrupt. . . .Even to become politician it doesn't mean to be an evil doer. . . .still you know God

and you practice justice. There were many people in the Bible who
dealt together with politics and God. . . .they were upright, they
were declared upright because they were focusing on God. . . .It's
hard, it's a long journey, it requires. . .not only finances but also
prayer.

Throughout their work the community referenced Biblical passages that communicated the Luba experience. The Luba ministers at the court at Kinkunki,
in my original interview with them, stressed the similarity between their way
of life and the practices commended in Hebrew Scriptures. The songs of Guy
Mande Muyombo used the image of the moral obligations of the warrior in
Luba and Hebrew tradition. Pastor Kahunda, leading relief efforts, cited Matthew 25. In words and deeds, Christian leaders preached sermons about the
meaning of the Christian life, specifically the care for widows, orphans and
sojourners. Rather than 'putting on' a different, colonial religion, Luba Christians found their own indigenous cultural experience to be reflected in Christian
scripture. Indeed, the distance is much shorter between the setting of the Hebrew and Christian scriptures and life's demands as experienced in rural Katanga than the distance between those same scriptures and life in modern and
postmodern western societies.

The witnesses in this book present many different models for holding Luba
and Christian tradition together. Several characters, including Bishop Ntambo
and Mama Sila, reject traditional religion. Even though Bishop Ntambo personally eschews many of the beliefs and practices with which he was raised,
his cultural genius and connection to his rural village of origin leads him to
honor traditional ways. Because he understands their spiritual sensibilities, he
easily fulfills the role of trusted leader with warlords, military and government
leaders alike.

Likewise, his community derives their values and methods of advancing
peace from the symbols of local tradition as they communicate their Christian
vision. "White lime" figures significantly into the mandate for peace given to
the *mulopwe* or *muholwe,* the traditional leader or chief, as it does in ceremonies
of seeking the advice of ancestors. The details of the presence of a symbolic
"white lime" substance, even as ordinary kitchen flour, demonstrates the power
of this symbol to express peace and celebration. When as a student at the University of Lubumbashi John Mutombo returned to his rural home in Kitenge,
his Methodist mother tossed white flour over him to celebrate his return; when,
years later, as a Methodist pastor and bishop's representative he undertook a
mission of reconciliation to Moba and Kalemie, he was equally comfortable
with white lime used in the community's final ceremony. In that case, in the

midst of the Christian ecumenical division, where Protestants and Roman Catholics could not partake the eucharist together, "white lime" served as a symbol around which the people of Moba and Kalemie could unify.

In other cases, the Luba and Christian systems of thought do not overtly contradict each other, and both enter into the interpretation of experience. Witnesses from Prophet Mechac's village never suggest a contradiction between their Pentecostal Christianity and the Luba assumption that spiritual power can disable Chinja-Chinja upon entering their village. Gaston Ntambo, a Congolese person with much experience in western culture, initially disbelieves the messengers who seem to know his business; but he, too, draws on the mysticism inherent in Luba spirituality and Christianity to come to understand his visitors as prophets who confirm his vocation.

In other cases, symbolized by Mama Alphonsine and her family who encounter the dead mother and live baby on the path, the witnesses find a contradiction between Luba and Christian tradition and negotiate between the two systems. Unlike Bishop Ntambo, Mama Aphonsine does not reject the claims of her culture, but she finds a way to mediate the differences.

When Christian interpreters seek to eradicate local culture, spiritual practice, and identity, Christianity leaves indigenous people bereft. First Nations people in Canadian Christian denominations have made this point clearly, and now draw on both Christian and indigenous traditions. So, too, in Congo. For some, like the communities around Bishop Ntambo and Prophet Mechac, this correlation of local culture and Christianity produces the strength that allows them to lay down their lives for peace. In the view of others, Christianity weakens local culture, and the spirituality of indigenous practice and Christianity barely holds the community together. The words of traditional chief Kanda-Fwanyinwabo of Ngoy-Mwana, in his interview in 2008, have haunted me, as a Christian well aware of the damage wrought by the colonial church in indigenous cultures:

> *John Mutombo, interpreting*: This is theological. He is saying. . .the Christian tradition and this traditional belief are totally different. Because, according to him, Jesus Christ is for the white person, and we have our own deities. The supreme God. . .is the one God but we have different intermediaries. . . .(The priests). . . .told us to forget about our deities. . . . You know, the people are brainwashed by the white. And our tradition is getting weaker and weaker. But for you to know our god, and it maybe to teach you, you don't know the procedure, how to call. That's why you have taught us Jesus, and we don't know even how to talk to Jesus. Jesus is far, and our deities are far, and we are now nowhere. We are

now lost. So we, the few people who are still leaning to our tradition, we know how to talk to them, how to get the power, how to protect people.

P: What do you think of Bishop Ntambo when he. . . . agreed with the governor to do the peace conference here and try to bring the Mai-Mai threat to an end?

M: I was one of the delegates.

P: Do you think the kind of leadership Bishop Ntambo provided was Luba leadership, in other words, the kind of leadership that extended the lime of peacemaking? Or was he primarily there as a representative of the Christian tradition, and therefore not a representative of Luba tradition? Or was he there as some kind of combination of both?

M: Bishop Ntambo, we call him God's messenger. I think if we look at him, this power is not physical power. The power in him is supernatural power. Because he had the power to unite with traditional people and the Christians, the bad people and the good ones, and he succeeded to bring both of us together.

Colonial Christianity, when it seeks to displace local culture, has the potential to make both Christianity and indigenous tradition ghost-like, lacking spirit-giving energy. In the stories of Kamina, neither colonial Christianity nor local tradition are bogeymen; indigenous people call on both traditions in their quest for the courage to make, keep and build peace.

An Organic Model of Peacebuilding

Local leaders became vehicles for the spirit of peace in at least nine identifiable ways: 1. calling on Luba and Christian tradition; 2. engaging in construction and agricultural projects; 3. caring for displaced guests, including widows and orphans; 4. maintaining and building capacities in infrastructure, including schools, hospitals, orphanages, guesthouses; 5. relating to leaders of other faiths, military, government, traditional chiefs and Mai-Mai commanders; 6. engaging American and European partners; 7. risking the peace of the local community for the sake of regional peace; 8. sending missions of reconciliation to church and communities in the former war zone and other places; and 9. promoting women into new roles and raising awareness of gender-based violence.

Portions of these activities provided resources that supported later activities—for example, because the leaders had rather innocently decided to open a guesthouse, they could transform a neutral space into a sanctuary for intense conversations necessary for peacemaking with the Mai-Mai. These local activities that contributed to peace occurred in a temporal space between the spectre of hunger and the intimate presence of the supernatural.

The Spirit of Building and Cultivating

Newly elected Bishop Ntambo created an ecclesial development plan based on stable, fired brick buildings that did not deteriorate under the power of the rains and agricultural training that taught people to feed themselves. Durable buildings quickly became the symbol of political stability, announcing the possibility that the country could withstand the forces that sought to overwhelm it. The spirit of building and cultivating countered the ghosts of hungry stomachs, leaking thatched roofs, torn clothing, and bare feet. During the war the building projects served as a psychological force, giving the local people and refugees the confidence to remain in Kamina.

Is it possible to adequately dramatize for a modern western reader the routine obstacles encountered during such projects? A ghost town has no fuel, vehicles, goods, factories, or production lines. The plodding work of pulling the stones from the fields of Kamisamba, negotiating for fuel, procuring and transporting cement and tin roofing, training labor and preventing theft fills what theologians call "kronos" time—the ordinary time of our existence—in which the hard, detailed work of peace occurs. The hopeful energy invested in each church completed, each parsonage updated, each class taught, each crop harvested provides a formed brick toward building the peace and a hedge against a release of frustrated, destructive energy expressed through looting and pillage.

The power of such projects, and the hope of rural people that the country will build capacities in education, medicine, transportation, electricity, and communcations, echoes around the countryside when religious, civil, and government leaders listen to the demands of the local Mai-Mai. Chinja-Chinja's requests in Kamina in 2004 reverberated in the discussions of the Bakata-Katanga in 2014: 'we need development in the rural areas.'

It's easy to lay the blame for the lack of rural development at the feet of the federal, provincial or town governments, or to blame individuals themselves for failing in the complicated task of upgrading rural areas, or to criticize the presence or absence of international aid. However, for all of these groups, the demands of urban development easing the lives of millions of people in Kinshasa, Lubumbashi, and the Great Lakes region tend to draw the emphasis away from the rural villages in a vast country often compared to the size of the United States east of the Mississippi River. In particular, the country is rarely remembered in its entirety by the secular international community. Its focus remains on the Great Lakes region, drawing attention and resources away from the rest of the country. Yet this story shows that war and peace in the rural and urban areas are intimately related.

As an example of this dynamic between the focus on the Great Lakes and the loss to the rest of the country, I recall then Secretary of State Hillary Clinton's August 2009 visit to the Great Lakes region that aroused her concern about the care of women who were sexually violated during the war. At that time, I had worked with a group to propose upgrading the church-run hospitals throughout the country so that they could house safe programs for women fleeing from violence. We had been told that the American embassy had supported the project and that it awaited funding. After Clinton's visit, we were told that all such funding had been prioritized for the Great Lakes region. The needs there are great—but violated, displaced women, including those internally displaced from the Great Lakes region, live throughout the Democratic Republic of Congo, with few resources near.

The ghosts of destruction and destitution in rural areas are replaced by the spirit of local leaders and their partners, including local and international NGOs and individuals, who envision rebuilding Congo's infrastructure. In some cases, the institutions are religiously based; in other cases, the government looks to the church as one place to find competent, experienced, local leadership for institutions such as government hospitals and schools.

The Spirit of Hospitality toward Guests

The image of men, women and children fleeing from towns, hustling and plodding down the lanes and paths, hiding from soldiers and militias, drinking from rain puddles and eating roots in the bush provides a background for the generosity and hospitality from others that helps people survive a war.

Even before the wars in Congo, the destitution, disease and early death of adults created a crisis of street children who did not have families to support them, leading to Mama Nshimba's and Mama Mujing's orphanage project. In that sense, the Congolese church carried on a Christian tradition much like the early sanctuary, the church's medieval monasteries, and post-Reformation orphanages for the care of children. Over the course of the war the orphanage turned into a children's soup kitchen, and care for orphans reciprocated as care for widows when the church hired displaced women to support the rapidly increasing number of children who needed to be housed, clothed and fed. These activities, in addition to feeding displaced people, fulfilled the Hebrew Scripture's mandate that the community should care for the orphan, widow and stranger in their midst.

When displaced families began trickling into Kamina, Congolese religious leaders responded much like those in North America, first contacting pastors

and collecting and organizing distributions in local congregations, then request-
ing food and goods from congregations within their judicatories, and, finally,
applying for aid from the denomination. In such a locale, where the food supply
was already limited, however, very few months elapsed between the beginning
of the crisis in August 1998 and the time when the local systems became overwhelmed in November. The initial impulse of hospitality quickly produced a
Congolese version of 'compassion fatigue,' exacerbated by a sense of helplessness produced by sympathy, as most Congolese people have experienced hunger and know what it means not to eat. The widely-touted African village ethic
of sharing—*bumuntu*—emerges, and people do contribute what food they have,
to the point of their own hunger. Still, Congolese religious leaders expressed
emotions experienced by disaster workers everywhere: they felt helpless when
the demand outstripped the supply, exhausted by overwork, and afraid of angry
retaliation by desperate people. Local hosts like Pastor Kahunda or displaced-
people-turned-aid workers, like Pastor Nyengele, experienced, wondered at,
and resented the spirit of ingratitude that emanated from some of the desperate
people they served. In addition, the local leaders found themselves shouldering
increasing levels of responsibility when they encouraged Bishop Ntambo and
his family, potential targets of political opposition, to leave.

Finally, church leaders such as Doctor Kasanka, Pastor Kora, Pastor
Kabongo and Pastor Ndlambda remained in the war zone, risking their own
lives to save others. Dr. Kasanka's story of courage and resilience at the
Kabongo Hospital remains one of the most extraordinary examples of risk-taking Christian vocation by a local hero who has received little recognition for
his years of sacrifice.

The Spirit of Peacemaking in the Mai-Mai Conference

Risk-taking Christianity correlated with Luba village tradition to make the Mai-
Mai peace conference possible. Kinship and village networks allowed the possibility that religious leaders could invite the Mai-Mai and that Pastor Kabongo
could persuade Chinja-Chinja to attend. Respect for spiritual leadership that
unites indigenous religion, cultural tradition, and Christianity made the conference a success. It underlines one finding arising from this research: *every decision for peace and violence in Congo has a religious or spiritual component.*

The witnesses reported that the willingness to risk the peace of Kamina was
motivated, for prominent leaders such as Bishop Ntambo and Prophet Mechac,
but also for local leaders, such as Bishop's cabinet, by the mandate of their
Christian faith. Multiple witnesses also reported that Mai-Mai participated because they trusted these religious leaders. Mai-Mai participants such as Kebe
Konkeka and observers of the Mai-Mai, such as Pastor Kabongo and Hubert,
reported that the Mai-Mai conducted their ceremonies and that their ancestors

directed them to send representatives or to appear themselves, as in the case of Bakanda Bakoka and, eventually, Chinja-Chinja.

How successful was this conference? After agreements were signed and the participants returned to their villages and towns, Bishop Ntambo told his followers, "Now we will see what happens." Success had been achieved at holding a conference with potential belligerents—including government, military, and Mai-Mai at odds with each other—without violence. But no one yet knew whether a larger peace would hold.

By what criteria did local townspeople and villagers deem this conference a success? When asked this question, they cited the following evidence: militia roadblocks were removed, allowing people to travel and reengage in commerce; the local militia groups largely disbanded, significantly reducing the villagers' fear of terror, looting and rape by the militias. When asked where these leaders are now, witnesses said that Maccabee became a farmer, Bakanda Bakoka's whereabouts were unknown, and Chinja-Chinja was arrested, imprisoned and held in Kinshasa without trial. Various stories and judgments circulate around Chinja-Chinja's arrest: according to former Governor Kisula Ngoy, Chinja-Chinja moved elsewhere, reengaged his former behavior, was arrested by the government and imprisoned. Some local witnesses judge Chinja-Chinja to be guilty of war crimes; for others, his arrest represents a miscarriage of justice.

The conference's success, from the standpoint of local participants, depended upon its spiritual leadership. Many political analysts and secular nongovernmental organizations have not adequately accounted for the reality of the importance of religion and spirituality for peace in the DRC. Most dismiss indigenous practice as magic and sorcery and ignore Christian practice. This lack in their work reflects their social location—one that reflects political, military, and diplomatic sources of knowledge. These frameworks often look at religion and spirituality with suspicion.

For example, The International Crisis Group (ICG), in its African Report 109, 9 January 2006, entitled "Katanga: Congo's Forgotten Crisis," mentions a "roundtable" with the Mai-Mai initiated by Governor Kisula Ngoy, which is deemed a failure based on an interview with an unnamed member of MONUC. (Witnesses in this book say that MONUC, fearing violence, avoided the conference, though I did interview one local Methodist, Olivier Monga, who worked for MONUC as an interpreter and did participate.) The ICG MONUC interviewee notes that the most significant Mai-Mai leaders either did not attend or sent representatives (without recognizing the widespread suspicion and fear between the government and the Mai-Mai, the religious practice motivating those who did attend, or the religious leadership who convened the conference). They considered the conference a failure because Ngoy's provincial government did not live up to its promises (though that conclusion suggests that enough Mai-Mai *did attend* to create an agreement that could have led to peace.) They claim that the relationship between government and Ngoy deteriorated when promises weren't kept.

The local witnesses in this book report a different perspective. Prior to the conference, the Mai-Mai had killed emissaries whom the government had sent to negotiate with them. The relationship between the Mai-Mai and the government had already become so broken that the government had no independent ability to negotiate with the militias. Local witnesses believed that the strain between the government and the Mai-Mai created the call to the religious community to convene the conference. After the conference, the local community noted its success, but the former governor said that Chinja-Chinja moved elsewhere and rabble-roused, inciting his arrest. Also, a bicycles-for-guns exchange was initiated by Devis Mulunda, a pastor who in the late 1990s left the United Methodist Church and founded his own religious group. He claims to have collected hundreds of firearms that were then handed over to the police; the ICG report claims that many bicycles were distributed, no guns handed over to the police, and that this program exacerbated the tensions between Mai-Mai groups when some received bicycles and others did not. The report also notes that this program competed with the mandate of National Demobilization and Reintegration Commission (CONADER), citing CONADER as its source.

The recommendations of the International Crisis Group focus mainly on military, political, and international strategies. Many recommendations are well placed. However, it expressly discourages local efforts like that of Mulunda's PAREC that might compete with military-based programs. It is beyond the scope of my story to report on and evaluate that particular project; however, the ICG reasoning ignores the local peacebuilding efforts that emanate from the beliefs and commitments of the local people. It never recognizes the possibility of collaborative efforts between religious and civil society leaders in Katanga, or the way that religion and spirituality may provide a coherent focus for such groups. Those efforts became important again in 2012, when the delegation of thirty-two religious and civil society members travelled to North America and Europe to lobby for peace in Congo in the face of the M-23 threat.

The Spirit of Post-Conflict Reconciliation

Many efforts of the church in the post-conflict situation have focused on missions of reconciliation that go hand-in-hand with missions of reconstruction. The fabric of Congolese society had been torn apart by more than a century of exploitation by colonial and oligarchic interests; the natural loyalties to family, village, kinship networks, linguistic groups and traditional kings and chiefs have been further frayed by war and militia violence. Reconciliation begins with whatever sentiments of connection remain. Leaders less traumatized sit with the alienated, accompany them in their suffering, and help them reach deep into their spirituality to acknowledge their Creator and through that, reconnect with people who have harmed them. This work of the church arouses the enduring desires of members of local communities for peace and flourishing. These concerns motivate the conflict resolution work of Congolese Christians such as John Mutombo, Kitenge Lumaliza Joseph, and Thomas Kalonda who undertook, on Bishop's behalf, conflict reconciliation missions in war zones Kalemie and Moba, and Bishop Ntambo's ongoing reconciliation work when he meets with political leaders who are at odds with one another.

The DRC has never had a Truth and Reconciliation Commisssion, and the work of reconciliation cannot be forced. But it can be invited by focusing local people on positive steps forward. Once the war retreated, Bishop Ntambo insisted that his pastors return to Tanganyika District to rebuild. In recent years the church has focused its church, parsonage and school rebuilding efforts on towns in the war zone, particularly in Kalemie and Moba.

The Spirit of Partnership

The importance of community partnerships threads throughout this story, culminating in the Mai-Mai conference. Over the years Bishop Ntambo had cultivated relationships with government, military, traditional, religious leaders and ordinary townspeople who now trusted him. Likewise, many of the Mai-Mai had community and kinship ties to the Christian church. This rhizomatic network of relationships proved to be essential to bringing the community together.

In order to focus these pages on the work of the Congolese people themselves, this story understates the importance of American and European partners. During the war Bishop Ntambo travelled throughout the United States with his church and parsonage model and a homemade video, raising funds for vital construction projects. The 2000 North Katanga Annual Conference minutes report nearly a million dollars raised from various donors. When he met with them, Bishop Ntambo said to his donors as he said to me: "This war will be over and then you will come."

This story recounts the first donors who arrived to see for themselves what was happening in Bishop's conference. Bishop Ntambo and his colleagues were clear about the psychological impact of these visits on the population: "If Americans come, the local people know the war is over." The first visits by Americans in this story represent only the beginning of a stream of visitors from seven different United Methodist Annual Conferences in the United States: formal relationships were established with Annual Conferences in Texas, Indiana, Ohio, New Jersey, Arkansas, Tennessee and New York who sent regular teams to visit. Other visitors, such as the Lions Club and Seventh Day Adventists from Texas, made significant contributions.

For the Congolese hosts, these visitors were always understood to be "missionaries." Throughout this time, however, many foreign missionaries sponsored by General Board of Global Ministries (GBGM), formerly served by persons from the United States and Europe, were replaced by Congolese persons-in-mission who had now been educated for the task. Eventually, Suzy and Guy Kasanka, Gaston and Jeanne Ntambo, and others became employed by GBGM in place of foreign missionaries.

The Spirit of Promoting Women

When I began this project, UNICEF statistics showed the DRC to be one of the poorest nations in the world, with enormous disparity between the education of Congolese men and boys and Congolese women and girls.

Luba culture offered trusted places to leading women in their role as mothers: the mother of the king advised him, and the wife of the king was the only person who could cook for him. Some women became diviners and traditional village chiefs, and some participated in battle. Indeed, Mai-Mai militias recruited women.

Regardless of any other title, the greatest honor for Congolese women lay in their role as mothers. The shadow side of this way of valuing women falls on women who cannot bear children or who are violated. In these cases, either a man may take an additional wife or the family of the man may pressure him to divorce a first wife and marry again. Villages may not deem rural girls worthy of the cost of education.

Congo remains a highly gendered society in which men and women are raised to believe that mothering is women's primary purpose and achievement. Large families, even among educated younger couples, remain the norm. Mothering contributes the primary skill that women in this story bring to the peace-building situation. Women like Mama Sila and Mama Alphonsine know how to be mothers and to care for mothers and for children. "It's what I know how to do," Mama Sila says, not apologetically, but with authority.

United Methodism in Kamina has promoted a variety of images of women. The original missionaries came during a time of Victorian values and might have contributed to the Luba valuing of women primarily as mothers, while also promoting the "one wife" nuclear family ideal. However, much has changed since the introduction of Christianity into Katanga: in North American Methodists valued women's education. The United Methodist Church now ordains women; it has a series of programs to promote women, especially women of color, into higher education and leadership roles.

In light of this checkered attitude toward women both in Luba culture and in Christianity, Bishop Ntambo's practices that model a countercultural attitude toward women are noteworthy. They include caring for the women who might have been discarded: employing internally displaced widows during the war and personally caring for his barren aunt after her husband died. He has ordained women and encouraged women to seek higher education, promoting women in to public leadership. Women participate in the large delegation that attends the quadrennial General Conference. Even though they have been prepared for and promoted into such roles, the culture and conditions in which Luba women live produces a swirl of conflict around them.

Peace for women remains one of the great tasks yet to be accomplished in Kamina. At the end of my first research trip four young women, the physician Dr. Mirielle Mikombe, the jurist Suzy Mwembe, and the clergywomen, Pastors Ilgha Ilunga Monga and Betty Kazadi Musau spent an evening with me discussing the ongoing issues women face in Kamina.

"I do not need to tell horror stories of rape. Others have done that. So how do I shape the women's story?" I had asked.

My questions began a long and animated conversation among these four young, educated women about the need for a church-based program to promote peace for women. "The church is part of the problem," Dr. Mirelle said firmly, "and the church must be part of the answer." They focused particularly on educating pastors, doctors and nurses about women's medical issues, attending to women's psychological issues as a result of war-related violence, and responding to violence against women in general.

On the next research trip, I returned with Dr. Jeanne Hoeft, a colleague who specializes in violence against women. We spent a week talking with the women, hearing from community women, and writing a grant proposal. The women entitled the proposal, "*"Stop aux violences faites à la femme.*" It centered on six strategies for empowering Congolese women to resist violence by 1) dispelling the "culture of silence" against violence against women; 2) using Bishop Ntambo's influence to engage community leaders in the campaign to resist; 3) educating at least one domestic violence counselor who could provide assistance at the Lupandilo Nursing School, supervised by Dr. Mirielle; 4) providing general education for physicians, nurses, and pastors on effective ways to respond to, reduce, and resist violence against women and follow-up reinforcement through Annual Conference meetings, 5) identifying 50 nurses and doctors and 50 pastors for intensive training, to equip them to lead educational workshops; and 6) equipping the church with educational and compassionate responses to women and girls who have experienced violence against women, including sermons, prayers, and Bible studies.

We were seeking funding when several tragedies undermined the project, mirroring the problem we were trying to address.

First, Dr. Mirielle, the co-principal investigator with me, died in childbirth. The significance of the loss of this highly educated and visionary woman cannot be overestimated. Kamina agonized—alternating between disbelief and shrieks of lament. However, Dr. Kasanka, by then the Health Ministries Coordinator for North Katanga United Methodist Church and Dr. Mirielle's supervisor, agreed to step into the proposal as co-principal investigator.

Simultaneously a second grief unfolded: Pastor Ilgha Iunga Monga, the talented woman who we identified as one with the gifts to be trained as the domestic violence counselor, had entered school to study with Dr. Hoeft. However, before leaving the DRC, she had had two miscarriages, and while she was gone, her husband sought a divorce to marry another woman.

Then the final blow came: Dr. Kasanka, the hero of Kabongo Hospital, suffered a debilitating stroke. He had to withdraw from medical practice in order to care for his own rehabilitation.

Death, discrimination, disease: these three ghosts plague the DRC. Some say Congo's greatest need is qualified leadership: but what if the leaders who exhibit sacrifice, courage and vision are struck down as they enter the prime of life, and few are prepared to take their place?

Peacebuilding, peacemaking, peacekeeping are organic, interconnected activities

Bishop Ntambo's peacebuilding in Kamina began as development—a dream that fired brick parsonages and churches could symbolically, socially, and ecclesially rebuild North Katanga and that agricultural training could "feed my people". When the coup against Mobutu and "Africa's World War" became the context for his dream, this development vision provided the cornerstone for a much larger, organic model of local religious peacebuilding. Peace is like a durable sanctuary—many people fire the bricks to build its walls, and all are invited to enter.

Appendix I

Characters in Order of their Appearance

A note about names: Luba people do not usually share family names. Customarily, children do not take the surnames of their fathers or mothers, and women do not usually change their names at marriage. Africans are often called by the first name listed, and it is the most important name, not a surname. Titles and roles (bishop, pilot, doctor) are often used instead of names. Papa and Mama are used as titles in ways that westerners might use Mr., Mrs., or Ms. Some Luba Christians choose to be known by their Kiluba names, and others by their French names.

The characters in this text are referred to by their familiar names. In cases where the same name causes confusion, two names or the most distinctive name may be used, with the witness's approval.

Bishop Ntambo Nkulu Ntanda (Bishop Ntambo), Bishop of the North Katanga Episcopal Area of the United Methodist Church, and his wife, **Thérèse Nshimba Nkulu (Mama Nshimba).** Bishop Ntambo retires from his position as Bishop of North Katanga in March, 2017. They live in Kinshasa, Kamina, and Lubumbashi, DRC.

Reverend Dr. Boniface Kabongo (Pastor Kabongo or **Boniface,** to distinguish him from the town of Kabongo**),** pastor and then district superintendent of Kamina during the war, became president of Kamina University. Tragically, he died of a stroke at age 50 on January 21, 2016.

Dr. Raymond Mande Mutombo Mulumiashimba (Raymond Mande or **Raymond,** to distinguish him from **Guy Mande),** the bishop's Lubumbashi-based assistant during the war, became acting governor of the newly-created province of Haut-Lomami in November 2015.

Reverend John Munkana Mwembo Mutombo (John Mutombo or **John,** no relation to Ilunga Mutombo**),** translator in Kamina and then public relations director in Kamina, now pastors churches and lives with his wife, **Aimerance Ngoie Kalenga Mutombo (Aimerance),** and their five children in Hartley, Iowa.

Chantelle (Chantelle) lived with **Mama Mujing, (Mama Mujing)** in Kamina, DRC, until adulthood; she became a student at Africa University.

Dr. Guy Kasanka (Kasanka), director of Kabongo Hospital during the war, lives in Lubumbashi with his wife, **Suzy Mwema (Suzy),** and their five children. At Kabongo hospital he worked with **Chaplain Masengo wa Katondo (Masengo).** After Dr. Kasanka's service in Kabongo, he was promoted to director of Kamina Health Ministries.

Pilot Gaston Ntambo (Gaston) flies for Wings of the Morning, the United Methodist medical evacuation service for poor villagers, in partnership with his wife, **Jeanne Ntambo,** who continues to monitor his flights to rural areas. They live with their five children in Lubumbashi.

Accounts of the actions of the traditional chiefs are based on interviews with **King Kayamba (King Kayamba),** king of a neighboring territory to Kamina, **Chief Kanda-Fwanyinwabo, (Chief Kanda-Fwanyinwabo),** chief of the groupement of seven villages of Ngoy-Mwena, and interviews with the ministers of the court of **King Kasongo Nyembo (Kasongo Nyembo)** in Kinkunki, near Kamina.

Pastor Nyengele (Nyengele) planted churches in Kitenge, was serving in Manono at the outbreak of the war, was internally displaced to Kamina with his wife, and supervised the distribution of relief in Kamina. He lives in Kamina. **Pastor Tschimwang (Tschimwang),** with whom he distributed relief, is deceased.

Ilunga Mutombo (Ilunga Mutombo, not to be confused with **John Mutombo,** the translator) supervised the depot, where relief and construction supplies were housed and dispersed. He continues to live and work for the church in Kamina.

Pastor Ngoy Kahunda wa Kazadi (Pastor Kahunda), Bishop's Kamina-based assistant during the war, now supervises the guesthouse in Kamina.

Headmaster Mbuyu Mwilumba Matthais (Mwilumba), principal of the United Methodist school in Kabalo and translator for the Zimbabweans, now leads a United Methodist school in Kalemie. His wife **Moma Kabila Alphonsine (Mama Alphonsine),** guided her own and other children to safety in Kamina where she cared for orphans. Their children include **Mwilambewe wa Mbuyu Esquin (Mbuyu),** who is now a physician; **Kongolo Kirongozi Patrice (Patrice),** who is trained as an engineer; **Mpungwe Baraka Cherita (Cherita),** who is a law student; **Mbuyu wa Katekamo Eschler (Eschler); Onda Kongolo Nizette Dada (Dada); Djete Kalwashi Harris, Mayombo Mwepu Nevadou, Ntambo Nkulu Ntanda Pierre Bishop.**

Mama Sila (Mama Sila) fled with her daughter **Chantelle Kalenga** and grandchildren from Kikondja, cared for orphans with Mama Mujng, and continues to provide for guests at the guesthouse in Kamina.

Reverend Dr. Guy Mande Muyombo (Guy, to distinguish him from **Raymond Mande,** no relation, both of whom are called **Mande** by Congolese associates), created the music program in Kamina. He now lives with his wife and five children in New York City and serves the United Methodist General Board of Global Ministries as Regional Offices HQ Unit Head.

Pastor Ndalamba (Ndalamba), pastor in Kamungu during the war, became district superintendent in Kabongo.

Pastor Mujinga Mwamba Kora (Kora) succeeded Pastor Kabongo as district superintendent in Kitenge. He continues to serve as pastor in North Katanga Annual Conference.

Pierre Kapata (Pierre) is a pseudonym. The former Mai-Mai studied criminology and wrote his thesis on his experience in the Mai-Mai.

Prophet Mechac (the Prophet or **Mechac)** continues to lead a large community of Pentecostals in Kaboto with his secretary, **Mutalala,** and other advisers.

Dr. Kisula Ngoy (Kisula) was governor of Katanga during the Mai-Mai conference; other government officials include **Mr. Ngoy Kyoni (Ngoy Kyoni)**, the district commissioner from Haut Lomami, and **Mr. Ngoy Kitwa Scholler (Ngoy Kitwa)**, governor's representative to Kabongo District.

Maccabee, Chinja-Chinja, and **Bakanda Bakoka** are Mai-Mai leaders who enter the story by the accounts of others who observed them; **Kebi Konkeka** provided a testimony. At the time of the interview he was training in the Congolese Army at Kamina Military Base.

Hubert (Hubert) continues as the driver for Roman Catholic Bishop Kalala in Kamina.

Pastor Kitenge Lumaliza Joseph (Pastor Kitenge, not to be confused with the town of Kitenge**)**, religious educator in North Katanga, traveled with **John Mutombo (John)** to Kalemie and Moba.

Katumbi Moise (Moise) became governor of Katanga after **Dr. Kisula Ngoy**. He is an opposition candidate for president in the 2016 election.

Citations

Note: The majority of the book is drawn from the testimonies of witnesses, whose names are listed in the Introduction. Historical information, as they knew it, was gathered from the witnesses themselves. I used secondary sources to verify and expand the events that the witnesses mentioned. I have referred readers to Michael Diebert's 2013 history, *The Democratic Republic of Congo: Between Hope and Despair* for the war and the political process as this book incorporates previous histories listed. When newspaper headlines are cited, the author of the article is not listed. When the content or a newspaper article is cited, the author, if named, is listed.

p. xv   7th -17th: Mary Nooter Roberts and Allen F. Roberts, *Memory: Luba Art and the Making of History*, p. 57.

p. xv   **November 25, 1965**: "Kasavubu Regime Ousted by Army Coup in Congo." Reuters, November 25, 1965. https://partners.nytimes.com/library/world/africa/651125kasavubu.html. Accessed August 21, 2016.

p. xv   **July 1999**: Emeric Rogier, "The Inter-Congolese Dialogue: A Critical Review," https://issafrica.org/uploads/CHALLENGESPEACEINTERCONGO. PDF. Accessed June 9, 2016.

p. xvii   **Joyce Dubensky…Volume II**: Pamela Couture, "'A Bishop for his People': Bishop Ntambo Nkulu Ntanda," in *Peacemakers in Action: Profiles of Religion in Conflict Resolution* Volume II, ed. Joyce Dubensky on behalf of Tanenbaum Center for Interreligious Understanding. (New York: Cambridge University Press, 2016).

p. 1   **Congo Lurches**: http://www.nytimes.com/2016/05/12/world/africa/congo-moise-katumbi-joseph-kabila.html?_r=0. Accessed August 21, 2016.

p. 2-3   **Gerald Monk…of our world**: Gerald Monk, John Winslade, Kathie Crocket and David Epstein, *Narrative Therapy in Theory and Practice* (Jossey-Bass, 1997), p. 32-52.

p. 3   **Social witness and recognition**: David Denborough, *Collective Narrative Practice*, (Dulwich Center Publications, 2008). See http://dulwichcentre.com.au/authors/david-denborough/. Accessed August 22, 2016.

p. 3   **Brian Mealer…naïve**: Brian Mealer, *All Things Must Fight to Live: Stories of War and Deliverance in the Democratic Republic of Congo* (New York: Bloomsbury, 2008), p. 150.

p. 4   **Jason Stearns'**: Jason Stearns, *Dancing in the Glory of the Monsters: The Collapse of Congo and the Great War of Afric*a (New York: Public Affairs, 2011), Kindle location 156.

p. 4   **Gérard Prunier's**: Gérard Prunier, *Africa's World War* (Oxford University Press, 2007).

p. 4   **Michael Diebert's**: Michael Diebert, *The Democratic Republic of Congo: Between Hope and Despair* (Zed Books, 2013).

p. 4   **My first decision**: Canadian author Camilla Gibb's experience, described on a panel at the Canadian Creative Non-fiction Collective Society, resonated with my own. She finished her dissertation in anthropology in Egypt using theoretical constructs. The project left her unsatisfied for reasons similar to the ones I document here. When she tried to use the same material to write a narrative, she found it impossible. Camilla Gibb, panel discussion, Canadian Creative Non-Fiction Collective Society, April 23, 2016, Calgary, Alberta.

p. 5   **Marc Gopin**: Marc Gopin, *Healing the Heart of Conflict: 8 Crucial Steps to Making Peace with Yourself and Others* (Rodale, 2004), p. xv.

p. 5   **John Paul Lederach**: John Paul Lederach, *The Moral Imagination: The Art and Soul of Building Peace* (Oxford University Press, 2005), 44ff.

p. 5   **Mutombo Nkulu N'Sengha**: Mutombo Nkulu N'Sengha, *Foundations for an African Philosophy and Theology of Human Rights: Rethinking the Human Condition in Post-Colonial Central Africa (1965-1997)*, Ph.D. Dissertation, Temple University, 2001, 91-219.

p. 16   **Congolese peacemakers...written**: William Grimes, "Gerda Lerner, A Feminist and Historian, Dies at 92," January 3, 2013. http://www.nytimes.com/2013/01/04/us/gerda-lerner-historian-dies-at-92.html?_r=0. Accessed August 22, 2016.

p. 16   **Congolese people...activities**: quoted by Linda Kerber and Sharron De Hart in *America: Refocusing the Past* (Oxford University Press, 1995).

p. 16   **Heather Walton**: Heather Walton, *Not Eden: Spiritual Life Writing for this World* (London: SCM Press, 2015).

p. 16   **Lee Gutkind**: Lee Gutkind, *You Can't Make This Stuff Up: The Complete Guide to Writing Creative Nonfiction from Memoir to Literary Journalism and Everything In Between* (Boston: Decapo Press, 2012).

p. 17   **indigenous essayists**: Rasunah Marsden, ed., *Crisp Blue Edges: Indigenous Creative Nonfiction* (Penticton, BC: Theytus Books, 2000).

p. 21   **"inaccessible" on humanitarian maps**: http://reliefweb.int/report/democratic-republic-congo/drc-monthly-humanitarian-bulletin-17-jul-17-aug-1999. Accessed August 22, 2016.

p. 23   **Where's the Peace**: http://articles.chicagotribune.com/2000-02-14/news/0002140010_1_peacekeepers-rwanda-and-uganda-hutu. Accessed June 9, 2016.

p. 25   **Mobutu...survive**: John Daniszewski and Ann M Simmons, "Mobutu, Zairian Dictator for 32 Years, Dies in Exile," *Los Angeles Times,* September 8, 1997. http://articles.latimes.com/1997/sep/08/news/mn-30058. Accessed June 9, 2016.

p. 26   **In Zaire**: http://www.nytimes.com/1996/09/13/world/in-zaire-they-finally-ask-who-follows-mobutu.html. Accessed June 8, 2016.

p. 29   **Zaire War**: http://www.nytimes.com/1996/10/26/world/zaire-war-breeds-a-human-catastrophe.html. Accessed June 8, 2016.

p. 33   **Last Chance**: http://www.nytimes.com/1996/09/06/arts/last-chance.html. Accessed June 8, 2016.

p. 33   **The rebel Kabila…Mobutu**: For further information, see summary of events in September 1996 through April 1997 in Diebert, *Congo*, kindle location 1174-1222.

p. 34   **…student massacre:** For more information, see http://www.unhcr.org/refworld/docid/3ae6a8654.html, accessed June 9, 2016. See also "Zaire—massacre of students at Lubumbashi" Lawyers Committee for Human Rights (U.S.), 1991; Diebert, *Democratic Republic of Congo (African Arguments)*, kindle location 885.

p. 36   **U.N. Presses**: http://www.nytimes.com/1997/01/25/world/un-presses-for-truce-to-help-refugees-trapped-in-east-zaire.html. Accessed June 8, 2016.

p. 39   **As Rebels Gain**: http://www.nytimes.com/1997/02/08/world/as-rebels-gain-in-zaire-army-morale-is-declining.html. Accessed August 14, 2016.

p. 43   **U.N. Chief Says**: http://www.nytimes.com/1997/02/14/world/un-chief-says-abandoning-aid-force-for-zaire-was-a-mistake.html. Accessed June 8, 2016.

p. 51   **A Three-Cornered Struggle**: http://www.nytimes.com/1997/04/13/world/a-three-cornered-struggle-to-redraw-zaire-s-political-map.html. Accessed June 8, 2016.

p. 53   **U.S. Decides**: http://www.nytimes.com/1997/04/30/world/us-decides-time-is-ripe-to-elbow-mobutu-aside.html. Accessed June 8, 2016.

p. 54   **There was a time…limbs:** This version of the story of the white lime as a tool of local peacemaking was shared with me by Luba ministers at Kinkunki. I learned then that any interviews with public officials would be attended by a variety of other members of the community. The entourage, which included John, me, a medical team also housed at the guesthouse, and other translators were invited to a conversation in a large *payotte*—an open, round, concrete structure with a thatched roof—where the ministers had assembled. They wore traditional garb—white waistcloths, animal skins, and wide-brimmed hats with tall feathers. Each introduced himself and his role as adviser to the king. When I asked whether the Luba have traditions of conflict resolution, I was immediately told this story. Thereafter, reference to white lime appeared in several interviews. The use of white lime (or chalk) on a diviner is shown in Polly Nooter Roberts and Allen F. Roberts' book, *Luba* (New York: The Rosen Publishing Group, 1997).

p. 55   ***kuboko kumo kubunga ke kololanga***: Mutombo N'Sengha, *Foundation for an African Theology of Human Rights: Rethinking the Human Condition in Post-Colonial Central Africa*, a dissertation submitted to Temple University, Leonard Swidler, Adviser, accepted May 22, 2001. p. 133. Accessed by pdf, December 12, 2015.

p. 55   **…own country**: Jason Sendwe and Moise Tschombe led Katanga in a failed attempt to secede from the Democratic Republic of Congo. For more information, see Gérard Prunier, *Africa's World War*.

p. 56   **The Congo Victors**: http://www.nytimes.com/1997/05/20/world/the-congo-victors-meet-the-zairian-vanquished.html. Accessed June 8, 2016.

p. 64   **On Visit**: http://www.nytimes.com/1997/12/13/world/on-visit-to-congo-albright-praises-the-new-leader.html. Accessed June 8, 2016.

p. 66   **A New Model**: http://www.nytimes.com/1998/03/25/world/clinton-in-africa-the-region-a-new-model-for-africa-good-leaders-above-all.html.   Accessed June 8, 2016.

p. 68   **One Year Later**: http://www.nytimes.com/1998/05/18/world/one-year-later-congo-seems-to-languish.html. Accessed June 8, 2016.

p. 73   **New Congo Ruler**: http://www.nytimes.com/1998/08/04/world/new-congo-ruler-facing-rebellion-by-former-allies.html. Accessed June 8, 2016.

p. 73   **For several months…at odds:** For the events of August 1996 see Diebert, *Congo*, kindle locations 1340-1385.

p. 80   **Congo Presents Evidence**: http://www.nytimes.com/1998/09/02/world/congo-presents-evidence-of-foreign-invaders.html. Accessed June 8, 2016.

p. 84   **Congo Peace Talks**: http://www.nytimes.com/1998/09/07/world/congo-peace-talks-open-in-zimbabwe.html. Accessed June 8, 2016.

p. 86   **Genocide With Spin Control**: http://www.nytimes.com/1998/09/01/books/books-of-the-times-genocide-with-spin-control-kurtz-wasn-t-fiction.html. Accessed June 8, 2016.

p. 90   **BOOKS OF THE TIMES**: http://www.nytimes.com/1998/10/16/books/books-of-the-times-no-ice-cream-cones-in-a-heart-of-darkness.html.   Accessed June 8, 2016.

p. 93   **Best Sellers**: http://www.nytimes.com/1998/10/25/books/best-sellers-october-25-1998.html?pagewanted=2. Accessed August 23, 2016.

p. 96   **Foreign missionaries…evacuated:** General Board of Global Ministries news reports say that US missionaries were evacuated and that Swiss and Danish mission boards were also considering evacuation. "United Methodist Missionaries to Leave Congo," August 19, 1998, updated September 25, 1998, www.umc.org/umns, now archived. The US missionaries went back to major cities three weeks later, but not to Kamina. Personal email correspondence with Ruth Zolliker, May 28, 2014.

p. 98   **Long War**: http://www.nytimes.com/1998/12/30/world/long-war-saps-spirit-and-money-in-congo.html. Accessed June 8, 2016.

p. 103   **"Trust and Obey"**: John H. Sammis, 1887. Public Domain.

p. 104   **Talks on a Cease-Fire**: http://www.nytimes.com/1998/09/09/world/talks-on-a-cease-fire-in-congo-end-peace-gets-only-lip-service.html. Accessed June 8, 2016.

p. 109   **A War Turned**: http://www.nytimes.com/1998/12/06/weekinreview/the-world-a-war-turned-free-for-all-tears-at-africa-s-center.html. Accessed August 23, 2016.

p. 115   **In Congo Carnage**: http://www.nytimes.com/1999/01/10/world/in-congo-carnage-how-many-died.html. Accessed June 8, 2016.

p. 116   **The African Question**: http://www.nytimes.com/1999/01/16/arts/african-question-who-blame-finger-points-west-congo-harsh-example.html. Accessed June 8, 2016.

p. 121   **PUBLIC LIVES**: http://www.nytimes.com/1999/04/20/nyregion/public-lives-in-congo-or-kosovo-a-compulsion-to-help.html. Accessed June 8, 2016.

p. 124   **Downside of Doing Good**: http://www.nytimes.com/1999/02/27/arts/down-side-of-doing-good-disaster-relief-can-harm.html. Accessed June 8, 2016.

p. 128   **Congo: Rebel Gains Claimed**: http://www.nytimes.com/1999/04/09/world/world-briefing.html. Accessed August 17, 2016.

p. 133   **Have We Forgotten**: http://www.nytimes.com/1999/05/27/opinion/have-we-forgotten-the-path-to-peace.html. Accessed June 8, 2016.

p. 136   **Q&A**: http://www.nytimes.com/1999/06/13/nyregion/q-a-dr-craig-etcheson-keeping-a-record-of-atrocities-of-war.html. Accessed June 8, 2016.

p. 142   **Beginning in…weeks:** "Democratic Republic of Congo: An Analysis of the Agreement and the Prospects for Peace," International Crisis Group, August 20, 1999. http://www.crisisgroup.org/en/regions/africa/central-africa/dr-congo/005-democratic-republic-of-congo-an-analysis-of-the-agreement-and-propects-for-peace.aspx. Accessed October 21, 2013.See also: Emeric Rogier, "The Inter-Congolese Dialogue: A Critical Review," http://www.issafrica.org/pubs/Books/CoPBookMay04/InterCongo.pdf. Accessed January 20, 2014. For events following see Diebert, *Congo*, kindle location 1428ff.

p. 143   **MONUC**: http://www.un.org/en/peacekeeping/missions/past/monuc/. Accessed June 9, 2016.

p. 143   **United Nations Expert Panel Report**: http://www.securitycouncilreport.org/atf/cf/%7B65BFCF9B-6D27-4E9C-8CD3-CF6E4FF96FF9%7D/DRC%20S%202001%20357.pdf. Accessed June 9, 2016.

p. 144   **Congo Refugees Flee**: http://www.nytimes.com/1999/07/02/world/world-briefing.html. Accessed June 8, 2016.

p. 149   **Congo Rebels**: http://www.nytimes.com/1999/08/25/world/congo-rebels-take-big-step-to-reviving-peace-plan.html. Accessed June 8, 2016.

p. 152   **"Blest Be the Tie That Binds"**: John Fawcett, 1782. Public Domain.

p. 152   **But that day…fought each other:** For more information, see Diebert, *Congo*, kindle location 1428.

p. 152   **Rebels Can't**: http://www.nytimes.com/1999/08/13/world/rebels-can-t-conquer-the-hearts-of-the-congolese.html. Accessed August 18, 2016.

p. 157   **Shaky Congo Peace**: http://www.nytimes.com/1999/11/12/world/shaky-congo-peace-pact-grows-more-so.html. Accessed June 8, 2016.

p. 163   **Congo's Leader Promises**: http://www.nytimes.com/1999/12/12/world/congo-leader-promises-cooperation-with-mediator-in-civil-war.html. Accessed August 18, 2016.

p. 167 **U.N. Says**: http://www.nytimes.com/1999/12/12/world/unicef-says-war-affects-poor-children-in-the-millions.html Accessed August 22, 2016.

p. 169 **Foes in Congo**: http://www.nytimes.com/2000/04/10/world/foes-in-congo-appeal-for-un-peacekeepers.html. Accessed August 22, 2016.

p. 174 **Mandela's Next**: http://www.nytimes.com/2000/01/13/world/mandela-s-next-job-trying-to-cool-one-of-africa-s-hottest-spots.html. Accessed June 8, 2016.

p. 180 **U.N. Faces**: http://www.nytimes.com/2000/01/31/world/un-faces-big-challenge-in-any-congo-peacekeeping-mission.html. Accessed June 8, 2016.

p. 183 **Congo's War**: http://www.nytimes.com/2000/09/18/world/congo-s-war-triumphs-over-peace-accord.html. Accessed June 8, 2016.

p. 187 **U.N. Peacekeeper**: http://www.nytimes.com/2000/03/29/world/un-peace-keeper-gives-council-a-gloomy-briefing-on-congo.html. Accessed June 8, 2016.

p. 192 **DANCE REVIEW**: http://www.nytimes.com/2000/09/20/arts/dance-review-driving-evil-spirits-away-with-song-and-pulsating-rhythm.html. Accessed June 8, 2016.

p. 198 **RELIGION JOURNAL**: http://www.nytimes.com/2000/05/13/us/religion-journal-repenting-racist-acts-and-recalling-genocide.html. Accessed June 8, 2016.

p. 202 **...filled with hope**: Interview with Dr. Raymond Mande Mutombo, January 7, 2009, Lubumbashi, DRC and personal correspondence, dated October 9, 2013; telephone conversation with Mark Harrison, General Board of Church and Society of the United Methodist Church, October 8, 2013; personal correspondence with Pastor Dr. J. P. Wogaman, 9/27/2013- 10/10/2013 and telephone conversation, October 10, 2013; *Daily Christian Advocate*, United Methodist General Conference 2000 *Daily Edition*, Vol. 4 No. 10, May 12, 2000, p. 2345-2346, http://www.gc2000.org/dca/pdf/0512/DCA%20Proceedings%202000%20for%20Pub%20Date%20May%2012%202000.pdf. Accessed October 9, 2013; Daily Christian Advocate Vol. 4., NO. 11, May 13, 2000, p. 2425. http://www.gc2000.org/dca/pdf/0513/DCAProceedings0513.pdf. Accessed October 9, 2013.

p. 202 **Security Council**: http://www.nytimes.com/2000/06/17/world/security-council-demands-that-rwanda-and-uganda-leave-congo.html. Accessed June 8, 2016.

p. 204 **As Peace Mission**: http://www.nytimes.com/2000/08/19/world/as-peace-mission-deteriorates-un-sends-an-envoy-to-congo.html. Accessed June 8, 2016.

p. 206 **Death Toll**: http://www.nytimes.com/2000/06/09/world/death-toll-in-congo-s-2-year-war-is-at-least-1.7million-study-says.html. Accessed June 8, 2016.

p. 209 **RELIGION JOURNAL**: http://www.nytimes.com/2000/09/16/us/religion-journal-back-from-africa-with-cry-for-help.html. Accessed June 8, 2016.

p. 212 **Congo Leader**: http://www.nytimes.com/2001/01/17/world/congo-leader-reportedly-dead-after-being-shot-by-bodyguard.html. Accessed June 8, 2016.

p. 213 **Who had assassinated…**: Stuart Jeffries, "Revealed: How Africa's dictator died at the hands of his boy soldiers", 10 February, 2001. http://www.theguardian.com/world/2001/feb/11/theobserver. Accessed June 8, 2016; Jason Stearns, http://congosiasa.blogspot.com/2010/02/who-killed-laurent-kabila.html. Accessed June 8, 2016; see also Deibert, *Congo*, kindle location 1498-1507.

p. 217 **…organized crime:** United Nations. http://www.un.org/en/sc/repertoire/subsidiary_organs/groups_and_panels.shtml. Accessed August 22, 2016.

p. 217 **The Inter-Congolese Dialogue…2002:** Rogier, *The Inter-Congolese Dialogue*, p. 30.

p. 217 **The people of Katanga…militias:** In 2006 the international Crisis Group reported Mai-Mai militias in other areas of North Katanga, but not in Kabongo and its surrounding areas. By that time, this area had been pacified. "Katanga: the Congo's forgotten crisis," Africa Report 103, January 9, 2006. http://www.crisisgroup.org/en/regions/africa/central-africa/dr-congo/103-katanga-the-congos-forgotten-crisis.aspx, accessed June 9, 2016.

p. 218 **Doubts on**: http://www.nytimes.com/2001/01/21/world/doubts-on-whether-kabila-s-son-can-lead-congo.html. Accessed June 8, 2016.

p. 223 **Who Runs Congo**: http://www.nytimes.com/2001/04/15/world/who-runs-congo-the-people-new-leader-says.html. Accessed June 8, 2016.

p. 226 **Prophet Mechac**: In January 2008 local witnesses in Kamina urged me to interview Prophet Mechac; then, I could only speak to him through a broken cell phone connection. In October 2009, during rainy season, I arranged to visit Mechac at his village, Kaboto, an hour's drive into the bush beyond Kabongo. In 2014 he visited me in Kamina to review the manuscript.

p. 226 **U.N. Delegation**: http://www.nytimes.com/2001/05/16/world/un-delegation-off-to-africa-sees-glimmer-of-hope-for-congo.html. Accessed June 8, 2016.

p. 230 **Front Line of U.N. Effort**: http://www.nytimes.com/2001/07/15/world/front-line-of-un-effort-to-take-guns-from-children.html. Accessed June 8, 2016.

p. 235 **WORLD BRIEFING: AFRICA: RWANDA**: http://www.nytimes.com/2001/07/07/world/world-briefing-africa-rwanda-former-allies-hold-talks.html. Accessed June 8, 2016.

p. 235 **Kitenge, eighty kilometers north of Kabongo**: In August 2001 the World Food Programme began providing relief in previously inaccessible areas near Kabongo and Kitenge. http://reliefweb.int/report/democratic-republic-congo/wfp-expands-food-assistance-war-victims-dr-congo. Accessed August 19, 2016.

p. 237 **Peace Talks to End**: http://www.nytimes.com/2001/10/17/world/peace-talks-to-end-war-in-congo-finally-begin.html. Accessed June 8, 2016.

p. 239 **WORLD BRIEFING AFRICA RWANDA**: http://www.nytimes.com/2001/11/24/world/world-briefing-africa-rwanda-charges-of-plunder-in-congo-denied.html. Accessed June 8, 2016.

p. 243 **Congo Peace Negotiations**: http://www.nytimes.com/2002/04/20/world/congo-peace-negotiations-end-without-accord-after-7-weeks.html. Accessed June 8, 2016.

p. 247 **Struggling to End**: http://www.nytimes.com/2002/08/02/opinion/struggling-to-end-africa-s-world-war.html. Accessed June 8, 2016.

p. 251 **Rwanda and Congo Sign Accord**: http://www.nytimes.com/2002/07/31/world/rwanda-and-congo-sign-accord-to-end-war.html. Accessed June 8, 2016.

p. 252 **War is Still**: http://www.nytimes.com/2002/11/21/world/war-is-still-a-way-of-life-for-congo-rebels.html. Accessed June 8, 2016.

p. 255 **WORLD BRIEFING AFRICA CONGO**: http://www.nytimes.com/2002/11/13/world/world-briefing-africa-congo-officials-suspended.html. Accessed June 8, 2016.

p. 256 **40 Nations**: http://www.nytimes.com/2002/11/06/world/40-nations-in-accord-on-conflict-diamonds.html. Accessed June 8, 2016.

p. 260 **U.N. Says**: http://www.nytimes.com/2003/01/16/world/un-says-congo-rebels-carried-out-cannibalism-and-rapes.html?_r=0. Accessed August 19, 2016.

p. 263 **WORLD BRIEFING AFRICA CONGO**: http://www.nytimes.com/2004/01/27/world/world-briefing-africa-congo-punishment-vowed-for-rapists.html. Accessed June 8, 2016.

p. 263 **Last week in February 2004**: MONUC investigated massacres against civilians by Chinja-Chinja (spelled Shinja Shinja) in February 2004. MONUC, http://reliefweb.int/report/democratic-republic-congo/drc-monuc-investigates-allegations-massacres-katanga. Accessed August 19, 2016.

p. 268 **Hopes and Tears**: http://www.nytimes.com/2004/04/21/world/hopes-and-tears-of-congo-flow-in-its-mythic-river.html. Accessed June 8, 2016.

p. 268 **April 29 Sermon 'The Fear of the Lord'**: http://archives.umc.org/interior.asp? ptid=17&mid=4320. Accessed October 6, 2014. Although posted on the UMCOM website, the copyright remains with Bishop Ntambo. Used with permission.

p. 273 **Warring Militias**: http://www.nytimes.com/2004/04/11/world/warring-militias-in-congo-test-un-enforcement-role.html. Accessed June 8, 2016.

p. 278 **The Saturday Profile**: http://www.nytimes.com/2004/07/10/world/the-saturday-profile-rescuing-victims-worldwide-from-the-depths-of-hell.html. Accessed June 8, 2016.

p. 279 **WORLD BRIEFING: AFRICA**: http://www.nytimes.com/2004/08/07/world/world-briefing-africa-white-rhino-numbers-cut-by-half.html. Accessed June 8, 2016.

p. 283 **Thatcher's Son**: http://www.nytimes.com/2004/08/26/world/thatcher-s-son-held-in-failed-africa-coup.html. Accessed June 8, 2016.

p. 285   **What about Bishop Ntambo and Bishop Kalala...**: Bishop Kalala's perspective is not represented because, though the interpreters extended multiple
invitations, he never made himself available to be interviewed.

p. 286   **Change Africa's Borders**: http://query.nytimes.com/gst/fullpage.html?res=
9D02E7DC1131F936A3575AC0A9629C8B63. Accessed June 8, 2016.

p. 289   **CLASSICAL MUSIC DANCE GUIDE**: http://www.nytimes.com/2004/09/
17/arts/music/classical-music-and-dance-listings.html.   Accessed   June   8,
2016.

p. 291   **Another Triumph**: http://www.nytimes.com/2004/09/25/opinion/another-
triumph-for-the-un.html. Accessed June 8, 2016.

p. 296   **Congolese Roots**: http://www.nytimes.com/2004/09/30/arts/music/congo-
lese-roots-now-helped-by-hiphop.html. Accessed June 8, 2016.

p. 300   **Fiction**: http://www.nytimes.com/2004/09/26/books/review/fiction-fireeaters
-flying-cats-and-pjoseph-conrad.html. Accessed June 8, 2016.

p. 303   **Friends Matter**: http://www.nytimes.com/2004/10/12/science/earth/friends-
matter-for-reclusive-creature-of-african-forest.html. Accessed June 8, 2016.

p. 305   **Juveniles**:   http://www.nytimes.com/2004/10/13/opinion/juveniles-and-the-
death-penalty.html. Accessed June 8, 2016.

p. 310   **The Listing; PERFORMING ETHNICITY**: http://query.nytimes.com/
gst/fullpage.html?res=9B01EFDF133DF93AA15753C1A9629C8B63.   Accessed June 8, 2016.

p. 315   **We've Seen the Enemy**: http://www.nytimes.com/2004/10/17/weekinre-
view/weve-seen-the-enemy-and-they-are-who-exactly.html. Accessed June 8,
2016.

p. 316   **Foes of Death Penalty**: http://www.nytimes.com/2004/10/20/world/africa/
foes-of-death-penalty-making-gradual-gains-in-africa.html. Accessed June 8,
2016.

p. 319   **In retaliation...betrayed.**: http://www.irinnews.org/report/54121/drc-Mai-
Mai-militiamen-kidnap-5-journalists-as-their-leader-is-arrested,   April   28,
2005. Accessed August 21, 2016.

p. 320   **Africans Pick Congo Leader, Not Sudanese**: http://www.nytimes.com/
2006/01/25/international/africa/25africa.html?_r=0. Accessed June 8, 2016.

p. 325   **Autocratic Leaders Who Improve Their Countries**: http://www.ny-
times.com/roomfordebate/2012/09/19/autocratic-leaders-who-improve-their-
countries. Accessed June 8, 2016.

p. 327   **Then, he had been chosen...Lubumbashi**: https://congomonde.wordpress.
com/2015/07/31/lubumbashi-le-d-g-mande-mutombo-de-linstitut-superieur-
de-commerce-un-batisseur/. 31 Juilliet 2015. Accessed December 8, 2015.

p. 328   **Canada condemns...Great Lakes Region**: http://www.international.gc.ca/
media/aff/news-communiques/2012/09/14c.aspx?lang=eng. Accessed February 18, 2015.

p. 328   **Rwandan...Eastern Congo:**   http://www.securitycouncilreport.org/atf/cf/
%7B65BFCF9B-6D27-4E9C-8CD3-CF6E4FF96FF9%7D/s_2012_843.pdf.
Accessed December 8, 2015.

p. 328   **Name: Ntambo Nkulu Ntanda... Prof. Mande Mutombo Mulumiashimba:**   http://archives.republicans.foreignaffairs.house.gov/hear-
ings/view/?1476. Accessed November 26, 2015.

p. 332   **Kagame notoriously left**: Kamuzini, "Kagame Storms Out of U.N. Meeting,"
29-09-2012. http://www.inyenyerinews.org/afrika/kagame-storms-out-of-un-
meeting. Accessed August 22, 2016.

p. 332   **Congo: Fighters Quit, Says U.N.:**   http://www.nytimes.com/2014/
01/15/world/africa/congo-fighters-quit-un-says.html. Accessed June 8, 2016.

p. 332   **Cessna Grand Caravan**: "Wings of the Morning" http://www.wes-
tohioumc.org/conference/wings-morning. Accessed December 8, 2015.

p. 333   **Bishop Ntambo had been elected...Haut Lomami**:   http://ar-
chive.wfn.org/2007/01/msg00383.html. Accessed December 8, 2015.

p. 341   **U.N. Envoy Rice**: http://www.nytimes.com/2012/12/10/world/un-envoy-rice-
faulted-for-rwanda-tie-in-congo-conflict.html. Accessed August 23, 2016.

p. 343   **The idea that...prohibiting regime:** Tuba Inal, *The Development of Global
Prohibition Regimes: Pillage and Rape in War,* a dissertation submitted to the
Graduate School of the University of Minnesota, July, 2008. Accessed through
dissertation abstracts, March 13, 2015.

p. 354   **...donors:** "Journal Officiel de la Conférence Annuelle 2000," July 2000,
p. 15ff.

Bibliography

Secondary Sources

For background on the popular image of the Congo in journalism I have relied on:

Butcher, Tim. *Blood River: The Terrifying Journey through the World's Most Dangerous Country*. New York: Grove Press, 2008.

Mealer, Bryan. *All Things Must Flight to Live: Stories of War and Deliverance in Congo*. New York: Bloomsbury, 2008.

Wrong, Michela. *In the Footsteps of Mr. Kurtz: Living on the Brink of Disaster in Mobutu's Congo*. Great Britain: Fourth Estate Limited, 2000.

For Congo in popular culture:

LeCarre, John. *The Mission Song*. New York: Little, Brown and Company, 2006.

Kingsolver, Barbara. *The Poisonwood Bible.* New York: HarperCollins, 1998.

Naipaul, V.S. *A Bend in the River.* New York: Vintage Books, 1979.

Nottage. Lynn. *Ruined.* New York: Theatre Communications Group, 2009.

Windle, Jeanette. *Congo Dawn*. Carol Stream, IL: Tyndale House Publishers, 2013.

For the prewar history of the DRC:

Hochschild, Adam. *King Leopold's Ghost: A Story of Greed, Terror, and Heroism in Colonial Africa.* New York: Houghton Mifflin Company, 1999.

Devlin, Lawrence R. *Chief of Station, Congo: Fighting the Cold War in a Hot Zone.* New York: Public Affairs, A Member of Perseus Books Group, 2007.

Reefe, Thomas Q. *The Rainbow and the Kings: A History of the Luba Empire to 1891.* Berkeley: University of Chicago Press, 1981.

For Luba culture, indigenous practices, and additional history:

Gabler, Rachel. "Where do we go from here? Radio Dramas based on the book 'A Letter to Africa About Africa' by Kasongo Munza", Part 1 and Part 2, TransWorld Radio, December 2009.

Roberts, Mary Nooter and Allen F. Roberts, *Memory: Luba Art and the Making of History,* exhibition catalogue of The Museum for African Art, New York City. Munich: Prestel-Verlag, 1996.

Roberts, Polly Nooter and Allen F. Roberts. *Luba.* The Heritage Library of African Peoples. Series Editor, George Bond, Ph.D. Director of the Institute for African Studies, Columbia University. New York: The Rosen Publishing Group, 1997.

For secondary source background on the history of the war in Congo and its aftermath:

Autesserre, Severine. *The Trouble with the Congo: Love Violence and the Failure of International Peacebuilding*. New York: Cambridge University Press, 2010.

Clark, John F, ed. *The African Stakes of the Congo War*. New York: Palgrave Macmillan, 2002.

Diebert, Michael. *The Democratic Republic of Congo: Between Hope and Despair. African Arguments*. London: Zed Books and the African Royal Society, 2013.

Nzongola-Ntalanja, Georges. *The Congo: From Leopold to Kabila: A People's History*. London: Zed Books, 2003.

Prunier, Gérard. *Africa's World War: Congo, the Rwandan Genocide, and the Making of a Continental Catastrophe*. Oxford: Oxford University Press, 2009.

Stearns, Jason. *Dancing in the glory of the Monsters: The Collapse of Congo and the Great War of Africa*. New York: Public Affairs, 2011.

Turner, Thomas. *Congo Wars: Conflict, Myth, Reality*. 2008. London: Zed Books.

Web resources (in addition to headlines from *The New York Times* listed in citations):

Daniszewski, John and Ann M Simmons, "Mobutu, Zairian Dictator for 32 Years, Dies in Exile," *Los Angeles Times,* September 8, 1997, http://articles.latimes.com/1997/sep/08/news/mn-30058

Grimes, William. "Gerda Lerner, A Feminist and Historian, Dies at 92," January 3, 2013. http://www.nytimes.com/2013/01/04/us/gerda-lerner-historian-dies-at-92.html?_r=0

International Crisis Group, "Democratic Republic of Congo: An Analysis of the Agreement and the Prospects for Peace," August 20, 1999, http://www.crisisgroup.org/en/regions/africa/central-africa/dr-congo/005-democratic-republic-of-congo-an-analysis-of-the-agreement-and-prospects-for-peace.aspx

International Crisis Group on expansion of food assistance to Kabongo and Kitenge. http://reliefweb.int/report/democratic-republic-congo/wfp-expands-food-assistance-war-victims-dr-congo

International Crisis Group. "Katanga: the Congo's forgotten crisis," Africa Report 103, January 9, 2006. http://www.crisisgroup.org/en/regions/africa/central-africa/dr-congo/103-katanga-the-congos-forgotten-crisis.aspx

IRIN. "DRC Militiamen Kidnap 5 Journalists as Their Leader is Arrested." *IRIN: The Inside Story on Emergencies.* http://www.irinnews.org/report/54121/drc-Mai-Mai-militiamen-kidnap-5-journalists-as-their-leader-is-arrested, April 28, 2005.

Jeffries, Stuart. "Revealed: How Africa's dictator died at the hands of his boy soldiers, 10 February, 2001. http://www.theguardian.com/world/2001/feb/11/theobserver

Kamuzini, "Kagame Storms Out of U.N. Meeting," 29-09-2012, http://www.in-yenyerinews.org/afrika/kagame-storms-out-of-un-meeting

MONUC, on alleged massacres against civilians by Chinja-Chinja (spelled Shinja Shinja), February 2004, http://reliefweb.int/report/democratic-republic-congo/drc-monuc-investigates-allegations-massacres-katanga

News24 Archives. "Rebels Threaten Aid Planes." August 14, 2003. http://www.news24.com/Africa/News/Rebels-threaten-aid-planes-20030814

Reuters. 'Kasavubu Regime Ousted by Army Coup in Congo.' November 25, 1965.https://partners.nytimes.com/library/world/africa/651125kasavubu.html

Rogier, Emeric, "The Inter-Congolese Dialogue: A Critical Review," https://www.issafrica.org/uploads/CHALLENGESPEACEINTERCONGO.PDF

Stearns, Jason. blog, http://congosiasa.blogspot.com/2010/02/who-killed-laurent-kabila.html

"Where's the Peace to Keep in Congo?," editorial, *The Chicago Tribune*, February 14, 2000. http://articles.chicagotribune.com/2000-02-14/news/0002140010_1_peacekeepers-rwanda-and-uganda-hutu

For background on illness in the DRC:

DRC Monthly Humanitarian Bulletin on inaccessible areas, 17 Jul - 17 Aug 1999, http://reliefweb.int/report/democratic-republic-congo/drc-monthly-humani-tarian-bulletin-17-jul-17-aug-1999.

Feierman, Steven and John M. Janzen. *The Social Basis of Health and Healing in Africa.* Berkeley: University of California Press, 1992.

Janzen, John M. *The Quest for Therapy: Medical Pluralism in Lower Zaire.* Berkeley: University of California Press, 1978.

Methodological and interpretive sources:

Denborough, David. *Collective Narrative Practice.* Adelaide, Australia: Dulwich Center Publications, 2008.

Gutkind, Lee. *You Can't Make This Stuff Up: the Complete Guide to Writing Creative Nonfiction from Memoir to Literary Journalism and Everything In Between.* Boston: Decapo Press, 2012.

Gopin, Mark. *Healing the Heart of Conflict: 8 Crucial Steps to Making Peace with Yourself and Others.* Emmaus, PA: Rodale, 2004.

Inal, Tuba. *The Development of Global Prohibition Regimes: Pillage and Rape in War,* a dissertation submitted to the Graduate School of the University of Minnesota, July, 2008. Accessed through dissertation abstracts, March 13, 2015.

Kerber, Linda and Sharron De Hart in *America: Refocusing the Past.* Oxford: Oxford University Press, 1995.

Marsden, Rasunah, ed. *Crisp Blue Edges: Indigenous Creative Nonfiction.* Penticton, BC: Theytus Books, 2000.

Monk, Gerald, John Winslade, Kathie Crocket and David Epstein. *Narrative Therapy in Theory and Practice.* San Francisco: Jossey-Bass, 1997.

N'Sengha, Mutombo Nkulu. *Foundation for an African Theology of Human Rights: Rethinking the Human Condition in Post-Colonial Central Africa*, a dissertation submitted to Temple University, Leonard Swidler, Adviser, accepted May 22, 2001.

Walton, Heather. *Not Eden: Spiritual Life Writing for this World.* London: SCM Press, 2015.

Church reports on missionaries:

"United Methodist Missionaries to Leave Congo," August 19, 1998, updated September 25, 1998, www.umc.org/umns, now archived.

"Wings of the Morning" http://www.westohioumc.org/conference/wings-morning

My prior writings on the DRC include:

"'A Bishop for His People': Bishop Ntambo Nkulu Ntanda," in *Peacemakers in Action: Profiles of Religion in Conflict Resolution* Volume II, ed. Joyce Dubensky on behalf of Tanenbaum Center for Interreligious Understanding. New York: Cambridge University Press, 2016.

"Religious Leaders Voice Concerns About Rwanda's Intervention in Congo," co-authored with Guy Mande Muyombo. *Sightings,* November 8, 2012.

"Victims, Perpetrators or Moral Agents: Children and Youth Survivors of the War in the Democratic Republic of Congo," *Journal of Childhood and Religion* 2:2, June, 2010, p. 1-17. http://www.childhoodandreligion.com/JCR/Welcome.html.

"Demystifying the War in the Democratic Republic of Congo," with Guy Mande Muyombo, in *International Conflict Resolution.* Pamela Couture, Guest editor with Emmanuel Lartey. *Journal of Pastoral Theology* focused edition. 2007. June. 15-26.

"Reading Adam Hochshield's *King Leopold's Ghost: A Story of Greed, Terror, and Heroism in Colonial Africa* Side by Side with Luis Rivera-Pagán's *A Violent Evangelism: The Political and Religious Conquest of the Americas*" in *The Journal of Pastoral Theology* 17:2, Fall, 2007, 37-55.

"Bible, Music, and Pastoral Theology," in *The Bible in Pastoral Practice: Readings in the Place and Function of Scripture in the Church.* Ed. Paul Ballard and Stephen R. Holmes. London: Dartman, Longman, Todd. 2005. 286-295.

Primary Sources

Government and United Nations sources include:

United Nations Expert Panel reports during the war, which can be found at http://www.un.org/en/sc/repertoire/subsidiary_organs/groups_and_panels.shtml

MONUC, http://www.un.org/en/peacekeeping/missions/past/monuc/

Canada's statement on the M-23 http://www.international.gc.ca/media/aff/news-communiques/2012/09/14c.aspx?lang=eng. Accessed February 18, 2015; now archived offline.

Records of the care of orphans and refugees, building projects, and donations were checked with Dr. Boniface Kabongo, translating, against the minutes of the North Katanga Annual Conference:

Journal officiel de la conférence annuelle. 27ième session de la conférence annuelle tenue à Kamina du 13 au 17 juillet 1997; Église méthodiste unie, Diocèse du Nord-Katanga, b.p. 459, Kamina.

Journal officiel de la conférence annuelle, tenue à Kamina du 28/06 au 3/07/98, 28ᵉ session; Église méthodiste unie, Diocèse du Nord-Katanga, b.p. 459, Kamina.

Journal officiel de la conférence annuelle, tenue à Kamina du 15/07 au 18/07/99, 29ᵉ session; Église méthodiste unie, Diocèse du Nord-Katanga, Kamina.

Rapport de la conférence annuelle du Nord-Katanga, 30ᵉ session présidée par Mgr. Ntambo Nkulu Ntanda, tenue à Kamina du 16 au 23 juillet 2000; Église méthodiste unie, Diocèse du Nord-Katanga, Kamina.

Rapport de la conférence annuelle, 32ᵉ session; présidée par Mgr. Ntambo Nkulu Ntanda, tenue à Kamina du 02 au 08 août 2002; Église méthodiste unie, Diocèse du Nord-Katanga, b.p. 459, Kamina.

Journal officiel de la conférence annuelle, présidée par Mgr Ntambo Nkulu Ntanda, tenue à Kamina du 13/07 au 18/07/2003, 33ième session; Église méthodiste unie, Diocèse du Nord-Katanga, b.p. 459, Kamina.

Journal officiel de la conférence annuelle, tenue à Kamina du 21-28 juillet 2004, 34ᵉ session par Mgr. Ntambo Nkulu Ntanda; Église méthodiste unie, Conférence du Nord-Katanga, b.p. 459, Kamina.

Journal officiel de la 35ᵉ session de la conférence annuelle, tenue à Kamina du 28/7 au 2 août 2005 par son excellence Mgr. Ntambo Nkulu Ntanda; Église méthodiste unie, Diocèse du Nord-Katanga, Kamina.

Procès-verbal de la conférence annuelle 2005-2006, tenue à Kamina du 09 au 14 juillet 2006, par son excellence Mgr Ntambo Nkulu Ntanda. Thème: « le surveillant est aussi surveillé », 36ième session; Église méthodiste unie, Diocèse du Nord-Katanga, Kamina.

Procès-verbal de la conférence annuelle 2006-2007, thème: « *tusimame, tujenge na tuache alama* » (Néhémie 2:18), tenue à Kamina du 15 au 21 juillet 2007, par son excellence Mgr Ntambo Nkulu Ntanda, 37ième session.

Prophet Mechac and Secretary Mutalala worked from written notes and in addition provided a document, *Le rôle du prophète en temps de guerre au Congo, Centre charismatique de Kaboto*, including the list of arms turned over the warlords in Kaboto and orphans cared for in Kaboto.

Papa Ngoy Nyengele provided original documents of the contract, interview, lists of registered internally displaced people, and distributions of food, Kamina, 2001-2004, funded by *Programme alimentaire mondial* (PAM; World Food Programme).

Student papers provided included:

Mutombo, Guy Mande, *The Mayi-Mayi as a civilian defence forces in the Democratic Republic of Congo*, Africa University 2002-2003.

Mutombo Munkana Mwembo, John. *On Laurent D. Kabila as an African Leader in Democratic Republic of Congo*, Africa University 2002-2003.

Ilunga, Ilgha Monga. *The Quest for Women's Self-Worth*. MACM thesis. Saint Paul School of Theology. 2013.

Documents by and about Bishop Ntambo and Raymond Mande Mutombo include:

Raymond Mande's petition to 2000 General Conference, "Proceedings of the 2000 General Conference of the United Methodist Church", *Daily Christian Advocate, Daily Edition* Vol. 4 No. 10, May 12, 2000, p. 2345-2346, http://www.gc2000.org/dca/pdf/0512/DCA%20Proceedings%202000%20 for%20Pub%20Date%20May%2012%202000.pdf

Daily Christian Advocate Vol. 4., NO. 11, May 13, 2000, p. 2425. http://www. gc2000.org/dca/pdf/0513/DCAProceedings0513.pdf

'The Fear of the Lord' April 29, 2004, United Methodist General Conference Sermon, http://archives.umc.org/interior.asp? ptid=17&mid=4320.

Linda Bloom, *United Methodist Bishop Elected Senator in Congo*. January 31, 2007. http://archive.wfn.org/2007/01/msg00383.html

Bishop Ntambo Nkulu Ntanda's testimony as part of the panel (with co-panelists Mark Schneider and Jason Stearns) on "Examining the Role of Rwanda in the DRC Insurgency," Committee on Foreign Affairs subcommittee on Africa, Global Health and Human Rights, chaired by Christopher H. Smith R-NJ, September 19, 2012, http://archives.republicans.foreignaffairs.house. gov/hearings/view/?1476

Announcement of Dr. Raymond Mande's academic appointment can be found at https://congomonde.wordpress.com/2015/07/31/lubumbashi-le-d-g-mande-mutombo-de-linstitut-superieur-de-commerce-un-batisseur/. 31 juillet 2015

Music includes:

"Blest Be the Tie That Binds," John Fawcett, 1782. Public Domain.
"Trust and Obey" John H. Sammis, 1887. Public Domain.